The Language of Disenchantment

D1603396

AAR
AMERICAN ACADEMY OF RELIGION

REFLECTION AND THEORY IN THE STUDY OF RELIGION

SERIES EDITOR
Theodore M. Vial, Jr., Iliff School of Theology

A Publication Series of
The American Academy of Religion
and
Oxford University Press

AMERICAN ACADEMY OF RELIGION

The Language of Disenchantment

Protestant Literalism and Colonial Discourse in British India

ROBERT A. YELLE

OXFORD
UNIVERSITY PRESS

OXFORD
UNIVERSITY PRESS

Oxford University Press publishes works that further
Oxford University's objective of excellence
in research, scholarship, and education by publishing worldwide.

Oxford   New York
Auckland   Cape Town   Dar es Salaam   Hong Kong   Karachi
Kuala Lumpur   Madrid   Melbourne   Mexico City   Nairobi
New Delhi   Shanghai   Taipei   Toronto

With offices in
Argentina   Austria   Brazil   Chile   Czech Republic   France   Greece
Guatemala   Hungary   Italy   Japan   Poland   Portugal   Singapore
South Korea   Switzerland   Thailand   Turkey   Ukraine   Vietnam

Copyright © 2013 by Oxford University Press

Published in the United States of America by Oxford University Press
198 Madison Avenue, New York, New York 10016

Oxford is a registered trademark of Oxford University Press in the UK and certain other countries.

Library of Congress Cataloging-in-Publication Data
Yelle, Robert A.
The language of disenchantment : Protestant literalism and colonial
discourse in British India / Robert A. Yelle.
p.   cm.
Includes bibliographical references (p.   ) and index.
ISBN 978-0-19-992499-8 (hardcover : alk. paper)—ISBN 978-0-19-992501-8 (pbk. : alk. paper)
1. Hinduism and culture—India. 2. Language and languages—Religious aspects—Hinduism.
3. Hinduism—India. 4. Protestantism—Influence. I. Title.
BL1215.C76Y45   2013
261.2'45—dc23   2012003473

1 3 5 7 9 8 6 4 2
Printed in the United States of America
on acid-free paper

To my parents, Louis E. Yelle and Judith M. Yelle

This light of the Gospel scattered all the fogs and mists of Gentile superstition . . . Apollo *complained that the oracles failed him, and that the Hebrew child had stopped his mouth. When it was proclaimed* . . . *that the great god* Pan *was dead, all the evil spirits were heard to howl and bewail the overthrow of their Kingdom* . . . *Such was the irresistible power of the two-edged sword which came out of Christs mouth, that nothing was able to withstand it.*

ALEXANDER ROSS, Pansebeia: or, A View of All Religions in the World, *2nd ed. (London, 1655), 181*

It is now the fittest season for Experiments *to arise, to teach us a Wisdome, which springs from the depths of* Knowledge, *to shake off the shadows, and to scatter the mists, which fill the minds of men with a vain consternation. This is a* work *well-becoming the most* Christian Profession. *For the most apparent effect, which attended the passion of* Christ, *was the putting of an eternal silence, on all the false oracles, and dissembled inspirations of* Antient Times.

THOMAS SPRAT, History of the Royal Society *(London, 1667), 362–63*

Contents

Preface

THE GERMAN SOCIOLOGIST Max Weber is famous for, among other things, his argument over a century ago now in *The Protestant Ethic and the Spirit of Capitalism* that the religious Reformation influenced attitudes and modes of conduct characteristic of modernity.[1] Recently Mark C. Taylor has pointed out that if Weber were rewriting his book today, he would have to call it *The Protestant Ethic and the Spirit of Globalization*,[2] in recognition of the fact that some of the patterns Weber described have been exported around the globe, where they have inspired the modernization of other cultures in directions he diagnosed as "disenchantment"—meaning, in the first instance, the decline of traditional religion and the banishing of miracles, magic, and mystery from the world.

This book contributes to the rewriting of such a history. While in deep agreement with both Weber's basic project and Taylor's suggestion for its revision, I should like to add that such a revision needs to take into account some considerations Weber neglected. To begin with, we have become increasingly aware, especially through the efforts of scholars in postcolonial studies, of the ethnocentrism of the concept of the uniqueness of the West as the embodiment of modernity, rationality, and secularism, a concept that informs our master narrative of progress and establishes European civilization as the protagonist and *telos* of world history. This master narrative depends on a set of antinomies—rational versus superstitious, secular versus religious, disenchanted versus enchanted, modern versus primitive, and West versus East—that caricatures other cultures, which appear in this narrative as antagonists and bit players, dangerous adversaries and exotic strangers, but not, under any circumstances, as heroes. Moreover, these antinomies structure an historical narrative of rupture, of the discontinuity and irreconcilability of before and after, past and present. One of the dangers of such a theory of a Great Divide[3] is that it invites us to lose a sense, both of connection with our own

traditions, and of our common humanity with those condemned to represent the past—even when they live in increasing proximity to us, obsolete
while still stubbornly present. Consequently, the project of disengaging
from or otherwise interrupting this master narrative is an imperative in
the contemporary multicultural world that we inhabit. Postcolonial historian Dipesh Chakrabarty has accordingly issued a call for historians to
"provincialize Europe," to expose and reject the ways in which Western
civilization has inserted itself as sovereign subject into the subtext of all
histories, and to reveal the contradictions inherent in its claims to represent simultaneously the universally human and the uniquely rational.[4]

The present work attempts to provincialize Europe not by getting
beyond its master narrative—by trying to write a history that does not
depend in any way on its presuppositions, a method that poses its own
difficulties—but by going behind or through this narrative and showing
its application by British Protestants in colonial India. My method has
been to extend Weber's insight that much of what we call rationality represents the inheritance of one particular religious culture, and that when
viewed within its proper historical perspective, which a study of the colonial encounter helps to provide, this inheritance may appear neither rational nor secular, nor universal and ineluctable. In particular, I focus on the
genealogical debt that the master narrative of rupture or disenchantment
in world history—including Weber's own version—owes to earlier Christian mythological narratives. These narratives have been deeply embedded
in modern culture, not only through their widespread dissemination in
sometimes thinly secularized forms, but also by the influence they have
had in denigrating or discouraging certain traditional modes of belief and
conduct. Disenchantment was simultaneously a mythical and a real event,
in the sense that the discourses and tropes that we inhabit have real consequences both for our experience of the world and for how we live in it,
particularly in relation to other cultures.

By describing disenchantment as an historical event, albeit one qualified by a deeper awareness of the theological presuppositions embedded
in this event, I am aware that my account runs the risk of substituting a
new history of modernity as rupture, and of reinstating, perhaps in modified form, some of the very antinomies it purports to interrogate. (This
despite the fact that my main focus is on some of the continuities between
Christianity and modern, secular culture.) It seems to me that this risk
cannot be eliminated without abandoning altogether the very possibility of
doing history, of describing the modes of continuity and change in the

transformation of cultural systems. What we must avoid doing is either simply adopting or blithely rejecting the antinomies upon which modernity is founded. By focusing on a reconstruction of the Christian genealogy of some British colonial projects for the reform of Hinduism, I have also, with a few exceptions, not extended my account to Hindu contributions to and contestations of these reforms. This may be seen as a further limitation of my project, though I believe a necessary and justifiable one given the constraints of time and academic specialization. Although my project may not escape the tendency to place European civilization at the center of history, it does explore more deeply the origins and causes of this tendency, toward the eventual overcoming of which this book may serve to contribute in some small way.

My approach has been informed in another way by attention to indigenous Hindu voices. Earlier in my career, as a graduate student at the University of Chicago, I studied classical India and wrote a dissertation on the Hindu ritual texts known as the *Tantras* that was subsequently published as a book.[5] The Hindu Tantric texts contain a linguistic ideology that contrasts starkly with that of European modernity. The Tantras affirm the magical power of words, and especially of the *mantras* or verbal formulas that are central to ritual practice.[6] Mantras exhibit a heightening of the poetic features of language, and especially its formality and repetitiveness. Such features are believed to enhance the efficacy of these formulas, and even their ability to alter the physical world. Mantras embody the dream of a natural language, one that perfectly reflects and can therefore influence reality. By imitating the cosmogony and other processes of creation, mantras aim to achieve a cosmic power. In the Tantras, language and reality—words and things—are not utterly distinct, but exist on a continuum that can be bridged through ritual practice. Such views of language, although foreign to modernity, bear a close resemblance to those found in many traditional cultures.

The reconstruction of the cosmology of the Tantras posed one sort of historical problem: the deep immersion in an alien (and ancient) cosmology, and the difficulty of reconstructing this cosmology through a sympathetic hermeneutical engagement. Once this problem had been solved, however, it raised an entirely different historical question, namely: What has happened to the worldview or cosmology represented by these texts? Not that it has disappeared entirely, as my experience of living in contemporary South Asia and comparative study of spells and ritual language had shown me. Yet such magical cosmologies were fundamentally incompatible with the more rational modes of belief and action dominant in modernity, which seemed, wherever it had touched, to have replaced such older cosmologies and banished their magic. I had recorded the formulas of snake-bite healers (*ojha*) in Rajshahi area, Bangladesh in 1998, even before beginning my work on the Sanskrit Tantras, and therefore knew that some were still using what are called folk mantras (*laukik mantra*). My skeptic's mind also recorded that these healers were active in the village, where there was no antivenin or other effective medicines. During the same trip, in Mymensingh, I attended a worship festival devoted to the goddess Manasa, patroness of snakes, which included the chanting of mantras; I noted that this was during the rainy season, in a fishing village where water-dwelling cobras were a constant threat. Such cases seemed to be explainable by a kind of simple functionalism, à la Bronislaw Malinowski.[7] They existed at the margins of modernity, in the gaps that still remained in the regime of technical or economic competence, and were evident around the world, not only in South Asian villages. I also purchased, when in India the next year, some contemporary anthologies of traditional mantras for magical purposes. However, these continuations of popular magic which, unlike the Tantras, did not amount to a coherent worldview, posed no threat to the dominant, rationalist cosmology of modernity any more than the horoscope embedded between the business and entertainment sections of the daily newspaper did. They seemed to exist in a safely isolated compartment, or clearly separate sidetrack. These cases were the exceptions that proved the rule that in modernity, we no longer (in general, or most of the time, or very much) believe in such things. Something had apparently intervened to disrupt the worldview of the Tantras and the practices that these texts recorded. The fact that I found no one during my entire year of dissertation research in India during 1999–2000 who could explain to me the cosmology of the Tantras, and had had to reconstruct this for myself, did nothing to dissuade me from this conviction.

That was the beginning of my study of the impact of British colonialism on India. I quickly discovered that there was a long tradition of colonial polemics against Hindu mantras and related forms of chanting, which led me straight back to John Calvin, the original source of the Puritan critique of "vain repetions" in prayer as a form of illicit rhetoric, magic, and idolatry.[8] This critique was based upon a fundamentalist, ostensibly literal reading of Christ's injunction in Matthew 6:7: "And in praying do not heap up empty phrases as the Gentiles do; for they think that they will be heard for their many words."[9] Many Puritans and other

Protestants applied this first against a range of Catholic practices, such as the chanting of the Hail Mary, the Our Father, and the Litany. During the ages of exploration and colonialism, they also exported this polemic around the globe, including to India, where for several centuries it was deployed in both explicitly theological and secularized forms by Orientalist scholars and colonial administrators—as well as, of course, Protestant missionaries.

This was the start of my engagement with the British Protestant theological tradition as a source for understanding the consequences of colonialism for the traditional, Sanskritic Hindu culture I had studied earlier. Gradually, I began to believe that this historical project had broader implications for our understanding of modernity—this space or place that we inhabit, which represents, among other things, a disenchanted cosmology, one denuded of divinity or contact with the Sacred. Like Weber and many others, I became convinced that the Reformation had contributed in an important way to disenchantment, and that the hermeneutical engagement with Protestant theology could be a fruitful method for approaching modernity.

At the same time, this method of doing history by tracing the continuities between theology and an ostensibly secular—meaning nonreligious, or religiously neutral—modernity, increasingly rendered problematic the very notion of the secular itself.[10] It raised the possibility that the secular was nothing but religion under another name, albeit a rather different sort of religion. This was the same possibility raised by earlier scholars (whom I had, by and large, not yet studied), including Karl Löwith, Carl Schmitt, and Marcel Gauchet.[11] My studies of colonial India posed the prospect of a broader critique of secular modernity, one that could potentially open paths that secularism had attempted to foreclose by neutralizing religion, above all by excluding any place for religion in our historical accounts. This prospect was—and still is—exciting, but also troubling, especially for someone who lives *extra ecclesiam.*

I have offered this brief account of the evolution of my thinking in order to provide some context for the present book; the following outline of chapters will serve to introduce its substance.

Chapter 1 provides an overview of the connections between the religious Reformation and British colonialism in India, situates my project in relation to both postcolonial studies and contemporary debates over secularization, and traces the outlines of the Christian myth of disenchantment that informed British attitudes toward Hinduism.

Chapter 2 examines the background of the colonial attack on Hindu mythology, which borrowed from an earlier critique, associated with Francis Bacon and scientific empiricism, of the habit of taking words as things. A deeper historical investigation shows that Protestant icono-clasm and literalism contributed to these polemics against verbal idolatry. A tradition of Christian comparative mythology that culminated in the Victorian scholar Friedrich Max Müller's theory of Hindu myth as a disease of language explained pagan idolatry and polytheism as a linguis-tic confusion. The effort to purify discourse by removing such distortions and creating a transparent, neutral medium for scientific description had theological dimensions, inasmuch as the smashing of verbal idols was identified with the restoration of the true name of God.

Chapter 3 describes colonial efforts to purify Indian languages by substituting for their diversity of scripts and modes of spelling a single, uniform system of transliteration based on the Roman alphabet. Often understood as a first step toward the creation of a universal language, or toward the elevation of English to this role, proposals for Roman translit-eration were deeply influenced by seventeenth-century projects for a uni-versal language or manner of writing. Like these earlier projects, Roman transliteration in the Indian context was seen by some as a means of re-versing the curse of Babel that resulted in the diversity of languages, and of reprising the miracle of Pentecost, at which the Apostles were able to communicate the Gospel in all tongues.[12] The idea of a universal language often expressed the desire for a universal religion based on Christian monotheism, and for the defeat of polytheism that colonialists explained as a result of linguistic diversity and ambiguity.

Chapter 4 studies the colonial attack on Hindu mantras, chants, and related forms of ritual language, which echoed an earlier Puritan critique of vain repetitions in prayer that was deployed initially against Catholics. The reconstruction of this theological polemic reveals that many Protes-tants objected to what they perceived as rhetoric, magic, and idolatry in repetitive chants: rhetoric for their poetic form and persuasive function, magic for their attempt to coerce or cajole God to intervene in the physical world, and idolatry for the anthropomorphism and belief in divine imma-nence on which such practices ultimately depended. These polemics may have been motivated in part by the introduction of the printing press, and the tendencies of thought that went along with it. Significantly, a number of the Hindu practices the British singled out for condemnation were closely associated with oral performance. This suggests the importance of examining not only the coordination of the religious Reformation and printing, but also the ideological dimensions of print culture.[13]

Chapter 5 addresses another aspect of the colonial critique of Hindu ritual. As part of their administration of India, the British incorporated the ancient texts of Hinduism known as the *Dharmaśāstras*, which they believed contained Hindu law. The Dharmaśāstras, however, contained not merely laws for inheritance, succession, and the enforceability of contracts, but also a cosmology, an ethic, and especially a ritual code premised on the caste system, which attempted to maintain the separation and purity of the castes through prescriptions of diet and social intercourse. To the British, such provisions were extraneous to a system of positive, secular law, and reflected a primitive stage at which law had not yet become distinct from religion. Far from religiously neutral, such attitudes toward Hinduism expressed theological presuppositions concerning the separation of religion from law, and of both of these categories from ritual. The Christian condemnation of Jewish ritual law as empty ceremonial replaced by the spiritual religion of the Gospel informed colonial comparisons between Hindus and Jews, as well as the forcible secularization of Hindu law and the disestablishment of its ritual dimensions.

A brief afterword to the book uses the historical studies in earlier chapters to reflect on the connection between Christianity and secular modernity as related soteriological systems, and on the question of the reality of the process of disenchantment that has been debated by theorists ever since it was announced by Weber.

As the above outline of my argument makes plain, this book makes only a beginning, or further step, in our knowledge of the Christian dimensions of disenchantment and the impact of such ideas on other cultures. It focuses primarily on disenchantment as a linguistic event, and only occasionally describes actual colonial reforms related to this event such as the substitution of English education for instruction in native Indian languages, the transliteration of those languages into the Roman alphabet, and administrative reforms of Hindu law. Unlike Weber's argument in *The Protestant Ethic*, my argument is simultaneously more ambitious, in attempting to describe an encounter between two cultures rather than a development internal to one, and more humble, in that I make no claim that Protestantism caused either colonialism or the reforms it introduced. My argument instead is that we must study the history of British Protestantism much more deeply than has been done until now in order to understand a good part of the meaning of British colonial discourse in

India, as well as some of the reforms this discourse appears to have influenced. I address political and economic developments only incidentally. My account is meant to augment, rather than replace, existing accounts of colonial discourse by adding missing theological dimensions. This requires, at times, patient excavation of Protestant theological disputes and other aspects of British intellectual history. On such occasions, I beg the indulgence of those readers who are interested mainly in India, and promise to try to reward their patience. I would suggest also that those readers who are interested primarily in British intellectual history or Protestant theology should pay more attention to colonial India. Although no one can acquire expertise in all of the traditions that converged in the colonial encounter, I have learned more by trying to understand both sides of this encounter than I ever could have learned from studying only one. The novelty and a great part of the value of the present work lies precisely in whatever merits it may have as a comparative study of religious ideas, albeit one in which traditional Indian culture appears mainly as a background, foil, and target for colonial polemics. A further acknowledged limitation of the work is that I do not attempt to present a balanced portrait of all Christian or even all Protestant attitudes or missionary activities in India. My aim instead is to demonstrate in a few key cases how what we think of as colonial rationality was deeply influenced by certain trends in Protestant—and especially Puritan—theology. The colonial encounter highlights and reveals the peculiarities of some aspects of the ideology of secular modernity that we have come to take for granted. In fact, we can never study modernity as a whole, but only in concrete cases and examples, as I have tried to do here.

Acknowledgments

THIS BOOK HAS taken a number of years to write, and several more to make it into print. Along the way, I have been fortunate to receive assistance and advice from many people and institutions. Without this support, the completion of this book would have been impossible. I would therefore like to express my deep gratitude, first to those institutions that have afforded me sustenance over the period during which I was researching and writing this book. I began researching these topics during the tenure of a Mellon postdoctoral fellowship at the University of Toronto during 2003–2005; continued the research during 2005–2006 on a fellowship from the Illinois Program for Research in the Humanities at the University of Illinois at Urbana-Champaign; and wrote the majority of the manuscript during 2006–2007 as a fellow of the John Simon Guggenheim Memorial Foundation. The generous support of the latter foundation funded trips to both Kolkata, India and England during which I completed the research on the manuscript. Since 2006, the University of Memphis Department of History has been my home, and has given me the space in which to edit the manuscript and see it through to publication. I would also like to acknowledge the assistance and hospitality of the following institutions and their staff: the Department of History, the Centre for South Asian Studies, the Centre for the Study of Religion, and Robarts Library at the University of Toronto; the Program for the Study of Religion (now the Department of Religion) and the University Library at the University of Illinois at Urbana-Champaign; the National Library, the Asiatic Society, and the West Bengal State Archives in Kolkata; Serampore College, especially Dr. Lalchungnunga, principal, and Sunil Kumar Chatterjee, librarian; Bennie Crockett and Myron Noonkester of William Carey University; the Rare Books Reading Room and Asian and African Studies Reading Room at the British Library; the Boston Athenaeum; and the libraries of the University of Chicago, the University of Memphis, and Harvard, Oxford, Yale, and Columbia universities.

Among the many individuals who have contributed their advice or ideas to the formation of this project are Ritu Birla, John Brooke, Debashish Datta, Caleb Elfenbein, Mark Elmore, Timothy Fitzgerald, Naomi Goldenberg, Greg Johnson, Christopher Lehrich, Spencer Leonard, Ruth Mas, Tomoko Masuzawa, Frank Reynolds, Bruce Rosenstock, Michael Silverstein, and Ananya Vajpeyi. Hena Basu assisted with the research in Kolkata. My understanding of the colonial encounter between Indians and Europeans has been enriched by discussions with S. N. Balagangadhara and his colleagues, especially Sarah Claerhout, Jakob De Roover, and Raf Gelders, at the Research Center for the Comparative Science of Cultures at the University of Ghent. Special thanks are due to Winnifred Fallers Sullivan, with whom I have collaborated on a number of endeavors, and who has frequently served as an advisor, critic, and sounding board.

Portions of the research and draft chapters were presented at the University of Toronto, the University of Illinois at Urbana-Champaign, the University of Heidelberg, the University of Chicago, and the annual meetings of the American Academy of Religion, the North American Association for the Study of Religion, the Law and Society Association, and the Association for the Study of Law, Culture, and the Humanities. Chapter 5 was originally written for a conference on "The Politics of Religion-Making" convened by Markus Dressler and Arvind Mandair at Hofstra University in October 2007. The volume that emerged from that conference has been published in the same series as this one. While my own contribution to the Hofstra conference ultimately grew too long to be included in the conference volume, it was previously published as "The Hindu Moses: Christian Polemics against Jewish Ritual and the Secularization of Hindu Law under Colonialism," *History of Religions* 49 (2009): 141–71. Part of chapter 3 was taken from "Images of Law and its Others: Canon and Idolatry in the Discourses of British India," *Culture and Religion* 6 (2005): 181–99. I thank the University of Chicago Press and Taylor and Francis, respectively, for permission to reproduce this material here.

Ted Vial, editor for the American Academy of Religion Series on Reflection and Theory in the Study of Religion, saw the potential in this work. I am indebted to him, to Cynthia Read, the religion editor for Oxford

University Press, and to Lisbeth Redfield, the assistant editor for the press, for their support and assistance in seeing it through to publication.

Last but certainly not least, I am grateful for the support of my family, especially my wife Lynda and daughter Maya, during the years it took to see this book to fruition. Against the debt I owe to them, this book represents at best a down payment.

Abbreviations

THE FOLLOWING ABBREVIATIONS will be used to refer to Friedrich Max Müller's works:

ALS   *Auld Lang Syne.* Second series. London: Longmans, Green and Co., 1899.

AR   *Anthropological Religion.* London: Longmans, Green and Co., 1892.

ASL   *A History of Ancient Sanskrit Literature.* Varanasi: Chowkhamba, 1968.

BW   *Biographies of Words and the Home of the Aryas.* London: Longmans, Green and Co., 1912.

Chips   *Chips from a German Workshop.* 5 vols. New York: Charles Scribner's Sons, 1895–1898.

CSM   *Contributions to the Science of Mythology.* 2 vols. London: Longmans, Green and Co., 1897.

HS   *A History of Ancient Sanskrit Literature so far as It Illustrates the Primitive Religion of the Brahmans.* London: Williams and Norgate, 1859.

India   *India: What Can It Teach Us?* New ed. London: Longmans, Green and Co., 1892.

Intro SR   *Introduction to the Science of Religion.* London: Longmans, Green and Co., 1882.

Intro ST   *Three Introductory Lectures on the Science of Thought.* Chicago: Open Court, 1898.

LE 1   *Last Essays.* First series. *Essays on Language, Folklore and Other Subjects.* London: Longmans, Green and Co., 1901.

LE 2   *Last Essays.* Second series. *Essays on the Science of Religion.* London: Longmans, Green and Co., 1901.

LL   *The Life and Letters of the Right Honourable Friedrich Max Müller.* Ed. Georgina Adelaide Müller. 2 vols. London: Longmans, Green and Co., 1902.

NR   *Natural Religion.* London: Longmans, Green and Co., 1889.

OGR   *Lectures on the Origin and Growth of Religion.* London: Longmans, Green and Co., 1901.

PR   *Physical Religion.* London: Longmans, Green and Co., 1891.

RR   *Rammohun to Ramakrishna.* Calcutta: Susil Gupta, 1952.

RV   *Rig-Veda-Sanhita: The Sacred Hymns of the Brahmans, together with the Commentary of Sayanacharya.* 6 vols. London: W. H. Allen, 1849–1874.

SBE   *The Sacred Books of the East.* 50 vols. Oxford: Clarendon Press, 1879–1910. Reprint ed. Delhi: Motilal Banarsidass, 1962–1966.

SL   *Lectures on the Science of Language.* 2 vols. London: Longmans, Green and Co., 1877.

SR   *Lectures on the Science of Religion, with a Paper on Buddhist Nihilism, and a Translation of the Dhammapada or "Path of Virtue."* New York: Charles Scribner's Sons, 1872.

SS   *The Six Systems of Indian Philosophy.* London: Longmans, Green and Co., 1899.

ST   *The Science of Thought.* 2 vols. New York: Charles Scribner's Sons, 1887.

TLSL *Three Lectures on the Science of Language.* London: Longmans, Green and Co., 1889. Reprint ed. Varanasi: Indological Book House, 1961.

TPR   *Theosophy or Psychological Religion.* London: Longmans, Green and Co., 1903.

VP   *Three Lectures on the Vedanta Philosophy.* London: Longmans, Green and Co., 1904.

The Language of Disenchantment

I

Orientalism and the Language of Disenchantment

> *Europeans made the discoveries of the old Eastern and the new Western world, expanding their missionary zeal to the ends of the earth. . . . Is it perhaps Jewish Messianism and Christian eschatology, though in their secular transformations, that have developed those appalling energies of creative activity which changed the Christian Occident into a world-wide civilization?*[1]

"Orientalism is Christianity"

Gil Anidjar, developing some of the implications of Edward Said's thought, has argued that "Secularism is Orientalism. And Orientalism is Christianity."[2] The very distinction between religion and the secular was originally a Christian distinction,[3] which has been accompanied historically by a host of other dichotomies, including that between "the (religious) Orient" and "the (secular) West." In the process of defining other cultural traditions as religious, European civilization has "judged itself no longer Christian, no longer religious . . . [and] named itself, . . . *reincarnated* itself as secular."[4] Through such a stratagem, Christianity has apparently (but only apparently) "transcended" religion,[5] by becoming free from the contingencies of historical tradition, and potentially universal, as is supposedly the distinction between the religious and the secular itself. This device served the interests of European rule over other cultures. By defining the terms of the discourse in such a way as to make the question of the origins and limits of the secular unthinkable, Christian colonialism rendered its own, ostensibly secular form immune to the objectifying and transformative power it directed against other traditions and, by the same token, made

itself invisible, and therefore potentially invulnerable. Anidjar argues further that the paradigm for this hierarchical opposition between European
secularism and Oriental religion was, first, that between Christianity and
Judaism, and subsequently, and no less dramatically, that between Christianity (or its secular descendants) and Islam. Paradoxically, some of the
origins of modern secularism can be located in anti-Semitism, or more
accurately anti-Judaism, as this depended on a concept of religious rather
than racial difference.

Anidjar's contention raises significantly the stakes for the self-
understanding of European modernity. If it could be shown that secularism
is not, in fact, nonreligious or religiously neutral, but embodies a particular
theology inherited from Christianity, then the very basis on which secularism has asserted its separateness from and superiority over other traditions identified as religious—including especially colonized cultures—would
be challenged. Such a genealogy would undermine the pretensions of secularism to constitute an ideology that is universal in potential if not in fact,
by demonstrating that, to the contrary, the roots of this ideology lie deep in
the soil of one particular religious tradition and have been transplanted
elsewhere only as an artificial, and possibly unsuccessful, graft.

Anidjar's provocative thesis remains precisely that: an insight, or the
statement of a philosophical or political position, which is part of his broader
critique of modern culture and attacks one of that culture's foundations—
namely secularism—in which several large cracks have lately appeared.
Moreover, it is presented in the context of an exegesis of Edward Said's
seminal work *Orientalism*,[6] as an effort to read, against the grain or between
the lines, a theory of secularism (and therefore of religion) within the text
of the master, where it must no doubt be found, unless we acknowledge in
his work a relative silence regarding one of the issues that has emerged as
central in contemporary accounts of modernity: the status of the secular
given the (apparent) resurgence of religion. However, what Anidjar's thesis
serves to highlight is how little attention has actually been paid to the
religious dimensions of colonialism in postcolonial studies generally.
Although, to speak only of Hinduism, we have had valuable accounts of
both Romantic and colonial representations of that tradition,[7] of the consequences of colonialism for Hinduism (extending even to claims that the
British invented that tradition),[8] as well as of the activities of missionaries
in India[9] and of their debates with Hindu scholars,[10] few studies have examined in detail the range and depth of the Christian dimensions of colonialism itself. Peter van der Veer's statement applies: "A great deal of work

has been done to show that colonial rule was based on a colonial sociology of India and the ways in which this knowledge was constructed. But it has not been sufficiently realized that the nature of the colonial project was profoundly Christian."[11] This is for various reasons, including, among others: the predilection of many postcolonial scholars for forms of material and social history in which religion does not appear as an important factor; prior normative commitments to secularism; the understandable desire to avoid the legacy of Orientalist accounts of a primitive and superstitious East, in which an emphasis on the religious dimensions of South Asian culture was implicated; and, last but not least, the limitations of academic specialization. Unfortunately, the neglect of the Christian dimensions of colonialism has reinforced the self-image of a secular, modern Britain opposed to a religious and primitive India. Anidjar's insight is therefore exceptional, and all the more impressive given the fact that it is not supported by a robust tradition of scholarship, at least as concerns colonial India. His insight poses a challenge to postcolonial studies to scrutinize more carefully the Christian dimensions of both colonialism and secularism alike.

There are, of course, exceptions to the general neglect of the Christian dimensions of British colonialism in India,[12] including—to name a few of the most important—both van der Veer's[13] and Gauri Viswanathan's work on colonialism as a mode of "conversion to modernity";[14] R. S. Sugirtharajah's studies of the applications and transformations of the Bible and Christian theology in colonial and postcolonial India;[15] and Richard King's description of the colonial transformation of Hinduism into philosophy and mysticism.[16] Among other things, King traces the influence of Protestant literalism, with its emphasis on the authority of scripture, which represented Hinduism also as a textual religion.[17] One of the most cogent observers of the impact of Christianity on colonial and contemporary representations of Hinduism is S. N. Balagangadhara.[18] Balagangadhara presents the thesis that the religion named Hinduism is an object created by European categories of analysis, and that the very distinction between the religious and the secular is a Christian dichotomy that has been universalized by Europeans and applied in a manner that distorts other cultures. He argues that "Christianity secularizes itself in the form of, as it were, 'de-de-Christianized Christianity' . . . dressed up as 'secular' (that is, not in recognizably 'Christian') clothes. . . . The enlightenment thinkers have built their formidable reputations (as opponents of 'all organized religion' or even 'religion' tout court) by 'selling' ideas from Protestant Christianity as though they were 'neutral' and 'rational.'"[19]

This occurred because "Christianity could become universal only if it ceased being specifically Christian."[20] As we see, there are striking resonances between Balagangadhara's investigation of secularization in the Indian context and Anidjar's thesis that both Orientalism and secularism are Christian. Both theorists emphasize the dependence of an ostensibly universal secularism on contingent Christian foundations.

Although the project of exposing these foundations has not proceeded very far, it does find precedent in Dipesh Chakrabarty's call to provincialize Europe. The exposure of the deployment of Weber's Protestant (and therefore provincial) ethic in the colonial context constitutes one response to this call. Chakrabarty notes that "the so-called universal ideas that European thinkers produced"—and secularism would certainly be chief among these ideas—"in the period from the Renaissance to the Enlightenment" (and let us not forget about the Reformation that occurred in between these two events) "and that have since influenced projects of modernity and modernization all over the world, could never be completely universal and pure concepts . . . For the very language and the circumstances of their formulation must have imported into them intimations of pre-existing histories that were singular and unique . . . Irreducible elements of these parochial histories must have lingered into concepts that otherwise seemed to be meant for all."[21]

Indeed, without a knowledge of the theological categories that the British imported into India, smuggled in the words of the English language, it is frequently impossible to understand colonial discourse, and to illuminate its parochial origins. Chakrabarty is aware of the Christian origins of some of those colonial categories,[22] including especially of the narrative of disenchantment, which posited an incommensurability of social logics between reason and superstition: "The first logic [i.e, that of reason] is secular . . . it derives from the secularized forms of Christianity that mark modernity in the West, and shows a similar tendency toward first making a 'religion' out of a medley of Hindu practices and then secularizing forms of that religion in the life of modern institutions in India. The second [i.e., that of superstition] has no necessary secularism about it; it is what continually brings gods and spirits into the domain of the political."[23]

Chakrabarty affirms the existence of enchantment in some form, yet regards this as coeval and continuous with humanity, not as a stage in human evolution. The idea of disenchantment as a temporal break from a superstitious past is a crucial part of the master narrative of European civilization. Indeed, the very coexistence and contestation in colonial India of different cosmologies and modes of practice already exposes the incompleteness of the process of disenchantment and poses a challenge to its supposed ineluctability. Consequently, Chakrabarty declines to "reproduce any sociology of religion"[24]—including Weber's—partly in order to avoid reiterating the dubious narrative of disenchantment. The present work, by examining the Christian roots of this narrative in India, further exposes the mythical dimensions of this narrative and contributes to the project of provincializing Europe.

What is "Disenchantment"?

So many discussions of secularization have been marred by a lack of clarity in their terms, beginning with the notion of the secular itself. "Secular" is often used to mean nonreligious, while "secularization" commonly refers to the decline of religion due to the progressive encroachment of the nonreligious realm on the traditional institutions, domains, and prerogatives of religion. Much of the current debate over secularization still takes as its point of departure Max Weber's argument, in *The Protestant Ethic*, that modernity is the result of a process of disenchantment: the decline of belief in miracles, mystery, and magic.[25] This signaled also the withdrawal or disappearance of the gods: another synonym for disenchantment that Weber borrowed from the poet Friedrich Schiller was "dis-godded" (*entgöttete*), or denuded of divinity.[26] What had supposedly replaced the earlier, enchanted cosmology reflected in Greek and other pagan myths was a rationalized technique designed to achieve certainty and eliminate the irruption of chance represented by the miracle or the *deus ex machina*. According to Weber's later definition, rationalization "means that there are no mysterious, incalculable forces that come into play, but rather that one can, in principle, master all things by calculation. This means that the world is disenchanted."[27] Not only science, but also other aspects of Western culture exemplified this process of rationalization. In *The Protestant Ethic*, Weber's focus was on the rise of capitalism as a mode of increasingly systematized economic conduct.

The novel thesis of Weber's argument was that behind this process of rationalization or disenchantment there lay a core of irrationality. Although we regard capitalism and other modern institutions as secular, these institutions reflect certain patterns of belief and conduct inherited from the Christian tradition. In Weber's view, this helped to explain why such a process of rationalization had occurred only in Western civilization. Weber traced this process back to ancient Judaism and its insistence on the radically transcendent nature of God, and accompanying prohibition against idolatry,[28] which contributed to the decline of belief in spirits, if not in religion itself, and ushered in the disenchantment of the world. Drawing on older traditions, Protestant and especially Puritan iconoclasts rejected the immanence of the deity, as well as those rituals by which humans had appealed to Heaven for the achievement of both worldly goals and salvation. Protestants dismissed such rituals as both ineffective and sinful. This attack on the ritual economy of the medieval Catholic Church opened the space that subsequently came to be occupied by a very different soteriology, one defined by utilitarian rather than ritual conduct and by capitalist striving and accumulation.

So much as an initial description of Weber's thesis. In the century that has intervened since Weber first made his argument concerning the religious genealogy of modernity, there has been a vigorous debate over different aspects of what is now called the secularization thesis.[29] Some have disputed Weber's contention that Protestantism was a causal factor in the rise of capitalism; others have attacked the notion that religion is in decline; others have interrogated the ethnocentrism of Weber's depiction of the West as the engine of modernity and unique possessor of rationality. The present work neither recounts nor engages with these scholarly debates, except incidentally in pursuit of its main concern, which is with the notion of the disenchantment of the world. As Weber suggested, a kind of disenchantment has occurred in modern culture, and some of its roots, at least in colonial India, appear to lie in Protestant or, more particularly, Puritan theology, in coordination with other factors. The British engaged in a series of attacks upon indigenous South Asian beliefs, practices, and institutions. They condemned Hindu mythology, rituals, languages, and laws, and attempted to reform these by either outlawing them, marginalizing them, or converting them into more rational, utilitarian forms. Although aspects of these developments have often been described by historians as a Renaissance or Enlightenment of Hindu tradition through its encounter with the West,[30] strikingly absent from the majority of such accounts is an awareness of the degree to which what we call secularization in the context of colonial India would more accurately be described as a Reformation, a hangover from or echo of the Protestant movement that had already occurred in Britain and was exported by that country to South Asia under colonialism.

The common colonial designation of Hinduism as idolatry was only the first and most obvious example of the imposition of Reformation categories.

Protestant iconoclasm at a deep level informed many criticisms of Hindu culture, beginning with its worship of multiple gods or images (*mūrti*) of these in stone, metal, or wood. Not only plastic images but also the verbal images of Hindu language and mythology were designated as idolatry, together with many Hindu rituals, which colonialists believed (in some cases correctly[31]) to be premised on a conception of the deity as both anthropomorphic and immanent in the world, a conception that Protestants regarded as a violation of the Second Commandment. A profound difference in cosmology and its included conceptions of divine nature and agency motivated many British polemics against Hinduism. These polemics were in many instances simply transferred from Catholics to Hindus as their target, with little if any modification. Such was the case not only with the worship of images, but also with attacks on the various forms of chants that Hindus used—mantras, Vedic recitation (*svādhyāya*), and the like—which, to many British, resembled the chanting of the Ave Maria by Catholics.

What we stereotypically refer to as Protestant literalism underlay many of these complaints, as well as associated efforts to purify Hinduism of its corruptions by going back to an original written standard that prohibited such idolatrous practices. Such efforts expressed the Protestant doctrine of *sola scriptura*—that scripture alone is the sole source of religious authority—announced by Martin Luther. Colonial projects for the codification of Hindu tradition, meaning its reduction to standardized, printed texts, and related attacks on customary or oral traditions were influenced by a Protestant privileging of the text, especially as literally interpreted. Protestant so-called plain style described both a style of language and a broader aesthetic that pared ornamentation to a minimum.[32] Poetry was held responsible for the personifications and polytheism of pagan mythology. The vain repetitions of Catholic and heathen prayers were labeled a form of rhetoric premised on the belief in an anthropomorphic deity, one susceptible to human persuasion and given to work magic in the world. Behind these developments lay a new or renewed insistence on the divinity as transcendent, rather than immanent in nature and embodied in language. Attacks on mythology and ritual banished the Sacred from the world, placing it beyond the power of words to picture or influence. If Protestant literalism insisted on a uniform reading of scripture, this reflected a conviction in the unity and universality of God. The ambiguity or polyvalence of mythological language supposedly accounted for pagan polytheism. Accordingly, the restoration of a uniform, univocal language would mean the triumph of monotheism and the reversal of the curse of confusion of tongues that had happened with the fall of the Tower of Babel. In colonial India, Protestant iconoclasm, in coordination with print culture, inspired attacks on oral custom, myth, and poetic ritual language, contributing to the opening of secular modernity as a space opposed to these traditional religious forms. Despite the diversity within both British and Indian traditions—not all British opposed, nor Indians used, repetitive prayers, for example—the overall patterns highlight a clash of cosmologies that owed much to Protestant iconoclasm and related ideas of language.

Arvind Mandair has astutely captured the coordination between the religious and linguistic dimensions of colonialism in India: "Recent theorizing of the nexus religion-language-subjectivity has shown that language and religion, far from being separate, are inextricably linked. Indeed, it could be claimed that the work of monotheism and monolingualism that is central to the formation of nationalist ideologies can be considered part of a single process that might be termed *mono-theo-lingualism*."[33] Mandair has in mind the way in which, in order to overcome the barriers of translation endemic to the colonial encounter, linguistic communities had to be homogenized and reified, in a process that contributed to nationalism and the repression of heterogeneous language traditions.[34] The codification of Indian traditions by British colonialists was also, at the same time, a standardization of their languages and religions, under a new master idiom in which both the English language and English ideas of language were dominant. Mandair also recognizes that this drive toward linguistic uniformity had a missionary dimension: "The goal of conversion to Christianity could not be realized unless there was at first a correspondence of concepts, one language: one religion,"[35] which first required a standardization of Indic traditions. Chapters 2 and 3 of this volume provide demonstrations of this coordination of objectives signaled by the term mono-theo-lingualism. Both Müller's project of comparative philology and colonial efforts to codify and transliterate South Asian languages associated polyglottism or the lack of a linguistic standard with idolatry, and the conformation of languages with monotheism.

Colonial projects for the reform of Hindu law showed another side of Protestant thinking. As part of their administration of India, the British had to establish authoritative sources of law. Their treatment of the ancient Sanskrit texts known as Dharmaśāstra—literally, the "science of *dharma*" (meaning what is right, good, and ritually proper)—as Hindu law exemplified broader processes of colonial codification and Protestant scripturalism.

Beyond this, in the course of their partial incorporation into the colonial legal system, these texts, and the traditions they represented, were radically altered to conform to British presuppositions concerning the separation of law from religion. Although such a separation fits precisely the common definition of secularization, in this case it was influenced by a Protestant concept of true religion as opposed to empty ritual. This distinction went back to Saint Paul's original definition of Christian "grace" as opposed to Jewish "law."[36] Following Paul, later Christians divided the Mosaic law into its natural, civil, and ceremonial components. Ceremonial laws in particular, which included animal sacrifice, were held to be mere "types" or symbols that foreshadowed Christ's Passion. Following this sacrifice to end all sacrifices, such Jewish rituals were supposedly neither necessary nor effective as a means of salvation. A typological reading of the so-called Old Testament was central to the claim that the Gospel had dissolved all distinctions based upon tribal ritualism, and instituted a universal dispensation that superseded Mosaic and other traditions. During the colonial period in India, the British compared Hindus to Jews, a comparison based especially on resemblances in their rituals; applied to Hindu law the same categories they had applied to Mosaic law; and used distinctions derived from Christian theology to forcibly disestablish the ritual elements of Hindu law. The secularization of Hindu law coordinated with Christian soteriology.

In keeping with Weber's general theory, each of these forms of rationalization, which aimed to disenchant or secularize Hindu tradition, reflected at a deep level presuppositions and tendencies found in Protestantism, and especially Puritanism, including the insistence on the transcendent nature of the deity and an associated iconoclasm and suspicion of ritual. What we call colonial secularism denotes a cosmology that, unlike some traditional Hindu cosmologies, rejected the immanence of the divinity. Colonialism, like capitalism as described by Weber, frequently transformed concepts inherited from Christian soteriology and modeled itself on that religion's self-presentation as a mode of universalism and supersessionism.

These colonial developments illustrate the dependence of the secular Enlightenment on key Christian categories. Secularism invoked and inverted the religious distinction between canon and idolatry, true religion and false, the Sacred and the Profane, so as to exclude the forms of traditional religion, and secure the foundations of modernity as distinct from an irrational, religious past. Moshe Halbertal and Avishai Margalit have pointed out the parallel between such secular polemics and religious iconoclasm: "Our discussion of the causes of error . . . is based on an important conceptual chain composed of the following links: the criticism of folk religion by the monotheistic religions, the criticism of idolatry by the monotheistic religions, the criticism of folk religion by the religious Enlightenment, the criticism of religion in general by the secular Enlightenment, and finally the criticism of ideology. The claim is that at every link of this chain the same intellectual moves were made."[37]

If this parallel between religious and secular iconoclasms is accurate, then the standard autobiography of modernity that recounts the triumph of reason over religion[38] stands revealed as not an objective narrative, but a work of fiction, and an exercise in amnesia. Iconoclasm is not a peripheral, but a central and distinctive, though not entirely unique, feature of Christianity and the other Abrahamic traditions, Judaism and Islam.[39] To identify modern rationality as a species of iconoclasm therefore raises significantly the stakes of the genealogical inquiry into the roots of modernity. Here, at its most distinctive, modernity appears to coincide with religion, or even to constitute a religion, albeit one of an admittedly peculiar sort that, borrowing Jan Assmann's terms, could be described as a "counterreligion," one that inherited the "Mosaic distinction" between true and false religions.[40]

This book provides further confirmation of the contention that British colonialism in India was informed and structured, at a deeper level and to a greater extent than has been described previously, by Protestant categories. Part of my account depends on the claim of a difference, at times profound, between traditional Hinduism and British Protestantism, a difference reflected in the vehemence of colonial polemics against Hindu beliefs and practices. As noted in the preface, it was these differences of cosmology or religious practice that, for me, inspired a deeper inquiry into the peculiarities of the modern West, and the consequences of these peculiarities for other cultures that were colonized by Europeans, especially those consequences I have labeled as disenchantment. Not only were colonial efforts to disenchant the languages of Hinduism deeply influenced by Protestant theology: As we shall see, the very idea of disenchantment as a discursive event goes back to earlier Christian soteriological myths.

The Myth of Rupture

Weber's account of disenchantment represented modernity as an event of rupture, a break or discontinuity between past and present, tradition and modernity, East and West, although the extent of this rupture was qualified already by the continuity he posited between modern and earlier

Christian (and Jewish) projects of disenchantment. This rupture was spatial as well as temporal, as Peter Berger sums up eloquently: "Protestantism . . . broke the continuity, cut the umbilical cord between heaven and earth,"[41] closing off the channels of mediation through which humanity had communicated with the Sacred.

Scholars of colonialism have often made similar claims; Sudipta Kaviraj, for example, has argued that "the colonial transformation of knowledges was an epistemic rupture on the vastest possible scale, one of the greatest known in history."[42] However, as Chakrabarty warned us, such accounts may reproduce a category error. Colonial modernity affirmed its own radical break with tradition as a concomitant of those dramatic changes that it sought to bring about, and as a reinforcement for the ideological justification of domination, of the superiority of colonizer over colonized. Historical narratives of colonialism as rupture, and especially as disenchantment, may express symptoms rather than a diagnosis of colonialism. As postcolonial historian Saurabh Dube has cogently articulated, "the idea of modernity rests on rupture. It brings into view a monumental narrative—the breaching of magical covenants, the surpassing of medieval superstitions, and the undoing of hierarchical traditions. The advent of modernity . . . insinuates the disenchantment of the world."[43] A growing literature challenges both of these self-characterizations of modernity as founded on rupture and as disenchanted by arguing alternatively that the image of an enchanted past is a projection, that disenchantment was unsuccessful, or that modernity possesses its own, possibly different forms of enchantment.[44] The deployment in the colonial context of the dichotomy between a superstitious past and an Enlightened present appears to highlight both the untenability of this dichotomy, and the political motivations that reinforced it.[45]

The rejection of these founding myths of modernity is a basic theme of various forms of postmodernism. Theorists of religion influenced by poststructuralism have emphasized the arbitrary and shifting nature of categories such as religion, myth, and ritual, and the contingent and strategic manner in which such categories are deployed.[46] Such categories often represent nothing in themselves, but are invested with apparent content through their relation and especially opposition to other categories in a broader conceptual network. Our understanding of myth, for example, has been indelibly marked by the Platonic opposition of myth (*mythos*) to logic or reason (*logos*).[47] Within this opposition, myth is a negative category, a placeholder for whatever we would like to oppose to reason, which is (usually) the more valued or privileged category. What we inherited from the Greeks was primarily this habit of privileging some forms of thought as reason, rather than any externally, that is, objectively coherent concept of myth. Protestant iconoclasm appears to constitute another example of this tendency, one that also marks European civilization as particularly intolerant. On this interpretation, the category of idolatry would also refer to nothing in itself, but would instead provide the excuse for a range of social practices of exclusion.

One implication of such analyses is that the mythic past many moderns imagine may be a mere figment, not a real past at all but a representation projected, perhaps quite recently, for strategic purposes. When it comes to mythology or an enchanted past, "there is no there there."[48] The critique of the thesis that disenchantment was an actual historical process, or that secularization is a sociological reality, appears to proceed ineluctably, according to the following logic: If no myth, then no demythologization; if no magic, then no disenchantment. (One might even say, If no religion, no secularization.) Thus, in his outline of an anthropology of the secular, Talal Asad states that "the notion that these experiences constitute 'disenchantment'—implying a direct access to reality, a stripping away of myth, magic, and the sacred—is a salient feature of the modern epoch. It is, arguably, a product of nineteenth-century romanticism, partly linked to the growing habit of reading imaginative literature—being enclosed within and by it—so that images of a 'pre-modern' past acquire in retrospect a quality of enchantment."[49]

Like Asad, Dube, and Chakrabarty, I believe that the self-definition of the contemporary era as having emerged from enchantment to reality is an important characteristic of secular modernity, and that a more critical genealogy of the idea of disenchantment would represent a significant contribution to an understanding of our age. I will suggest, however, that this genealogy leads us back beyond Romanticism, to earlier Christian traditions. I will argue further that a recognition of the theological or mythological basis of the idea of disenchantment does not fully dispose of the idea itself. Disenchantment describes a particular cosmology, eschatology, and soteriology, which have had broader consequences for our experience of, and mode of living in, the world. To a certain extent, the idea of disenchantment has created its own reality, has induced its own break or rupture with history, and precipitated a different mode of relation to the past, which can never be separated from our imaginings of it, such that this break can be located with some accuracy, or rather at particular nodal moments, including most proximately the Reformation. Although disenchantment is a myth, it is a myth that by virtue of being believed in and widely disseminated has become, to a certain extent, a cultural reality.

Criticisms of the idea of disenchantment or secularization require us to think more carefully about what, precisely, we mean by these terms. Obviously, there was never a time when gods walked the earth and magic was effective. Consequently, disenchantment cannot be taken literally, as the description of an objective change in physical reality. To have any meaning, this term must describe some subjective or cultural transformation. The rise of polemics against myth and magic signaled such a profound change in religious attitudes. This development would be worthy of study even if there were no evidence of a decline in the practices described by the terms myth and magic, and even if these terms were neither adequate nor even coherent as descriptions of aspects of premodern religious traditions. Despite the inability of these categories to provide any accurate information regarding the past, they would still provide an illuminating glimpse of the rhetorical structures of modern thought. This is part of the rationale for Asad's genealogical analysis of the discursive oppositions and attendant evaluations embedded in the concept of the secular, as well as for the historian Peter Burke's account of the "repudiation of ritual" as characteristic of the modern era, a characteristic that has been noted also by other scholars.[50]

We must keep in mind, however, that there was also some social reality to the phenomenon of disenchantment. Protestant iconoclasm itself was real enough. Its most noticeable effects were on the liturgy, ritual practices, symbolism, and aesthetics of the Catholic Church. Iconoclasm was a flagrant and often violent attack, not only on the theology of the Church, but also on its physical manifestations: Stained-glass windows were smashed, icons were defaced, images were toppled and broken, and precious relics despoiled and relegated to the scrap-heap.[51] Following in the wake of this iconoclasm, many of the Reformed churches adopted the plain style, which involved, among other things, aesthetic minimalism, an absence of pictorial and other imagery, and a stripped-down version of the liturgy. This aesthetic extended beyond the confines of the churches, into the attire of the faithful and the architecture of the buildings, both of which eschewed ornateness. In some places, the repression of artistic expression led to a prohibition of theatrical performances. The Protestant understanding of idolatry, although obviously polemical and normative rather than merely descriptive, did mark a change in the spiritual economy of representation. Of course, one can always question the extent to which theological concepts of idolatry drove individual events of popular icono- clasm. Other motivations, such as political protest, were also certainly involved.

Moreover, the attack on vain repetitions was not utterly inapposite as an account of the practices against which it was deployed: On the contrary, it served rather well as a description of some features of such practices, and marked a real shift of attitudes. British Protestants identified vain repetitions in prayer as a form of rhetoric, magic, and idolatry. To a great extent, Hindu mantras agreed with this description: They were in fact repetitive; were stated by many of those who used them to possess the capacity to transform physical reality; and were premised on a conviction in the immanence of the deity. That they further constituted a form of rhetoric or persuasion—one that underwrote the belief in their efficacy— is a necessary inference from their poetic form and pragmatic function, as I have argued elsewhere.[52] Leaving aside the pejorative connotations of the label, then, the category of vain repetitions served rather well as a descrip- tion of certain ritual practices. Indeed, it anticipated some modern anthro- pological theories of ritual as a mode of rhetorical performance.[53] For similar reasons, Jonathan Z. Smith has acknowledged the canniness of the Protestant complaint against the emptiness of ritual.[54] Peter Burke also noted the association between ritual and rhetoric when he stated that "like rhetoric, with which it has not a little in common, ritual became a bad word in parts of western Europe in the course of the early modern period."[55] Although this was only a debate over words, it nevertheless had profound consequences for our understanding and experience of the world.

The rise of polemics against myth and magic presumably had some effect on whatever practices went under these terms.[56] That there formerly existed a greater level of belief, or of social investment, in myth, ritual practices, and the nearness of the gods, is a fact so massively and redun- dantly attested by the historical and anthropological data that it appears to have lost the ability to shock us. If Mircea Eliade's "archaic ontology"— which defined myth and ritual as both an irruption of the Sacred and the repetition of its creative power[57]—was a representation, this representa- tion was constructed, in the first place, by those who adhered to it, and only secondarily by those who described or opposed it as outside observers or polemicists. (One example is Tantric mantras, which repeat the cos- mogony in verbal form as a means of producing powerful speech that is supposedly capable even of bringing the gods to life.) To conclude other-wise would be to silence the voices of these other cultures and engage in a form of ethnocentrism potentially as bad as that embodied in the use of the label primitive. Of course, the archaic ontology is not nearly so mono-lithic as Eliade made it out to be. It is also true that we moderns have our rituals and myths. Yet it does not follow from this that modern literature is the same as premodern myth—even if some persist in applying the same canons of interpretation to both genres—or that our behavior as capitalist utility-maximizers is ritualistic in the same way that medieval Christian sacraments were. Weber already recognized the continuity between these manifestations of *homo religiosus*, but he focused, quite appropriately, on the discontinuity between them, and on the conditions that had served to bring about such changes. Whatever the nature of the premodern condition(s) described, more or less accurately, as constituting the archaic ontology or the mythic or magical worldview, the fact remains that disenchantment was central to the project of modernity, and in many more ways than have previously been recognized. In this regard, as will become apparent, modernity continued earlier, specifically religious pro-grams for establishing a regime of images, including verbal representa-tions, as a crucial pillar of the ideology of monotheistic universalism.

In order to understand disenchantment—and modernity itself, to the extent that it is founded on this concept—it is not enough to point out that disenchantment is a myth, no more than the rejection of the trope of rup-ture described by this myth serves, in itself, to produce a viable, alternative account of what actually happened. It is necessary to locate this myth, to identify its nature, origins, and consequences. This leads us straight back to Christianity. Asad suggests that the Romantics invented the idea of dis-enchantment in the nineteenth century. The thesis that the idea of disen-chantment is of recent invention could be taken to undermine its relevance and accuracy as a description of historical processes that occurred in the early modern period. Asad indicates as much with his statement that dis-enchantment is strictly a retrospective category. However, this idea is actu-ally much older than the eighteenth or nineteenth century. The very notion of a break from a religious past was itself in part an inheritance from Christianity, the echo of an earlier soteriology or scheme of salvation, according to which the coming of the Messiah had put an end to the reign of the demons, silenced the pagan oracles, and rendered magic inopera-tive. Romanticism merely inherited the notion of disenchantment, and provided it with a different value.

As Weber and Marcel Gauchet, among others, have suggested, disenchantment drew on ideas native to early Christianity or even ancient Judaism. Protestants reinterpreted and applied these ideas in new and powerful forms. According to the original version of the myth, the central event in human history was Christ's incarnation and sacrifice.[58] This was, supposedly, what had disenchanted the world. The Incarnation occurred once and for all time; this event was supposedly simultaneously unique and universal. As Gauchet emphasizes, following the Incarnation, any similar, repeatable or continuously renewable passage between the human and the divine became problematic, if not impossible. For these reasons, Gauchet has labeled Christianity "the religion for departing from religion" and the chief agency behind the "disenchantment of the world."[59] For Christians, the Crucifixion was the sacrifice to end all sacrifices; it redeemed us all, for all time. From then on, the efficacy of Jewish sacrifice and other rituals, and with this any obligation to perform the same, ceased. This singular event was signaled by the rending of the Temple Veil in Jerusalem,[60] and by other wondrous occurrences. According to Eusebius (d. 339 CE), it was the death of Christ that silenced the pagan oracles, by driving the demons from the world and ending their misleading pronouncements. Many Protestants insisted further that, with the Passion, all miracles, magic, and mystery ceased, and the obscurely figurative language of both the pagan oracles and Jewish rituals was replaced by the illuminated "plain speech" of the Gospel.[61] A brief account of the history and especially the modern transformation of these myths will reinforce my claim that it is precisely this shared myth of rupture or break from a superstitious past that highlights the continuity between Christianity and secular modernity. This will also illustrate the connections between Protestant literalism and the linguistic dimensions of disenchantment under colonialism.

The Silence of the Oracles

> *By bards foretold the ripen'd years are come,*
> *Gods fall to dust and oracles are dumb.*
> *Old ocean murmurs from his oozy bed,*
> *A maid has born a Son, and Pan is dead.*[62]

The Greek philosopher Plutarch's (ca. 45–120 CE) story of the decline of the oracles considered why these living voices of the gods, who communicated in riddles and verse, have stopped speaking to us. In pursuing one explanation for this phenomenon, Plutarch recounted a story that became famous: While at sea by night, the sailor Thamus heard a voice instruct him to proclaim in a loud voice as his ship went by the island of Palodes the following words: "Great Pan is dead!" Having completed his assignment, the sailor and all of his crew and passengers heard a great wailing and lamentation, as if the world had come to an end. For Plutarch, this meant that the gods, too, could die and so leave the world.[63]

This story suggests that the idea of disenchantment was not entirely foreign to classical paganism. However, it took Christians to elevate this to the central event of human history. Beginning with Eusebius, Christians argued that the event to which Plutarch's story referred was none other than the redemption effected through Jesus's birth, death, and resurrection. Christ had driven the demons from the world and so caused the oracles to cease.[64] Such readings of Plutarch's story fit into an ancient Christian mode of assimilating paganism into a universal history centered on the goal of redemption. According to such allegorical or typological readings, non-Christian histories, as well as histories recounted in the Hebrew Bible or so-called Old Testament, often contained disguised or confused references to some of the true events of the sacred history of the Gospel. Samuel Mather, the eighteenth-century New England Puritan theologian, interpreted Plutarch accordingly:

> The Devil, in imitation and abuse of this Ordinance of God [not to consult oracles], had his Oracles, and gave Answers in the old Pagan times: But his Answers were usually Sophistical and Ambiguous. And after the Death of Christ God was pleased to chain him up: Therefore *Plutarch* an Heathen Philosopher, in his Morals, hath a Discourse upon it, why the Oracles are ceased; and he hath an Expression for the resolving of it, which hath more of Truth in it than himself understood. Amongst other Things he gives this Account of it, that it was because the great God *Pan* was dead. It was indeed because *Jesus Christ*, who is the great God and the great Shepherd of the Sheep, had suffered Death, and thereby conquered *Satan*, and hath therefore stopt the Devil's Mouth from giving answers in that way ever since.[65]

What is most interesting about this passage is neither its allegorical reading of Plutarch's story as a distorted version of events depicted in the Gospels, nor its attack on the confusion and obscurity of the oracles

themselves, but rather the manner in which it illustrates the convergence
of these two tropes. No longer merely an account of the triumph of Christ
over the demons, Plutarch's story, in its form as well as its content,
described the replacement of one mode of speech by another. The oracles
were "Sophistical and Ambiguous," a mode of rhetoric that perpetuated
rather than alleviated enigmas. The clarity of the Gospel replaced and
silenced all such doubts, obfuscations, and mysticism, revealing the true
sense underlying paganism.

The trope of illumination dispelling the darkness of error was a
common theme in Christian retellings of the death of Pan,[66] providing the
logic for George Hakewill's (1578/79–1649) pun: "Since the incarnation of
the *Sonne of God* our blessed *Saviour* . . . the delusions of these spirits have
vanished as a mist before the *Sun*";[67] and the theme for William Vaughan's
(1575–1641) poetry: "Thou hast, *O glorious Saint*, beheld her Pure,/Like to
the *Sunne* dispelling Clouds obscure./ When Shepheard *Pan* deceas'd,
then *Oracles*/ From that time ceas'd through *Christian Miracles*."[68]

As Christian skepticism regarding these pagan practices merged with
other forms of skepticism, for which theology served as a matrix and point
of departure, the trope of enlightenment through the Son gave way to the
idea of a more general Enlightenment.[69] Purveyors of a new naturalism
aimed to discredit popular beliefs in the reality of magic. Motivated by an
opposition both to claims of magical powers and to the persecutions of accused witches, they argued that magic was ineffective—merely a delusion—
and that many of the spirits and demons supposed to be behind supernatural
phenomena did not really exist. Oracles and other magical practices were
forms of imposture abetted by the greed of priests and cunning men and
the gullibility of common folk. In these accounts, strains of a burgeoning
secular sensibility can be heard in their interaction with more traditional
Christian themes. Reginald Scot's *Discovery of Witchcraft* (1584) still
affirmed that the oracles, and other forms of magic, though formerly
effective, had ceased with the coming of Christ: "Whatsoever hath affinity
with such miraculous actions, as witchcraft, conjuration, &c. is knocked
on the head, and nailed on the crosse with Christ, who hath broken the
power of devils."[70] Plutarch's story alluded to this event. However, Thomas
Ady, in *A Candle in the Dark* (1655), depicted the oracles as a form of fraud
from their very origins, involving ventriloquism and an alteration of the
voice.[71] He allowed that Plutarch's story might refer to Christ, but only
as a rhetorical device used by the sailor Thamus to grain credibility.[72]
John Webster's *The Displaying of Supposed Witchcraft* (1677) argued that

Plutarch's story, like other such stories of apparitions, was merely a fairy tale.[73] Such false images were often traceable to natural or artificial causes, and could be accounted for scientifically.[74] However, Webster affirmed the real existence of some spirits as described in the Bible.

These authors exhibited a growing strain of radical skepticism regarding the reality of magic. Attacks on ritual practices and on the existence of intermediate spirits, short of the one true God, combined with a heightened rationalism. Polemics that were nominally directed at the oracles of the pagan priests could also be taken to apply to religion in general and to Christianity in particular. Some, therefore, concluded that the attack on the effectiveness of magic, or on the existence of spirits, was really just a cover for an undisclosed atheism.[75] Plutarch had already proposed certain natural causes for the oracles' decline, including the cessation of the subterranean vapors that inspired them and the rise of skepticism regarding certain purveyors of oracles, who clothed their pronouncements in enigmatical or flowery language.[76] The seventeenth-century French scholar Bernard Fontenelle aimed "to prove that *Oracles*, were they of what nature soever, were not delivered by *Daemons*, and that they did not cease at the coming of *Jesus Christ*."[77] His primary concern was to discredit the claim that either the oracles, or their decline, could be attributed to a supernatural agency. Fontenelle argued that the deceptions of the pagan priests were the true cause of many of the so-called oracles, the decline of which was brought about not only by the gradual recognition of their inherent obscurity and falsehood, but also by Greek skepticism, Roman neglect, and finally the hostility of Christians to all things pagan.[78] Fontenelle presented the decline of the oracles as an inevitable result of the onward progress of reason and time in jointly exposing the oracles as frauds, and their predictions as false.

Daniel Defoe argued similarly in his *Political History of the Devil* (1726): "The Christian Religion spreading it self universally . . . into all Parts of the World, the Oracles ceas'd; that is to say, their Trade ceas'd, their Rogueries were daily detected, the deluded People being better taught, came no more after them, and being asham'd, as well as discourag'd, they sneak'd out of the World as well as they could; in short the Customers fell off, and the Priests, who were the Shopkeepers, having no Business to do, shut up their Shops."[79]

The second edition of the *Encyclopaedia Britannica* (1781) still accepted the existence of demons as the underlying cause of some oracles, but regarded as more numerous a "second sort of oracles, which were pure artifices and cheats of the priests of false divinities."[80] It became possible, finally, to substitute this more radical, naturalistic skepticism, verging on irreligion, in place of Christianity as the cause of the death of the oracles: "From all the foregoing Arguments against the common *delusive* Idea of *Witchcraft*, *Truth* emerges from Obscurity, *Error* is exposed, *Superstition* brow beaten, the *Cheat* detected, and the celebrated *magical* Oracle struck dumb (as *Plutarch* speaks of the antient one) 'GREAT PAN IS DEAD.'"[81]

In this anonymous account by a Deist author in 1788, reason has almost completely replaced Christianity as the agency that disenchanted the world. Such interpretations, however, originated in a theological background in which Christianity and rationality were understood to be indistinguishable. Both forms of skepticism, the earlier theological and the later naturalistic one, were united in attacking the oracles as a false mode of speech, rightly relegated to the past.

The Romantics inherited this ancient Christian myth, and echoed Plutarch's line that "Great Pan is dead!" with a tone of mourning for those gods recorded in mythology who had fled this world.[82] Friedrich Schlegel's (1772–1829) call for a "new mythology" embodied in a new poetry responded to this event, at second or even third hand.[83] For this event was part of the original autobiography of Christianity, and of the self-definition of that tradition as against Judaism and paganism. Reinterpreted and adapted during the Reformation, the event of disenchantment was narrated by radical Protestants in strident and triumphal tones before being experienced and voiced by Romantics in tones of lamentation.

"We use great plainness of speech . . ."

The myth of rupture that links modernity to its Christian past also refers to a transformation in modes of speech, semiotic styles, or "linguistic ideologies."[84] In the wake of the linguistic turn and the focus on discourse and especially on genealogies of language in the human sciences, it has become a commonplace that modernity is, to some extent, a figure of speech, a style of discourse that has defined itself as plain, objective, and rational, in opposition to the ambiguity and obscurity of figurative discourses such as metaphor. This reinforces the analogy between modernity and Christianity, which, already in ancient times, identified the event of disenchantment as the Gospel's replacement of earlier, obscure forms of speech, represented by pagan oracles, Jewish ritual, and the types of the Old Testament. Such earlier ideas contributed to the movement we refer to, stereotypically, as Protestant literalism. The self-designation as a plain style of speech, although central to modernity, is not unique. It had roots in earlier Christian traditions, which had also framed their autobiographies around the narrative of a purification of discourse. The phrase "plain style" or "plain way" of speech was used originally by British Protestants to describe either the language of the Gospels or Saint Paul's method of preaching,[85] as in the King James translation of Second Corinthians 3:12– 13: "Seeing then that we have such hope, we use great plainness of speech: and not as Moses, which put a veil over his face."[86] Paul defined Christianity against the "veiled" religion of Judaism. According to later Christians, Mosaic ritual especially was merely a "type" or "figure" that foreshadowed the clear light of the Gospel and its message of Christian redemption, which illuminated and replaced the obscurities of such ritual symbolism together with the enigmas of pagan oracles.[87]

Although Paul affirms, earlier in the same chapter, that "the letter killeth, but the spirit giveth life," many Protestants elevated precisely the literal sense of scripture in the name of the new dispensation. One paradox here is the manner in which a mode of allegorizing—a densely symbolical hermeneutic of scripture—gave way to one that was opposed precisely to such figurative readings: as the polysemousness of Dante's *Comedy*, and of medieval Christian hermeneutics more generally, gave way to Protestant literalism and plain style. Second Corinthians 3 already describes that moment of transition from one mode of discourse into its opposite. The paradox is partly resolved when we consider what, in their origins, such allegorical or typological readings represented.[88] Typology constituted not an embrace of but a violence against the symbol. Christian typological interpretations of the Hebrew Bible, which Christians now called the Old Testament, demoted and devalued the symbol in favor of what it symbolized. The figure of Moses, like other figures in the Old Testament, found its true meaning and importance, indeed its coherence, only as a symbol and prefiguration of something in the New Testament. Moses was only a type of Christ, who constituted the antitype. In the same way, the almost-sacrifice of Isaac signified the perfect consummation of Christ's sacrifice on the cross, which ended the obligation of animal sacrifice that had obtained under Jewish law. We may gloss the contrasted terms type and antitype with the modern terms sign and referent: The former had value only insofar as it pointed to the latter, which constituted the reality. The term "to foreshadow" or "shadow forth" finds its genesis in precisely such typological interpretations: The type was also called a shadow which, in this case, is cast before the substantial reality that it merely traces, as if the sun lay before us, and were too bright to gaze at directly. John Weemes (ca. 1579–1636) expanded on the semiotic dimensions of salvation in his book on the Jewish ceremonial law: "It was a great benefit to learning, when the obscure Hieroglyphicke, in Egypt were changed into letters, and the darke and mysticall writings of Plato were changed by Aristotle, into a cleare and plaine forme of writing: It is a farre greater benefit, when the Lord hath changed these darke figures and shadowes, into the clear light of the Gospel."[89]

The idea that Jewish law was one of the mysteries made plain by the Gospel was central to the Christian claim to have superseded Judaism. The reference to hieroglyphics was not peculiar to Weemes.[90] It echoed a long tradition according to which Jewish ritual was an antidote for or a prophylaxis against Egyptian idolatry.[91] Deists only deepened the ridicule of such symbols, as when John Toland (1670–1722) mocked modes of biblical interpretation that refer to "type, symbol, parable, shadow, figure, sign and mystery."[92] The roots of the Protestant devaluation of the sign were therefore already present in orthodox Christian interpretation. Protestant literalism was a logical development from typology, though to call it a necessary development would be to succumb to teleology.

An emphasis on the literal interpretation of scripture was central to the Reformation. Luther's doctrine of *sola scriptura*—scripture alone—located the source of religious authority squarely in the original text of the Bible, as opposed to subsequent customs, whether oral or written. The intensified engagement with scripture placed additional emphasis on the importance of fixing the meaning of the Holy Word as a guide to belief and conduct. Scripture provided both the proof that the Catholic Church had deviated from the pure doctrine of primitive Christianity, and a replacement for that Church's lost authority. This was more than an insistence on the primacy of the text. Practices of reading the Bible changed dramatically following an increase of translations in the vernacular languages and of their distribution through the recently introduced medium of the printed book. Protestants elevated the importance of the literal sense of scripture, and demoted its allegorical and other symbolic senses.

Protestants of course held a wide variety of opinions regarding liturgy and the correct interpretation of scripture, as evidenced, for example, by Puritan attacks against those vain repetitions that remained in the liturgy of the Church of England.[93] Quakers were at one extreme in rejecting all set forms of prayer or liturgy. Pagan myths might be interpreted literally, or as figurative expressions of monotheism. Some of these differences of opinion are discussed below. However, broadly speaking, the Reformation inspired a movement toward literalism, meaning both a valorization of the semantic content of language and a devaluation of its poetic and magical functions, which contributed to the rise of polemics against both ritual and mythological language. Under the conviction that Christianity had been corrupted through the introduction of pagan beliefs and ceremonies, Protestants also attacked the myths and rituals of the heathens or Gentiles directly. The urgency of this mission was enhanced by the recovery of classical texts, both pagan and Christian, that contained such mythologies, and by the discovery of living pagans through exploration and trade, which confronted Christians with alternative histories and realities. The British encounter with Hinduism exemplified this process.

The common thread among British polemics against the language and symbolism of Hinduism was not only that they were directed at a reformation of discourse, one that complemented a broader religious Reformation. At a deeper level, each of these polemics expressed a variant of iconoclasm, an extension of the prohibition against image-worship from plastic or pictorial to verbal images—from statues, paintings, and stained glass, to the metaphors and rhetorical flourishes of language, beginning with religious language. As Peter Harrison recognized, "iconoclasm with respect to images directly parallels literalism with respect to texts."[94] The contrast between the canon of scripture and Hindu idolatry was only the most obvious form of this linguistic iconoclasm. Like many Protestant interpretations of scripture, the attacks on Hindu mythology and on vain repetitions in prayer frequently equated literalism with monotheism, and its absence with idolatry and polytheism. In the case of myth, the failure to interpret words in their proper sense, in an awareness of the appropriate division of labor between the literal and metaphorical uses of terms, produced the mistaken belief in the existence of the pagan gods. The critique of vain repetitions attempted to limit prayer to the strictly semantic function of expressing inner intentions, and to exclude magical uses of language, which were believed to be premised on an idolatrous application of rhetoric to God, as if he were a mortal man. The poetic dimensions of ritual discourse as a mode of performance were severely circumscribed.[95]

Some British Protestants regarded the profusion of Hindu languages and ceremonies in the same way that they regarded the proliferation of Hindu images, as forms of gross polytheism. The reformation of language would, accordingly, represent the triumph of Christian monotheism. The Biblical story of the Tower of Babel (Genesis 11) accounted for the diversity of not only languages, but religions as well. The communication of the Gospel in all languages, as had happened at Pentecost (Acts 2), would provide the remedy for this confusion. The dream of a purified, univocal language, in which each word would stand for one, really existent thing, and each thing would be represented by only one word, was associated with the movement for an empirical science; but the idea of such a universal language coordinated for many with the hope of a universal, monotheistic religion identified with Christianity.

Protestant literalism and the more Enlightened scientific discourse that it ushered in constituted a new linguistic ideology, one that attempted to establish a different relationship, not only between language and material reality—as exemplified in the transition from the discourse of magic to that of empirical science—but also toward the materiality of the text. Literalism was facilitated by the objectification of the text that occurred with the rise of a culture of the printed book beginning in the fifteenth century. The solidity of the text lent an appearance of immutability to its meaning. However, literalism was more than an emphasis on texts—a natural outcome of the growth of printing and literacy, and accompanying subsidence of oral culture. Protestant literalism constituted an attempt to fix both the meaning of language, and its connection to the world. Michel Foucault has told us that "In every society the production of discourse is at once controlled, selected, organised and redistributed by a certain number of procedures whose role is to ward off its powers and dangers, to gain mastery over its chance events, to evade its ponderous, formidable materiality."[96] Protestant literalism established such a mode of restriction or, to borrow Foucault's term, an "imposed scarcity."[97] Among the various possible meanings and uses of language, only certain ones were permitted. Other meanings and uses were correspondingly prohibited. Discourse was supposed to behave simply as a medium of expression, a conduit for content, rather than as an independent power, obdurate structure, or site where meaning might slip away from us. The Reformation was one of those crucial moments during which there occurred a new ordering of discourse, a renegotiation of the boundaries between truth and fiction, poetry and prose, and even language and the world. As Foucault put it in the parallel case of Plato's Athens, where philosophy contended with poetry and sophistry: "Efficacious discourse, ritual discourse, discourse loaded with powers and perils, gradually came to conform to a division between true and false discourse."[98] Such distinctions were deployed also during the colonial era by the British to disenchant the languages of India.

Anthropologist Webb Keane has emphasized the closeness of the connection between Protestantism and the linguistic ideology of colonial modernity in his description of the difference in "representational economies" involving both language and other modes of signification that became apparent in parts of modern Indonesia as a result of the encounter between natives and Dutch Calvinist missionaries.[99] Traditional Sumbanese emphasized the formal, textural characteristics of ritual language, especially its fixed nature and repetitive, poetic structure.[100] They also affirmed the role of speech in carrying out efficacious and even magical action.[101] Protestants, on the other hand, regarded the normative functions of language to be reference and predication.[102] Words were demoted to signs of thought, rather than powers in their own right.[103] Protestants eschewed the sensuous dimensions of language, including both Sumbanese formal prayer and the Catholic rote recitation of texts. Keane's account of how Dutch Calvinists' insistence on spontaneity and sincerity led them to reject such practices, and to seek an unmediated connection with divinity, corresponds to what I have referred to as Protestant literalism. Protestants regarded these material forms of language as idols or fetishes, or simply as insincere.[104] Part of the danger of such forms was that they attributed either too little or too much agency to human beings, by displacing that agency onto idols, texts, or other external objects, or by encouraging humans to arrogate to themselves the power of altering reality.[105] This was also a usurpation of powers that belonged properly to God.[106] These are, of course, the classic elements of the concept of idolatry.

Keane notes the coordination of Protestantism and science in disenchanting the material world,[107] and emphasizes the role of the Reformation in precipitating the linguistic reforms that shaped modern notions of subjectivity.[108] Invoking Weber, Keane posits a genealogical relationship between Protestant iconoclasm and modern conceptions of language:

> These conflicts [among missionaries and Indonesians] ideologically align Protestant Christianity with the idea of modernity, referential language (as expressed in the values of transparency and truth) and the signifying practices that underlie abstract value (as expressed in money and commodities) in opposition to paganism, the past, performative and magical language, and ceremonial exchange . . . Protestantism and modernity (and, one might add, capitalism) alike, even conjointly, seek to abstract the subject from its material and social entanglements in the name of freedom and

authenticity. It is in this, I think, that we can see one suppressed link between modernist views of language and things, and the more theological concerns expressed by Protestant and other religious reformers.[109]

As Keane noted, Protestantism and modernity converged in promoting spontaneity, sincerity, and clarity in discourse, as opposed to formalism, esotericism, and ambiguity. This orientation underlay the valorization of semantic content and plain speech over the poetry of ritual and other traditional forms. Another example is Thomas Ady's account, in the mid-seventeenth century, of the oracles or "southsayers." Ady depicted the style of speech of these as a mode of inauthenticity, a kind of ventriloquism, in which the natural, human voice was submerged:

> *Mantes* [i.e., an oracle] was such a Witch, or false Prophet, as had that devillish imposture of harring in their throats to deceive the people, called of some *Ventriloquium*, a speaking in the belly, and they that practised this imposture were so perfect in it, that they would speak so strangely, that many times they dared to practice their imposture above ground [as well as in resonant caves], whereby they made it seem to silly people that the spirit of *Apollo*, or some other Idol (which they called gods) spake within them . . . This imposture of speaking in the Belly hath been often practised in these latter days in many places, and namely in this Island of *England*, and they that practise it do it commonly to this end, to draw many silly people to them, to stand wondring at them, that so by the concourse of people money may be given them.[110]

Ady accounted for Plutarch's tale in the same fashion.[111] The oracles deceive by making unnatural sounds, not only "harring" (growling or clearing the throat[112]), but also "muttering," "peeping," and "chirping" like birds.[113] From our contemporary perspective, what is striking is not only the utter naturalism of Ady's account, but also the connections he posited among subjectivity, authenticity, and the spoken voice. The oracles represented, at once, a denaturation of the voice, a mode of fraud and deception, and a displacement of both voice and agency onto some spirit or idol. By contrast, the form of modernity that he heralded associated authentic human agency—exhibited above all in the exercise of reason—with both honesty and speaking in one's own true, clear voice.

Protestant attacks on verbal idols attempted to institute a perfectly transparent order of communication. Following Keane's point, I would argue that this was also, at the same time, a bid for the autonomy of the speaking subject, as liberated from rhetorical suasion and the habit of tradition, or what Jeremy Bentham called "allegorical idols."[114] The bid for linguistic autonomy took as its paradigm the uniqueness of the deity. The establishment of a univocal language became a metaphor for the triumph of monotheism. In arguing that God could not be moved by human rhetoric, nor displaced by fictitious authorities that were merely artefacts of language, Protestants were constructing the image of a transcendental subject whose autonomy guaranteed, in turn, the autonomy of the human subject and its freedom from rhetorical influence. Communication was fixed and rendered certain, at the same time that it was subjugated to the authority of the speaker, for whom God served as a model. The fixing of language accomplished by literalism coordinated with a particular concept of the subject and its autonomy. Protestant literalism objected above all to the view of language as an independent power, capable of influencing the world and the deity. Although the decline of belief in the magical power of words curtailed, in certain respects, the agency of the would-be wielder of such a language, it substituted a different sort of agency, one that was premised on the expansion of a sovereign domain of reason. This coordinates with Charles Taylor's account of the rise, under disenchantment, of a "buffered" or autonomous subject, as opposed to the "porous" self of enchanted cultures, which was open to the encounter with spirits.[115] Modernity seems to be very much concerned with the erection of barriers, whether around God, the self, language, or religion, which was demarcated from the secular.

Keane's analysis of the interconnections among language, subjectivity, and materiality is especially helpful for understanding what occurred in the colonial Indian context, where the British attempt to reorder language aimed at a realignment of the relationship of the speaking (and listening) subject both to physical reality, and to the divine simultaneously. The disenchantment of language also worked to disenchant the material world, beginning with the idols or statues of the divinities in which their spirits were localized. There was a fundamental, iconoclastic logic underlying British polemics against Hindu image-worship, repetitive prayers, and the belief in the magical power of words.

Disenchantment as a Theological Trope

These genealogies of disenchantment as an event of discourse or conversion to a particular linguistic ideology reinforce Weber's insight that part
of what we think of as modern, secular rationality is actually an inheritance from and a transformation of Christian soteriology. An originally
Christian myth of disenchantment has become the myth of the emergence of the secular out of its religious past, with the breaking of the
power of tradition. Modernity presents itself as a new New Testament that
aims to supersede everything that came before. Ironically, this is also the
original behind Mark Lilla's idea of the Great Separation between religion
and politics, which he used as an argument against those who would seek
to reintroduce considerations of the theological dimensions of secular
modernity.[116] It is this separation itself that constitutes the myth of
secularization, which originally took the form of an eschatological
narrative specific to Christianity. Separation, silence, disenchantment: All
such metaphors refer to the same, mythical event.

Paradoxically, it is precisely in the shared self-designation as a break or
rupture that we find a continuity between secular modernity and its Christian past.[117] This provides further evidence for Karl Löwith's argument that
modern histories have borrowed some of their narratives from Christian
eschatology and soteriology.[118] The genealogy of the idea of disenchantment leads us to consider again the Christian antecedents and dimensions of modernity. If disenchantment was the nightmare of Romantics, it
had already been the fervent dream of numerous reformed Christians
who wanted nothing more than to banish the pagan gods from the world
and prohibit their worship. The categories of myth and magic may have
been imposed as alien (and, to use Asad's term, retrospective) categories,
by outsiders to the traditions they purported to describe. However, the
Romantics were not the first to impose these categories. When earlier
Christians attacked pagan idolatry and polytheism, they made the same
assumption that was later made by Schiller, other Romantic poets, and
Weber: namely, that the world had once been—or perhaps still was—
populated by spirits and genies, if only in the imaginations of some benighted souls. The difference is that they condemned this mythic world
and consigned it to oblivion precisely in order to create a vision of a new
religious order. Is it possible that, when the Romantics later mourned the
passing of the mythological vision, they were mourning a recent death?
One that had been brought about only on the threshold of modernity?

That the terms of this mourning were drawn from Greek mythology is not dispositive. Again, this does not mean that disenchantment was a reality, only that it was a dream shared by both the Romantics and their forerunners and opponents. Asad is partly correct: Disenchantment is not merely a Romantic literary trope, but a full-blown Christian soteriology, a myth in the fullest sense of the word. We must be very cautious not to simply reinscribe this mythic narrative as factual history, by assuming, as the myth itself does, that the world has actually been disenchanted. Moreover, as the history of this myth shows, the line between the Christian discourse of soteriology and the rationalist discourse of Enlightenment is exceedingly thin, exposing the vanity of the pretensions of the latter to afford, in Asad's words, "a direct access to reality, a stripping away of myth, magic, and the sacred."[119] A genealogy of the secular should dismantle the hierarchical oppositions that support the self-image of modern rationality.

While supporting Weber's account in certain respects—especially concerning the Christian origins of disenchantment—my analysis indicates the difficulties of distinguishing his supposedly descriptive account of secularization from normative theological accounts. In light of the genealogy of the myth of rupture as described above, it appears that Weber converted a Protestant theological position, which argued that disenchantment has already occurred, into an ostensibly objective view of history. To some degree, Weber's own theory is itself a theology.[120] Weber took the sectarian, polemical claim that "the world has been disenchanted" and re-presented it as an objective, value-free claim about the world—despite the fact that he uttered this claim in a tone of melancholy resignation. If this is the case, then the theory of secularization itself becomes increasingly difficult to distinguish from a particular theological stance, the presuppositions of which lead back to Christianity. Disenchantment would be, to this extent, a Protestant trope, confirming in this one case at least Balagangadhara's contention that "the modern day social sciences embody the assumptions of Christian theology, albeit in a 'secularized' form,"[121] and justifying Chakrabarty's refusal to "reproduce any sociology of religion,"[122] especially that which asserts the reality of disenchantment. Whether the world has or has not been disenchanted depends, to some degree, on one's theological position.

As Anidjar has suggested, the original model for the West's religious Other was the Jew as viewed from within a Christian imaginary. In this sense, the genealogy of Orientalism is inextricably tied to that of secularism, which preserved crucial structural elements of the Christian attitude toward

Judaism and paganism and transferred these to religion as the now super-seded Other. Such philosophical insights are perhaps most valuable when they prove capable of illuminating historical developments. Accordingly, this book explores the structural analogies and historical connections between these Christian soteriological concepts and the colonial encounter, in which British Protestants compared Hindus to both Jews and pagans, and attempted to relegate all of these non-Christian traditions to a past now thankfully transcended.

There is a strong structural analogy, reinforced by genealogical connec-tions, between Christianity and an ostensibly secular modernity. Isn't this precisely where Anidjar has directed us to look, by labeling secularism as both Orientalist and Christian, and thereby highlighting the parallels among secular oppositions to religion, Christian subordinations of Juda-ism, and colonial oppressions of the Oriental? Perhaps the best way to understand this continuity is to perceive the common strategy that informs both Christianity and secularism, each of which claims to be universal, and in order to make this claim plausible, further asserts its transcen-dence of carnal, reified tradition. Conversely, our recognition of this shared strategy, and of the historical connection between Christianity and secularism, directly undermines the latter's claim of religious neutrality, upon which its further claim of universality and, ultimately, its legitimacy depend. Hence the significance of Anidjar's thesis, and of the present historical investigation.

2

"A Disease of Language"

THE ATTACK ON HINDU MYTH AS VERBAL IDOLATRY

Words versus Things

One of the key targets of colonial projects for the reform of India was the subcontinent's languages. British observed the supposed tendency of Asiatic languages to prolixity and the excessive use of metaphor, figuration, and other forms of ornamentation.[1] Such devices were at best superfluous, and could also prevent the clear expression of ideas. Colonialists drew a contrast between European clarity and Indian obscurity of discourse. In one of the showpiece essays by the students of the College of Fort William in Calcutta at the beginning of the nineteenth century, W. B. Martin argued that "from the hyperbole and picturesque which reign throughout all Eastern literary productions; from the metaphorical and poetical dress which forms so striking a characteristic in all Eastern languages, we may reasonably conclude, that society among them, is as yet in a state of infancy; that they have not yet arrived at those more refined and cultivated periods, when . . . clearness and precision become the chief objects of attention."[2]

In his infamous 1835 *Minute on Education*, Thomas B. Macaulay (1800–1859) argued that government support for Sanskrit and Arabic learning was as wasteful as money spent on "chaunting at the cathedral."[3] This applied to India a complaint registered in his *Essay on Bacon* that, prior to the advent of science, "words, and more words, and nothing but words, had been all the fruit of all the most renowned sages of sixty generations."[4] Charles Trevelyan (1807–1886) similarly applied this criticism to South Asia, relegating it to the prescientific and pre-Reformation era:[5] "The time of the people of India has hitherto been wasted in learning languages as distinguished from knowledge—mere words as distinguished from things—to an extent almost inconceivable to Europeans."[6] The Scottish missionary Alexander Duff (1806-1878) argued that "*Things*, not *words*; knowledge, not mere speech; must be taught in order to insure a decided change in the notions and feelings of the people."[7] The Boden Professor of Sanskrit at Oxford, Sir Monier Monier-Williams (1819–1899), identified two forms of Sanskrit, the natural and the artificial: "In the one, words are made subservient to ideas; in the other, ideas are subservient to words."[8]

Colonial complaints against Indian languages signaled a shift of emphasis from literary form to content, in particular, to the empirical knowledge in which the English excelled. Many of these complaints were inspired, directly or indirectly, by Francis Bacon and the scientific tradition he helped inaugurate in Britain, which was deeply, even obsessively concerned with the reform of language as a path to the reform of knowledge. Hans Aarsleff noted that the Asiatic Society, the institution founded by Sir William Jones in Calcutta in 1784, was modeled, to some extent, on the Royal Society, the scientific association founded over a century earlier in England to promote the principles of science as laid down by Bacon, and to oppose the dominance of scholastic metaphysics.[9] Like those intrepid empiricists, Jones "considered languages as the mere instruments of learning," although often "improperly confounded with learning itself."[10] Aarsleff claims that this statement was "in the spirit of Bacon, Locke, and the Royal Society . . . designed to strike directly at universal grammar and etymological metaphysics."[11]

The learned pandit and Hindu reformer Isvaracandra Vidyasagar, in his proposal for revising the curriculum at the Calcutta Sanskrit College in 1850, described a Sanskrit philosophical treatise as "similar to that of the schoolmen of the middle ages of Europe . . . what Bacon would call a 'cobweb of learning."[12] He accordingly recommended its removal. Apart from serving as one of the inspirations for colonial reforms in language and education, Bacon also provided part of the curriculum in British India.[13] A list of texts used at the Calcutta Hindu College in 1848 included both Bacon's *Advancement of Learning* and his *New Organon*, the latter in a Calcutta edition.[14] One Indian edition of the *New Organon* directly applied Bacon's critique of idols or "fancies" of the mind to local examples: "From this aphorism it will be seen how far Bacon was from agreeing with those who imagine that the appropriation of the sounds current in Language was determined by God, instead of being settled by man. The Hindus are not the only people who regard certain sounds as having a natural fitness to represent certain notions."[15] Other fancies were illustrated by Hindu

astrology and the ancient plays of Kālidāsa. Such superstitions had supposedly been rejected in Britain by the Baconians of the Royal Society.

The attack on misleading language had been central to the definition
of the new science in seventeenth-century England. One of the first tasks
for reason was to purge language of its fictions, which obstructed the path
to knowledge. Bacon had identified certain mental errors as "idols of the
mind" including the "idols of the marketplace," linguistic errors including
"names of things which do not exist . . . to which nothing in reality corresponds."[16] Bacon said that these idols were "the most troublesome of all:
idols which have crept into the understanding through the alliances of
words and names. For men believe that their reason governs words; but it
is also true that words react on the understanding; and this it is that has
rendered philosophy and the sciences sophistical and inactive."[17]

Such intellectual rubbish needed clearing away before the advancement of scientific learning could occur. Thomas Hobbes, who had been
Bacon's secretary, similarly attacked the tendency of scholastic philosophy
and theology to reify abstractions, whether through misunderstanding or
a deliberate intent to deceive. If such ideas did not translate from Latin
into clear English, there was a good reason, namely that they were nonsensical.[18] John Locke, who echoed Hobbes on these points, also criticized
the habit of "taking words for things," or believing that they necessarily
reflect reality.[19] Although all conceptions, and all language, were ultimately derived from sense experience—there being no other source of
knowledge—human imagination could nevertheless err in producing
fanciful ideas of things not to be found in nature. Locke was followed
closely by the etymological philosopher John Horne Tooke, who, in *The
Diversions of Purley* (1798 and 1805),[20] traced all words back to their concrete
roots and described language as an abstraction from sense experience.
Words were both abbreviations and metaphorical deployments of such
concrete ideas, which could lead us astray unless we armed ourselves with
the etymological knowledge of their origins. At the end of the eighteenth
and beginning of the nineteenth centuries, echoing his predecessors, the
legal reformer Jeremy Bentham attacked the "fictions" of both law and
language.[21]

The critique of taking words for things was characteristic of the hard-
headed tradition of British philosophy, which led directly to the abandonment of metaphysics and an emphasis on more pragmatic considerations,
such as those embodied by science and utilitarian politics and economics.
The central concern of this tradition with language, and especially with

the purification thereof, culminated in analytical philosophy and the movement toward symbolic logic, as a replacement for the error-laden and radically imperfect vehicles of communication represented by the natural languages. The two terms most commonly applied to this tradition are nominalism and empiricism. Nominalism, a philosophical school dating back to the Middle Ages, was opposed to realism. Realists—the original of whom was Plato, with his theory of Ideas or Forms—affirmed the real existence of those abstract qualities, such as Justice, or Whiteness, named by words. Nominalists insisted that such terms were only abstractions from experience. Individual beings were the only existent things, and the abstract qualities named by more general terms and concepts enjoyed no real existence, whether in this world or the next. The gap between language and reality could become a serious problem, requiring a purge of metaphysical terms and a closer adequation between language and the natural world. This is where the empiricism of the seventeenth century came in. By emphasizing the necessity of attending to nature as it is, and of adjusting our language to sense experience rather than projecting our linguistic conceits into the world, empiricism, based on scientific experimentation, would solve the problem of which the nominalist critique of language had made us aware.

The colonial attack on Indian languages, which borrowed these Baconian ideas, expressed not only the English sense of scientific superiority, but also a difference in linguistic ideologies and language practices. In a classic article on the command of language in colonial India, Bernard Cohn characterized the difference between the traditional South Asian understanding of language and the British understanding in the following way:

> Europeans of the seventeenth century lived in a world of signs and correspondences, whereas Indians lived in a world of substances ... Meaning for the English was something attributed to a word, a phrase, or an object, which could be determined and translated, at best with a synonym that had a direct referent to something in what the English thought of as a "natural" world. Everything had a more or less specific referent for the English. With the Indians, meaning was not necessarily construed in the same fashion. The effect and affect of hearing a Brahmin chant in Sanskrit at a sacrifice did not entail meaning in the European sense; it was to have one's substance literally affected by the sound. When a Mughal ruler issued

a farman or a parvana, it was more than an order or an entitlement. These were more than messages . . . In drawing up a document, a letter, or a treaty, everything about it was charged with a significance that transcended what might be thought of as its practical purpose. The paper, the forms of address, the preliminary phrases of invocation, the type of script, the elaboration of the terminology, the grammar, the seals used, the particular status of the composer and writer of the document, its mode of transportation, and the form of delivery—all were meaningful.[22]

In this terse formulation are compressed a number of claims. One is that English emphasized the meaning or content of language, at the expense of both its ritual form and its performative or transformative power. This corresponds to the difference between what linguists call the semantic and pragmatic functions of language.[23] English stressed the referential function of language, the manner in which it pointed to both particular meanings, on the one hand, and particular things in the real world, on the other, thereby guaranteeing their reciprocal, one-to-one connection. This view was naturalistic or scientific, as it subordinated language to the empirically observable world, which language merely represented and reflected. Both linguistic empiricism and the belief in referentiality coordinated with the British emphasis on codification, or the authority of the written (i.e., printed) text, whether such texts were in original Indian languages or translations from those languages into English. Such translations were founded on the idea of an underlying semantic content that could be reproduced in one linguistic form as easily as in another. Translation became an act of lexical substitution—the replacement of one word by its counterpart in another language—a process that was both enabled and typified by dictionaries. The coherence of this view of translation depended on the grounding of language on an extra-linguistic substratum. What guaranteed the possibility of exchanging a word for its foreign counterpart, was their common reference to some really existent thing.[24]

Cohn suggests that in traditional Indian culture, language was viewed quite differently than it was among the colonial British. As against semantic content, Indians emphasized the ritual form and performative or pragmatic function of language. Rather than merely a medium that passively recorded and transmitted propositional statements regarding the natural world, or the inner intentions of communicants, language was also an active force. Language did not merely point to a substance, on which it depended. Rather, it was often taken for or as a substance in its transformative power.[25]

It is not correct to state that Indians lived in "a world of substances." Obviously, both Europeans and Indians lived in "a world of signs and correspondences," that is to say, of representations constructed largely of words. Indians did not walk around stumbling into words. What Cohn seems to be suggesting is that Indians did not always recognize the semiotic dimensions of their discourse, which they mistook, on occasion, for substantial, unmediated reality. This comes very close to the colonial complaint that Indians took words for things. In any case, under the traditional Hindu religious cosmology, the boundary between language and material reality was indeed regarded as more permeable, a point of continuity rather than an absolute barrier.

To further specify the distinctions between these linguistic ideologies, it will be necessary to expand on Cohn's account. As Sheldon Pollock has noted, "we cannot know how colonialism changed South Asia if we do not know what was there to be changed."[26] British caricatures of Hindu chants and related practices were not entirely fictitious, despite the fact that they reflected biases inherited from Reformation-era polemics against Catholics. Hindus practiced a variety of forms of recitation, especially of their most sacred texts, the *Vedas*, and of formulas called mantras that were either verses from these scriptures or, especially in later forms of Hinduism, ritual formulas designed for either religious worship or pragmatic purposes. The uses of these formulas coordinated with a particular linguistic cosmology. Beginning over 1000 BCE in the Vedas, Speech (*Vāc*) was regarded as one of the primary creative forces, and worshiped as a goddess.[27] The efficacy of speech was preserved among the Brahmins, the highest caste, whose name denoted their possession and mastery of the ritual formulas or sacred words (*brahman*) that allow one to control the gods themselves. Beginning around 500 BCE, the *Upaniṣads*, especially the *Chāndogya* and the later *Māṇḍūkya*, elaborated the meaning of the most powerful syllable, the sacred *om*, in cosmic terms. In the *Atharva Veda* and the early Upaniṣads, verbal formulas figured prominently in rites of practical magic. The Tantras, a class of texts that appeared beginning around 600 CE in Buddhist and Hindu variants, continued and extended these ideas. They inflated the emphasis on the power of language, and especially of the mantras, so much that Hindu Tantra is also referred to as the science of mantras (*mantraśāstra*). Tantric mantras were, with few exceptions, a new sort of mantra, different from, although to some extent modeled on, their Vedic predecessors. They incorporated numerous, apparently nonsensical and often rhythmic seed syllables (*bīja*), which were regarded as especially efficacious. The repetition (*japa*) of mantras, even thousands of times or more, was considered a means of increasing their power. Such repetitions could be counted on a rosary (*japamālā, akṣamālā*) consisting of beads, seeds, or jewels.

As I have shown elsewhere, the procedures prescribed in numerous North Indian Hindu Tantras for making mantras successful or effective (*siddha*)—especially the enveloping (*saṃpuṭa*) of the mantras by adding certain bījas at the beginning and end in forward and reverse order respectively—converted mantras into diagrams of various processes of creation, including the cosmogony and sexual reproduction.[28] Enveloping shaped mantras into quasi-palindromes that imitated the cosmic cycle of creation and destruction in their forward and backward motion. By the same device, mantras were also made to imitate the in-and-out movement of sexual intercourse and the cycle of reproduction, or leaving and returning to the womb. By being assimilated to other, especially creative forms of activity, mantras became effective as instruments of ritual power, or what have been called speech acts.[29] Through the addition of special symbolic letters, mantras also represented the evolution of the five elements from abstract to concrete, from ethereal space to solid earth. The beginning of the mantra, in the cosmic ether, coincided with the traditional belief that sound or speech was the beginning of the cosmogony. By tracing the evolution of the elements from their most subtle form until the point at which they assumed substantial existence in the element of earth, mantras symbolized the transformation of sound into matter. This underwrote the Tantric belief in the magical power of words: the idea that mantras could produce tangible results, such as those defined by the six magical rites (*ṣaṭkarmāṇi*).[30] Arthur Avalon neatly expressed Tantra as a theory of "natural name": the belief in the co-origination of speech and reality.[31] The articulation of the mantra was similarly understood as the coming-to-embodiment of the divinity that it named. The bīja was literally the seed or sperm out of which the god arose;[32] and the mantra constituted the subtle body of the divinity that could otherwise be represented in a solid image (*mūrti*) of stone or wood. It was not for nothing that Cohn stated that Sanskrit chanting was understood to affect one's very substance. Despite the existence of alternative viewpoints,[33] the role of language in many traditional Vedic and Tantric practices reflected a belief in the cosmic power of language, and its consubstantiality with reality, meaning both its substance-like status and its ability to alter the natural world. Although notions of literal interpretation existed, they were frequently subordinated to symbolic, metaphorical, or poetic treatments of language.

The linguistic ideology of modernity contrasts with that of some traditional forms of Hinduism on a number of key points, several of which were raised already by Cohn. The British emphasized the semantic function of language—its meaning-bearing function—as opposed to its pragmatic function as a mode of poetic or ritual performance. Both cultures aimed to make language reflect nature, and so accord with reality. For some Hindus, this relationship of resemblance between language and reality could work in both directions: Language could not only imitate reality, but also alter it. In contrast, for most British the relationship between language and reality was uni-directional. Language should be made to reflect reality, through empirical categorization and the elimination of metaphysical terms. However, the relationship could not be inverted in such a way as to manipulate reality prospectively by means of language, as if by magic. This contrast describes a difference in the linguistic cosmologies of the two cultures. In traditional Hinduism, language could be ontologically prior to the physical world, whereas in modern Britain, it could not.

The difference thus described appears to coincide with a shift in linguistic episteme that occurred during the seventeenth century in Europe. Brian Vickers has described this as a change in "the relationship between language and reality," a shift from the "identity" between words and things posited by occult traditions, to the "analogy" posited by scientific traditions: "In the scientific tradition . . . a clear distinction is made between words and things and between literal and metaphorical language. The occult tradition does not recognize this distinction: Words are treated as if they are equivalent to things and can be substituted for them."[34]

Vickers associates this transformation in linguistic ideology with the critique of the habit of taking words for things advanced by Bacon, Hobbes, Locke, and others,[35] which anticipated the modern doctrine of the arbitrariness of the linguistic sign formulated by Ferdinand de Saussure.[36] Other proponents of a cultural Great Divide between past and present have pointed to the premodern, irrational conflation of words and things, or of different registers of language (such as poetic and semantic), and the modern, rational separation of these.[37] The opponents of such a divide naturally reject such a distinction.[38] However, in some cases, such as that of the colonial encounter between British and Hindus, such a divide, however it is described, seems to have been not entirely a figment of the moderns' own imaginations, although we must be careful not to exaggerate its magnitude. The question of the existence or nonexistence of a Great Divide is fraught with teleological and moral bias, and as I have suggested, owes much to an earlier Christian narrative of the disenchantment of the world through the coming of Christ, and the triumph of the plain speech of the Gospel over the obscurity and mystery of pagan oracles. By raising this question again in terms of an opposition of styles of discourse—a difference that, although charged with rhetorical and religious motives, nevertheless possesses some cultural reality—I shall try to steer the narrow course between either denying the specific difference of modernity or confirming modernity's own characterization of this difference. In colonial South Asia, the various critiques that the British leveled against traditional, Sanskritic Hindu linguistic culture helped to bring about a shift of mentalities or a new episteme that progressively encroached on, when it did not render obsolete, the older tradition.

The introduction of Protestant literalism, mediated by a new textual economy of the printed book, precipitated, for those whom it affected, a radical qualitative transformation in the order of discourse, one that fundamentally altered the Hindu linguistic cosmos and redrew the boundaries and relations among language, thought, and reality. Crucial to a reconstruction of the meaning of linguistic reform in the colonial context is an appreciation of how the basic Christian opposition of monotheism to polytheism and idolatry had been transposed into the domain of language. Various critiques of verbal idolatry—the normative opposition of a scriptural canon to heathenish custom, the attack on the personifications of mythological language, and the polemic against vain repetitions in prayers and magic spells (as described in chapter 4)—were applied to Indian linguistic theories and practices, as they had been applied previously to Catholic and sectarian practices in Britain. The soteriological dimensions of a perfect language as the fulfillment of the monotheistic ideal underlay a number of proposals for linguistic reform in colonial South Asia. The recovery of the historical roots of the British reordering of South Asian discourses in religion, and specifically Protestant iconoclasm, challenges the self-representation of colonialism and of the modernity that it ushered in as simply rational or utilitarian, as opposed to the primitive superstitions of the colonized Others. Although postcolonial studies have done much to dispel the "white mythology" of rationality that conceals the epistemological violence of colonialism,[39] so far the properly religious dimensions of this mythology have not been adequately addressed.

The colonial situation in many ways reveals most clearly the contours of linguistic iconoclasm and its connections with processes of modernization. "Idolatry" is a category of cultural comparison, a label applied by one group to the beliefs or practices of another, which depends on a distinction between (our) true and (their) false religion. Even the briefest study of the beginnings of comparative religion in the early modern period shows that the traditional Christian category of idolatry deeply influenced the initial assessment of other cultures, and remained a central category of comparison for centuries. Such comparisons are always also acts of communication, and of translation. What is often ignored is the fact that, in the colonial context, translation occurred on two levels simultaneously. The lingual level, that of dictionaries, which involved the word-for-word replacement of the categories of one culture by those of another, was only the first and most obvious. The second and more important level was metalinguistic, and consisted in the replacement, either partial or total, of one linguistic ideology by another. The colonial attack on Indian idolatry—verbal as well as visual—was part of a broader opposition of one regime of representation, one linguistic cosmology, to another.

Although I have used the shorthand expression "Protestant literalism" to refer to this divide, it is important to recognize that literalism alone is an inadequate description of it. The Tantras were also literalist in the sense that they assumed at least the potential of a perfect correspondence between words and things. From one perspective, Protestant and later Enlightened styles were distinguished by a sharpened distinction between the literal and metaphorical uses of language, combined with a new empiricism and a devaluation of the symbol. An example of this is Huldrych Zwingli's (1484–1531) insistence that Christ's statement "This is my body" had to be taken in a symbolic rather than a literal sense, for to do otherwise would lead to the false doctrine of transubstantion: the belief that, in the Eucharistic meal, the bread and wine are literally transformed into the body and blood of Christ.[40]

Protestant Literalism, Scientific Nominalism, and the Attack on Verbal Idolatry

Whatever the degree of reality possessed by British complaints against the tendency of Indian languages to take words for things, such complaints represented both more and less than the opposition of science to superstition.

They also reflected deeply held Protestant presuppositions concerning the nature and function of language, as well as Christian historical ideas regarding the triumph of the Gospel over pagan idolatry, as described in the previous chapter. One problem with the familiar history of the ascendancy of science and reason, which constitutes part of the autobiography of modern culture at least within the English-speaking world, is that it significantly underestimates the connections of philosophical nominalism with theology. Although the attack on the habit of taking words for things did constitute a general theory of language and reality, it was also closely connected with religious iconoclasm. In order to understand these dimensions of British polemics against Indian languages, we must spend some time investigating their historical and theological background.

The simplest example of such linguistic iconoclasm is Bacon's use of the term "idol" to describe the various cognitive fallacies.[41] Subsequent thinkers in the Baconian tradition continued, well into the nineteenth century, to employ overtly religious rhetoric in their critiques of language. In this tradition, the religious crime of idolatry was converted into a kind of linguistic confusion, a cognitive error: the false inference from the existence of a name, to the existence of the thing named. The prototype for this error was the belief in the reality of the pagan gods. Some of the most important British thinkers generalized this cardinal mistake of the Gentiles to the point where it appeared as the root cause of much contemporary epistemological error and theological strife. The reconstruction of this dimension of seventeenth-century language reforms sheds important light on the connections among Protestantism, science, and the new philosophy. It also explains a number of polemics against Indian languages and traditions. Following an account of earlier British examples of linguistic iconoclasm, subsequent sections of this chapter show the impact of these ideas on Friedrich Max Müller's nineteenth-century explanation of Hindu and other mythologies as a disease of language.

Attacks on the idolizing of words provided one of the central themes of Thomas Sprat's *History of the Royal Society* (1667), an apology for the nascent Royal Society of London for Improving Natural Knowledge founded in 1660, the preeminent body for the advancement of science in England during the second half of the seventeenth century, which was founded on Baconian principles. Sprat adopted a version of the standard Protestant sacred history according to which a pure, original Christianity had been corrupted by paganism.[42] He modified this narrative for the purpose of championing the cause of science. He extolled the Royal Society's emphasis on "*Works* before *Words*"[43] as the basis for a true science: "*The Royal Society* . . . did not regard the credit of *Names*, but of *Things*."[44] The distinction was between the sophistical and merely verbal knowledge of the grammarians and schoolmen, and the concrete knowledge of nature advocated by the new experimentalists. Hence the Society's motto "Nullius in Verba," which translates roughly as "we place faith in the words of no one," and expresses a rejection of the authority of tradition.

Sprat's polemic against verbal knowledge drew deeply on the rhetoric of iconoclasm. The dedicatory poem by Abraham Cowley depicted Francis Bacon as a Moses leading his people forth from the land of false gods, "Countries where yet instead of Nature, we/ Her Images and Idols worship'd see."[45] He elaborated with the image of the scarecrow:

> Authority, which did a Body boast,
> Though 'twas but Air condens'd and stalk'd about,
> Like some old Giants more Gigantic Ghost,
> To terrifie the Learned Rout
> With the plain Magique of tru Reasons Light,
> He chac'd out of our sight,
> Nor suffer'd Living Men to be misled
> By the vain Shadows of the Dead:
> To Graves, from whence it rose, the conquer'd Phantome
> He broke that Monstrous God which stood
> In midst of th'Orchard, and the whole did claim,
> Which with a useless Sith of Wood,
> And something else not worth a name,
> . . . made Children and superstitious Men afraid.
> The Orchard's open now, and free;
> Bacon has broke that Scar-crow Deitie;
> . . .
> From Words, which are but Pictures of the Thought,
> (Though we our Thoughts from them perversly drew)
> To Things, the Minds right Object, he it brought . . .

Thomas Hobbes had also used the image of the scarecrow to describe how, in the universities, the schoolmen would use Aristotle's "doctrine of separated essences"—that is, the idea of a soul or spirit independent of the body—to "fright [people] from obeying the laws of their country with empty names, as men fright birds from the corn with an empty doublet, a hat, and a crooked stick."[46] Like Hobbes, Cowley diagnosed idolatry as, above all, a linguistic offense. The body of this idol was "but Air condens'd." This echoed the nominalist doctrine that some words are *flatus vocis*, mere words or breath. Such religious words are the most windy ones, full of nothing substantial. Yet puffed up, they can cast a giant shadow able to frighten us, quite literally, out of our sound minds. The image of the scarecrow further served to make such idolatry appear ridiculous.

In the main body of the work, Sprat continued these themes. The first part provided an account of the history of knowledge. The Egyptians obscured the knowledge of nature by wrapping it up in "the dark Shadows of *Hieroglyphicks*."[47] Paganism infected Christianity primarily through Greek philosophy,[48] which led to arguments over words: "Warrs of the Tongue"[49] or a "Notional Warr."[50] Prior to Christianity, the world was darkened by superstition. Heroes like Bacon freed us from the "slavery to dead Mens names . . . which lye like Monsters in their way."[51] Sprat concluded this part of his history by contrasting two modes of respect for tradition, one wholesome, and the other not. The names of the dead could be preserved by pictures or by children. Whereas the former more closely resembled the deceased, they were merely "dead *Pictures*, or *Statues*, . . . [rather than] *Genuine Off-spring*."[52] We should accordingly respect tradition as its children, by adding our own vigor and ideas, even if these diverged from the past. The "slavery to dead Mens names"—an unthinking continuation of tradition in which no particle is ever changed, and nothing new ever added—was at once a form of idolatry and a prescription for sterility and stagnation. Sprat defended the methods of the Royal Society against the claims of tradition by distinguishing freedom of thought and revisionism as the true religion, opposed to idolatry or a veneration of the images of the dead. The celebrated battle of the moderns versus the ancients—of Baconian experimentalism against the dead hand of changeless tradition, represented by the dreaded Aristotle—thus took on the character of a holy war that emulated and extended the religious Reformation.

Hobbes, although never a member of the Royal Society, directed a withering nominalist critique at talk of spirits and pagan deities. He described the "Demonology" of the Gentiles, which "filled almost all places with spirits called *demons* . . . and a whole kingdom of fairies and bugbears."[53] This foreshadowed the later Romantic conception of the world of paganism as an enchanted one, with the crucial difference that, for Hobbes, this was not some vanished dream, but an all-too-real nightmare from which his philosophy was designed to awaken us. He criticized the overactive imaginations of the

Gentiles that had populated nature with innumerable spirits of different varieties, all of which were "idols of the brain."[54] He associated the concept of idolatry with the Greek root *eido-* (to see) and its derivatives, such as *eidolon* (image),[55] and transferred the label of idolatry to both Plato's forms (*eidola*) and Aristotle's categories. The Catholic Church had inherited such pagan mythology and idolatry and other relics of the Gentiles, together with the vain philosophy of the Greeks, which, like their mythology, asserted the real existence of fictitious conceits.

Hobbes attributed the belief in such phantasmic creatures to confused language. The poets were responsible for inventing such nonsense.[56] He insisted that all talk of "incorporeal substances," such as one heard from the scholastic theologians, was a contradiction in terms.[57] He connected such abuses of words, including especially the reification or turning into noun substantives of qualitative or adjectival terms, with the false doctrine of transubstantiation that held that the bread of the Eucharist was literally transformed into Christ's body.[58] Hobbes argued that originally in scripture the word "spirit" (Latin *spiritus*) meant only breath, and the word "angel" (Greek *angelos*) meant a messenger.[59] Taking these terms to signify incorporeal beings deprived them of all sense. Similarly, the terms Satan and Devil were actually "appellations" meaning "enemy" and "destroyer," which, when left untranslated, gave the false impression that they were "the proper names of *demons*."[60] Hobbes defined idolatry as "the worship not of other, (for there is but one God), but of strange gods; that is to say, a worship though of one God, yet under other *titles, attributes,* and *rites,* than what were established by Abraham and Moses."[61] If other gods than the One did not exist, then it followed logically that, in worshipping other gods, one was worshipping only their names, or worshipping the One God under a false name. In either case, polytheism was not the real worship of other gods, but only a form of linguistic confusion. Idols could be figured in plastic or verbal form: "And whereas a man can fancy shapes he never saw, making up a figure out of the parts of divers creatures, as the poets make their centaurs, chimeras, and other monsters never seen, so can he also give matter to these shapes, and make them in wood, clay, or metal."[62] Such impersonations needed to be stripped of authority to make way for the legitimate sovereign, represented by another idol or fictive person, the Biblical image of the Leviathan.

Although Hobbes claimed an absolutely rigorous fidelity to the original meaning of scripture, his materialist literalism, especially as applied to the concept of spiritual beings, could clearly provoke skepticism regarding the existence not only of spirits and idols, but of God himself. Emphasizing this point, early opponents including Bishop John Bramhall accused him of atheism. Leaving aside the debate over Hobbes's religious convictions, it is clear that he exemplified a number of important critical tendencies characteristic of the Reformation. Above all, in his attacks on idolatry, on the remains of the Gentiles or pagans, on the doctrine of transubstantiation, and on the authority of the Church that, as he thought, depended on all of these, Hobbes continued and extended Protestant, anti-Catholic iconoclasm.[63]

John Locke endorsed these attacks on the habit of "taking words for things."[64] Following Hobbes's etymologies of the same terms, Locke observed that "*Spirit*, in its primary signification, is breath; *angel*, a messenger."[65] Locke's references to idolatry, however, were much less frequent and obvious than Hobbes's.[66]

A century later, John Horne Tooke adapted Locke's idea that all words are based, ultimately, on sensory impressions, by tracing the etymologies of literally thousands of words back to concrete roots that depended, finally, on sense experience. All language was an abstraction from these roots, and could mislead us unless we became aware, through etymological analysis, of their origins. Tooke borrowed from not only Locke, but also Bacon's attack on the idols of language,[67] and attributed many of the ills of language to the poets, with their habit of *prosopopoeia* or personification.[68] Eching several of his predecessors, Horne Tooke explained that terms such as "Heaven, Hell, . . . Fiend, Angel, Apostle, Saint, Spirit" were not even true nouns, but "Participles and Adjectives, not understood as such, [which] have caused a metaphysical jargon and a false morality, which can only be dissipated by etymology. And, when they come to be examined, you will find that the ridicule which Dr. Conyers Middleton has justly bestowed upon the Papists for their absurd coinage of Saints, is equally applicable to ourselves and to all other metaphysicians; whose moral deities . . . are not less ridiculously coined and imposed upon their followers."[69]

More than simple empiricism, such critiques encoded the displacement of Protestant iconoclasm into the domain of language, and viewed the purging of linguistic idols as part of the work of religious Reformation. Both religion and science were united in their efforts to disenchant the world by expunging fairies, sprites, miracles, and other enchantments.[70] The combination of nominalism with iconoclasm attacked the linguistic fictions of pagan mythology and the scholastic discourse that continued such heresies. Christianity and empiricism jointly promoted a reorientation toward the concrete.

Such a coordination of methods and goals was already alleged by Sprat in his *History*. He sought to refute the charge of atheism directed at the members of the Royal Society[71] and identify their experimental scientific method with Christianity through their common endeavor in eradicating superstition, or disenchanting the world: "It is now the fittest season for *Experiments* to arise, to teach us a Wisdome, which springs from the depths of *Knowledge*, to shake off the shadows, and to scatter the mists, which fill the minds of men with a vain consternation. This is a *work* well-becoming the most *Christian Profession*. For the most apparent effect, which attended the passion of *Christ*, was the putting of an eternal silence, on all the false oracles, and dissembled inspirations of *Antient Times*."[72]

As an apologist, Sprat's motives are of course suspect. Yet he points to some affinities between religion and science that we would do well to take seriously, especially as these have been noticed again by modern scholars.[73] Sprat argues that the severe discipline of experimental philosophers resembles religious mortification.[74] Submitting to the revision of our former, erroneous hypotheses parallels the corrections of religious repentance. The scientist who undertakes pains to serve the cause of natural knowledge more closely approaches Christian humility than does the vain purveyor of speculative school-knowledge.[75] Whereas Catholicism is inimical to the scientific mind, the searching criticism practiced by the Royal Society is a direct continuation of the religious Reformation:[76] "The present *Inquiring Temper* of this Age was at first produc'd by the liberty of judging, and searching, and reasoning, which was us'd in the first *Reformation* . . . The *Church of England* therefore may justly be styl'd the *Mother* of this sort of *Knowledge*; and so the care of its *nourishment* and *prosperity* peculiarly lyes upon it."[77]

Indeed, the Society even represents the true spirit of the Reformation, which has now brought religion down to earth, where it belongs: "Men must now be told, that as *Religion* is a *hevenly thing*, so it is not utterly averse from making use of the Rules of *human Prudence*. They must be inform'd, that the *True Holiness* is a severity over our selves, and not others."[78] Of course, we have the advantage over Sprat in knowing later chapters of the story, in which the fissures between science and traditional Christianity deepened. Few today would claim a simple continuity between the two.[79]

Arguments concerning the relationship between science and religion in the seventeenth century have often focused on their common linguistic ideology. Already in the 1930s, Robert Merton noted the coordination of religion and science in promoting a reform of language away from poetic, metaphorical, and ornamented styles toward a mode of prosaic literalism. Merton claimed that the redirection of the Puritan ethos into the scientific domain "was at the immediate expense of literary, and ultimately, of religious pursuits."[80] Citing the theologian John Smith's retelling of Plutarch's account of the decline of the oracles and the rise of a clear language of prophecy—an event that Smith identified with the advent of the Gospel of Christ[81]—Merton argued that earlier decades of the seventeenth century witnessed a decline of interest in poetry or a loss of its social prestige, which scholars attributed to a variety of sources, especially "Puritanism, the new philosophy and science."[82] The Royal Society's interest in promoting the knowledge of things rather than words—factual rather than merely verbal knowledge—and a correspondingly plain style of language established an "affinity between Puritanism, Baconianism and the new science."[83] Whether or not the Reformation gave birth to science, as Sprat claimed long before Merton, it does appear to have contributed to the definition of science as a discursive domain opposed to the fictions of pagan mythology.[84]

A perusal of these proposals for the reform of language in seventeenth-century England suggests that the birth of the scientific movement was even more endangered and agonistic than standard histories of that movement would indicate. The triumph of science was achieved only after a long struggle with a series of monsters—scarecrows, centaurs, ghosts, and other horrors—all of which creatures had to be banished to establish and enforce the borders of the kingdom of science. A mere convergence of terminology between science and Protestant iconoclasm of course does not amount to an identity of interests and intentions.[85] The use of religious rhetoric may be an unconscious mirroring of traditional categories, or a deliberate and strategic deployment of those categories for rhetorical purposes, including persuasion and dissimulation: an attempt to present essentially philosophical arguments to a broader, religiously oriented populace, or to conceal one's own secular motivations. However, there are several reasons to regard such iconoclastic rhetoric as the indication of a deeper connection between theological and secular, scientific modes of thought. Attacks on verbal idolatry suggest a close convergence of theology and science in their conceptions of language and of representation more generally. Iconoclasm is a central, not a peripheral feature of the Christian theological tradition; and to find it occupying a prominent role in the discourses of science and philosophy calls into question the degree of independence from theological thought that these domains have often been thought to possess. In a number of cases, such as the critique of vain repetitions discussed in chapter 4, these criticisms appear to have originated in theology, and only subsequently made their way into the scientific tradition. Moreover, the attacks on the names of pagan gods and of spirits by the scientists seem to have originated in an earlier and contemporaneous tradition of Christian, and especially Protestant, comparative mythology that explained pagan idolatry or polytheism as stemming from a linguistic confusion, in which the proliferation of names for the deity was mistaken for the actual existence of other deities. Mythologists such as Gerard Vossius (1577–1649) and John Selden (1584–1654), as discussed below, may have served as the source for Hobbes's linguistic reduction of the names of pagan gods. This tradition reemerged most notably in the late nineteenth century in the person of Friedrich Max Müller, who extended these critiques of mythological language to Hinduism in the course of creating what he called a Science of Religion. This suggests that, on the issue of historical priority, science followed rather than led religion in its attack on verbal idolatry.

Friedrich Max Müller's Comparative Mythology

> At first, the names of God, like fetishes or statues, were honest attempts at expressing or representing an idea which could never find an adequate expression or representation. But the eidolon, or likeness, became an idol; the nomen, or name, lapsed into a numen, or demon, as soon as they were drawn away from their original intention.[86]

> Do you still wonder at polytheism or at mythology? Why, they are inevitable. They are, if you like, a parler enfantin of religion. But the world has its childhood, and when it was a child it spoke as a child, it understood as a child, it thought as a child; and, I say again, in that it spoke as a child its language was true. The fault rests with us, if we insist on taking the language of children for the language of men, if we attempt to translate literally ancient into modern language, oriental into occidental speech, poetry into prose.[87]

Viewed in the context of earlier British critiques of linguistic idolatry, colonial contrasts between European prose and Indian poetry no longer appear as simple reflections of the difficulty of communicating with Indians and the desire to overcome the translation barrier. Such contrasts also often encoded religious distinctions, and even had soteriological dimensions. The transition from enigmatic to plain speech supposedly paralleled the passage from spiritual childhood to maturity. The two quotes above—both from Friedrich Max Müller, the most famous nineteenth-century critic of Indian languages and mythology—traced idolatry to a "disease of language" that infected especially, but not only, tropical India. Müller's views of linguistic and religious evolution, which placed Indians in the position of children, deliberately echoed both the Protestant identification of the Gospel as plain speech and Paul's conversion narrative (from 1 Corinthians 13:11, KJV): "When I was a child, I spake as a child." The reform of Indian languages would, accordingly, effect both a linguistic and a religious Reformation, one that Müller devoted much of his life to accomplish. This section lays the groundwork for appreciating some neglected theological dimensions of Müller's project.

Müller was a German expatriate who had taken up residence in England in 1846 to work on the first printed edition of the *Rig Veda* and ended up as Professor of Comparative Philology at Oxford, with a list of honorary titles, degrees, and academy memberships too numerous to mention, and an equally long bibliography of published works ranging from Sanskrit literature to the comparative study of language, mythology, and religion.[88] Today he is remembered primarily for his theory of myth as a disease of language that can be cured through historical linguistics or etymological analysis.[89] According to Müller, myths, as represented most clearly by the hymns of the Hindu Vedas (ca. 1500–1200 BCE), were originally descriptions of natural occurrences, such as the rising of the sun. Terms drawn from the experience of nature were used initially as metaphors for the divinity. These terms were later corrupted and erroneously taken to refer to anthropomorphic deities. Hence Müller's famous formula that in myth, "nomina become numina": Names become spirits (or demons); the names applied to God are taken as gods themselves.

Müller's theory of myth was debunked in his own lifetime by Andrew Lang, and his "solar mythology" became the target of parody.[90] This explains the common interpretation of Müller as largely irrelevant to the contemporary discipline of religious studies.[91] Ritually invoked as a totemic ancestor, his own works scarcely read, he has reemerged in recent decades in the context of a debate over the origins of the modern study of religion. The debate turns on the degree to which the study of religion was, and is, theological in its origins and orientation; and when, if ever, it emerged as a scientific discipline in its own right, separate from theology. For religious studies, Müller is a father figure in a dysfunctional family with a contested lineage.[92] Whereas there is general agreement that he was personally a committed Christian,[93] the disagreement is over the connection of his private religion with his public theories.[94]

Müller's theory of myth resembled somewhat the theories of his contemporary Adalbert Kuhn (1812–1881) in Germany and, somewhat later, Michel Bréal (1832–1915) in France.[95] However, the view that mythology was an effect of language was much older. Müller's attack on mythological language drew from the tradition of Bacon, Hobbes, and Locke, as well as from a Christian and especially Protestant tradition of comparative mythology, which included such figures as John Selden and Gerard Vossius, who had already interpreted pagan polytheism as a linguistic confusion.[96] This tradition anticipated certain of Müller's specific ideas and terminology, such as the formula that in myth "nomina become numina," which echoed nominalism,[97] and the explanation of polytheism as stemming from polyonymy, or the proliferation of poetic and metaphorical names for the deity, which were, in their origins, only names for natural phenomena, and especially for the sun, that with the passage of time were no longer understood to be metaphorical.

Müller's theory described in detail the process by which language becomes diseased. Mythology refers to many deities who, from our perspective, do not exist. How is it that such false beliefs arise? Müller's answer was that, originally, the names of these deities were simply the names of natural forces, such as the sun or the wind. For example, one of the chief Vedic gods, Agni, denoted the fire into which the sacrifice was offered. Gradually, such words for natural forces lost their status as appellations or adjectives and were taken instead as proper names:[98] "The mischief begins when language forgets itself, and makes us mistake the Word for the Thing, the Quality for the Substance, the *Nomen* for the *Numen*."[99] Mythology sprang from turning "nouns of quality into nouns of substance."[100] At that moment, there occurred a personification of terms originally understood to be metaphorical. The grammatical division of nouns according to gender in many languages such as Sanskrit also facilitated personification.[101] This process of mythologizing depended on the original meaning of language having been forgotten, subject to recovery only through historical study.[102] For example, the sun was originally referred to as a "shiner," and subsequently, this descriptive was taken to refer to an actual being or agent that was both divine and resplendent with light. Eventually, this name became fossilized and was then prone to phonetic shift over time. The common Indo-European term for God as "sky-father," evidenced by the Vedic Sanskrit *dyaus pitar*, had in other Indo-European languages become the proper names Zeus and Jupiter, which obscured the original etymological reference. The word "shining" (Sanskrit *divya*) was the root of the words for god found in the various Indo-European languages: Sanskrit *deva*, Greek *theos*, and Latin *deus*. A variation of the same process also explained pagan polytheism, or the belief in multiple gods so prevalent in mythology. One substantive, such as the sun, was given numerous names according to its different qualities, such as bright, warm, and so on. With the passage of time, it was forgotten not only that these names were mere adjectives or appellatives, but also that they referred to the same thing. Thus, "the *polyonymy* of [mythological] language . . . is what we are accustomed to call *polytheism* in religion."[103] Müller referred the term polyonymy to the Stoics,[104] although there were other, more recent precedents for his use of this term.

Müller's idea that many myths were originally literal tales concerning the rising and setting of the sun, and its revolutions during the course of the year, affirmed that natural bodies or phenomena were, in some sense, appropriate metaphors for the divinity. His account of the original naturalness and spontaneity of mythological expression was a necessary corollary of his scientific approach to mythology. Müller emphasized that human beings can use only the materials of language to express any concept, even the concept of divinity. Nothing else is available for us. Together with Locke, he insisted that all language and all thought begin with perception. All words had originally a concrete reference.[105] Müller paraphrased Locke's famous statement that "nothing is in the intellect that has not come from the senses,"[106] substituting "religion" for the "intellect."[107] Although we cannot perceive divinity directly, we can perceive and name the sun,[108] and then apply such names, by metaphorical extension, to the deity.

Although Müller claimed to be engaged in the creation of a Science of Religion—a feat of demythologizing that combined empiricism with historical philology—his theory of myth was deeply invested in the theological categories of the Reformation, and above all in polemics against linguistic idolatry. Müller cited Bacon's critique of the different idols of the mind,[109] and often made favorable reference to Locke's,[110] Horne Tooke's,[111] and especially Hobbes's[112] theories of language. He followed Hobbes's and

Locke's etymological reductions of spirit, angel, and related terms:[113] "Spirit was one of the many names by which human ignorance tried to lay hold of the perceiver as distinguished from the perceived. It is a poor name, if you like; it meant originally no more than a puff or whiff, a breeze, a breath."[114] Moreover, Müller's argument that mythological names for deities were originally "appellatives,"[115] "adjectives" or "qualitative terms,"[116] or "predicates"[117] that had falsely been converted into substantives, echoed these earlier thinkers. Hobbes had argued against taking "appellations" of the Devil as "proper names." Horne Tooke had argued that terms such as "Heaven, Hell, . . . Fiend, Angel, Apostle, Saint, Spirit" were not even true nouns, but "Participles and Adjectives."[118] Like the British nominalists before him, Müller identified mythology as a form of linguistic idolatry. In agreement with Hobbes, Müller advanced a linguistic interpretation of the pagan gods as merely empty names: "It was a mistake of the early fathers to treat the heathen gods as demons or evil spirits . . . They are masks without an actor,—the creations of man, not his creators; they are *nomina*, not *numina*; names without being, not beings without names."[119]

The rhetoric of iconoclasm recurred throughout Müller's writings. His reference to mythology as a shadow echoed Bacon's similar complaint against the "shadows thrown by words."[120] Müller glossed "shadow" with the same Greek word, *eidolon*, meaning "image" or Plato's "ideas": "We speak, for instance, of the *shades* of the departed, which meant originally their shadows. Those who first introduced this expression . . . evidently took the shadow as the nearest approach to what they wished to express; something that should be incorporeal, yet closely connected with the body. The Greek *eidolon*, too, is not much more than the shadow."[121] This passage connects *eidolon* or "shadow" with the notion of a separate soul or immaterial spirit, a favorite target of Hobbes, who complained persistently against "incorporeal beings" and "disembodied essences." Müller employed the terms *eidolon* and "idol" interchangeably,[122] echoing Hobbes's explicit equation of the two terms.

Several versions of Müller's famous formula that mythology involves the mistaking of *nomina* for *numina*, or names for spirits,[123] identified this cognitive error with idolatry: "Names have a tendency to become things, *nomina* grow into *numina*, ideas into *idols*, and if this happened with the name *Dyu* [for Zeus, Jupiter], no wonder that many things which were intended for Him who is above the sky were mixed up with sayings relating to the sky."[124] An example of this is when an abstract term is, quite literally, transformed into a statue and worshiped as a goddess, as happened with the Latin word *virtus* (virtue).[125] The same process could be observed in modern times, as in the worship in Revolutionary France of "the Goddess Reason."[126] Müller condemned a long list of abstract terms used in modern philosophy and politics, the successors of medieval Scholasticism: "such terms as *Nature, Law, Freedom, Necessity, Body, Substance, Matter, Church, State, Revelation, Inspiration, Knowledge, Belief.*"[127]

As Tomoko Masuzawa points out,[128] the Nomina-Numina formula is a pun that illustrates what it denotes: metaphorical extension and change of meaning by a simple process of phonetic substitution, or in this case a change of vowel. The Ideas-Idols formula, which works better as a pun for an English-speaking audience, was chosen for the same reason; and it may also have been suggested by Bacon's and Hobbes's earlier associations of the Platonic ideas with idolatry. In this way Müller depicted mythology as a poetic corruption of language of the sort that occurs in folk etymologies, or in the modern game of telephone, in which a message at one end of a human chain is passed along until, inexorably, it is corrupted and garbled beyond recognition.

Early Christian Comparative Mythology and the Attack on Linguistic Idolatry

Where did Müller get his ideas, and the formulas in which he expressed them? The Nomina-Numina formula had been used by earlier comparative mythologists writing in Latin, for whom the use of this pun made intuitive sense.[129] The English Orientalist and legal scholar John Selden may have been one source for Hobbes's attacks on linguistic idolatry.[130] In both *Titles of Honor* (1614) and *De diis syris* ("On the Syrian Gods") (1617), a book on the pagan gods named in the Bible, Selden explained that polytheism was the result of a proliferation of names and titles for God[131] and, together with Gerard Vossius, whom he may have influenced, was one of the first to use the Nomina-Numina formula.[132] The following statement by Selden is illustrative: "Where at first there were only various names (*nomina*), there came to be various divinities (*numina*). Thus the moon which was called Isis, Lucine, Diana, Trivia, Hecate, in the end gave rise to as many goddesses: each *nomen* became a particular *numen*."[133] Like others before and after him, including "solar mythology" Müller, Selden attributed polytheism and idolatry to the worship of celestial bodies, including the sun.[134] The twelfth-century Jewish scholar Maimonides was a primary source for these views, which had also been advanced by some earlier thinkers.[135] Edward, Lord Herbert of Cherbury (1583–1645), who advanced a concept of natural religion and of the origins of idolatry that anticipated the Deists,[136] held similar views, as the titles of two of the chapters in his work *On Pagan Religion* (*De religione gentilium*) illustrate: "Why there were so many Names given to God, and what they were" and "The Worship of the Sun and his Several Names."[137] Herbert cautioned that "wise people did not think that the Sun itself . . . was the Supreme God."[138] John Tillotson (1630–1694) also contended that the supreme God was often identified as the sun.[139] In 1687, John Turner referred to the sun as a "*multifarious* and *Polyonymous Numen* . . . who was Worshipped by antiquity under a Thousand names as the *Supream Numen*."[140] All of these thinkers preceded Müller in connecting the thesis of the origin of idolatry in sun-worship with the interpretation of pagan polytheism as a linguistic confusion.

The explanation of idolatry as a linguistic confusion—one that took the names of deities, as well as of lesser spirits and demons, as guarantees of their existence and reality—was central to British nominalism, which extended this idea into a general critique of language. According to Joseph Spence's *Polymetis* (1747), this explanation appeared already in classical Greek and Roman accounts of mythology, including those of Cicero, Varro, Seneca and Pliny:

> The old Romans, as well as the rest of the heathen world, were very expert at making distinctions by names; where, according to their own notions, there was no manner of difference in the things. The thinking part of them believed that there was but one great Being, that made, and preserved, and actuated all things: which is just as much as to say that they believed there was but one God, in our sense of the word. Their best authors say this expressly, in books which they published in their life-time; and some of them go so far as even to give the reasons why they talked vulgarly of so many gods. When they considered this one great Being as influencing the affairs of the world in different manners, they gave him as many different names; and hence came all their variety of nominal gods.[141]

From the fifteenth century onward, similar explanations by the ancients were encountered through the humanist study of classical traditions, including pagan mythology. At the same time, increasing knowledge of contemporary, non-Abrahamic traditions as a result of European exploration contributed to the desire for an explanation of those traditions that would reconcile them to the master narrative of sacred history presented in the Bible. This desire contributed significantly to the birth of the modern, comparative study of religion, which traces part of its parentage to Christian theology. For Christians, sacred history was anchored on the goal of salvation and the triumph of monotheism. The discovery, whether historical or ethnographic, of civilizations that to all appearances worshipped other gods or even several gods at once, called this historical narrative into question. Christianity perceived polytheism as both a spiritual threat and a philosophical problem. Polytheism disturbed the always-fragile relationship of religious revelation to natural reason and historical justification.[142] From a Christian perspective, the interpretation of pagan polytheism as a function of linguistic diversity fit within the Biblical narrative of the Tower of Babel, which accounted for the existence of the many languages as the "curse of confusion" that would ultimately be undone only by the plain language of the Gospel (see chapter 3 in this volume).

During the Renaissance, forerunners of comparative religion such as Marsilio Ficino (1433–1499) and Giovanni Pico della Mirandola (1463–1494) emphasized the unity of religions in reason. The different traditions reflected a common truth; some of them were perhaps even better at doing so than Christianity. This unifying truth was, in fact, the truth of the unity of the deity, the central tenet of the so-called *prisca theologia*—meaning the pure, ancient wisdom or theology—as communicated in the Hermetic corpus of texts.[143] Until Isaac Casaubon (1559–1614) demonstrated that these neo-Platonic texts were not older than 200–300 CE, they were believed to be older than Christianity or even Moses, part of the Egyptian wisdom that was handed down, possibly in less than pristine form, in Christianity itself. Recovery of this ancient theology was thought to have the potential to heal the divide among the different religions. Casaubon's demonstration returned historical priority to the tradition of Biblical revelation. However, the problem of reconciling sacred history with the remains of paganism, and of confirming the primacy, whether historical or philosophical, of monotheism over polytheism, continued to vex many Christians. One cardinal problem for the thesis of an ancient monotheistic theology was the counterevidence provided by the ruins, and relics, and literary remains testifying to widespread polytheism in the ancient world, including among the Egyptians, Greeks, and Romans. If these peoples—beginning with the Egyptians, who would seemingly worship anything from the animal, mineral, or vegetable kingdom—were truly committed to monotheism, then how do we explain their apparent commitment to the existence of multiple deities? The thesis of an ancient theology answered this question by distinguishing between an exoteric and an esoteric doctrine: a religion of polytheism for the masses, and a religion of monotheism for the spiritual elite, especially the priests. The hypothesis of an esoteric monotheism underlying pagan polytheism enjoyed tremendous longevity, as some seventeenth- and eighteenth-century Deists used it for a similar purpose, namely to explain the proliferation of external forms of worship in the face of their claims that natural religion consisted of a simplified, philosophical monotheism. In such later interpretations, the esotericism of the priests was often interpreted as a stratagem for personal gain, a form of "priestcraft": The true religion was withheld from the common folk not because it was above their comprehension, but so that the priests could steal the sacrifices and amass wealth and power. In its origins, however, the esotericism of the ancient theology often received a more positive value, as designed to protect a hidden truth, possibly too difficult for ordinary folk to comprehend.

The linguistic interpretation of polytheism could be pursued to divergent conclusions. If the pagans—or at least the more intelligent among them—were indeed cognizant that the many gods were really One, then this could open a path to a positive interpretation of paganism, as a valid manifestation of the true religion or perennial philosophy, or at least a precursor of Christian monotheism. On the other hand, as just noted, the thesis of an esoteric doctrine could bolster charges of priestcraft or the deliberate corruption of external religion.[144] Both of these interpretations required that some pagans actually be aware that polytheism was either false or, at any rate, not the highest form of religion. This is precisely what many opponents of the thesis of an ancient theology denied, by asserting that paganism was a real polytheism, not a polytheism in name only. Those who held this position defended the uniqueness of the Jewish and Christian revelations, and were generally opposed to the idea of a natural, much less universal, monotheistic theology.

These debates played out in England, where, as we have seen, Selden and Hobbes affirmed that idolatry depended on a linguistic confusion of the pagans, although the former allowed that more enlightened pagans confessed the truth of monotheism. Alexander Ross, in his *Pansebeia: Or, a View of All Religions in the World* (1655) argued that "however the *Gentiles* might seem to worship divers chief gods, because they expressed them by divers names, and effects, or Offices; yet indeed the wiser sort understood but one supream Deity, which they worshipped under divers Names, Epithets, and Operations."[145] Thomas Fuller (1608–1661) allowed that the wiser pagans were guilty only of "symbolicall Idolatry,"[146] as they worshipped the true God falsely, under a diversity of names: "Though very many [are] the Idols mentioned in Scripture, yet our mistake may make them more then they were; if erroneously conceiving *Quot nomina, tut numina*, that every severall Idols name we meet with, was a different and distinct Deity by them adored. O no! As our *one and onely* God is known to us by severall names, *Jah, Jehovah, El, Elohim, Adonai* &c. so in apish imitation thereof, some one heathen God took a principall pride, to have severall names imposed upon him, and pleased himself much in *polyonymia*, in *multitude of titles.*"[147]

Others were of the same opinion.[148] Ralph Cudworth, the foremost of the Cambridge Platonists, in his *True Intellectual System of the Universe* (1678), a work designed in part to refute Hobbes's opinions of religion,[149] claimed that among the pagans "much of their polytheism was but seeming and phantastical only, and really nothing but the polyonymy of the one God . . . the worshipping him under several personal names."[150] Cudworth endorsed the idea of an "arcane theology," beside the "vulgar" one, that explicitly affirmed the existence of one, supreme God.[151] For support, in addition to the classical authors, he quoted Gerard Vossius's statement that "The more sagacious [pagans] . . . affirmed all these [gods] to be but one and the same God [*numen*]; to wit the nature of things, which, though really but one, yet according to its various effects, both received divers names [*nomina*], and was worshipped after different manners."[152]

Edward Stillingfleet (1635–1699), in his *Origines Sacræ* (1662), provided a different linguistic interpretation of polytheism, as resting on a metaphorical use or interpretation of scripture: "Another fountain of *Heathen Mythology*, was the taking the Idiom of the Oriental Languages in a proper Sense . . . A third way observable, is, the alteration of the Names in the ancient Tradition, and putting Names of like importance to them in their own Language."[153] Stillingfleet asserted that there was an "ambiguity of sense in the Oriental languages" that contributed to the apparent luxuriousness of their mythology, which seemed to be populated by an extravagance of deities.[154] Given this fundamental ambiguity, and the frequent use of poetic figures, mythology could come about in two ways: either by taking figures of speech in an improperly literal sense or, conversely, by taking literal meanings figuratively.[155] Either error could lead to reading mythology into the text of the Hebrew Bible. Stillingfleet's concern was to inoculate scripture against the charge of mythology, just as Müller was later to attempt for the Vedas. And his analysis depended on the same attribution of ambiguity or, in Müller's term, "radical metaphor" to ancient, Oriental languages.

The thesis that pagan polytheism was apparent, and not real—a mistaken inference on the part of outsiders—lent support to the rationality and universality of monotheism, yet it also, at the same time, called into question the uniqueness of the Christian revelation. John Edwards (1637–1716) objected vigorously to Cudworth's interpretation. Edwards argued that the idea that the heathens merely gave different names for the same god was "a mistaken Notion without doubt; for they were not looked upon by some of the *intelligent Heathens themselves* as mere Denominations . . . and 'tis certain they were not so esteemed as such by the *Vulgar* . . . In brief, the *Idolatry* of the Heathen World was worshipping a Multitude of Persons and Things which they took to be Gods, but were not."[156] Edwards did not dispute the idea that polytheism arose from linguistic confusion. Indeed, in an earlier work, he affirmed that "the Heathens had the *Names of their Gods*, and the pronunciation of them sometimes, from the *Names* and *Titles* of the *True God*."[157] Echoing Selden, Edwards argued that the names of several pagan gods, as well as of the Jewish god, were corruptions of Jehovah.[158] Such borrowings confirmed the priority of the Biblical revelation.[159] Polytheism may have been a linguistic mistake, yet it was a mistake of the pagans themselves, and not of later interpreters who falsely attributed to them a real belief in their nominal gods. This should make Christians grateful for the divine revelation that delivered us from idolatry.[160]

William Warburton, in his massive *The Divine Legation of Moses Demonstrated, on the Principles of a Religious Deist* (1742–1758), in a similar bid to preserve the authority of divine revelation, attacked the thesis of Cudworth, Vossius, and Kircher, that "*Brutes were deified only as the Symbols of the first Cause*."[161] Animal worship, the most odious and a peculiarly Egyptian form of idolatry, did not originate in polyonymy, but in the use of hieroglyphics,[162] which did not, as some thought, conceal a secret monotheism but rather encouraged idolatry through their emphasis on pictorial representation:[163] "Language . . . was out of mere necessity, highly figurative, and full of material images . . . The Genius of the *most ancient Hieroglyphic* Writing was again revived for Ornament in *Emblems* and *Devices*, the Custom of their Poets and Orators in personalizing every thing, filled their *Coins*, their *Arches*, their *Altars*, &c. with all kinds of imaginary Beings."[164]

Warburton quoted Shakespeare to describe this error: "As imagination bodied forth/ The forms of things unknown, the artist's hand/ Turn'd them to shape, and gave to airy nothing/ A local habitation and a name."[165] Finally, the hieroglyphics degenerated into magic and mystery[166] and, abetted by priestcraft, led to animal worship.[167] For this reason, the Second Commandment against idolatry had been aimed directly against hieroglyphic writing: "All Hieroglyphic Writing was absolutely forbidden by the second Commandment, and with a View worthy the Divine Wisdom; Hieroglyphics being, as we shall shew hereafter, the great Source of the most abominable Idolatries and Superstitions."[168] Therefore, Moses had been forced to alter the shape of the letters.[169] As Jan Assmann noted, Warburton's assertion of a connection between hieroglyphs and idolatry foreshadowed Müller's theory of myth.[170] Echoes of another possible connection are discernible in Müller's comments that Egyptian hieroglyphs may have influenced the popular mind to zoolatry,[171] and that even in the letters of our present alphabet "there lies embedded the mummy of an ancient Egyptian hieroglyphic."[172]

"To the Unknown God": Monotheism, Polytheism, and the Vedas

These debates over the historical priority of either monotheism or polytheism in pagan religion continued into the Enlightenment. Hobbes had contended that the original form of natural religion was polytheism, although his interpretation of idolatry and polytheism as the confused worship of the One God otherwise agreed with Müller's views.[173] David Hume, in his *Natural History of Religion* (1757), also argued that polytheism was the first religion:

> It appears to me, that, if we consider the improvement of human society, from rude beginnings to a state of greater perfection, polytheism or idolatry was, and necessarily must have been, the first and most ancient religion of mankind . . . But farther, if men were at first led into the belief of one Supreme Being, by reasoning from the frame of nature, they could never possibly leave that belief, in order to embrace polytheism . . . There is an universal tendency among mankind to conceive all beings like themselves, and to transfer to every object, those qualities, with which they are

familiarly acquainted, and of which they are intimately conscious. We find human faces in the moon, armies in the clouds; and by a natural propensity, if not corrected by experience and reflection, ascribe malice or good-will to every thing, that hurts or pleases us. Hence the frequency and beauty of the *prosopopoeia* in poetry; where trees, mountains and streams are personified, and the inanimate parts of nature acquire sentiment and passion.[174]

Significantly, Hume identified one of the causes of polytheism as poetry: more specifically, the tendency of poetry to personify its characters and produce the appearance of agency and intention where none may exist, for dramatic effect, pathos, and to accord with the natural tendencies of human understanding. This is not very far from Müller's account of how the roots and radical metaphors of primitive language attribute agency to different natural forces. Yet despite Hume's argument that religion and human knowledge advance toward perfection, his granting of priority to polytheism could still be taken to undermine the authority of biblical monotheism and the orthodox depiction of idolatry as a degeneration from either true revelation or natural religion, as described already by Paul in Romans 1.

Müller's argument that polytheistic mythology was a later corruption of language indicated his preference for the priority of monotheism. He attacked Charles de Brosses's theory of the origin of religion in fetishism, which gave priority to polytheism.[175] Müller's refutation, through philological analysis, of the thesis of an original polytheism closely resembled earlier Protestant efforts to rescue a pure, primitive Christianity from the clutches of a supposedly idolatrous Catholic Church by recovering the original meaning of the Bible. His own position was complicated by the recent discovery, at the end of the eighteenth century, of the Sanskrit language and its historical relationship to Greek, Latin, and other Indo-European languages. Müller's mammoth labor to publish an edition of the *Rig Veda* was motivated by the discovery of the familial relationship among the Indo-European languages, and the conviction that, among these, Sanskrit was the "eldest sister."[176] Therefore, by going back to the oldest scriptures of the Hindus, one might discover what the original religion of the Indo-Europeans, and possibly of all humankind, had been. What was at stake in these otherwise drab discussions of the dating and periodization of texts was nothing less than the defense of monotheism. The prestige of origins would accrue to whatever proved to be the original form of religion. Without the claim of historical priority secured for monotheism by evidences of its universal or at least wide distribution in primitive times, Christian sacred history might be called into question. The problem was that a *prima facie* reading of the Vedas appeared to endorse the conclusion that these oldest surviving Indo-European scriptures were polytheistic, like the very different beliefs and traditions of contemporary Hinduism. Müller's comparative mythology had to come to terms with this problem in some way.

In his 1784 essay "On the Gods of Greece, Italy, and India," which Müller had read,[177] William Jones already identified poetry as one of the causes of primitive polytheism: "Numberless divinities have been created solely by the magick of poetry; whose essential business it is, to personify the most abstract notions, and to place a nymph or a genius in every grove and almost in every flower."[178] Müller was not even the first to apply the concept of an original monotheism and the related linguistic interpretation of pagan polytheism to Indian religion. In 1847, William Westall invoked Paul Ernst Jablonski (1693–1767) in arguing that "there appears to have existed among all ancient nations some faint idea of the one true God . . . The Upanishads, or doctrinal books of the Hindoos, undoubtedly inculcate the belief of one Supreme God, in whom the universe is comprehended; but already had they begun to address the Deity by different appellations, a practice which was, perhaps, among the first causes of polytheism."[179] Westall quoted the Sanskritist Henry Thomas Colebrooke's account of the Vedas for the proposition that the different names of Hindu deities "are all resolvable into different titles . . . ultimately of one God."[180]

Another precedent for Müller's theory was Robert Chatfield's 1808 comparison between the North Indian Devanāgarī alphabet and Egyptian hieroglyphs: "In the days of ignorance, superstition became a vehicle for ambition; the Priests resorted to craft and concealment, and the people were content to follow their ordinances in blind obedience. The Egyptian Priests had a sacred sacerdotal language, and hieroglyphic character, the use of which, was forbidden or unattainable by the vulgar. The Brahmins had their Devanāgarī (or the language of angels), which, they said, was delivered to the people by Brahma, in the same manner, as the elements of the sacerdotal language of Egypt, were supposed to have been imparted by the elder Hermes."[181] Chatfield cited Cudworth's thesis that the Egyptian priests secretly affirmed the unity of the Godhead, but rejected the application of this defense to Hinduism.[182]

Within an older tradition of Christian comparative mythology that had already been applied to India, Müller's originality lay in his ability to elaborate some basic ideas into a complete theory of mythology and language, based upon his extensive knowledge of comparative philology, as one of the first Europeans to acquire a deep knowledge of Sanskrit. Müller's effort to defend the priority of monotheism or, failing that, to disprove the thesis of an original polytheism was buttressed by a series of linguistic arguments. In his essay on "Semitic Monotheism," Müller attributed the difference between the monotheism of the Jews and the polytheism of the Aryan peoples such as the Indians and Greeks to a difference in how their respective languages formed predicates from roots.[183] Hebrew words preserved more obviously the three-letter roots from which they derived. This supposedly made it more difficult for their etymologies to be forgotten and for these words to be taken as independent entities. Hobbes anticipated this view when, in his analysis of the Nicene Creed, he argued that, unlike Latin and Greek, Hebrew lacked the copula and "could not have those names which are derived from the copula *est* (as, *essentia, entitas,* and *esse*), nor anything equivalent to them."[184] Scholastic metaphysics began with the Greeks, who imposed their grammatical myths on Jewish monotheism. Both thinkers argued that Hebrew had built-in grammatical defenses against the mythological personification of words. However, Müller added that neither Aryan nor Semitic languages were, in their origins, polytheistic:

> The primitive intuition of God . . . was in itself neither monotheistic nor polytheistic, though it might become either, according to the expression which it took in the languages of man. . . . It is too often forgotten by those who believe that a polytheistic worship was the most natural unfolding of religious life, that polytheism must every-where have been preceded by a more or less conscious theism. *In no language does the plural exist before the singular.* No human mind could have conceived the idea of gods without having previously conceived the idea of a god. It would be, however, quite as great a mistake to imagine . . . that therefore a belief in One God preceded everywhere the belief in many gods. A belief in God, as exclusively One, involves a distinct negation of more than one God.[185]

The bold claim Müller made in this passage was that the origins of language in sense experience guarantee that, even if primal religion was not truly monotheistic, it also could not have been truly polytheistic.[186] Every word originally applied to a single existent thing, or to a quality or attribute of that thing. Plural and class terms are already partial abstractions from experience. For this reason, the idea of multiple gods must have been a later development.

It is well known that Müller coined a new term, "henotheism" (from the Greek words *henos*, one, and *theos*, god) or "kathenotheism," to describe the religion of the Vedas.[187] This referred to a stage of religion, neither polytheistic nor properly monotheistic, at which the different names of God, if not different gods, might be worshipped in turn as supreme. If the Vedas must be placed in one or the other category—either monotheism or polytheism—then they were clearly the latter. However, unlike the fully-formed polytheism of the Olympian pantheon, with Zeus at the head, in the Vedas "whenever one of these individual gods is invoked, they are not conceived as limited by the powers of others, as superior or inferior in rank. Each god is to the mind of the supplicant as good as all gods . . . This surely is not what is commonly understood by Polytheism. Yet it would be equally wrong to call it Monotheism. If we must have a name for it, I should call it Kathenotheism."[188] Whereas henotheism viewed individual gods as successively supreme, and polytheism acknowledged the supremacy of one god among many,[189] only monotheism entailed the outright denial of multiple divinities. The creation of a new category of henotheism allowed Müller to reject the claim that the original, natural religion was polytheism—indeed, he called henotheism "a kind of monotheism"[190]—while also affirming an evolutionary scheme in which Jewish and Christian monotheism could be regarded as a precious achievement.

Müller argued that many of the names of divinities in the Vedas were still recognized as appellatives and disclosed their natural basis: Agni, for example, still clearly meant the "fire" into which the sacrifice was made; and Surya (the sun), Ushas (the dawn), and the Maruts (the storm gods) referred to material things or events.[191] So long as the names were recognized as referring to natural phenomena, they were not yet mythological.[192] With the passage of time, however, the commentarial tradition lost the sense of the hymns and mythology reared its ugly head,[193] as had already happened in Homer and the Greek myths, in which the gods were fully personified, and the original reference of their names to natural phenomena had become obscured.[194] The names Zeus and Jupiter no longer pointed to the heavenly Sky as clearly as the Sanskrit Dyaus Pitar did.

Similarly, Müller argued that the Vedas, unlike ancient Greek religion, did not condone image-worship.[195]

Müller's location of the Vedas in the dawn of henotheism, at a stage before the crystallization of polytheism and idolatry, colored his interpretation and presentation of these texts. His translation of selected Vedic hymns in the *Sacred Books of the East* series began with *Rig Veda* 10.121, a philosophical hymn arguably exhibiting monotheistic tendencies that, like others in the same section, is generally agreed to be of later date than other hymns of the *Rig Veda*.[196] By thus rearranging the order of the hymns, so as to deviate from both their traditional arrangement and their chronological sequence, Müller granted priority to the monotheistic dimensions of Vedic religion.[197] The refrain of this hymn is: "Who is the God to whom we shall offer sacrifice?" Müller claimed that subsequently, by Brahmin priests, the interrogative pronoun "who" (*ka*) was taken as the name of a god: a prime example of the mythological corruption of language.[198] To reinforce his interpretation of this hymn, Müller added a title, "To the Unknown God,"[199] a reference to St. Paul's preaching among the idolatrous Athenians:[200] "I found also an altar with this inscription, 'To an unknown god.' What therefore you worship as unknown, this I proclaim to you."[201] Müller's use of this line as a title for *Rig Veda* 10.121 located this text within a Christian tradition of assimilation of pagan religions, which presented the Gospel as a fulfillment of those religions, and in particular as a clarification of their obscure pronouncements. Although the one unknown God may have been a late revelation among the Greek philosophers, who was to say that the Vedas had not arrived at this proto-Christian revelation at an earlier point?[202] Müller simultaneously reinforced his argument that the most primitive stage of religion was monotheistic or at least nonpolytheistic, and located the Vedas in an evolutionary scheme or developmental trajectory in which they could be seen as a worthy preparation for Christian theology.

In this way, Müller attempted to have his cake and eat it too—the cake in this case being the other religions, especially Hinduism, to which Müller granted a limited truth in accordance with the apparently ecumenical idea that "Truth is one, but it is called by different names."[203] Müller quoted a line from Krishna in the *Bhagavad Gītā*: "'Even those who worship idols, worship me.' Whatever we do, however pure and abstract our language may be, in one sense we are all idolaters, we idolise the deity in the imperfect ideas which we have formed of it, and under the ever-varying names which we have given to it."[204] This seems to place Müller among the more

liberal exponents of Christian comparative mythology. However, while acknowledging both that other religions possessed some truth and that
Christianity was perhaps imperfect, Müller still affirmed a hierarchy among
religions according to which Christian monotheism, with its doctrine of the
Incarnation, was both first among equals and the perfection of what had
been only dimly glimpsed by other religions.

At its foundation, Müller's theory of language was an attempt to rework
the doctrine of Christ as the incarnate word (Greek *logos*), so as to put this
on a firmer and more universal basis in both nature and the study of
language. Lourens van den Bosch rightly noted that "Müller thus placed
himself clearly in the tradition of Logos theology, but employed the concept of Logos in a syncretistic manner by combining it with his views on
the philosophy of history and the Vedanta."[205] Understood in terms of
Christian theology, as Müller understood it, the problem of the Logos was
the problem of how the divine might be incarnated in language, how finite
words might express the infinite, how the matter of words might give
voice to the spirit. All religions and mythologies responded to the same
problem, of how to body forth and give expression to the transcendent: "As
soon as the existence of a Beyond, of a Heaven above the earth, of Powers
above us and beneath us had been recognised, a great gulf seemed to be
fixed between what was called by various names, the earthly and the heavenly, the material and the spiritual, the phenomenal and the noumenal, or
best of all, the visible and invisible world . . . and it was the chief object of
religion to unite these two worlds again, whether by the arches of hope
and fear, or by the iron chains of logical syllogism."[206] Both Aryan and
Semitic thought had adopted distinctive answers to the problem posed by
the distance between God and man. Whereas the "physical religion" of
the Aryans looked for the divine in nature, the religion of the Jews refused
this answer and, by insisting on a God beyond nature, sharpened the
problem of relating the divine and the human: "Nowhere had the invisible
God been further removed from the visible world than in the ancient
Jewish religion, and nowhere have the two been so closely drawn together
again and made one as by that fundamental doctrine of Christianity,
the divine sonship of man."[207] The problem posed by the Jewish notion of
an invisible God remained without adequate resolution until the Christian doctrine of the Incarnation. What united the visible and the invisible was the Logos.[208] For Müller, it was language itself—in the form of
the divine Word—that bridged this gulf, solved the dilemma, unraveled the
conundrum.[209]

Müller's theory of myth rested on a complete identification or conflation of linguistics with Christian theology. Religion, language, and thought were ultimately one and the same. The problem of language was the problem of expression: How to capture thoughts by means of words, mere phonic matter, and convey them to others? If all expression, indeed all thinking, required us to descend into verbal matter, how could we avoid falling into gross idolatry, and reascend by means of language to union with the divine spirit? First, through the etymological analysis of names that would reveal they were after all "just matter" that had been used metaphorically to express a nascent intuition of the divine. Second, by the achievement of a language adequate to the realization of the perfect unity of the finite with the infinite, or of matter with spirit.

If, for Müller, polyonymy equaled polytheism, then univocality, the opposite of polyonymy, would be the restoration of the one true name of the deity, the triumph of monotheism. Müller's scholarly project reflected a kind of linguistic iconoclasm, a transposition of monotheism and the prohibition against idolatry to the domain of language. Through the codification of the Hindu scriptures, etymological analysis, and above all the critique of myth as idolatry, Müller pursued a Science of Religion and Language that, although ostensibly secular, now appears to have its roots deep in the Reformation. This so-called Science of Language had patently soteriological dimensions, and aimed to remedy the confusion of tongues or Curse of Babel:[210] "The Science of Language thus leads us up to that highest summit from whence we see into the very dawn of man's life on earth, and where the words which we have heard so often from the days of our childhood—'And the whole earth was of one language and of one speech'—assume a meaning more natural, more intelligible, more convincing, than they ever had before."[211] Comparative philology would restore the unity of human language that had been lost with the fall of the Tower of Babel. In so doing, it would follow the path laid out by the Apostles who, inspired by the Holy Spirit at Pentecost, had acquired the ability of preaching to the different nations in their own languages (Acts 2: 1–13): "The science of language owes more than its first impulse to Christianity. The pioneers of our science were those very apostles who were commanded 'to go into all the world, and preach the gospel to every creature;' and their true successors, the missionaries of the whole Christian Church."[212] Through the conquest of a new etymological science, Müller could at last reveal to all those bowing before unknown gods the true name of the one God to whom they had really been praying all along.

Müller applied Protestant scriptural literalism to Hindu mythology and attempted—especially with his edition of the *Rig Veda*—to reduce Hinduism to its supposedly canonical sources. His explicit equation, in the field of mythology, between polytheism and polyonymy—the existence of multiple names for a single thing, including the deity—reflected an attempt to establish the triumph of monotheism on a linguistic basis. In this regard, Müller's endless fascination with establishing the etymological identity of God—the cognate status of Greek *theos*, Latin *deus*, and Sanskrit *deva*—was exemplary of a broader view that the conformation of all languages and religions was a work of redemption, a linguistic soteriology. His proposed Science of Religion, which converted the dark, shadowy language of mythology into a transparent and veridical discourse of scholarship, echoed the Protestant mode of typology, which replaced the obscurity of pagan oracles with plain speech.

Earlier Christians had preceded Müller in the effort to reconcile the tenets of the sacred history of the Bible with the evidence of Gentile beliefs and practices. The Europeans' discovery of other cultures during the era of exploration and colonialism was accompanied by the rise of a method of philological criticism originally developed through the investigation of the Bible and of classical pagan literature. Both sources of new information—the philological or historical, and the ethnographic or contemporary—complicated the efforts of orthodoxy to save the appearances of biblical chronology, and to verify the accuracy of the history presented in scripture. Such efforts were made especially difficult by the discovery of the Indo-European language family, and of the common ancestry of Sanskrit with Greek and Latin.[213] This discovery displaced the historical priority of Hebrew, revealed the existence of a history not contemplated in the Bible, and suggested a divide or potential conflict between "Aryan" and "Semitic" languages. The proponent of one of the last truly popular and academically authoritative versions of Christian sacred history, or alternatively of one of the first secular versions of such a history, Müller illustrated the tensions of reconciling Christian theology with the burgeoning knowledge of the religious traditions of other cultures. The growing knowledge of diverse mythological systems cast the name of God itself into doubt. Müller's attack on linguistic idolatry was an attempt to certify this name. His theories of language and mythology occupied an intermediate stage and a point of connection between Protestant criticisms of idolatry and modern, secular studies of religion. These conclusions afford scant comfort to the view that religious studies is now scientific, and has transcended its theological past, as Müller died barely a century ago.

Conclusion

The British colonial attack on Hindu language and especially mythological tales as idolatry—as exemplified by the work of Friedrich Max Müller— reveals a series of intersections and coordinations between the work of scientific and that of religious reformation. Ostensibly the triumph of empiricism over superstition, the demythologization of Indian languages echoed an earlier Christian eschatology according to which the Incarnation of the Logos had brought an end to the obscurity of both the Old Testament and the pagan oracles. Just as the Gospel had supposedly replaced each of these with a form of plain speaking—a mode of exposition that revealed and dispelled all enigmas—the colonial reformation of Indian languages promised to make plain what Indians had really meant and, in so doing, to displace their false or imperfect religions with the true religion of Christianity. More than simply a concern to stabilize the meanings of terms for practical purposes, such as trade or translation, some British attacks on the misleading nature of Indian languages demonstrated a conflation between the purification of language and the goal of salvation. Whether pagan polytheism and idolatry were viewed as a form of original sin testifying to the childlike nature of primitive humanity, or conversely as a degeneration and decline from an honest effort to express intimations of the divine, Christianity represented the solution: both an entry into spiritual maturity and a return to the pure expression of divinity. European colonialism and science frequently deployed Christian eschatological and soteriological narratives, in strategically altered variations, to subordinate the religion of the Hindus and even their very languages, as later chapters in this volume will demonstrate.

3

"One Step from Babel to Pentecost"

COLONIAL CODIFICATION, UNIVERSAL LANGUAGES,
AND THE DEBATE OVER ROMAN TRANSLITERATION

> As the confounding of tongues divided the children of men
> and scattered them abroad, so the gift of tongues, bestowed
> upon the apostles (Acts ii), contributed greatly to the gath-
> ering together of the children of God, who were scattered
> abroad, and the uniting of them in Christ, that with one
> mind and one mouth they might glorify God, Rom. Xv.6.[1]

> Let it be granted that the first object is to disenchant the
> popular mind of India: Do you propose to break the spell
> which now binds it by the facilities and attractions of the
> English language?[2]

Printing and Proselytism

In colonial India, the diagnosis of mythology as a "disease of language," a form of idolatry stemming from both the fetishization of native words and the ambiguity or polyvalence of such words, led to a series of proposals for the treatment of this disease. Müller's comparative philology, which used etymological analysis to disenchant mythological language, was a relatively late entry among these proposals. At the heart of Müller's project was the desire to produce, if not a universal language, at least the possibility of ac-curate translation, above all of the name of God. Other proposals sought to treat the linguistic idolatry of the Hindus by standardizing and codifying their languages and texts; by transliterating these into versions of the Ro-man alphabet; or by simply replacing them with English. A number of these proposals were motivated by the soteriological objective of instituting the true religion—that is, Christianity—by reversing the confusion of tongues that began at Babel. Like Müller's comparative mythology, they conflated monotheism with monolingualism. Müller himself contributed to these other proposals by creating a "missionary alphabet" and advocating for the Roman transliteration of Indian languages.

The colonial valorization of a textual canon—a single, uniform linguistic standard—prompted numerous condemnations of the diversity of languages and traditions in India.[3] Many British saw the religious, political, and linguistic variety of India as a problem, one they sought to address with a series of linguistic reforms. Codification embodied the dream of a perfect language capable of translating between the universal and the particular and overcoming the vagaries of communication in the colonial context. To understand some of these reforms, however, we must appreciate how they expressed the Christian ideas of a religious Reformation and the triumph of monotheism over idolatry.[4] For many British, codification would both demonstrate and bring about the universal translatability of the Christian gospels. If, as the twentieth-century missionary in India R. V. De Smet stated, "Pentecost is the antitype of Babel,"[5] then the effective institution of English as the universal language would contribute to the eventual victory of Christian monotheism.

Of the various projects for the reform of Indian languages, the one that has received the most attention is the colonial propensity for codification. A host of materials, in both Indian and European languages, was reduced to print, including classical Indian literature, the Vedas, and the sacred law books of the Hindus; grammars, dictionaries, and primers in classical and contemporary Indian languages; Bibles and other Christian writings; and secular European literature. One of the significant contributions of postcolonial studies has been its excavation of the reordering of Indian discourses that occurred as a result of colonial projects for the codification of South Asian languages and cultural traditions.[6] The British gradually substituted the authority of the printed text for that of oral traditions and customs. Codification performed an objectification of traditions that facilitated their further representation, organization, and control. The location of authentic, authorized culture in texts secured the possession of symbolic and often real power as well. The effect of this textual bias on both British and Hindus is a noteworthy legacy of colonialism. This bias distorted the actual shape of Hinduism, displacing living traditions in favor of a written standard that in many cases was ancient, irrelevant, or even incomprehensible to many Hindus.

Although Bernard Cohn's classic account of colonial language reforms scarcely mentioned the religious dimensions of codification, other scholars have noted that the Protestant bias toward the location of religion in written texts distorted, in some cases profoundly, our knowledge of Indian religions.[7] Despite such intimations, the connection of these events with Protestant ideas has not been explored with the attention it deserves. This chapter accordingly examines the religious dimensions of codification and related proposals for the Roman transliteration of indigenous languages in colonial India, and takes seriously the suggestion that these developments constituted—at least from the colonialists' own ideologically motivated perspective—a linguistic Reformation, rather than a Renaissance or a simple exercise in colonial domination.

The propensity for codification united two otherwise distinct moments in colonial policy toward India, customarily referred to as Orientalism and Anglicism. The British at first supported instruction in native languages, including Sanskrit and Arabic. This was the Orientalist phase personified by Sir William Jones (1746–1794) and symbolized by the Asiatic Society he founded in Calcutta in 1784. Following attacks on this system by the Anglicists such as Charles Trevelyan and Thomas Babington Macaulay, the colonial government in 1835 diminished its support for traditional education and moved to replace this with a system of instruction in English language and subjects.[8] Although opposed in their estimations of the value of traditional Indian learning, both Orientalists and Anglicists were united in their support for codification. However, the texts chosen for codification were subject to change, from those in classical Sanskrit, Arabic, and Persian literature to those in modern vernaculars and, increasingly, those translated into English. An overemphasis on the transition from Orientalism to Anglicism can obscure the continuity between the two periods. Not only did Orientalist approaches continue after 1835, as Müller's massive labor to codify the Vedas illustrates, but both Orientalism and Anglicism shared certain assumptions regarding the nature and uses of language, assumptions which in many cases were drawn from a common Protestant heritage.

The shift to Anglicism signaled a further devaluation of native languages and the knowledge they contained. For Macaulay and other Anglicists, the antidote for such false knowledge was the substitution of the English language itself for native languages as the medium of instruction: "I have never found one among [the Orientalists] who could deny that a single shelf of a good European library was worth the whole native literature of India and Arabia . . . Whoever knows [English], has ready access to all the vast intellectual wealth, which all the wisest nations of the earth have created and hoarded in the course of ninety generations."[9]

English was not only the equal of any language that ever existed, but contained, in condensed form, all of the useful knowledge of every language. Trevelyan similarly extolled the virtues of an English language that although composed of diverse intermingled linguistic sources, had forged these into an indissoluble whole.[10] This contrasted favorably with the disorganized array of languages in polyglot India, and suggested a model for the linguistic assimilation of that country.

The role of printing in inspiring colonial codification was significant. Although manuscript writing had been used in South Asia for millennia, the introduction of the printing press from Europe and the massive expansion of book publishing under the British colonial administration transformed both European knowledge of Indian cultures and, to some extent, these cultures themselves. Francis Bacon claimed that printing, gunpowder, and the compass had "changed the whole face and state of things throughout the world . . . so much that no empire, no sect, no star seems to have exerted greater power and influence in human affairs than these mechanical discoveries."[11] Although the British deployed all three of these inventions in their conquest of India, their possession of the printing press arguably secured for them the most enduring victory by the impact it had on indigenous mentalities and their conversion to modernity. Apart from contributing to an attack on oral traditions, print culture standardized the orthography of the Indian languages, complete with European punctuation marks previously nonexistent in these languages.

This apparently mundane change was thought by some of those who introduced it to constitute a salvific moment, a religious Reformation overturning both polytheism and the curse of Babel. Indeed, the introduction of print culture into India does appear to have had some long-lasting effects that, while encouraged by the new medium of communication, also reflected a new linguistic ideology that emerged from Protestantism and the Enlightenment. As missionary Joseph Mullens pointed out in 1852,

> One of the Calcutta Deists[12] writes that the present position of England is owing to the invention of printing and to the spread of the Baconian philosophy. He forgets what it was, that printing spread abroad. It was the Bible, copies of which were multiplied faster than they had ever been and were received with the greatest avidity. Printing is not an end but a means. The result depends on *what* is printed. In England men printed the Bible, and it was by the increase of Scripture

knowledge that the people were so improved. . . . The Baconian philosophy is the *result* of such a [Christian] spirit, not its cause.[13]

Despite the polemical motive and theological bias behind Mullens's
claim, there is some truth to what he says. Protestantism, and not printing
and Baconian thought alone, inspired a number of colonial reforms in
India, even if it is an exaggeration to credit Christianity with the domination of that country, as Mullens does.

In the seventeenth century, Royal Society member John Aubrey argued
that printing had frightened away Robin Goodfellow and other fairies, and
disenchanted the English countryside.[14] Similarly, some British colonialists in nineteenth-century India anticipated that printing would end the
monopoly of Brahmin idolatry.[15] An article "On the Effect of the Native
Press in India" compared that country to pre-Reformation England and
prescribed the same remedy, namely the printing press. By being widely
distributed through printing, mythological tales would lose their appeal.
Revealing the secret rites of the Hindus would break the power of the
Brahmin priests, just as the publication of the Bible had broken the
monopoly and authority of the Roman Church. Paganism would follow
the same path of decline that it had taken in Europe: "Idolatry has more
of the nature of a charm than of a fixed and vigorous principle; when once
the spell is broken, its disjointed and disorganized fragments can never be
re-assembled into the same uniform and powerful system . . . There was a
time when the mythology of Greece exercised an almost omnipotent sway
over the most polished nation in the world;—it has now passed away, and
exists only in the fervid lines of the poet or the pages of the pantheon."[16]
Printing would kill the living idols of India, and substitute for these a
harmless textual relic. At the same time, the printing press would allow
the wider dissemination of the Gospel. Those Indians who, upon seeing
the printing press set up by the Baptist missionary William Carey (1761–
1834) north of Calcutta in 1798, believed they were viewing the image of
the English God, may not have been entirely mistaken.[17]

For a number of British, including not only missionaries but also professional scholars and government officials, codification would provide
the remedy for verbal idolatry. This judgment reflected the Protestant
ideal of a scriptural canon opposed to the idolatry of custom. Codification
would perfect language and fix it in textual form through a combination of
critical etymology, scientific observation, and judicial fiat. This was a work
of linguistic soteriology, a true scriptural Reformation. Müller's long labor

to produce the first printed edition of the *Rig Veda* was succeeded by his editorship of the fifty-volume *Sacred Books of the East* series, through which many Europeans were first introduced to the religious traditions of Asia in translation. This series, in Müller's view, constituted a new canon that would serve as the necessary point of departure for any science of religion. His effort to fix the religious traditions of the world—or at least the scriptural traditions or "book religions"—in published editions and translations of their original and authoritative texts was a corollary of his study of philology or etymology, which sought to arrive at the original meaning of words and thus remedy linguistic idolatry.

Müller emphasized what important consequences the invention of writing had for the development of culture,[18] and its close connections to the religious Reformation.[19] He believed that, just as the humanistic study and translation of the Bible had produced a renewal of Christianity, an edition of the *Rig Veda* was a necessary step toward a Hindu Reformation:

> Some of the questions now being agitated in India are just the same as the questions which led in the end to the reformation of our own Church. If with us the chief question was that of the authority of the Bible replacing that of the Pope and Councils, with them it is the authority of the Vedas. And if it was the first printed edition of the Greek New Testament by Erasmus that gave the strongest impulse to our own Reformation, it was the first printed edition of the Veda that gave the most powerful incentive and the strongest weapon to the founders of the Brahma-Samaj in India. Let us hope that India may be spared a Thirty Years' War before it can consolidate the work [of religious reformation].[20]

Echoing Protestant attacks on the secrecy and elitism of the Catholic Church, Müller condemned the obscurity in which Brahmins had maintained the Veda.[21] He also supported the codification of Buddhist texts undertaken by Henry Olcott, who produced a Buddhist catechism with strongly Protestant overtones,[22] and encouraged Anagarika Dharmapala, an associate of Olcott's, to pursue the project of purifying Buddhism.[23] Sharada Sugirtharajah points to another, ulterior motive Müller had in codifying the scriptures of other traditions: Once these were accessible, their various absurdities would supposedly discredit them and prepare the ground for conquest by Christianity.[24] Indeed, Müller often spoke of the reformation or conversion of Hinduism to

Christianity,[25] and his study of Comparative Mythology was, as we saw, another means to this end.

In his speech before the World's Parliament of Religions held at Chicago in 1893, Müller stressed the superiority of written to oral tradition. He lamented the fact that the representatives of the various traditions had not been asked to state the "most essential doctrines "of their respective traditions, giving "Yes or No" answers to key questions, and citing "chapter and verse." He cast doubt upon the authority of the speakers at this event, which he argued was inferior to "the Parliament of Religions, the record of which has been assembled in forty silent volumes," namely his own *Sacred Books of the East* series (which later grew to fifty volumes).[26] He expressed his commitment to scripturalism, original intent, and literal interpretation, which takes the form of a catechism. Scientific knowledge of religious traditions could be derived only from their authoritative scriptures: "Book-religions . . . must be judged, first of all, out of their own mouths, i.e., out of their sacred writings. . . . There must always remain, to the historian of religion, an appeal to the statutes of the original code with which each religion stands and falls, and by which alone it can justly be judged."[27]

Müller's location of authentic, authorized religion in printed texts followed an old Protestant pattern. Earlier in the century, the Abbé Dubois (1765–1848) provoked a controversy with his argument that missionary efforts in India would fail to produce converts. The Serampore missionaries, who engaged in one of the earliest and most sustained efforts to translate and print the Bible in India, criticized Dubois's and other Catholics' techniques of imparting Christianity through verbal teachings, which served only to corrupt the religion thus imparted with idolatrous customs. The fact that few converts had been secured in this manner proved the superiority of a written or printed translation as a means of proselytizing. Whereas oral instruction was limited to those in range of hearing, written copies of the Gospel, multiplied by the printing press and circulated far and wide, would be a thousand times as effective as a tool for the propagation of Christianity, and would serve to check and correct the errors of preachers.[28]

Sharada Sugirtharajah argues that "for Hindus, the meaning of a text is not confined to nor firmly entrenched in the written word."[29] Despite this, the Protestant concept of textual authority exemplified by Müller's discourse greatly influenced the traditions that have been called "reformed" or "neo-Hinduism."[30] Both Rammohun Roy (1772–1833) and Dayananda Sarasvati (1824–1883)—two leading early Hindu reformers—treated the Vedas in the manner in which Protestants treated the Bible, resolving religious questions on the basis of scripture rather than custom and accumulated tradition.[31] Each of these reformers translated or elucidated the Vedas in vernacular languages,[32] paralleling Protestant efforts to do the same for the Bible. The Protestant influences on both of these thinkers are well known.[33] Rammohun sympathized publicly with Unitarianism, and Dayananda called idolatrous Brahmins "Popes."[34] One episode of Dayananda's biography reveals how deeply he may have absorbed Protestant ideas of scriptural authority. During a debate early in his career, a Brahmin opponent quoted a verse from the Vedas that Dayananda disputed. When Dayananda asked for a copy of the disputed line to be shown, his opponents countered that he was sufficiently refuted and ended the debate, declaring their own victory.[35] Part of Dayananda's disagreement with his opponents was whether ultimate authority was located in a text or, on the other hand, in oral traditions as represented by certain persons and as demonstrated through performance. Dayananda demanded the citation of chapter and verse. Echoing Müller's insistence on a yes or no answer from scripture, Dayananda argued for a literalist hermeneutic of the Vedas:

> Q. Idol-worship may not be efficacious. But it is not a sin.
> A. Injunctions are only in two forms, "do this" [and] "do not do this" e.g., the Vedas say "thou shalt speak the truth["] or, "Thou shalt not tell a lie." The commission of these "do's" is virtue and their omission is vice. Similarly the omission of the "don't's["] is virtue and their commission is vice, when you worship idols which is a forbidden action, why are you not a sinner?[36]

Upon what he regarded as a literal reading of the Vedas, Dayananda reached the conclusion that the Vedas did not condone idolatry. Not only was this the same conclusion that Müller reached upon a reading of these texts, but it echoed, unsurprisingly, Protestant readings of the Bible that had been deployed for centuries against Roman Catholic practices.[37]

Indian Languages as the Font of Idolatry

The institution of a uniform linguistic standard through codification reflected a colonial anxiety over the diversity of Indian languages. British complaints concerning the over-luxuriousness of Asiatic poetry were complemented by more general objections to India as a jungle:[38] a place of monstrous diversity, a motley mixture of races, classes, and creeds that represented both an over-whelming growth of nature and a lack of civilization or *tabula rasa*.[39] From a Christian perspective, India displayed both a bewildering profusion of gods and an absence of true religion.[40] Such diversity posed a problem of epistemo-logical and political order to which codification provided one response. Some rejected the idea that the codification of the Hindu scriptures would be enough to cure their idolatry. Alexander Duff, a Scottish missionary influential in the early institution of English education in Calcutta, referred to Hinduism as a "Gigantic System,"[41] a "false religion . . . which seems to embody the largest amount and variety of semblances and counterfeits of divinely revealed facts and doctrines," which in its effrontery most clearly resembled Roman Cathol-icism.[42] Faced with such a bewildering multiplicity produced by illegitimate accretions, how are we to know what Hinduism truly is? Duff rejected oral tradition and directed us to the "original written standard itself," as an anti-dote to the "boundless vagaries of sect, schism, and heresy."[43] Upon appeal to its authentic scriptures, however, unlike Müller, Roy, and Sarasvati, Duff found in original Hinduism the evil of idolatry.[44] Declarations of the one supreme Brahman, which appeared to converge with Christian monotheism, were dismissed as descriptions of an "infinite nothing."[45] The reality was that Hindus worship "not the high and the holy One that inhabiteth eternity, *but three hundred and thirty millions of deities instead.*"[46] Hindu attempts to recon-cile belief in the One and the Many were dismissed out of hand. The Holy Bible was the sole antidote for such multiplied errors.

Around the time that Müller was beginning work on his *Rig Veda*, the missionary and Sanskritist John Muir (1810–1882) also argued for the importance of a written standard of religious authority. Although all reli-gions in the world sprang from one original form, they subsequently parted ways through lack of a written tradition. The proof of this was the Hindu designation of religious tradition as "*Sruti* and *Sruta*, i.e., some-thing which has been heard" rather than received through writing. This lack of a scripture led to the corruption of the original revelation, as oral tradition is variable, "and since truth is uniform and error multiform, many false religions sprung up in different lands according to the fancies of men."[47] That the "truth is uniform," however, meant ultimately not merely any written standard, but the single standard of the Christian Bible.

Such agreements over the value of a scriptural standard left room for disagreement concerning the propriety of translating the Christian scrip-tures into Indian languages. William Carey regarded the connection of Sanskrit and other Indian languages with idolatry as circumstantial and correctable: "The people do not venerate the language for the idolatrous ideas it contains, but the ideas for the dress they wear. . . . Instead of pulling down the temple around which the worshippers are assembled, let us displace the idol, and present for the veneration of the people, a new and legitimate object of regard, arrayed in new vestments."[48]

Just as the Greek language, although pervaded by mythological notions, had been converted to a holy purpose, so too would Sanskrit be. The scholars of the Reformation had purged classical tradition and the Bible itself of erroneous interpretations, by a dual strategy that involved the philological study of the original texts and their publication in the vernacular languages. Similarly, the study and publication of Sanskrit would tend to disenchant this language, rendering it suitable for the expression of Christian ideas. Accordingly, Carey supported learning and instruction in the native Indian languages as a vehicle for religious reform[49] and, together with his associates, pursued perhaps the most ambitious project of translating the Christian scriptures ever undertaken. He utterly rejected the argument that the mere study of ancient languages and texts originally consecrated to idolatry could revive or spread false religion: "Once a system of idolatry has fallen into disuse, the study of the works which treat of it, can never recall it into active and vigorous operation. . . . If therefore anyone imagines that by keeping up a knowledge of the language, there will remain some aperture by which in the lapse of ages, the Hindoo gods may return and take possession of the mountains, lakes, and rivers formerly consecrated to them, . . . he is greatly mistaken. No system of image worship, either in whole or in part ever experiences a resurrection."[50]

Duff, taking the opposite view, concluded that the languages of Hinduism were hopelessly beyond redemption. The translation of Christian doctrine into Indian languages was all but impossible, as the obvious and literal translation was a false simulacrum of the true Gospel. This was because every indigenous term that might be used to communicate Christian truth was already indissolubly linked to "what is erroneous in faith, idolatrous in worship, blasphemous in principle, or abominable in practice."[51] Similarly, Charles Cameron (1795–1880) argued for the prohibition of the study of classical Indian languages in the universities on the grounds that these languages were inextricably connected with "pagan theology."[52]

Duff argued that, whereas native Indian languages were irredeemably particular, especially in their religious errors, the Bible constituted a universal language that was capable of translating across both space and time. The original apostles were aided by the "gift of tongues," whereby "*every man* heard the apostles speak *in his own language*": "Into whatever city or region an apostle entered, he found himself instantly, without any previous study, and solely by supernatural communication, enabled to address the native inhabitants in their own vernacular dialect."[53] Lacking this gift, modern missionaries would have to rely on converts who could proselytize in their native tongue. But Duff's faith in the ultimate communicative power of the Bible was never in doubt. Transcending the contingencies of linguistic convention, it existed both within and outside of language.[54] Although Classical Greek was "saturated throughout with the spirit of a polytheistic mythology," Septuagint Greek was "the only language generally understood,, which could at once, without alteration, convey the mind of the Spirit to man."[55] Duff eulogized the universality of the Gospel, which was an "ever germinant seed" capable of flourishing in any climate, even that of India: "Christianity is . . . wholly independent of earthly change. It is the same in the temperate as in the torrid zone: the same in the torrid as in the frigid. It is not scorched by heat, nor benumbed by cold. Age does not diminish the freshness of its bloom: soil does not affect its nature: climate does not modify its peculiar properties. Amid the burning sands of Africa: amid the frost-bound solitudes of Greenland: amid the wildernesses of America: amid the fertile plains of India: it still shoots up and flourishes."[56]

There were some obvious inconsistencies in Duff's claims. The very attribute he extolled in Biblical language, namely, the ability to communicate theological ideas, he condemned in Indian languages. Moreover, did not this resistance of Indian languages to Christian ideas challenge the thesis of the universal communicability of the Gospel? Duff's solution to these problems was to make English the sole medium of education. Whereas every term in Sanskrit was inextricably linked with idolatry, so that learning that language would make one "*tenfold more* a child of Pantheism, idolatry, and superstition than before," learning English would have the opposite effect.[57] For Duff, the explicit end of English education in India was the overthrow of Hindu idolatry and the triumph of Christianity.[58] In addition to promoting English language instruction, he also advocated the transliteration of Indian languages into the Roman alphabet, a policy hotly debated during the 1830s and 1850s, as described below. Both of these policy proposals exhibited a conflation, on the part of Duff and some others, of the triumph of a common language or alphabet with the triumph of the universal religion, Christianity.

Even some who promoted the translation of the Bible acknowledged that this would require a thorough transformation—a Christian baptism and rebirth—of South Asian languages.[59] David Allen stated that "the language of heathen nations" needed to be Christianized before it would be capable of conveying the "plain and intelligible" meanings of the Gospel.[60] The problem of how to translate the name of God illustrated the entrenched polytheism of the various South Asian terms that were possible candidates for this translation. The most common candidate was Sanskrit *deva* and its cognates in the vernacular languages, a term that, as we have seen, Müller connected etymologically with Latin *deus* and Greek *theos*. However, the term *deva* was already appropriated for the many gods of Hindu mythology, leading to obvious possibilities of misunderstanding.[61] For this reason, another term such as *īśvara* (lord) was sometimes chosen.[62] The association of the term *deva* with polytheism was affirmed by William Hodge Mill in his *Proposed Version of Theological Terms* in 1828.[63] Precisely because of this association, Mill chose to appropriate the term *deva* to express the one true God and deny the existence of other gods. To claim that there was one highest divinity was to do no more than most Hindu sects already did, with their assertions of the supremacy of Viṣṇu or Śiva, or of the impersonal (*nirguṇa*) Brahman; whereas to deny the existence of the popular Hindu devas was as radical as Jewish iconoclasm originally intended to be. The force of the monotheistic proposition would have been blunted by adopting a different word for god(s): "The word expressing this [word *theos* or God] in any language should be such as in enumerating the proposition 'God is One'—*Deus unus*—should convey a marked denial of the polytheistic proposition *Dii plures sunt*, or there are more Gods than one. Therefore, in the language of every heathen country, the word for the one only living and true God, should be the same universally that idolaters affix to their false gods."[64]

Mill changed his mind, however, after Rammohun Roy, who confirmed the association of the term *deva* with polytheism, objected that "the introduction of this word *Deva* to signify God . . . would require a change in the vernacular language of this country and unintentionally tend to confirm irrevocably Polytheism among the Hindoos." Richard Fox Young states that "thereafter *deva* was restricted to the idea of false gods."[65]

Opportunities for miscommunication in the translation of the Bible were ripe. The Calcutta Baptist Missionaries observed one source of potential confusion in the transliteration of unfamiliar names, which acquired, in the new language, inappropriate meanings: "Care has been taken, that no proper name should coincide exactly with a Bengali word of obvious significancy. If the name Mary were spelt according to the Greek, it would either mean having beaten (*māriyā*) or having died (*mariyā*)."[66] Accordingly, they suggested the transliteration *mariyam*. This particular problem was compounded by the lack of distinction between capital and lower-case letters in South Asian alphabets, a lack also pointed out, as we shall see, by proponents of the transliteration of Indian languages into the Roman alphabet.

The Debate over Roman Transliteration

The apparently mundane topic of spelling reform illustrates the religious dimensions of some colonial projects for the reform of Indian languages. One of the goals of codification was to standardize the Indian languages, to fix both the meanings of words and their orthography in printed dictionaries and grammars, which began the process of converting regional dialects into transregional idioms and establishing a uniform model for prose writing. Complaints over the lack of a uniform standard of orthography or spelling were common in these early projects. The *Hints Relative to Native Schools* (1816) authored by William Carey, Joshua Marshman, and William Ward—the famed "Serampore trio" of Baptist missionaries operating at Srirampur, north of Calcutta—traced the deficiencies in the natives' learning—which were so bad that they could not even read each others' scrawls—to the lack of books: "And as to manuscripts, they have scarcely one in prose."[67] The first step toward *"improving them in the knowledge of their own language"* was to print Indian letters "with the utmost accuracy."[68] The missionaries' attitude reflected the difference between their own culture of printing and prose, and the Indians' tradition of spoken language, supplemented by handwriting and traditional manuscripts often composed in verse.

At the same time that various prophets of language reform in Britain were proposing that the unnecessarily irregular, idiosyncratic, and tradition-wedded orthography of English be replaced by one or another system of regularized phonetic spelling, linguistic missionaries in India were proposing that literature in the different Indian languages and scripts should be printed in the Roman alphabet used by English and most other European languages.[69] Both groups included a healthy proportion of Protestant evangelists. Sometimes the two groups overlapped, perhaps most notably in the figure of Müller, who early in his career proposed a "missionary alphabet" for Indian and other languages,[70] and also became involved in the movement for phonetic spelling in England.[71] In the Indian context, the level of polyglottism and diversity of scripts was of course infinitely greater than in England. Some colonialists saw this as a problem, both for their administration of the country and for Indian intellectual culture. Trevelyan stated that "next to the multiplicity of languages, the intellect of India is oppressed by the multiplicity of letters."[72] Monier Monier-Williams described Hindustani as a "mixed language," formed like English by the merger of different races, but "even more composite in its structure."[73]

Roman transliteration was proposed by William Jones in the first volume of *Asiatic Researches* (1788), the new journal of the Asiatic Society founded in Calcutta, as a means of standardizing the communication of the knowledge being assembled by Orientalists.[74] Jones's system was taken up initially by fellow Orientalists and later by proponents of a broader project of printing Indian languages in Roman type. His system had some competition from another created by John Borthwick Gilchrist (1759–1841), the pioneering scholar of Hindi.[75] In 1854, Baron Christian Bunsen, Müller's patron, sponsored a series of meetings at which different proposals for a universal alphabet were considered, including Müller's own *Proposal for a Missionary Alphabet* and another by Richard Lepsius.[76] Supporting missionary endeavors was a primary motive for Bunsen and his associates.[77] The debate over Roman transliteration heated up in the early 1830s, and then again surrounding the Indian Rebellion of 1857, just a few years after the Bunsen conferences. In 1859, Monier-Williams edited an anthology of essays by proponents and opponents of the use of Roman type in printing Indian languages, and expressed his own strong support for Jones's system of Roman transliteration.

During the first round of debates in 1834, Charles Trevelyan associated Romanization, which he supported, with the policy of Anglicization advocated with much greater notoriety one year later by Macaulay in his famous *Minute on Indian Education*.[78] Trevelyan's initial opponents included James Prinsep, the noted Orientalist, as well as the Serampore missionaries, who condemned the scheme as "utterly preposterous."[79] Roman transliteration was one facet of the broader movement to Anglicize Indian culture. This movement contended that British support for education in the traditional literatures succeeded only in perpetuating a system of false knowledge that was not, on its own, economically viable. The government should instead devote its energies to promoting education in English. Obviously, the convergence of Romanization with full Anglicization would require the eventual demise of traditional literature, which would be replaced by literature in English and suitably rationalized modern Indian languages: "All the existing Muhammadan and Hindu literature will gradually sink into disuse, with the exception of such portions of it as are worthy of being turned into the new letters."[80]

A principal motivation for spelling reform was religious pedagogy: the facilitation of the acquisition of a knowledge of the Christian scriptures. This had also been one of the motivations behind earlier projects of codification. The first book translated into Bengali and printed in the Bengali alphabet by Carey at Serampore in 1800 had been the Gospel of Matthew, followed one year later by the complete New Testament.[81] Similarly, the first book printed in Romanized Hindustani was the Sermon on the Mount.[82] A Romanized Bengali version of the Sermon on the Mount was supposedly adopted at an orthodox Hindu school where a version in Bengali character would never have been allowed.[83] Another proponent illustrated the utility of the Roman alphabet by transliterating versions in different Indian languages of the first verse of the Gospel of John: "In the beginning was the Word."[84] The reduction of these translations to a common alphabetic standard rendered their similarities more apparent, serving to underline the universal translatability of the Christian Logos. It was not for nothing that some of its proponents called the Roman alphabet "the Christian character of the North-West Provinces,"[85] naturally opposed to Devanāgarī, the "alphabet of the gods,"[86] in which many Hindi and Sanskrit texts were written.

These debates showed a coordination between the missionary and economic goals of the British in India.[87] Romanization would be an aid to the diffusion of Christianity: "The moral conquest of India is to be effected by a process less rapid and less obvious to public view, than that of its subjugation physically and politically by the courage of our soldiers, and the wisdom of our legislature."[88] Alexander Duff, under the pen name "Alpha," was one of the strongest proponents of Roman transliteration, which complemented his efforts to promote English language instruction for Indians as a means of propagating Christianity. Trevelyan's own motivations were scarcely less missionary, although often couched in the language of utility. Some of the principal advantages claimed for Roman transliteration were that, in the short term, it would save money, as Roman characters took up less space on the printed page; and, in the long term, it would promote commerce. Among both evangelicals and utilitarians were found individuals who viewed the adoption of Roman transliteration as a step toward the ultimate unification of India under a common language, for either religious or commercial purposes, or more commonly both.[89] Monier-Williams summed up this view: "Let us gradually and in a Christian spirit of conciliation, induce our Indian fellow-subjects to adopt our views of religion and science, to study our language and literature, to benefit by our mechanical knowledge and our various appliances for economising time, labour, and money."[90] Trevelyan claimed that Romanization would "create a tendency towards a common Indian language, of which English will be the connecting link, and the Christian religion the source of inspiration."[91] "But the greatest advantage of all the use of these letters is, that it will cut up the existing native literature by the roots, and give rise to a new and purified literature, unconnected with the abominations of idolatry, and impregnated with the Spirit of Christ."[92] Adoption of the Roman alphabet might be only a small step toward these high goals, but it was a step nonetheless. Trevelyan argued that the fact that William Jones's proposal for Roman transliteration had not succeeded yet after mere decades, was no reason to assume that it could never succeed. After all, the truths of Christianity had been confined to the Holy Land for 1,500 years, in the form of Judaism, before the appearance of Christ and his apostles.[93]

The convergence of these imperial and religious objectives was illustrated by a comparison between Britain and the Roman Empire, in its Christian and pre-Christian versions. Rome was the source of the alphabet in question and the cause of its initial dissemination. Just as Christianity had emerged to be the lasting legacy of the Eternal City, Duff argued that the spiritual conquest enabled by Rome's alphabet would be more noble and enduring than her martial conquests.[94] The subtext, that the British Empire had better look to its own more lasting spiritual legacy, was obvious.

Back in England, phonetic spelling was also often depicted in religious terms. In Müller's view, the adoption of phonetic spelling for English would be comparable to the Protestant Reformation in its potential benefits.[95] Another anonymous proponent described it as a "Phonetic Reformation . . . second only in importance as it is to the introduction and establishment of Printing itself." For many, the Bible remained a "sealed book—a mere assemblage of unmeaning hieroglyphics." To amend this sorry state would require instituting "perfect coincidence between written and spoken language." This was the intention of the phonotypers in Bath, England, who printed the first sheets of the phonetic Bible in 1845, following Gutenberg's earlier contributions to "the causes of Civilization and

Christianity." The author noted that "already, several missionaries have determined to apply the Phonetic principle, in reducing to form barbarous and hitherto unwritten language, and thus test its capabilities by actual experience."[96]

Earlier Universal Languages and Their Religious Dimensions

Movements for the simplification and standardization of spelling in both nineteenth-century England and her Indian colony represented an historical legacy of the schemes for a universal language or system of writing proposed in the seventeenth century, a number of them by individuals associated with the Royal Society.[97] Such a language would institute between words and things, or between either of these and their mode of written notation, a stable and uniform relationship analogous to that which empiricism was aspiring to establish between scientific understanding and the physical world. The universal language proposals coordinated also with technological developments in orthography, shorthand, and printing.[98] The institution of a perfect, universal, or philosophical language or mode of writing that would accurately reflect the natural world was an obvious desideratum of any empirical science worthy of the name. Yet this goal, as pursued by many, was more than mere empiricism. The universal language schemes often expressed a more fundamental desire for a perfect mode of communication as a panacea for social, intellectual, and religious problems. As Paolo Rossi states, "the religious dimension was, in fact, often foregrounded in the writings of the theorists of universal language . . . It is quite clear . . . that these new 'languages' were not intended simply to clarify the semantic problems of natural philosophers, but had much broader and more ambitious aims. They were designed as instruments of total redemption, and a means for deciphering the divine alphabet."[99]

The idea of a univocal language—that is, of a language in which one thing would be represented by exactly one word (or written character), and/or one sound by one letter, served in many cases as a metaphor for the triumph of monotheism. Such a language would provide an antidote for the errors of language that promoted idolatry,[100] and by ending the diversity of languages, would end as well the diversity of religions. The universal languages would remedy the curse of Babel and repeat the miracle of

Pentecost, at which the Apostles, speaking in tongues, disseminated the word of the Gospel.

In *The Advancement and Proficiency of Learning* (1605), Bacon suggested that a "real character" might be framed that would represent things rather than words.[101] The different languages used different words to express the same things. Absent and in lieu of a universal spoken language, a rationalized system of writing would allow perfect communication by instituting a direct correspondence between a mark or character, on the one hand, and a thing or an idea, on the other. Such a philosophically rationalized system of writing would both perfect language and permit universal communication by bypassing the tremendous variety of spoken languages. This provided the inspiration for a number of later proposals for a perfect, universal language, the most ambitious of which was John Wilkins's (1614–1672) *An Essay towards a Real Character, and a Philosophical Language* (1668). Wilkins attempted, in one, large volume, to fulfill several great aspirations: to classify all concepts according to a philosophically and empirically rationalized scheme; to create a system of written marks to express such concepts (the "real character"); and to create an alphabet that would allow the expression of such concepts in spoken form (the "philosophical language"). Well into the nineteenth century, and even beyond, a variety of individuals, often working in obscurity or outside the margins of the official academic establishment, continued to produce such schemes.

According to Bacon's original proposal, a real character would represent things immediately, rather than through the words of ordinary language. For precedent, Bacon invoked both Chinese characters—which carried the same meaning in different dialects even though pronounced differently—and Egyptian hieroglyphs, which had already been interpreted by some Europeans as naturally expressing the things they symbolized.[102] The word "character" had a prior history in natural magic, where it denoted pictorial figures with a special connection to reality. Bacon's proposal continued the desire for a character that would immediately access—in the sense of communicating, rather than influencing—the world of things.[103] Hence, his call for a character that, like the Chinese, would be "real" rather than "nominal." He acknowledged that there could be, in some sense, a natural fit between a character and the thing denoted by it, just as hieroglyphs and gestures could signify iconically (*ex congruo*), through their pictorial resemblance to the things denoted. However, his real character, like the Chinese, would be artificial or instituted by convention (*ad placitum*), and he rejected the idea that such a character could be effective in magical operations.

Some who followed Bacon's original proposal expressed the hope that such a real character or universal language might be made to bear a natural resemblance to things.[104] Although Wilkins allowed the possibility of inventing a natural character or alphabet "that should not signifie *words*, but *things* and *notions*,"[105] he concluded that such an endeavor would be extremely difficult.[106] Accordingly, his real character was what Bacon had originally proposed: an artificially instituted system of written symbols that signified by convention or agreement, rather than by nature or by virtue of a resemblance to that which they expressed.[107]

These universal language projects illustrate a broader semiotic shift toward an insistence on the arbitrary or conventional status of linguistic and other signs, as well as the lingering hope to transcend the restrictions this imposed on language. Despite John Locke's deep skepticism concerning the possibility of a universal language, and his persuasive insistence on the arbitrary nature of words,[108] a number of later proposals for a universal language or system of writing echoed Wilkins's desire that such a mode of communication be, in some sense, natural.[109] Vickers's identification of the shift, in the late seventeenth century, from occult to scientific mentalities is largely correct, but took longer than he indicated, and was in fact progressive and incomplete. Like the magical languages that preceded them, a number of scientific proposals for a universal language or character were enchanted by the prospect of a language that was capable of mirroring nature, and promised practical results that bordered on the magical.

The universal language proposals were a product of the Reformation in several respects. The breakdown in the unity of the Church, especially over the interpretation of scripture, as well as the rise of the vernaculars, highlighted the need for a common linguistic standard as a vehicle for communication. As Sidonie Clauss notes, "the idea of forming a new universal language to replace Latin grew in part out of nostalgia for international Christendom."[110] The additional weight placed on the correct interpretation of scripture as a guide to religious knowledge and practice further exposed the depredations visited upon language by the vagaries of time and the diversity of cultures. Against this backdrop there emerged several proposals for a universal language or mode of writing—proposals that, while coming mainly from the scientific community, frequently carried strong religious and even magical connotations.[111] Several scholars have suggested that the universal language schemes were inspired also by the rise of print culture.[112] It certainly made more sense to argue for the benefits of a universal mode of writing after literacy had itself begun to become more widespread, in part as a result of printing. Similar to printing, a real or universal character would standardize and stabilize knowledge.

The universal language schemes also reflected an important continuity with orthodox Christian soteriology. The creation of such a language was seen by many as a salvific event, a work of redemption. The authors of such languages commonly invoked the story of the Tower of Babel (Genesis 11)[113] and, less frequently, the story of Pentecost (Acts 2). The dispersal and differentiation of languages after the destruction of the Tower served as the explanation of the problem of linguistic diversity to which such universal characters would provide the solution. In the Garden of Eden, Adam had called the different creatures "by their own names" (*nominibus suis*: Genesis 2:16–17, Vulgate version). This had two possible meanings: Either he established their names by convention, as Locke insisted,[114] or he somehow knew their secret, true names. Interpreters often embraced the latter position, and held that Adam spoke a perfect, natural language—namely, the original form of Hebrew.[115] John Bulwer, for example, interpreted the diversity of languages as a fall from humanity's original condition in the Garden of Eden, where Adam knew the language of nature.[116] Expulsion from the Garden preceded and foreshadowed the loss of the perfect language at Babel. The story of Pentecost, however, at which the first apostles had displayed the gift of preaching the gospel in every conceivable tongue, provided a precedent for the idea of a universal mode of communication that would overcome the language barrier and, at the same time, restore the state of grace. Margreta de Grazia states that "a tradition extending back to Augustine and continuing through the Middle Ages regarded this event [i.e., Pentecost] as God's explicit revocation of the penalty He had imposed at Babel."[117] A number of universal language schemes aimed at the recovery of the lost perfect language, or of an effective replacement for it, as had happened at Pentecost.[118] Such universal languages were understood as a work of redemption, as well as a tool for propagation of the Gospel.[119] As Vivian Salmon notes, "there was one particular purpose . . . for which men of all shades of religious opinion envisaged a universal language . . . that of [fulfilling] the linguistic requirements of missionaries."[120] This was exemplified, in many individual proposals, by the translation into the new character or language of Biblical or other religious texts, including Genesis 1, John 1, and the Lord's Prayer, that highlighted the divinity of language or communication between humans and the divine.[121] Robert Stillman has rightly emphasized the soteriological dimension of the universal language schemes: "Intensely conscious of the salvific power of the Word, from the 'Let there be' of creation to the descent of the logos in the incarnation, Bacon, Hobbes, and Wilkins are drawn to conceptualize perfect languages as a model and sometimes a means for achieving a salvific form of knowledge."[122]

The religious dimension of these proposals was present already in Bacon and Wilkins. Although Bacon's discussion of the real character in *The Advancement* gave no indication of this, one of his most popular works, *New Atlantis* (1626), did.[123] This book depicted a fantastic voyage to the fictional land of Bensalem. A ruler and priest of this land recounts how, after the death of Christ, a pillar of light off the coast of their land pointed the way to an ark that held a Book, containing versions of the Old and New Testaments, and a letter from Saint Bartholomew: "There was also in both these writings, as well the Book as the Letter, wrought a great miracle, conform to that of the Apostles in the original Gift of Tongues. For there being at that time in this land Hebrews, Persians, and Indians, besides the natives, every one read upon the Book and the Letter, as if they had been written in his own language. And thus was this land saved from infidelity (as the remain of the old world was from water) by an ark."[124] In this episode, a type of real character appears as a means of salvation, a device for the universal propagation of the Gospel that repeats the event of Pentecost.[125]

In an early treatise on cryptography published a quarter century before his *Essay*, Wilkins expressed the hope of inventing a mode of writing that would reverse the curse of confusion imposed at Babel: "The perfecting of such an invention were the only way to unite the seventy two Languages of the first confusion."[126] In his *Essay*, the religious motive remained paramount. Such modes of communication promised to reverse the "Curse of the Confusion" imposed at Babel,[127] and by spreading true religion and the "clearing of some of our Modern differences in Religion" would be the most effective design "next to the Gift of Miracles, and particularly that of Tongues, poured out upon the Apostles in the first planting of Christianity."[128] Wilkins's prime example of the corruption of language was the transformations in the Lord's Prayer that rendered earlier Saxon and English versions incomprehensible to modern readers.[129] Toward the end of the work, he translated the Lord's Prayer in both his philosophical language and real character,[130] and gave specimens of the Prayer in fifty languages, as a demonstration of the value of his proposal.[131]

One of the basic ideas of the universal languages was the removal of ambiguity or polysemousness in interpretation. Wilkins described one of the deficiencies of language as its use of "equivocals," terms that had more than one meaning: as Latin *malus* could designate either evil, or an apple tree, or the mast of a ship.[132] A perfect language, on the other hand, would so "contrive the Enumeration of things and notions, as that they may be full and *adequate*, without any *Redundancy* or *Deficiency* as to the Number of them, and *regular* as to their Place and Order."[133] Consequently, the universal languages sought to institute the rule of "one word for one thing," meaning not only that each word (or character) would have only one referent, but also that each referent would be signified by only one word (or character).[134] The fundamental idea of a perfect language was expressed elegantly in Jeremy Bentham's rhyme: "Whene'er the same nature,/ The same nomenclature" (*eadem natura, eadem nomenclatura*).[135] In the case of an alphabet, this meant that each letter should have one and only one sound.[136]

Especially when opposed to linguistic idolatry and polytheism, the idea of a univocal, universal language served as a metaphor for the triumph of Christian monotheism. In the early 1870s, Robert Hunt—admittedly one of the crazier exponents of English as a universal language that preserved the "pre-Babel vocalization"—clearly expressed this association: "The *scope* of the whole scheme is ONE LORD, ONE LAW, ONE LANGUAGE, and PARADISE REGAINED."[137]

"One Step from Babel to Pentecost"

In colonial India, the apparently more modest proposals for a missionary alphabet and Roman transliteration followed the pattern set by the universal language schemes in England, and occasionally shared the utopian or even messianic goals of these schemes. William Jones's original proposal expressed the need for a "natural character" that could transcribe accurately all languages:

> The letters, by which they [the labials] are denoted, represent in most alphabets the curvature of one lip or of both; and a *natural character* for all articulate sounds might easily be agreed upon, if nations would agree on any thing generally beneficial, by delineating the several organs of speech in the act of articulation, and

selecting from each a distinct and elegant outline. A perfect language would be that, in which every idea, capable of entering the human mind, might be neatly and emphatically expressed by one specifick word . . . and on the same principle a perfect system of letters ought to contain one specifick symbol for every sound used in pronouncing the language to which they belonged.[138]

In Jones's natural character, the shape of the letters would imitate and express their sounds. According to him, in most alphabets the labials, formed by the curving and closure of the lips, are signified by equally sinuous shapes: for example, English "p" and "b." Jones may have been thinking of Devanāgarī, which he also praised for being "more naturally arranged than any other" alphabetic system.[139] It is the case that, in Devanāgarī, several of the labial letters are curved (e.g., those for "pa" प and "ba" ब). However, this is also true of many other letters. In the end, although he called English spelling "disgracefully and almost ridiculously imperfect,"[140] Jones endorsed the idea of using the Roman alphabet, suitably modified by diacritics, to transliterate Indian languages. Apparently, given the absence of agreement on what would have been more desirable, namely, a natural character, Roman transliteration was an acceptable substitute.

Jones's proposals echoed Bacon's and Wilkins's proposals for a real character. Other proponents of Roman transliteration imbibed their influences either directly from these earlier sources, or indirectly from Jones. Duff invoked Wilkins for this purpose,[141] as Müller was later to cite Wilkins in support of both his missionary alphabet and his Science of Language: "What Leibniz suggested, and what Bishop [John] Wilkins carried out to a certain extent, a completely new philosophical language, would be the best cure for that malady of language which has afflicted our race as long so we know it [sic], though even that could only give temporary relief."[142]

Jones was not even the first to apply these Baconian ideas to South Asia. Almost half a century prior to his proposal there appeared a work entitled *The Methodist: or, A New Method of Reading, Writing, and Printing, all Languages in Short-Hand, by a New and Universal Alphabet; and of Learning All Arts and Sciences, by a Real Character and Philosophical Language* (1741). The title of this work already indicated its indebtedness to Wilkins's earlier proposal. *The Methodist* created a new set of characters for its universal alphabet, which supposedly had several advantages (apart from its universality): It would enable the writing and printing of languages in shorthand, so that "the Substance of a large Folio, perhaps may be reduc'd to the Size of a portable Pocket Volume, and thus render'd at an easier Rate," adding to the cost-savings of a single font of types; and it would serve as the basis of a "Real Character . . . expressing the natures of Things by the simple *Lines* of the same," as well as of a "Philosophical Language expressing the several *Lines* of the Character by distinct *Sounds* proper to Each, and hereby signifying the Natures of *Things* by their several *Names*."[143] Evidently, the author of this work also aspired, like Jones and some others within the Baconian tradition, to a natural character rather than to one that signified merely by convention. The primary goal of *The Methodist* was to support the work of missionaries in translating the Bible, particularly in India. Noting the efforts of the missionaries at Tranquebar and elsewhere, the work expressed the desirability of finding some universal alphabet that could be used to print the Bible in any language.[144] Toward that end, the author requested of his missionary correspondent samples of the alphabets, grammars, and lexicons of the various Indian languages, together with translations into those languages of the Gospel of John ("In the beginning was the Word").[145]

As we saw, seventeenth-century proposals for a perfect philosophical language or character frequently depicted the creation of such a language as a salvific event, a work of redemption that would reverse Babel and repeat Pentecost. Many later colonial projects for linguistic reform were similarly inspired; Müller's Science of Language was only one example. As Brian Pennington states, William Jones "attributed all later elaborations on or deviations from [an] initial rational, monotheistic state to . . . the scattering of linguistic groups after the fall of the Tower of Babel."[146] By implication, the establishment of a uniform system of writing would be a means of countering the unholy nexus of polytheism and polyglottism. Proponents of Roman transliteration sometimes invoked the Babel legend much as we do, as a metaphor for linguistic confusion, suitable in their view for describing the contemporary diversity of Indian languages and writing.[147] In other cases, however, the soteriological dimensions were unmistakable. Trevelyan, for example, declared that the Roman alphabet would "become the universal written character of the whole world" and "continue to advance . . . until that day shall arrive when the curse of Babel will be removed, and all mankind will be united in the enjoyment of a common language and a common mode of expressing it."[148] On another occasion, he affirmed that "next to the establishment of a universal language . . . the establishment of a universal system of orthography will most tend to the production of unrestricted freedom of intercourse between all the families of the human race."[149] Accordingly, James Prinsep, who opposed Roman transliteration, ridiculed its utopian dimensions. In his view, the prospect for success was "as chimerical as the establishment of an universal language, or the 'removal of the curse of Babel.'"[150]

In his arguments for English-only education, Alexander Duff argued that the unity of language and the unity of religion would proceed hand-in-hand: "Is it chimerical to anticipate the prevalence of one tongue, the utterance of one lip, wherever Christianity and free trade are maintained? At Babel languages were confounded because men became impiously proud . . . Is it Utopian to anticipate that one language may prevail, when mankind shall become one brotherhood in truth?"[151] However, under the Orientalists, "divine honours were paid to the Sanskrit, and its deva nagree [i.e., Devanāgarī, the principal alphabet used in northern India] was consecrated with a lustration."[152] Opposing such verbal idolatry, Lord William Bentinck, Macaulay, and Trevelyan had induced a "reformation" comparable to that of Luther and Bacon.[153]

The missionary and Tamil scholar George Uglow Pope read the late 1850s debates and, in his *One Alphabet for All India* (1859), argued for the extension of Roman transliteration to the South Indian languages.[154] The epigraph of this tract read, "That they all may be ONE," an obvious reference to the goal of Christianization. Pope acknowledged that the objective was to assist the missionary in his endeavors.[155] Although the goal of a single language—Dravidian, but English-infused—for South India appeared remote or even "chimerical," that of a single alphabet was more feasible. The Roman character would be "one step from Babel towards Pentecost," and would "break down one more of the barriers which keep the races of men apart . . . [thus] advancing civilization," meaning Christianity.[156]

One of the primary objectives of such language reforms, as we saw earlier, was to end the ambiguity of reference of the various languages by instituting a univocal language or system of writing. Jones explicitly invoked the idea of "one word for one thing" and argued that, similarly, a phoneme should always be represented by the same letter.[157] Müller later made the same connection between the idea of a perfect, univocal language and spelling reform: "As in a perfect alphabet the same letter ought always to have one and the same sound, and the same sound ought always to be represented by one and the same letter, so, in a perfect language, the same word ought always to have one and the same meaning, and the same meaning ought always to be represented by one and the same word."[158]

Such arguments depended on a conflation of language with nature. Words were the audible, and visible, embodiment of reality. A single word should ideally correspond to a single entity in the physical world. The danger was that this correspondence might not exist, as in the empty verbal knowledge of Catholic scholasticism or traditional Sanskrit.

Brian Houghton Hodgson (1800–1894), the early scholar of Buddhism in Nepal, explicitly attacked this view of language in defending the use of the vernaculars against the Anglicists: "That language is an express image of thought is an old and exploded error. Words do *not* expressly embody ideas—the function of language being limited to putting and keeping two minds in the same train of thought."[159] (Here Hodgson anticipated modern theories of the pragmatic function of language-in-use.) Although mathematical and scientific expression are precise, the same precision is impossible for philosophy and the moral sciences. Hence, the hope that a future Bacon would produce a true philosophical language was likely vain. However, Hodgson did not entirely reject his opponents' arguments. He reversed their analogy between English education and the Protestant Reformation. A vernacular medium had always been the best means of confounding priestly deception and domination;[160] in India this mandated the use of local languages instead of English. The Anglicists were reprising the role, not of the fathers of the Reformation, but of the Roman Church.[161] They were idolizing the words of the English language instead of Latin: "Those who are accustomed to consider the despotic influence of words over ideas—an influence which even that intellectual giant Locke declared his frequent inability to subdue when it was connected with a foreign language, save by rendering the passage *into his own tongue*—will be able to appreciate [my objection to the Anglicists]."[162] Hodgson still affirmed the goal of converting Indians to Christian modernity, but through the use of local languages and customs rather than their immediate and total replacement by English.[163]

Proponents of Roman transliteration and associated language reforms in colonial India sometimes confounded monotheism, as an order of images or representation, with the chimerical ideal of a universal and univocal language. The triumph of monotheistic Christianity as the universal religion of India would proceed hand-in-hand with the triumph of the Roman alphabet, the "Christian character of the North-West provinces." This would also represent the correction of Hindu polytheism, and justify the name of God.[164] Reprising his label of *Rig Veda* 10.121 as a hymn "To the Unknown God," Müller provided a transliteration of this hymn into the new missionary alphabet.[165] What the language of Hinduism rendered obscure, the Gospel would make plain.[166]

As with other colonial projects for linguistic reform, some proponents of a phonetic alphabet of "one word for one sound" advocated an ideal of linguistic monotheism, and opposed the proliferation of different alphabets that supported Hindu polytheism. Monier-Williams argued that, if opponents could contend that Indians have a "prescriptive right" to their own native alphabets, then they could also contend that "the Hindu has a prescriptive right to his own religion with its million gods."[167] Müller stated: "Where there is no important national literature clinging to a national alphabet, . . . the multiplicity of alphabets—the worthless remnant of a bygone civilisation bequeathed, for instance, to the natives of India—should be attacked as zealously by the Missionary as the multiplicity of castes and of divinities."[168] (The first, conditional clause may have exempted Sanskrit from obliteration.) If orthographic variation amounted to idolatry, it was only natural that Christians would wish to write the name of their Lord always in the same way. The problem was that the "j" sound found in English "Jesus" was absent in many languages. Despite this, Müller allowed that missionaries might wish to retain the letter "j" in their alphabets, as "it would enable us to spell uniformly the name of our Lord—and in all the translations of the Bible . . . that one name at least would stand unaltered and uncorrupted in all tongues and all ages." This could be the sole exception to phonological accuracy. Alternatively, Christ's name could be allowed to change into diverse forms, so that "the very variety of the name will proclaim the unity of Him who has promised to all tongues the gift of His Holy Spirit."[169]

Apart from Roman transliteration, the application of European typographic conventions to the printing of Indian languages also assumed religious significance for some. In traditional Sanskrit manuscripts, the writing proceeds unbroken. One word flows into another, in accordance with the established conventions of euphonic combination (*sandhi*). Moreover, there are no capital letters, and the only punctuation is a line or double-line ("stick": *daṇḍa*) to mark the end of a paragraph or section. This state of affairs, which coordinated with an emphasis on the oral recitation of Sanskrit texts, for which manuscripts played a supporting role, also facilitated a genre of poetry called *śleṣa* in which the long strings of letters could be carved up different ways to produce different meanings, and even entirely different poems.[170] This brought the traditional proclivity of poetry for polysemousness to new heights. For some colonialists, however, the goal was not polyvalence but univocity, and the traditional way of writing Sanskrit detracted from that goal. Punctuation was introduced into the printing of Indian languages by the Serampore missionaries and the scholars of the College of Fort William at the beginning of the nineteenth century.[171]

For some colonialists, even the pursuit of correct punctuation carried religious overtones.[172] In his inaugural lecture on *The Study of Sanskrit in Relation to Missionary Work in India* (1861), Monier-Williams argued in favor of applying European typographic conventions to the printing of Sanskrit texts.[173] Echoing the principle of one word for one thing, he argued that the words for individual things should be separated when printing Sanskrit texts. Typography, spacing, and punctuation would all smooth the process of reading for the Western eye especially. Monier-Williams attacked the older system of writing, which was wedded to an oral and esoteric priestly tradition, designed for the ear rather than the eye, to convey the sound rather than the sense, and in which ideas are subservient to words instead of the other way around. Suitably reformed, however, Sanskrit would serve as a powerful vehicle for the missionary: "Such, indeed, is the exuberance and flexibility of this language and its power of compounding words, that when it has been, so to speak, baptized and thoroughly penetrated with the spirit of Christianity, it will probably be found, next to Hebrew and Greek, the most expressive vehicle of Christian truth."[174]

Duff argued that traditional Oriental writing, unmarked by punctuation or capital letters, displayed a "homogeneous uniformity" that resembled "the plains of Bengal . . . [with] no undulations of soil, no elevations, . . . [nothing] to diversify the scene . . . Go where you may, it is one wearisome unvaried sameness, one interminable interchange of flat paddy fields and close dingy jungle. Similar is the appearance of an Oriental work. It looks like one dull monotonous mass, without beginning, middle, or end."[175] In Duff's polemic, the metaphor of India as a jungle—a diversity at once boundless and empty—was applied to the country's languages. This jungle needed to be cleared, surveyed, and demarcated by European punctuation.

Pope employed a similar geographical metaphor, comparing native writing to "the Tinnevelly *têris*, or sand plains, a dreary monotonous pathless waste." The lack of capital letters, italics, and other devices meant that no one can quickly gather an idea of the content of a page printed in native characters. The absence of punctuation posed special problems for the translation of Christian scriptures:

In translations of the Holy Scriptures . . . it is of the last importance that sacred names and the names of places, strange to native ears, should stand out apart from the other words of the sentence, as in English they are made to by the aid of capitals. . . . And again, how necessary is the use of italics in translations of the Holy Scriptures to distinguish words not in the original, but the insertion of which is rendered necessary by the idioms of the language into which they are rendered. The absence in native works of all these expressive marks, by which precision and distinctness are attained in works printed in the Roman character, is of itself reason sufficient for the change now proposed.[176]

The lack of distinctions among words printed in Indian alphabets exacerbated the habit of verbal idolatry, instead of promoting the recognition of the uniqueness of words and, by extension, their one-to-one correspondence with objects in the physical and moral worlds. Although apparently motivated by empiricism, this complaint also disclosed anxiety over the religious problem of how to affirm the uniqueness of biblical places and persons in the absence of capital letters, as we saw earlier in the case of the name of Mary. This paralleled the concern over translating the name of God as *deva*, a plural class noun that could never, in Indian scripts, be capitalized so as to confirm the uniqueness of the Christians' personal God.

One of the striking features of colonial proposals for Roman transliteration, especially as compared with their seventeenth-century precursors, was how clearly they reflected diminished expectations. Bacon and Wilkins aspired to a perfect philosophical language that would record the world without distortion, by classifying completely all beings and concepts, and would communicate universally by bypassing the medium of spoken languages. Colonial proposals were much less ambitious. The transliteration of existing languages replaced the institution of a universal character. English phonetic spelling aimed to make it a bit easier to learn how to read. The Roman transliteration of Indian languages similarly aimed to make these languages easier to learn. Presumably, a certain measure of reality had intruded into the utopian schemes for a universal language. The stubborn fact of linguistic diversity made the idea of a universal language progressively less plausible. Despite this, proponents of spelling reform often continued to make grandiose claims for the utilitarian value and even salvific power of their systems.

An Empire of Language

Colonial proposals for language reforms obviously had political as well as religious motivations. These motivations often converged, to the point of being indistinguishable. As Joseph Mullens argued, British colonialism in India blended Baconianism with Christianity. However, there were also fractures between the official colonial policy and the objectives of the missionaries. The British colonial administration only grudgingly opened to the proselytizing activities of the missionaries in 1813. Prior to that time, proselytizing was prohibited, ostensibly because of the possibility that it would disturb native sentiment. William Carey and his associates had to operate from Serampore, in Danish territory. Missionaries were blamed for the massacre at Vellore in 1806, as well as for the much more serious challenge to British domination of the subcontinent represented by the 1857 Rebellion. The second round of debates over Roman transliteration occurred soon after this event, and reflected a certain hardening of opinion regarding the causes of the Rebellion. Opponents of transliteration pointed to the need to respect native traditions, while proponents regarded assimilation to English learning as a means to the pacification of the colonized. Müller—who, though primarily what we would call an Orientalist, also supported a missionary alphabet and evaluated Hinduism in terms of his own Christian categories—illustrates the range and complexity of colonial British attitudes. This complexity is apparent in his contributions to the debates over the causes of the Rebellion. One popular explanation was the insensitivity of the British to Indian religions, as illustrated by the famous charge that the native troops had rebelled against using bullets greased with pig and beef fat, which would be anathema to Muslims and Hindus. Trevelyan (under the name Indophilus) attributed the rebellion to this cause.[177] Müller (under the name Philindus) argued that the cause was the neglect and suppression of the Indian languages.[178] If the British had possessed a better knowledge of South Asian languages, at least, the Rebellion might not have caught them by surprise. He further attacked the view that the study of Oriental languages was worthless, and that English would become the common language of India. The two interlocutors both supported the creation of a college for the teaching of Oriental languages, to replace Haileybury, although they disagreed as to whether Sanskrit should be part of the required curriculum along with the vernaculars.[179]

After the Rebellion, Müller authored an anonymous article, "The English Alphabet Applied to the Languages of India," in which he reviewed proposals for Roman transliteration—including his own, which he of course favored—and reiterated his support for a universal system of writing as a means for both political and religious uniformity.[180] He rejected as chimerical the project of making English the universal language of India at that time, but advocated Romanization in government schools and official publications: "Last but not least . . .in all missionary publications the native alphabets should be discarded."[181] He then quoted Trevelyan's argument that, as the Gospel had, after a long delay, converted the parochial tradition of Judaism into a worldwide religion, there was still hope that the Roman alphabet might succeed in India. Despite their disagreement on tactics, Müller still supported Trevelyan's general strategic goal of a universal mode of communication to complement and advance the universal religion, Christianity.

Whatever position one took in these debates, the decision of which language and educational policy to pursue appeared key to the success of the colonial endeavor. The "command of language," as Bernard Cohn argued, reinforced the "language of command."[182] For similar reasons, the author of the first Spanish grammar in 1492 told Queen Isabella that "language is the perfect instrument of empire."[183] Even the sophisticated and arguably Indophilic Müller affirmed a connection between linguistic (or more broadly epistemological) and political domination. He claimed, with typical extravagance, that *"the discovery of the Sanskrit language and literature has been of more value to England in the retention and increase of her Indian Empire, than an army of a hundred thousand men."*[184] Yet "a man-of-war is built in less time than an Oriental scholar can be launched ready to converse with natives."[185] Of course, these statements were partly self-serving: an attempt to justify the expenditure of the government's largesse on philological projects that were of uncertain importance to the continuation of the Empire.

Colonial projects for the reform of Indian languages shared with both Baconian tradition and Christian monotheism the ideals of unity and universality, as well as the objectives of epistemological certainty and cultural and political domination. These connections are highlighted by the structural analogy between monotheism and empire, in which the Few control the Many. The missionary William Ward affirmed a causal connection between monotheism and colonial power: "I fear more for the continuance of the British power in India, from the encouragement which Englishmen have given to the idolatry of the Hindoos, than from any other quarter whatever."[186] Müller also linked monotheism and polytheism with different types of social formation or political organization. Henotheism corresponded to the stage of autonomous hamlets that were not yet villages,[187] or tribes that have not coalesced into nations: "[Henotheism] is, if I may say so, anarchy, as preceding monarchy, a communal as distinct from an imperial form of religion."[188] Polytheism, which, according to Müller, was not simply several gods but a pantheon with a chief god, corresponded to larger and more centralized polities. He argued that a nation's gods reflected its own political system: a monarchy among the pantheon implied a monarchy among the people.[189] If such a correlation obtained between the political and religious domains, what would be the appropriate form of religion for the British Empire? Perhaps only Christian monotheism, which evacuated other gods and, with them, any competing sources of political authority. Projects for the reform of Indian languages served this strategic objective, if only symbolically.

4

"Vain Repetitions"

THE ATTACK ON HINDU MANTRAS

The favour of God is not obtained with a vaine heape of woordes: . . . their superstition is heere conde[m]ned, which thinke they pleasure God and doe him service with their longe murmured praiers, with which errour wee see Poperie so infected, that the greatest force of their prayer is supposed to consist in many wordes. For the mo wordes any manne hathe muttered, the more effectually he is accounted to have prayed.[1]

The Hindus themselves, in immense multitudes, begin to doubt about the power of the Mantras; and especially of those which are said to have the power of bringing God by distinction into a stone.[2]

"Chaunting at the Cathedral"

When Macaulay argued that colonial government support for Sanskrit learning was just as wasteful as money spent on "chaunting at the cathedral,"[3] he was echoing Protestant condemnations of the repetitive prayers of Roman Catholics, the Ave Marias and Paternosters that they repeated in Latin without even understanding the words. Macaulay's argument represented, in some respects, the culmination of a very long tradition of polemics against Indian prayers, whether Hindu, Muslim, or Buddhist. One of the earliest European accounts of travel in India, written by Edward Terry, a pastor who accompanied Sir Thomas Roe to the court of the Mughal Emperor around 1615, described the method of prayer among Muslims in India: "The Priests doe neither reade nor preach in their Churches, but there is a set forme of prayer in the *Arabian* tongue, not understood by most of the common people, yet repeated by them as well as by the *Moolaas*. They likewise rehearse the Names of God and *Mahomet* certayne times every day upon Beads, like the misse-led Papist, who seemes to regard the number, rather than the weight of Prayers."[4]

In this brief passage we see already what were to become some of the standard tropes of the colonial critique of Indian chants: The heathens emphasize the sound of words rather than their sense, and mechanical repetition over sincerity of intention, just as Catholics do.[5] The identification of Hinduism, Islam, and other Indian religions with Catholicism was central to these polemics.[6]

One of the first applications of these criticisms to Hinduism appeared in Henry Lord, *A Display of Two Forraigne Sects in the East Indies* (1630), which stated that Brahmins are

> enioyned to certaine prayers in their Temples, which may hold some resemblance with common Seruice, were it purged of super-stitious Ceremonie; the summe of which deuotion, is the repetition of certaine names of God, dilated and explained, where also they vse processions, with singing, and loud tinckling of Bels, which chaunt-ing is of their Commandements, with offerings to Images, and such like impertinent seruices. . . . These *Bramanes* as they dis-charge their Ministeriall function . . . straine their bodies into cer-taine mimicall gestures . . . They must neuer reade of the booke deliuered to Bremaw, but it must be by a kinde of singing, and quauering of the voice.[7]

Although overlaid and partly obscured by Lord's anti-ritualist senti-ment, many of his descriptions fit authentic Hindu practices. The repeti-tion of divine names is enshrined in the Hindu compositions that elaborate one hundred (*śatanāma*) or one thousand names (*sahasranāma*) of a god or goddess. Lord refers also to the musical mode of chanting the scrip-tures. His condemnation of repetitive prayers occurs in the course of a wholesale parodizing of ritual behaviors, such as gesture and singing, which he caricatures as a form of possession or enthusiasm, a St. Vitus's dance of irrational exuberance, anchored by the superstition of idolatry.

Behind British condemnations of Hindu chants lay a difference of opinion regarding the powers and right uses of language. Whereas, according to the linguistic ideology of the Tantras at least, certain re-peated prayers were capable of producing magical effects, and even of embodying the divine, the British rejected all of this as idolatry. Between the two cultures lay a difference of religious cosmologies. Some branches of traditional Hinduism affirmed the consubstantiality of language with both nature and the divine, as well as, more generally, the immanence of the deity, which could be embodied not only in language, but also in images of stone, metal, and wood. British Protestants instead insisted that the deity was utterly transcendent and incapable of being influenced by prayer. This theological proposition, as Weber already noted, coordinated with a broader disenchantment of the world, and not only of ritual language. To appreciate this difference of linguistic ideologies, we must understand Reformation polemics against repetitive chants.

The Protestant Critique of Battology

In 1673, the Puritan divine Richard Baxter published *A Christian Directory*, his comprehensive guide for the faithful, which included a blistering diatribe against the ritual practices of Catholics:

> *It much glorifieth God to worship him, according to the glory of his wisdom and goodness, and it dishonoureth him to be worshipped ignorantly and carnaly, with spells and mimical irrational actions, as if he were less wise than serious grave understanding men. . . .* The second Commandment is enforced by the Jealousie of God about his Worship. Ignorant, rude, unseemly words, or unhansome gestures, which tend to raise contempt in the auditors; or levity of speech which makes men laugh, is abominable in a Preacher of the Gospel, And so is it to pray irrationally, incoherently, confusedly, with vain repetitions and tautologies, as if men thought to be heard for their babling over so many words, while there is not so much as an appearance of a well composed, serious, rational and reverent address of a fervent soul to God. To worship as the Papists do, with Images, Agnus Dei's, Crucifixes, Crossings, Spittle, Oyl, Candles, Holy Water, kissing the Pax, dropping Beads, praying to the Virgin Mary, and to other Saints, repeating over the Name of Jesus nine times in a breath, and saying such and such sentences so oft, praying to God in an unknown Tongue, and saying to him they know not what, adoring the consecrated Bread as no Bread, but the very flesh of Christ himself, choosing the tutelar Saint whose name they will invocate, fasting by feasting upon Fish instead of Flesh, saying so

many Masses a day, and offering Sacrifice for the quick and the dead, praying for souls in Purgatory, purchasing Indulgences for their deliverance out of Purgatory from the Pope, carrying the pretended bones or other Relicts of their Saints, the Popes canonizing now and then one for a Saint, pretending miracles to delude the people, going on Pilgrimages to Images, Shrines or Relicks, offering before the Images, with a multitude more of such parcells of Devotion do most heinously dishonour God, and as the Apostle truly saith do make unbelievers say, *They are mad*, 1 Cor. 14.23. and that they are *children in understanding*, and not men: v. 20.[8]

The list of practices Baxter would prohibit reads like a complete inventory of the ceremonies of the reviled Papists. The very length of this list served to reinforce rhetorically the absurdity of the profusion of ungodly rituals in the unreformed Church. Baxter enumerated a wide variety of practices, including verbal, gestural, and other behaviors. The common denominator of all of these is that they violate the Second Commandment, that is, the prohibition against idolatry, meaning both the worship of other gods, and the making and worship of images. Baxter's inflation of the concept of idolatry, and his extension of iconoclasm beyond the images of the saints, reflected a common Protestant pattern. The worship of images was just one, special case of a more general error of mistaking matter for God, or as Baxter puts it, following Paul's scriptural distinction, worshipping "carnaly," that is, in the flesh, rather than "in Spirit."[9] Also characteristic was Baxter's attack on the repetitive nature of Catholic ceremonies, which he identified as one form of a more general error of multiplying the number and duration of rituals, or using "a multitude more of such parcells of Devotion."

Baxter singled out verbal repetitions for special condemnation, whether these involved saying the name of Jesus, the rosary, other prayers, or an entire mass. Echoing his prohibition, earlier in the passage, against spells, he criticized prayers made "irrationally, incoherently, confusedly, with vain repetitions and tautologies, as if men thought to be heard for their babling over so many words." This was a close paraphrase of Christ's injunction in Matthew 6:7, during the Sermon on the Mount, which in the King James Version runs: "But when ye pray, use not vain repetitions, as the heathen do: for they think that they shall be heard for their much speaking."[10] During the Reformation, Protestant theologians resuscitated this scriptural provision and applied it against a variety of types of ritual speech. They identified "vain repetitions" as a form of rhetoric, magic, and idolatry. The prototypical target of this charge was the Catholic's incessant muttering of Hail Mary's. Although such practices had long been followed by a large number of Christians, the new Protestant detractors of such popular practices believed that they were returning to the original, literal intention of the Messiah, and applying this strictly. Protestantism in this way constituted a literalism in at least two dimensions. First, the injunctions of the Bible, including Jesus's command not to pray repetitively, were taken at their (supposed) face value. Second, the particular injunction in question elevated the semantic content of prayer over its magical and rhetorical functions.

Baxter's diatribe signaled the decline of what has been called the magical view of the world. Apart from his attack on specific ritual practices, he cut off, one after another, the means of intercession between this world and the next. Any of those points at which the Sacred might be found to breach the barrier into this world—whether in those places specially touched by the divine presence, as in pilgrimage sites or the images or physical remains of holy men and women—were sealed off. Our prayers, although they may be heard, may not influence the course of suffering of those in Purgatory, nor coerce the deity as magic spells are supposed to do. Nor is the Eucharist transubstantiated into the actual flesh and blood of Christ. All of this was characteristic of the Protestant condemnation of Catholic sacramentalism as idol-worship. The attack on vain repetitions as a form of rhetoric, magic, and idolatry was related logically to other manifestations of Reformation iconoclasm, and especially to other applications of the prohibition against idolatry to language. In England from the sixteenth century onward, the polemic against vain repetitions informed the distinction of proper, sanctified prayer from illegitimate, prayer-like uses of language.[11] By playing a crucial role in separating lawful prayers from unlawful spells, this polemic contributed to the construction of the modern notions of prayer and of ritual. Such polemics, as we shall see, have echoed down to the present day.

Of course, what we call Protestant literalism is not a monolithic tradition, but a diversity of theological opinions. Protestants have held a wide variety of views on prayer. The critique of vain repetitions in prayer was a legacy of Puritanism, traced below directly to John Calvin himself. Some, especially later groups, such as Pentecostals and other Evangelicals, embraced ecstatic forms of ritual involving, *inter alia*, speaking in tongues (*glossolalia*). This was very far from, and in some respects a reaction against, the sober and austere plain style adopted by other, and especially earlier, Protestants. A common theme, however, was the rejection of formalism and the insistence on sincerity in prayer. Taken in one direction, these virtues recommended simplicity in prayer; in another, an utter spontaneity and immediacy marked by the signs of grace and possession by the Holy Spirit. In any case, it was the earlier, Puritan strain of this tradition that appears to have had the greater impact on the development of modern, rationalist attitudes toward prayer and ritual.

What was at stake in the critique of vain repetitions in prayer, and in ritual more broadly? This critique was, as already noted, not entirely new, but a reinterpretation of Christ's injunction in the Sermon on the Mount.[12] Coming immediately before the Lord's Prayer, which prescribes a model for how to pray, Matthew 6:7 is one of the verses that tells one how *not* to pray.[13] The modern Revised Standard Version of this verse reads: "And in praying do not heap up empty phrases as the Gentiles do; for they think that they will be heard for their many words." What was new was not the prohibition itself, but rather the way in which it came to be interpreted and applied in the course of Reformation debates over the propriety of certain forms of ritual. Such debates occurred, at least implicitly and in the first instance, in the course of exegesis of the relevant gospel verse. Renewed attention to this verse arose as part of a more general search for a canonical basis for existing ritual practices. Part of the method of Protestant literalism was to hold any customary practice against the standard of the biblical text. If there was no textual warrant for a practice, that practice was deemed illegitimate, a spurious invention introduced by willful man. The further danger inherent in any unauthorized ritual was that it might have a nonbiblical source, in paganism or heathenism, and therefore constitute a form of idolatry. The Puritans directed the scriptural prohibition of vain repetitions against Catholics and other Protestant groups deemed to be insufficiently reformed. Originally employed against Catholics, the verse in question came to be employed also against a number of repetitions remaining in the liturgy of the Protestant Church of England, which, as Puritans believed, had not gone far enough in excising these superstitious formulas. Similarly, Quakers—in part on the basis of another scriptural injunction, "Let your words be few" (Ecclesiastes 5:2)—abandoned all set forms of liturgy.[14]

The classical Puritan interpretation of Matthew 6:7 can be traced to John Calvin (1509–1564), who fully developed the association of vain repetitions with rhetoric and idolatry, as well as with Catholicism.[15] He stated that Jesus "does not forbid us to pray long or frequently, or with great fervour of affection; but he forbids us to confide in our ability to extort any thing from God by stunning his ears with garrulous loquacity, as though he were to be influenced by the arts of human persuasion."[16] Elsewhere, he glossed "use not muche babling"[17] more expansively:

> He [Christ] reprehendeth an other fault in praier: namely much babling. And he useth two wordes, but in the same sense. For *Battologia* signifieth a superfluous and unsaverie repetition [*supervacua est et putida repetitio*]: but *Polulogia* is a vaine babling. Christ reprooveth also their foolishnesse, which, that they might perswade and entreate God, do powre oute many woordes. . . . Also the favour of God is not obtained with a vaine heape of woordes: but the godly heart doeth rather sende oute his affections, which as arrowes shall pearce the heavens: yet their superstition is heere conde[m]ned, which thinke they pleasure God and doe him service with their longe murmured praiers, with which errour wee see Poperie so infected, that the greatest force of their prayer is supposed to consist in many wordes. For the mo wordes any manne hathe muttered, the more effectually he is accounted to have prayed. Also they doe daily resounde out in their churches long and tedious songs, as though they would allure God's eares. . . . For from whence commeth this foolishnesse, that men should thinke that they have profited muche, where as they weary God with their muche babling, but because they imagine him to be like a mortal man, which hath nede to be taught and admonished. . . . And he acknowledgeth it to be a thinge absurde and to be laughed at, to deale with God rethorically, as if that hee were bowed with copye of woordes.[18]

The first question of interpretation was how to render the Greek phrase *me battologesete*, a negative imperative based on the implied root verb *battologein*.[19] This exceedingly rare verb[20] lent itself to different interpretations. The 1560 edition of the Geneva Bible, which as its name indicates was translated by Puritan exiles in Calvin's city, chose the translation "vain repetitions." The King James or Authorized Version of 1611 followed suit. The first edition of the Geneva Bible (1557) originally had "bable not much," in agreement with Thomas Cranmer's translation, "babbling."

The term "vain repetitions" itself had been used earlier, by Thomas Wilson in *The Arte of Rhetorique* (1553).[21] Wilson also labeled rhyme as—in Christopher Hill's words—"a popish invention":[22] "I thynke the Popes

heretofore (seeyng the people folie to be suche) made al our Hymnes &
Anthemes in rime, that with the singyng of men, plaiyng of organnes,
ringyng of belles, & tunyng of Hymnes, & Sequencies the poore ignoraunt
might thinke the Harmonie to be heavenly, & verely beleve that the Angels
of God made not a better noise in heaven."[23]

In his Preface to the *Book of Common Prayer* (1549), Thomas Cranmer
explained that, with the passage of time, the purity of the ancient rites had
been corrupted by "uncertain Stories, and Legends, with multitude of
Responds, Verses, vain Repetitions, Commemorations, and Synodals,"
with the result that insufficient time and attention had been given to communicating the entire Bible, and its meaning, to the people. These usages
of the term vain repetitions indicate that the condemnation of such forms
of rhetoric began in England even prior to the 1560 Geneva Bible.

One of the few modern analyses of the debate over the translation of the
term *battologein* as vain repetitions, written by the Catholic priest Joseph
F. Sheahan over a century ago, contended that the attack on repetitive
prayers was an innovation by Protestants based on an erroneous interpretation of Matthew 6:7: "Christ never condemned repetition of any kind, . . .
[and] there is no condemnation of repetition anywhere in the Scriptures. . . .
Until the sixteenth century neither Jews, Christians, Mohammedans nor
Pagans ever saw any harm in repetition."[24] There is little reason to believe
that Sheahan's last claim at least is factually inaccurate. The Protestant
condemnation of vain repetitions in prayer constituted a transformation in
the history of prayer and devotional practices, one that illustrates a key
point of connection between the religious Reformation and the repudiation of ritual—including the condemnation of ritual repetition—that some
scholars have identified as characteristic of modernity.[25]

It is possible that *battologein*—in English, "battology" or, less commonly,
"battalogy"—is an onomatopoetic term that imitates, by a form of reduplica-
tion, that which it denotes, just like "babbling," "stammering," or the Greek
"barbaroi," which labeled non-Greeks as barbarians because of their incoherent speech.[26] Another etymology of this term traced it to some actual
person named Battus.[27] This was often said to be a poet mentioned by Ovid,[28]
"who made long Hymns consisting of many Lines full of Tautologies,"[29]
such as: "There they were under that mountain; there they were under that
mountain" (*montibus, inquit, erant, & erant sub montibus illis*). Others traced
it to the mythical King Battus of Cyrene, who supposedly stuttered.[30]

More important than the etymology of the term battology itself was
the behavior it denoted, and the motivations attributed to such behavior.

Archbishop John Whitgift (1530–1604) and the Puritan Thomas Cartwright (ca. 1535–1603) debated the proper translation as well as the application of this verse to the Church of England liturgy.[31] Cartwright defended the translation "vain repetitions," and sought to prohibit not only repetitive prayers, but even any prescribed form of prayer, including the Lord's Prayer, which he regarded as merely a nonbinding example of how to pray. Whitgift, on the other hand, preferred the translation "babbling," and claimed that it excluded only prayers made in "many words, without faith and the inward affection of the mind." He quoted Erasmus's gloss that "yet are not long prayers here condemned, but those that are vain, fond, and superstitious." This did not apply, in his opinion, to the Lord's Prayer and other prayers based on scripture, even if repeated. There are numerous places in the Bible, such as the Psalms, where repetitive prayers are depicted as perfectly acceptable and indeed holy.[32] The Jesuit John Percy (1569–1641), alias John Fisher, noted several of these places—including Christ's own repeated prayer at Gethsemane—in defending the repetition of the Paternoster, Ave, and Creed.[33]

Not every form of repeated or extended prayer was proscribed, not least because there were scriptural examples that clearly authorized such prayers, under the right conditions or frame of mind.[34] Battology was interpreted variously as babbling, incoherent, or slurred speech; as speech that was needlessly multiplied or prolonged; or as speech that repeated the same meaning or the same words over again.[35] Sometimes, then, repetitions that were vain could be distinguished by their form alone. In other cases, the distinction was primarily a question of intent: prayers devoid of the requisite purpose or attention, and so merely repeated without the proper devotion, were vain.[36] The meaning of the prohibition varied depending on the interpreter. However, there was a relatively stable set of categories associated with the term vain repetitions, including, most notably, rhetoric, magic, and idolatry. Battology was regarded as a form of superstitious rhetoric, designed to persuade if not compel God to perform miracles or magic. The prototypical Biblical examples were two notorious groups of idolaters: the priests of Baal who opposed Elijah in 1 Kings 18:26, and who prayed all day and all night for their god to bring fire down from the sky; and the opponents of the Apostle Paul in Acts 19, who cried: "Great is Diana of the Ephesians!" over and over.[37]

The contemporary target of such illustrations, however, was Roman Catholics.[38] Various Catholic practices were singled out, especially the use of prayer-beads and the recitation of Hail Mary's, Our Father's, the Litany, and the Jesus Psalter.[39] Jeremy Taylor called Catholicism "a Religion that numbers their murmurs by berries fil'd upon a string."[40] John Fisher rebutted the claim that Catholics believed their prayers to be more efficacious because more numerous: "The Catholike Church . . . attributes no merit to prayers in regard of their number, further then the number awakes in us devout thoughts, which is the only thing that by the number we ayme at."[41] Of particular fault, according to Protestants, was the underlying view of such practices as a kind of work or penance that was by nature tedious, and could be contracted out to others so as to spare oneself the effort.[42] The reduced versions of these practices that remained in the Protestant Church of England were similarly attacked.[43] Sometimes other groups, such as Jews[44] or "the Pharisees,"[45] were accused of the offense.

If the speech was incoherent, or not understood by the speaker, it could be vain for that reason alone. This fit the definition of battology as "babbling." William Annand defined battology as "*inarticulata vox* [inarticulate speech], like the talk of young children."[46] A number of commentators, including Baxter, singled out the Catholics' rehearsal of formulas in a Latin tongue they did not comprehend.[47] This readily extended into a critique of the mere recital of words without understanding. Such attacks made recurring reference to the squawking, senseless, mimical speech of members of the bird kingdom. George Downame criticized "a bare recitall of a set form of words without any inward grace; such as parrots might be taught to make."[48] John Downe extended the avian analogy: "Such are all they, who pray in a language they know not: like unto *Parrats*, or the *Cardinalls Jay*, that could repeat the whole Creed, but understood not a word thereof."[49] John Rawlet stated that such prayers were "fitter for Mag-pies and Parrots than for reasonable creature[s]."[50]

The vain repetitions themselves could, as previously mentioned, take a number of different forms. They could refer to the kind of poetic parallelisms supposedly employed by the classical poets Battus and Aeschylus, "who has near an hundred Verses at a time made up of nothing but Tautologies."[51] They could refer to the repetition of names of Jesus, or other Christian figures, in the fashion of the worshippers of pagan gods, "with thundring Names repeated over and over again."[52] One of the most common glosses of vain repetitions was "tautology."[53] Tautology is a common rhetorical device defined by the modern scholar of rhetoric Richard Lanham as "repetition of the same idea in different words."[54] During the Reformation, there was a fusion between this device of classical rhetoric, referred to in earlier texts, and the vain repetitions ostensibly prohibited by the Bible. Some critics of such devices in prayer extended tautology to mean not only the repetition of the same sense in different words, but even of the same exact words, a defect supposedly common among heathens.[55] Thomas Hobbes, in his treatise on rhetoric, glossed tautology as "vain repetition," and further defined this as "when the same thing in effect, though not in words, is repeated," citing the Gospel of Matthew as his authority.[56] The scriptural charge against repetitions in prayer was thus adopted into general rhetoric and treated as an error of logic.[57]

One problem for these interpretations was that the Bible itself contained numerous repetitions, especially in the Psalms. The use of parallelisms, which repeat the same idea or sentiment a second time in slightly different language, had been noted as a common device in ancient Hebrew poetry, even before Bishop Robert Lowth wrote his ground-breaking treatise *On the Sacred Poetry of the Hebrews* (1787).[58] Although such repetitions were ordinarily excused as divinely inspired,[59] or even as deliberate imitations of foolish speech,[60] John Lightfoot attacked the Jews for their use of synonyms, which, though repeating the same idea rather than the same words, was just as blameworthy: "The sin is equally the same in using different words for the same thing, as in a vain repetition of the same words; if so be, there were the same deceit and hypocrisie in both; in words only multiplied, but the heart absent."[61]

The association between vain repetitions and rhetoric appeared self-evident to many seventeenth- and eighteenth-century Protestants.[62] James Blair stated that "The chief Fault of it . . . lay in turning Devotion from the affectionate Work of the heart, to the Work of the Invention, Memory or Tongue."[63] However, "all Rhetorick and fair Words signify nothing with" God.[64] Offspring Blackall forbade "rhetorical and ornamental Forms of speaking in our Prayers,"[65] as "there is no Need of using Motives or Persuasives, or Rhetorical Flourishes, to move [God] to Compassion."[66] Such forms of rhetoric are of no effect in persuading the deity, as Thomas Manton emphasized:

> A frothy Eloquence, and an affected Language in Prayer, this directly comes under Reproof: As if the Prayer were more grateful to God, and he were moved by Words and Strains of Rhetorick, and did accept Men for their Parts, rather than Graces. Fine Phrases, and quaint Speeches, alas! They do not carry it with the Lord: They are but an empty Babble in his Ears . . . Prayer, it is not a Work of

Oratory, the Product of Memory, Invention, and Parts . . . Too much
Care of verbal Eloquence in Prayer, and tunable Expressions, is a
Sin of the same nature with Babling. . . . When Prayer smells so
much of the Man, rather than of the Spirit of God, alas! 'tis but like
the unsavoury Belches of a rotten Breath in the Nostrils of God. We
should attend to Matter, to the Things we have to communicate to
God, to our Necessities, rather than to Words.[67]

The Catholics who produced the Douay-Rheims Bible (1582), which
translated the phrase in question as "speak not much," argued that "Long
prayer is not forbidden . . . but idle and voluntary babbling, either of Heathens to their gods, or of heretickes, that by long Rhetoricall prayers think
to perswade God."[68] Against this interpretation, Thomas Cartwright
argued that rhetorical prayers were not prohibited, only repetitive prayers
similar to those of the heathens. Although God could not be moved by
prayer, petitioners might through rhetorical prayers "endeavour to perswade their own consciences."[69] Both sides agreed that such rhetoric was
objectionable when addressed to God with the intent to persuade.

The root of the problem with vain repetitions was not the use of rhetoric in prayer per se, but rather the false conception of God from which
this use drew its rationale. When Baxter referred all spurious forms of
worship, including vain repetitions, to the Second Commandment, he
did not elaborate on their connection with idolatry. Annand similarly
said that such repetitions are vain "When they are Idolized,"[70] invoking
a generic sense of idolatry as pagan or carnal worship, or as the fetishization of external ceremonies. Others, however, argued that the epistemological error underlying the vanity of repetitive prayers went deeper.
Calvin explained that such rhetorical forms of prayer were regarded as
effective "because they [the heathens] imagine him [God] to be like a
mortal man."[71] Manton's connection of vain repetitions with idolatry
echoed earlier Christian identifications of idolatry as the original sin:
"The original Mistake of the Heathens (and that which compriseth all
the rest) was this, a Transformation, or changing of God into the Like-
ness of Man . . . Because Man is wrought upon by much speaking, and
carried away with a Flood of Words, therefore they thought so it would
be with God. This Transformation of the Divine Nature into an Idol of
our own shaping and picturing, the turning of God into the form of a
corruptible Man, this hath been the Ground of all the Miscarriage in the
World."[72]

Such practices ran afoul of not only the Second Commandment against idolatry, but also potentially the Third Commandment against taking the name of the lord in vain, which was sometimes extended to incorporate swearing by false gods or idols, or using the true God's name for "cursing, enchanting, or conjuring."[73] As a form of rhetoric designed to persuade or compel God, or the gods, to do one's bidding, vain repetitions also constituted a form of magic.[74] Baxter, as we have seen, complained about Catholic "spells and mimical irrational actions." Later in the same work, he opined that it is not unlawful per se to repeat the same words in prayers, so long as we do not affect a "ludicrous Canting . . . as if God were moved by them as by a Charm."[75] The anonymous author of *A Whip for the Devil, or the Roman Conjurer* (1683), described the formulas of a Catholic exorcism as "vain Repetition and Tautology."[76] Jeremy Taylor attacked the Catholic view of ritual as encouraging such magical views of language: "They teach, That prayers themselves *ex opere operato*, or by the natural work it self, do prevail: For it is not essential to prayer for a man to think particularly of what he says; it is not necessary to think of the things signified by the words . . . For prayers in the mouth of the man that says them are like the words of a Charmer, they prevail even when they are not understood."[77]

At the root of the Protestant critique of vain repetitions was the condemnation of both idolatry and a magical view of language. Presented as a mode of fidelity, both to the literal commands of scripture and to the idea of a transcendent God, this critique coordinated with a rejection of divine immanence and of the consubstantiality of language with physical reality. As such, it reinforced other attacks on the immanence of the Sacred, including attacks on verbal fetishes and pagan myths.

"The Indian Rosary"

During the age of exploration and colonialism, these polemics against ritual chanting, which were originally part of an internal debate within European Christianity, were exported to different parts of the globe. Given that the historical examples of vain repetitions involved non-Christian Gentile groups, the prototypical idolaters, it was natural for this critique to be applied abroad. Early applications of this critique to living as opposed to historical non-Christian peoples began as soon as Europeans began to study the religious practices of other, contemporary cultures, whether as the result of the burgeoning textual study of Oriental languages that came out of the Renaissance and the philological study of the Bible, or as the result of early traveler's accounts in the Age of Exploration. Catholics occasionally joined Protestants in condemning such heathen practices, despite a greater willingness to accommodate such indigenous forms which, after all, resembled some of the devotions followed in their own churches. Some of the earliest such critiques were of Muslim prayers, as in Edward Terry's account quoted above.[78]

As Europeans acquired a more direct knowledge of Hindu beliefs and practices, the Protestant critique of vain repetitions in prayer served a locative function that allowed Hindu mantras to be fitted to presuppositions concerning the distinction between true prayer and illicit magic. William Ward wrote a treatise on Indian religion entitled *A View of the History, Literature, and Mythology of the Hindoos* (1822), in which he condemned Hinduism as "the most puerile, impure, and bloody of any system of idolatry that was ever established on earth."[79] He described the Hindu belief in the efficacy of mantras: "Repeating the name of the gods . . . is considered as one of the most efficacious acts of devotion prescribed in the shastras. The oftener the name is repeated, the greater the merit."[80] Ward affirmed the ubiquity of such practices in the daily life of Hindus, who "repeat incantations, when they retire to rest, when they rise, when they first set their foot on the ground, when they clean their teeth, when they eat, when they have done eating, when it thunders, when they enter on a journey, when their head or belly aches, when they see an idol, when they put on new clothes, when they want to kill or injure a supposed enemy, when they wish to cure the scab in sheep, &c."[81] Their faith in the power of mantras was unfalsifiable. If a mantra failed, they concluded it was because it had not been spoken properly.

Ward highlighted the pervasiveness and irrationality of the Hindu practice of *mantrajapa* (the chanting of mantras). A section of his tome was entitled "Illustrations of Scripture from Hindoo Manners and Customs."[82] This consisted of passages of the Bible together with Indian illustrations. The purpose was twofold: first, to provide evidence of scripture, and especially of its relevance to the understanding of a contemporary, albeit savage culture on the far side of the globe; and second, to describe, place, and control the phenomenon of Hinduism. Ward used mantras to illustrate Matthew 6.7: "In this the heathen are followed by all the Christian churches who have preserved least of the true spirit of Christianity: the Roman, Armenian, and Greek Christians in India, as well as the Musulmans, are continually practising 'vain repetitions.'"[83] In this way, he fitted Hinduism to the pre-existing label of idolatry.[84]

The degree of preinterpretation thus imposed on Hindu practices was indicated already by the English terms chosen to translate the Sanskrit word mantra, which, although sometimes glossed as "prayer," was more likely to be referred to as a "spell," "charm," or "incantation."[85] One early Bengali-English dictionary defined mantra as "a text of the veda, a charm, a mystical verse or incantation, a mode of addressing a being of real or pretended divinity."[86] The Abbé Dubois' early account of Hindu mantras already highlighted their association with magic.[87] However, this association was strongest among Protestant sects in India, which appear to have avoided "mantra" as a translation of "prayer," in part because of the term's association with both magic and Catholic practices.[88]

The translations of the New Testament produced at the beginning of the nineteenth century by William Carey and other Baptist missionaries at Serampore incorporated such ideas. The first book printed by Carey was a Bengali translation of the Gospel of Matthew in 1800, followed by the complete New Testament in 1801.[89] The Revised Standard Version translates Matthew 6:7 as follows: "And in praying do not heap up empty phrases as the Gentiles (*ethnikoi*) do; for they think that they will be heard for their many words." The Greek word *ethnikoi*, translated here as "Gentiles," originally meant something like "the other peoples," "the non-Jews," or even possibly "those ordinary, nonorthodox or religiously deficient Jews."[90] However, Carey's 1801 Bengali New Testament rendered this *pratimāpūjakerā*, which meant precisely "idol-worshippers."[91] *Pratimā* and *mūrti* are the two Sanskrit words standardly used to denote the images or statues of deities propitiated in worship.[92] Subsequent translations replaced this with *devapūjakerā*, or the Sanskrit equivalent, which is a compound meaning "god-worshipper."[93] In theory, "god" could be either singular or plural. However, in this context, *devapūjakerā* could not possibly be taken to mean "worshipper of the one true God." It must have meant either "worshipper of the many gods," that is, "polytheist," or "a worshipper of one or more of the class of beings known as *devas*," with *deva* carrying the association of a devil, false god, or idol.[94]

Others affirmed the association of *deva* with idolatry. As described in chapter 3, there were varying opinions as to whether this term should be used to translate the one God.[95] The Calcutta Baptist Missionaries, who took up the work of Bible translation after Carey, continued to use the phrase *deva*-worshipper in the translations of Matthew 6:7 in their Bengali editions of 1833 and 1845 and their Sanskrit editions of 1844 and 1851.[96] At some point on or before 1886 they adopted the more neutral and accurate term *parajātīyajana*, which means, like the Greek *ethnikoi*, simply "those other folks or tribes."[97] This change had already been made by some earlier translators including John Ellerton, William Hodge Mill, and others.[98] In comparison with such modern, neutral readings, the older translations by the Serampore and Calcutta Baptist Missionaries overdetermined the association between chanting and idolatry, and read this association back into the original Greek text. Presumably, they were reflecting the Puritan association of repetitive prayer with idolatry. Through Bible translations, this association was conserved and disseminated well into the nineteenth century. As a channel for the dissemination of the association between repetitive prayer and idolatry, the various Bible translations, and particularly those in Sanskrit, were probably less important than the statements of professional scholars and colonial administrators, which played a more direct role in shaping attitudes and policies toward such Hindu practices. The Bible translations represented a monumental effort that showed few results in terms of converts, especially among Brahmins and pandits, who were the only class qualified to read the Sanskrit translations, and the least disposed to do so.

A debate conducted in print between the Hindu theologian Mora Bhatta Dandekara and the missionary John Wilson (1804–1875) in the early 1830s reveals that the point of contention was the efficacy of image-worship and the status of mantras as speech acts able to influence the deity. Wilson's *An Exposure of the Hindu Religion* included a translation of the Bhatta's tract, the *Hindudharmasthāpana* (*Vindication of Hindu Religion*), which compared the power of mantras to the power of a king's commandment or a medicine. The Bhatta even defended the traditional belief in the power of mantras to embody the deity: "By means of the Mantras the Deity is, according to the rules laid down in the sacred books, called into the image, and thus the immaterial God obtains an imperceptible imagined body . . . We conclude, therefore, that by the due performance of image-worship and similar good works, God is found and enjoyed . . . You will say that all this is to be received implicitly,—that there is nothing tangible about it. I reply that those whose attention is fixed night and day on the image, to them the form of God makes its appearance."[99] Invoking the Logos doctrine, the Bhatta further countered that such ideas were not foreign to Christianity: "The Son [i.e., Christ] . . . is sometimes in the form of word."[100]

Rejecting the Bhatta's argument that Hindus do not really believe the idols to be God,[101] Wilson distinguished between true speech acts and the magical powers traditionally claimed for mantras: "There is a great power in a king's commandment, I allow; but it must not be forgotten that the Mantra is not a commandment from the king to the subject; but a commandment from the subjects to the king, and even to the greatest of all kings! How will it then prevail?"[102] Wilson proceeded to contend that "the Hindus themselves, in immense multitudes, begin to doubt about the power of the Mantras; and especially of those which are said to have the power of bringing God by distinction into a stone."[103] If the Bhatta already appears to have reduced his claims for the efficacy of mantras and their ability to bring the gods to earth—the god makes an "appearance" in an "imperceptible imagined body"—this is in response to his Christian opponents' claims that "there is nothing tangible about" the divinity thus established in the image. Wilson reminds him of the extravagant claims made in some of the Hindu sacred texts. Of course, one may question to what degree these texts were representative of popular opinion, but the doctrinal contradiction to which Wilson pointed was accurate. When the Bhatta presents an early version of the theory that the mantra is a speech act, possessing a power in itself, or because of the nature of its author, Wilson indicates the inadequacy of the mantra and its human author to affect their intended audience, namely God. Wilson's distinction among different types of speech acts echoes the Protestant critique of vain repetitions as both idolatry and a mode of rhetoric or false magic which, although intended to influence the deity, lacks the power to do so. His further claim that Hindus themselves were beginning to lose faith in mantras may have been merely wishful thinking, although the Bhatta's revisionism suggests some influence of these Christian polemics even on orthodox elements of the Hindu population by this time. As we shall see, some Hindus went further in their rejection of the efficacy of mantrajapa.

Another missionary polemic directed against the members of the Hindu reform group, the Tattvabodhini Sabha, in 1845, illustrates a wholesale rejection of the value of any sort of repetition of Hindu prayers or recitation of the Vedas to an audience that lacks comprehension of their meaning.[104] Although this text claims to be authored by "a Native Friend," it is clearly of Protestant origin. The Friend argues that "from an idolator of imaginary beings, animate and inanimate matter, and figurative personifications of abstract words, you have descended to deify some letters of the Sungskrit alphabet." He condemns the repetition of the *Gayatri* mantra supposed to be chanted daily by orthodox Brahmins: "If you believe that the repetition of the *Gayetree* a certain number of times, is likely to expiate all our worldly sins, and to secure our final beatitude, what objection can you have, to the *Hurreenam* [*harināma* or name of the lord (i.e., of *Viṣṇu*)] of a Bhoistub [*Vaiṣṇava* or follower of *Viṣṇu*], or any other kind of Jop [*japa*], or to the *Tusbeeh* of a Mahomedan, or the *beads* of a Roman Catholic?" The Friend contrasts such practices with sincere and inward prayer: "I do not like the idea of another man repeating within my hearing, for his own sanctification, or my edification, names of the Almighty, like a Mahomedan crier." The Friend acknowledges that the repetition of sacred texts may inculcate "the impression of the sublime truths contained in" them: "I admit without any degree of modification, that the repetition of the Gayetree and the Vedaic text is better adapted to enable the audience to hear them better, and oftener, and thus to learn them." However, our efforts should be expended on explanation and understanding—on "sermons" rather than "service"—and this mandates abandoning formulas in Sanskrit, "the old enigmatical and out-of-use language of the Vaids," as well as repetition itself, which answers only the ends of superstition: "You must attach the same importance to the reading of the text, as the benighted portion of the Hindoos do to a *path* [*pāṭha*, a reading or recitation] and the Mahomedans to *Telawut.* You must presuppose the efficacy of *magic*, before you can hope to drive out superstition from the minds of your ignorant countrymen, by the virtue of reading *over*, that is, *to* them, the Vedaic text. Attraction may be the end of the musical performance, but I do not find the utility of vociferating the hard and unintelligible passages from your sacred volumes."

Protestant missionaries might be expected to reflect such attitudes toward Hindu ritual. More surprising is to find that such reformed Christian ideas concerning prayer permeated the attitudes of Orientalist scholars and colonial administrators as well, to greater or lesser degrees.[105] We have already heard Macaulay's analogy between Sanskrit pedagogy and "chaunting at the cathedral." The pioneering 1808 account of the Vedas by Henry T. Colebrooke in *Asiatic Researches* attacked the traditional practice of reciting these most ancient hymns of the Hindus "in various superstitious modes: word by word, either simply disjoining them, or else repeating the words alternately, backwards and forwards, once or oftener." Like the Koran, the Vedas were "read by rote, for the sake of the words without comprehension of the sense."[106] As if this were not bad enough, in later corruptions of the Vedic tradition, mantras degenerated into "the unmeaning incantations of the *Mantra-sastra*, or *Tantras* and *Agamas*," in which "supernatural efficacy is ascribed to the mere recital of the words of a *mantra*."[107]

Another Sanskritist, Monier-Williams, carried such ideas forward until nearly the end of the nineteenth century. His English-Sanskrit Dictionary translated battology as "meaningless repetition" (*nirarthaka punarukti*).[108] Monier-Williams's account of religion in modern India included a chapter on "Indian Rosaries" that began by noting the canonical Christian injunction against vain repetitions: "Rosaries seem to be common in nearly all religious systems which attach more importance to the repetition, than to the spirituality, of prayers."[109] Hindus were guilty of valuing the sound of prayer over its sense.[110] He translated the Hindu term for rosary, *japamālā*, as "muttering-chaplet."[111] Hindus were worse than Catholics in this regard, as the latter no longer affirmed the efficacy of repetition.[112] Monier-Williams singled out the Hindu Tantras for special vilification, as in these texts the mantra "becomes a mere spell or charm."[113] He attributed such beliefs in the power of sound to the Mīmāṃsā view that sound (*śabda*) is eternal or original (*autpattika*).[114]

Monier-Williams also attacked a variety of analogous Buddhist practices, including the use of manually rotated prayer wheels.[115] He singled out the "trivialities and senseless repetitions" of the Buddhist scriptures,[116] which, as more sympathetic scholars have noted, do indeed rely on extensive repetition as a key organizing stylistic device.[117] This compared unfavorably with the simplicity of style of the Christian scriptures, which "attaches no mystical talismanic virtue to the mere sound of its words," unlike the Buddhist scriptures, the sound of the words of which are "believed to possess a meritorious efficacy . . . Then as to the words themselves, contrast the severely simple and dignified style of the Bible narrative, its brevity, perspicuity, vigour, and sublimity, its trueness to nature and inimitable pathos, with the feeble utterances, the tedious diffuseness, and I might almost say the 'inane twaddle' and childish repetitions of the greater portion of the *Tripitaka* [the Buddhist scriptures]."[118]

Monier-Williams's account of the decline or degradation of Hinduism and of mantras from the Vedas to the Tantras of course echoed another Protestant trope, that of Catholicism as a corruption, under the influence of paganism, of an originally pure Christianity. Similar accounts of the decline of religion into magic were voiced by missionaries such as the Reverend John Robson in 1893: "Whenever a religion attains a high spiritual advance, the magical tendency at once begins to drag it down . . . The hymns or prayers that were the sincere expression of the faith of those that uttered them, are repeated by their followers. At first they are repeated with some realisation of their meaning and some of the same faith as the authors had. By and by they come to be repeated as mere forms, in the mere repetition of which there is some virtue."[119]

The mantra was for Robson an example of prayer having been reduced to the status of a magic formula that, the more it is repeated, "the greater the obligation on the part of the god becomes." This was, as we have seen, the heart of the Protestant critique of vain repetitions. Robson also emphasized the excessive ritualism of the Hindus, who, "when not otherwise employed, mechanically turn round their rosary and mutter the name at each bead. This system of invocation may also be said to be the foundation of the way of works. The repetition of the name comes to be a work."[120] Robson attacked repetitive prayers on several grounds, as the slavish continuation of traditional forms, the mechanical muttering of prayers, and the incantation that depends on a superstitious belief in its magical efficacy. All such practices belong to the "way of works," which regards the ritual itself as effective for salvation. This interpretation assimilated mantrajapa to the Protestant denigration of "salvation through works," and embrace of "salvation through faith alone" as the true path of religion.[121]

Yet if magic was a degeneration of true religion, this process of corruption could be reversed through missionary activity. Wilson's claim that the Hindus themselves had begun to doubt the power of mantras was not entirely wishful thinking. The polemics against vain repetitions in South Asian traditions articulated by early travelers, colonial administrators, Protestant missionaries, and academic Sanskritists or professional Orientalists had some effect on Hindu self-understanding. The association between idolatry and chanting was adopted by the Hindu reformers Rammohun Roy and Dayananda Sarasvati. Rammohun's Protestant-influenced monotheism excluded most forms of ritual practice, including image-worship and mantrajapa. He dismissed the repetition of divine names as a form of magic and rejected the belief in the efficacy of such practices to procure salvation.[122] Roy further established the connection between chanting and idolatry in his discussion of the "Precepts of Jesus," where he advocated a strict form of Unitarianism and ridiculed arguments for the Trinity:

> What are we to think of such reasoning as that which finds a confirmation of the doctrine of the Trinity in the thrice repeated term "holy," in verse 3, ch. vi. of *Isaiah?* Following this mode of argument, the repetition of the term "Eli, Eli" or "My God, My God," by Jesus [in Matthew 27:46] . . . equally establishes the duality of the Godhead. So also the holy name of the Supreme Deity being composed

of four letters [in different languages] . . . clearly denotes the quadral-
ity of the Godhead!! But these and all similar modes of argument
that have been resorted to, are worthy of notice only as they serve to
exhibit the extraordinary force of prejudice and superstition.[123]

Rammohun dismissed the argument that image-worship was merely
symbolic, and affirmed that some really believed that in the rites of establishing the breath or vital force in the image of the deity (*prāṇapratiṣṭhā*),
which use mantras, the image is "changed from that of the mere materials
of which it is formed, and that it acquires not only life but supernatural
powers."[124] This complaint echoed Protestant polemics against the Catholic doctrine of transubstantiation.[125]

Dayananda, while influenced by Protestant scripturalism and iconoclasm, hewed more closely than Rammohun to an orthodox Hindu interpretation of the Vedas. Yet he also attacked repetitive chanting during a
long diatribe against "Idolatory" (sic), which took the form of a mock
dialogue:

A. Mere remembrance of name is of no avail, as the word "sugar" does not
   taste sweet nor the word *"neem"* [a bitter plant] taste bitter unless you
   actually taste it [i.e., the actual leaf] in your mouth.
Q. Is repetition of name altogether useless? They speak so highly of reciting name.
A. Your method of repeating names is not right. The way in which you
   recite names in useless.
Q. What is our method?
A. It is against the Vedas.
Q. Now please let us know what is the Veda-enjoined way of reciting name.
A. The name should be repeated in this way. Take the word "just" for
   instance. "Just" is the name of God because He is partial to none and
   deals with every body with justice . . . In this way the remembrance of
   even one name is quite sufficient to improve the condition of men.[126]

Dayananda's line "the word sugar is not itself sweet" was copied from
Mīmāṃsā, which used the same analogy to argue against the belief in
names that have a substantive connection to the things they denote.[127] Significantly, both of these Hindu reformers, like Protestants before them,
identified repetitive chanting as a form of idolatry. Their well-known emphasis on the literal meaning of scripture[128] complemented the exclusion of the

performative or pragmatic uses of ritual language, which uses depended on the belief in the consubstantiality of language with reality. While drawing on indigenous sources, Rammohun's and Dayananda's views appear to owe more to their encounter with Protestantism and their desire to reformulate Hinduism as a more rational, simple form of devotion, suitable for modern modes of living. That both Rammohun and Dayananda broke with tradition is evidenced by their respective rejections of the efficacy of repetition, belief in which had long been central to Hindu tradition.

A different sort of reaction may be observed among those Hindus and Westerners who have, more recently, reinterpreted mantras as psychologically efficacious, reconceived as a type of meditation—a form of concentration, exercise, and relaxation, profitable for both body and mind—and not, as in traditional yoga, a ritual practice leading to the attainment of magical powers (*siddhi*, a word closely related to the word *siddha* used by the Tantras to describe a mantra that has been perfected and rendered successful). Not that this dimension of yoga had not existed previously, but its contemporary prominence has been achieved precisely through a repression of the formalism and magical thinking that characterized many earlier practices of mantrajapa. The idea of the consciousness of the mantra (*mantra-caitanya*) and the importance of concentration represented an indigenous anticipation of a psychological or spiritual account of the efficacy of mantras. In response to Christian polemics against idolatry and the magical uses of mantras, such aspects of the Hindu tradition were emphasized, as in Mora Bhatta Dandekara's debate with John Wilson.[129] Despite such rationalizations, the descriptive accuracy of many of the colonial polemics against mantrajapa must be acknowledged. The Tantras clearly affirmed that repetition would make a mantra effective, and that the mantra was the verbal embodiment of the god, capable of bringing statues to life.

British Literacy versus South Asian Orality

The encounter between British and Hindu cultures reflected not only religious differences, but also differences in these cultures' attitudes toward the relative roles and values of writing and oral performance.[130] Although Hindus had possessed manuscript writing for millennia, they lacked the printing press until it was introduced by Europeans, and oral performance accordingly held a more important status in India. The traditional Hindu ritual system especially placed primary emphasis on hearing and repeating the sacred word.[131] In the Vedic and later Tantric traditions, the recitation of sacred texts or formulas played a central role in pedagogical transmission and devotional and magical practices. Repeated recitation (*svādhyāya*) was a primary mode of learning the Vedas, the oldest and most sacred Hindu texts.[132] A student of the Vedas spent years acquiring these compositions through a laborious process of memorization.[133] Given the sanctity of the hymns, which for most of the last 3,000 years constituted fixed compositions in an archaic form of Sanskrit, the meaning of which was opaque until supplemented by exegesis, elaborate techniques of recitation were developed to maintain every syllable unaltered by the passage of time. The basic methods of recitation involved the repetition of the syllables of the Vedas both individually and in combination. These methods were supplemented by other patterns of increasing complexity that involved such devices as chanting syllables twice in a row, or in reverse order. Most scholars agree that these devices reflected the oral nature of Vedic culture. Manuscript writing, on palm leaves or bark, existed from an early date. However, writing was always regarded as subordinate to the spoken word. The most sacred scriptures were called "that which is/was heard" (*śruti*), and their transmission took place within an oral, face-to-face system of pedagogy in which the teacher (*guru*) enjoyed a superior, and even quasi-divine status vis-à-vis the student (*śiṣya*). Learning the Vedas was permitted only to males from the three upper or "twice-born" (*dvīja*) castes (*varṇa*). The Tantric tradition (beginning ca. 600 CE) circulated by means of an esoteric, hieratic system of oral transmission. Women and lower-caste individuals (*śudra*) were denied the right of learning certain mantras, and especially of pronouncing the sacred *om*.[134] The transmission proceeded from teacher to student, who received the bīja and other mantras from the lips of the teacher. It was forbidden in some cases to read the mantras from a book, or to pass them outside the chain of oral transmission. Thus, one of the so-called "flaws" (*doṣa*) of mantras, which would render them ineffective or dangerous, was the flaw of being "burned" (*dagdha*) for having been "gone into six ears" (*ṣaṭkarṇaga*)—that is, having been heard by more than the four ears of teacher and student combined.[135] The continuing oral nature of transmission of mantras in the Tantric era may explain the proliferation of techniques of recitation, such as the technique of "enveloping" described in chapter 2, that recombined the syllables of the mantras in ways that resembled those employed in Vedic recitation.

When the British arrived in India, they singled out for condemnation many of these practices of oral recitation. Bernard Cohn summarized the colonial view that traditional Indian pedagogy emphasized rote meaning over comprehension, and sound over sense.[136] We have already seen Colebrooke's early, negative judgment of Vedic recitation. In 1823, A. D. Campbell stated that "great attention was being paid in the [Hindu] schools to proper pronunciation of syllables of a 'poetical' language but not to the meaning or construction of words in this language . . . The result was that the students had a 'parrot-like capacity to repeat, but not to understand what they had learned.'"[137] In an 1833 Minute arguing for the discontinua-tion of Dr. Tytler's plan of disseminating Western scientific knowledge in Arabic, Charles Trevelyan, who was opposed to all such schemes of native instruction, argued that the education imparted at the Calcutta Madrassa and other such institutions was of "parrotlike superficial letters" and "cannot be called learning."[138] A similar complaint appears in a tract that may have been authored by Rammohun Roy: "You buy a block of stone or earth . . . and call it your God. . . . Further, you do not get your chil-dren instructed in the [true astronomy] . . . but you teach them, like parrots [*suker nyaya*], the fables contained in the Poorans [Purāṇas] and other books, in which religious and moral instruction is conveyed by means of parables."[139] William Adam's reports on indigenous education in nineteenth-century Bengal, although sympathetic to native practices in general, singled out for condemnation the elementary Arabic schools: "The teachers possess the lowest degree of attainment to which it is pos-sible to assign the task of instruction. They do not pretend to be able even to sign their names; and they disclaim altogether the ability to understand that which they read and teach. The mere forms, names, and sounds, of certain letters and combinations of letters they know and teach, and what they teach is all that they know of written language, without presuming, or pretending, or aiming to elicit the feeblest glimmering of meaning from these empty vocables."[140]

The objection voiced by the British in many cases was directed against the rote learning of letters—even if this involved the recitation or imita-tion of what had previously been written—rather than against oral perfor-mance per se. Yet such complaints may have reflected, in part, the distinction between a primarily oral culture and one based on printed texts. Frances Robinson has described the dependence of South Asian Islam on oral modes of pedagogy and cultural transmission, and an ac-companying resistance, by both Muslims and Hindus, to the profound changes introduced by a culture of printing during the colonial era.[141] It appears significant that a number of the practices the British singled out for condemnation as vain repetitions were strongly associated with modes of oral transmission and performance. Colebrooke's attack on the so-called superstitious modes of Vedic recitation; the many polemics against Tantric mantrajapa; and even Monier-Williams's critique of the "senseless repetitions" in the Buddhist *Tripitaka* all provide examples of this. As Rupert Gethin has argued, the repetitions and various other mnemotech-nics in the Buddhist scriptures indicate that these texts were composed and transmitted orally, like the Vedas.[142] Such oral traditions were vari-ously revalued, repressed, and transformed under colonialism, with poetic repetition at the receiving end of some of the most violent polemics.

Pejorative attitudes toward traditional South Asian forms of poetry and oral performance represented the introduction of not merely print cul-ture, but also an ideological bias. The valorization of print, and of prose, over poetry had theological dimensions, as we saw, for example, with John Muir's condemnation of the oral nature of Hindu revelation (*śruti*). An article from the Serampore missionaries, "On the Progress and Present State of the Native Press in India," argued that the press had a natural tendency to suppress such "idolatrous" works as the "thousand names of Doorga," both by exposing their inherent absurdities and by encouraging the cultivation of prose: "To the operations of the press the country is in-debted for a growing partiality towards Prose works. Heretofore no trea-tises existed in the vernacular tongue, which were not written in measured feet. No language however, is capable of promoting the progress of knowl-edge, unless it is employed in prose. The early productions of almost every nation which has risen to celebrity have been composed in verse, for which prose has been gradually substituted as society has advanced and ideas have been multiplied. . . . A similar progress may be expected in India."[143] Such metrical Indian compositions as the *Lalitā Sahasranāma* (the thou-sand names of the Goddess) were doubly idolatrous, on account of both their subject matter and their form. With the clarity of thought encour-aged by prose, and by the printed word, both of these errors would in time subside.

An essay authored in 1836 by Kylas Chunder Dutt, a student at the Hindu College in Calcutta—one of the premier institutions for the dissemination of European, secular learning among the native population—told the sacred history of "the Divine Art of Printing." At first, "to preserve from oblivion the religious ceremonies, laws and renowned actions of sages and heroes, mankind, in the primitive ages of the world, had recourse to metre." But oral tradition was uncertain and corruptible, and contributed to superstition. Although opposed by the Roman Catholic Church, which promoted such ignorance, printing triumphed, ushering in an Enlightenment and "a complete revolution in the human mind."[144]

In a chapter entitled "Ideologies of Sacred Sound," Arvind Mandair has focused attention on the contrast between colonial British and indigenous Sikh ideas and practices of language, in which different valuations of oral vis-à-vis written tradition played a role.[145] He highlights the importance of musical and poetic performance in the recitation of Sikh texts.[146] Mandair recognizes the association of colonial projects for the codification of Indian traditions with the dominance of print culture in Europe, but regards as intensely problematic contemporary scholarly efforts to reverse the effects of these projects by Romanticizing indigenous oral traditions.[147] Both approaches—either the colonial insistence on a written standard or the postcolonial recuperation of a lost oral tradition—depend on the dichotomy of "presence" and "lack," which essentializes traditions by locating them in either scriptural or oral form. Mandair contests the reduction of Sikh traditions either to the Western model of the book or to the Brahmanical ideology of sound, which he acknowledges privileged oral performance.[148] While endorsing Mandair's caution, I would nevertheless emphasize that, for many Hindu traditions at least, both colonial codification and the complementary attack on mantras as vain repetitions appear to have been strongly influenced by the European bias toward writing and against orality.

Modern Echoes of the Polemic against "Vain Repetitions"

The attack on vain repetitions in prayer that began in the Reformation and continued in colonial India has endured into modernity. The norm reflected in such polemics—that true prayer expresses an internal state of devotion, and eschews both empty formalism and pretensions to magical efficacy—has persisted down to the present, and has become the orthodox view within the Christian world and even beyond. Supposedly objective, scholarly accounts of prayer are often simply restatements of Protestant theological polemics. The article on "Prayer (Tibetan)" in James Hastings's *Encyclopaedia of Religion and Ethics* (1908–1927) states that "the supposed efficacy of the mechanical repetition of prayers as devotional exercises has led in Tibet, as in the Roman

Church, to the extensive use of the rosary."[149] Another example is Friedrich Heiler's *Prayer* (1921), a modern classic on the subject.[150] Heiler defined prayer as "a spontaneous emotional discharge, a free outpouring of the heart,"[151] which over time degenerates into a fixed formula, especially one designed to influence the deity:[152] "The prayer formula completely loses its character as prayer and is degraded to become a magic spell when there is ascribed to the words of the prayer an *unfailing*, immanent, and magical power which, either by an absolute compulsion exercised on higher beings, or by excluding entirely all activity on their part, directly and automatically realizes the wish of the reciter of the prayer."[153]

Heiler recited all of the elements of the Protestant attack on Catholic prayer as idolatry: the original nature of prayer as spontaneous; its corruption into formalism ("The prayers are recited either with ceremonial stiffness and frigid officialism or they are gabbled in a purely mechanical manner"[154]) and magic, defined as the belief that the deity can be coerced. Although his primary target was formalism, Heiler associated this with musical and repetitive forms, such as the Litany.[155] Views of prayer that originated in the Reformation have continued until almost the present day to be represented as scholarly fact.[156] The possibility—even probability—that such prejudices still govern our views of prayer and similar linguistic acts, makes it all the more crucial to understand their origin.

Protestant attitudes toward prayer may have affected even the practices of the Roman Catholic Church. The main document on the liturgy to emerge from Vatican II, the *Sacrosanctum Concilium* or Constitution on the Sacred Liturgy, stated as a general principle that "in the revision of the liturgy, the following general norms should be observed: The rites should be distinguished by a noble simplicity; they should be short, clear, and unencumbered by *useless repetitions*; they should be within the peoples' powers of comprehension, and normally should not require much explanation."[157] The document itself does not apply the description "useless repetitions" to the case of the rosary or other repetitive prayers. However, Pope Paul VI a decade later promulgated an encyclical in which he appeared to confront this particular case:

> There has also been felt with greater urgency the need to point out once more the importance of a further essential element in the Rosary, in addition to the value of the elements of praise and petition, namely the element of contemplation. Without this the Rosary is a body without a soul, and its recitation is in danger of

becoming a *mechanical repetition* of formulas and of going counter to the warning of Christ: "And in praying do not heap up empty phrases as the Gentiles do; for they think that they will be heard for their many words" (Mt. 6:7). By its nature the recitation of the Rosary calls for a quiet rhythm and a lingering pace, helping the individual to meditate on the mysteries of the Lord's life as seen through the eyes of her who was closest to the Lord. In this way the unfathomable riches of these mysteries are unfolded.[158]

Of course, it would be difficult to prove here the influence of a specifically Protestant understanding of prayer, given that the authority Paul VI cited, Matthew 6:7, belongs to Catholics as well as Protestants. However, as we have seen, the application of this verse to prohibit repetitive prayers appears to have been an innovation of John Calvin. Paul VI arguably went too far toward the Protestant position, prompting his successor John Paul II to write, twenty-eight years later, a defense of the repetition of the rosary. John Paul II quoted his predecessor's warning against mechanical repetition.[159] However, later in the same encyclical, he added that

Meditation on the mysteries of Christ is proposed in the Rosary by means of a method designed to assist in their assimilation. It is a method *based on repetition*. This applies above all to the *Hail Mary*, repeated ten times in each mystery. If this repetition is considered superficially, there could be a temptation to see the Rosary as a dry and boring exercise. It is quite another thing, however, when the Rosary is thought of as an outpouring of that love which tirelessly returns to the person loved with expressions similar in their content but ever fresh in terms of the feeling pervading them.[160]

John Paul II himself placed emphasis on the fact that the rosary is *"based on repetition."* The method of repetition has a purpose, namely, to assist in assimilation, which presumably means the creation of a strong mental impression or association, and possibly as well, conjoined with this, a vivid remembrance or experience of the mysteries in question. John Paul II proceeded to note that Christ himself used repetitions on occasion. He ended with the exhortation to "confidently take up the Rosary once again."[161] It is difficult not to interpret this as a deliberate attempt to rehabilitate the rosary following a perceived attack upon its dignity.

In concert with such confessional views of prayer are some popular and scholarly views which attempt to rescue prayer from the attack on its magical and ritual dimensions by emphasizing that prayer, in its essence, is primarily a spiritual exercise, a manifestation of an inward devotion. This core feature of prayer supposedly has remained stable throughout the centuries in all cultures, and even into modernity. Philip and Carol Zaleski's *Prayer: A History* (2005) presents a sensitive, sympathetic study of prayer through the ages.[162] Defending prayer against its critics, the authors define prayer as *"action that communicates between human and divine realms."*[163] The authors are well aware of varying motivations for prayer and its wide range of manifestations.[164] They also acknowledge modern sociological and other evolutionary accounts of prayer, including Heiler's,[165] that criticize some forms of prayer as primitive and magical, as well as other factors that have contributed to the disenchantment of prayer in post-Vatican II Catholicism[166] and in modern culture more generally.[167] However, the overall picture they paint is an optimistic one, in which prayer remains available as a mode of contact with the divine, for example in Hinduism: "Sacrifice is not just an archaic practice preserved here and there in aspic, or fossilized in the depths of Indian culture, but a way of life to which nonsacrificing Hindus continue to feel drawn and to which prayer gives privileged access. . . . To this day not only the forms but also the ideals and lore of Hindu prayer bear the indelible mark of the old sacrificial system."[168]

One would like to believe in the perennial power and availability of prayer. However, what is missing from this history is an acknowledgement of the radical transformations that have occurred in our conceptions of prayer precisely as a mode of communication with the divine. A genealogy of modern views of prayer shows that prayer, like religion, is neither timeless nor universal. Indeed, rather than secular critiques of prayer, it was precisely a transformation in our understanding of the divine, and in our manner of relating to it, that precipitated a decline in the magical and ritual dimensions of prayer. The horizon of possibilities has now contracted for many of us, so that even many proponents of prayer now have shifted the grounds of their defence of the practice squarely within the this-worldly realms of culture and especially individual psychology.

The sixth edition of the *Encyclopaedia Britannica* (1822) still allowed one, tiny loophole for the efficacy of prayer: although God is all-knowing and therefore has no need of our information, governs by unalterable laws, and cannot be persuaded by petitions, still by His foreknowledge of both dangers and prayers he might have made prior arrangements for our rescue.[169] Some recent studies show, by their willingness to entertain the hypothesis that prayer might be efficacious in curing sickness, for example, that belief in the magical power of prayer is alive and well among some segments of the population in the industrialized world.[170] These studies still find scientists, subjects, and project funding at a time of scarce economic resources for medical research. The most current and authoritative research regarding the efficacy of prayer shows all the hallmarks of modern science, including highly controlled experiments that attempt to isolate the efficacy of prayer performed for the sake of another person's well-being without that person's knowledge. These studies have shown no beneficial effect of such prayers.[171] Of course, the efficacy of prayer for one's self, prayer performed with the knowledge of the person prayed for, and meditation are a different matter, and perhaps research in the future will be confined to measuring the potential benefits of such practices.

Reformation, Reason, and the Repudiation of Ritual

The Protestant critique of vain repetitions in prayer, as we have seen, was part of a more general movement in the history of religious ideas that we refer to as the Reformation, and exemplifies some of the characteristic features of that movement: a general repudiation of ritual, particularly in its magical dimensions; a distaste for ornament, including rhetorical and verbal; the favoring of plainness, simplicity, or a minimalist aesthetic; literalism, including not only the avoidance of allegorical interpretation and the insistence on the understanding or semantic comprehension of the liturgy and the Bible, but also the critique of certain metaphorical, symbolic, and poetical uses of language; and iconoclasm, or the prohibition against idolatry framed broadly so as to include both verbal and plastic images. The Protestant critique of vain repetitions identified the spiritual and cognitive defect in this sin as the belief in a form of superstitious rhetoric, one ultimately premised on an idolatrous confusion between the divine and the human, or the spiritual and the material. Other scholars, beginning with Weber, have noted previously that the Protestant insistence on the transcendent nature of the deity, which has often been interpreted as a return to Mosaic tradition, had the corollary effect of de-spiritualizing or disenchanting the world from which divinity was now decisively removed. Divinity may not be dragged down into the world through the application of magical formulas, nor may ordinary forms of rhetoric, designed to persuade human beings, exert influence on a nonanthropomorphic deity. The consequence is that language lost its magical power to coerce the deity and, by so doing, to control the world. The door between this world and the next was, at least from our side, slammed shut. This was expressed most explicitly in Protestant denials of the power of ritual works to effect salvation. According to this disenchanted linguistic cosmology, the prescribed functions of language are to describe the world and express the inner intentions of human beings, but not to function as a power or authority in its own right, for to do so would be to idolize speech itself. In this way, the very nature of linguistic performance was reconceived and, so to speak, relegislated. The functions of language that linguists call semantic came to be privileged over those that are called pragmatic, and the sphere of the latter was accordingly reduced. Recognition of this reinforces the religious dimensions of the reformation of language that accelerated in seventeenth-century England under the Baconians.

The rejection of the (supposedly) magical theory of *ex opere operato*, whereby the prayer or other rite or sacrament would be effective if properly performed, irrespective of the disposition or moral quality of the participants, signaled a shift to a deeper emphasis on the inward or intentional dimensions of prayer, and away from its external performance.[172] Keane identified the modern insistence on sincerity in speaking as a consequence of Reformation views of language. The Protestant critique of vain repetitions in prayer coordinated with a broader insistence on understanding the scriptures and the liturgy, at the expense of a traditional emphasis on ritual performance and efficacy. The oft-described valorization of belief over practice, or orthodoxy over orthopraxy, common to both Protestantism and secular modernity relocated true religion in the interior of the religious subject.

The reconstruction of the Protestant critique of vain repetitions in prayer shows the coordination of this critique with a broader logic of representation or linguistic ideology. In this ideology, the relative roles of addresser and addressee—of prayerful petitioner and the divinity to whom one prayed—was also renegotiated in such a way as to exclude any hint of compulsion of the latter. Accordingly, the rhetorical or pragmatic force of prayer had to be denied, along with the forms that supposedly provided such force. Although obviously not all forms of rhetoric were excluded—as a developed tradition of Protestant pulpit rhetoric shows, in addition to continuing debates over authorized forms of prayer—this did represent a significant curtailment of the power attributed to human speech. The elevation of the semantic content of prayer went hand in hand with the devaluation of its rhetorical form and pragmatic efficacy.

Behind all of this lay a renewed insistence on the remoteness and omnipotence of the deity, or its distance from the human. Whether or not this insistence was itself the original motive for the critique of vain repetitions, it served to reinforce the creation of a new Protestant subject for whom religious intentions and sincerity of speech were everything. The very notion of such a subject, who uses but is not used by speech, closely parallels the notion of an autonomous God immune to the influence of rhetoric. But whether this God was created in man's image, or vice versa, is difficult to say.

This revaluation of ritual performance was connected with the Protestant work ethic described by Weber. Puritans recommended the replacement of modes of ritual action with more utilitarian, and presumably more effective, modes of work. For one form of perpetual work, they substituted another. Weber already contrasted these divergent modes of work, the earlier, Catholic one according to which "the highest form of monastic productivity lay in the increase of the *Thesaurus ecclesiae* through prayer and chant," and the new, Protestant one represented by "[Richard] Baxter's . . . continually repeated, often almost passionate preaching of hard, continuous bodily or mental labor."[173] Weber explained that the shift in thinking regarding modes of work paralleled the Protestant denigration of "salvation through works" in favor of "salvation through faith alone." The Protestant devaluation of ritual works constituted part of a broader transformation in soteriology. While deeply influenced by Protestant theological categories, especially literalism and iconoclasm, the attack on vain repetitions in prayer is a quintessential example of what Weber called rationalization.

Apart from lingering echoes of the theological critique of vain repetitions in supposedly scholarly treatments such as Friedrich Heiler's, there are several points of continuity between Protestant views of ritual and some modern theories of ritual performance.[174] Protestant views of ritual reflect an awareness of the rhetorical dimensions of ritual discourse, and of ritual as an object of analysis: an existential stance that leads to a certain detachment or even alienation from ritual, and the substitution of a new relation to ritual that ranges from skepticism, to critical appraisal, to sympathetic or aesthetic appreciation. The Protestant attack on vain repetitions included within its range of targets poetic parallelisms, so-called tautologies, and sometimes even rhyme itself, all of which have been identified by modern theorists, such as Stanley Tambiah, as contributing to the power of ritual as a mode of rhetorical performance.[175] Protestants similarly focused attention precisely on the rhetorical function of such devices. This convergence suggests the possibility that what so distressed Protestants about the vain repetitions in some rituals was not entirely illusory—a figment of their own fevered brains—but rather an awareness, at times quite astute, regarding the manner in which ritual produces whatever magic it may produce.[176] Protestant theologians argued that the emptiness of such repetitive prayers lay above all in the fact that, although they were designed to persuade God to work magic, they could not possibly succeed in doing so. Although many Protestants continued, well into the Reformation, to affirm the efficacy of magic and the existence of spirits, witches, and the Devil, their interpretations of attempts to influence God as inefficacious and, therefore, a mode of vain rhetoric already displayed the hallmarks of the standard modern skepticism toward ritual. Therefore, it is not surprising to find that Protestant attacks on vain repetitions have been echoed by nineteenth- and twentieth-century secular scholars and theorists of ritual, long after the belief in magic ceased to be credible. In these observations of the characteristics of ritual, the Puritans anticipated modern theories of ritual performance. The Protestant position regarding ritual is already more than halfway toward the modern view that rejects the sense of ritual performance as magical power, and substitutes the more positive sense of a theatrical, aesthetic, or poetic performance.

Certain attitudes toward ritual, and especially toward repetitive prayers, that were first articulated during the Reformation continue to influence us nearly five centuries later. The Reformation assault on traditional Christian ritualism, and especially on its magical dimensions, represented one of the pivotal moments in the construction of modernity, which renegotiated the boundary between the religious and the secular domains, and between this world and the next, helping to usher in a broader secularization.

5

The Hindu Moses

CHRISTIAN POLEMICS AGAINST JEWISH RITUAL
AND THE SECULARIZATION OF HINDU LAW

The Christian Repudiation of Ritual
and the Secularization of Hindu Law

The British colonial attack on Hindu ritual was not limited to mantras. Although there have been a number of fine accounts of the transformation of indigenous South Asian legal traditions under colonialism,[1] none has given sufficient attention to a central aspect of this transformation: the rejection of the ritual elements of Hindu law,[2] or rather of *Dharmaśāstra*—the millennia-old Sanskritic tradition of religious law that defined the "science of dharma" or of righteousness for Hindus[3]—and the manner in which this rejection was informed, conditioned, and endorsed by Christian antinomianism, meaning the idea that religion is a matter of the spirit and not of law or ritual. This view of religion, which was originally applied by St. Paul to distinguish Christian "grace" from Jewish "law,"[4] was extended by Protestant theologians, who further valorized religious belief over ritual practice.[5] In colonial India, comparisons between Hindus and Jews as well as categories derived from Protestant attitudes toward Jewish ritual coordinated with the marginalization of the ritual aspects of Dharmaśāstra, or the forcible secularization of Hindu law.

Following Saints Paul and Augustine, Christians divided the Mosaic laws into natural or moral, civil or judicial, and ceremonial law, also called ritual or simply religious law.[6] Natural law transcended the ephemeral distinctions embodied in external modes of worship, and was therefore universally binding, even on the Gentiles to whom the Jewish law had not been revealed.[7] Civil law was the law of a particular nation or people considered as a political body, and ended at the boundary of that nation or with the demise of its sovereignty, as had happened with the Israelite kingdom.

Ritual law consisted of the external forms of worship of a people such as, in the case of the Jews, laws prescribing circumcision and certain dietary restrictions. Christians claimed that the Jewish ritual laws especially were mere "types" or "shadows" that had been fulfilled and abrogated by the Messiah, whose sacrifice on the cross consummated all previous sacrifices, rendering them both ineffective and unnecessary. Typological interpretations of scripture demoted Jewish ritual to the status of a symbol that was merely a prefiguration or foreshadowing, ultimately replaced and superseded by the Gospel. Christian supersessionism was most succinctly expressed in the use of the pejorative term Old Testament to denote the Hebrew Bible. The demotion of ritual signs progressed further during and after the Reformation, in coordination with Protestant scriptural literalism, plain style, and polemics against Catholic sacramentalism.[8]

In colonial India, such theological categories shaped British perspectives on and treatment of Dharmaśāstra. Traditionally, *dharma* encompassed much of what is understood by both of the categories law and religion, and was at once a legal code, a metaphysics, a cosmology, a system of morals, and a set of ritual techniques. British viewed this mixture, and especially its ritual elements, as evidence of a primitive stage of development in which law and religion had not yet assumed their proper and distinct identities. These evolutionary theories, although ostensibly secular and objective, emerged from and retained the traces of Christian theology. For many British and other Europeans, Hinduism confused or confounded law with religious and especially ritual precepts in a manner that recalled ancient Judaism. Just as Christians had earlier characterized such Jewish practices as circumcision and dietary restrictions as forms of empty ceremonial abrogated by the Gospel, the British in India evaluated analogous Hindu practices, and especially the institutions of caste, with their associated purification rituals, as marks of social and religious distinction incompatible with Christian universalism. Such omens may have prepared us for the strange figure of a Hindu Moses, a conflation between Hinduism and Judaism according to which these two traditions were related to each other through a common source—the legendary law-giver Manu, identified by some with Moses—as revealed by their shared propensity for ritual.[9] Despite its pretensions to religious neutrality, the British colonial view of Hindu law echoed an earlier Christian soteriological scheme according to which religious freedom meant, precisely, freedom from Jewish ritual law. Such Protestant presuppositions justified a colonial practice that excised the ritual elements of Dharmaśāstra. The British incorporated certain portions of the Dharmaśāstra into the colonial legal system while not incorporating other portions, especially those that Europeans identified as ritual. Both law and religion were redefined in such a way as to exclude ritual. The redefinition of law as positive and secular and of religion as spiritual, interior, and private (or at least personal and familial), constructed an exhaustive dichotomy from which ritual was excluded as a superfluous and pernicious third term.

Secularization is commonly defined as the separation of various domains of culture—newly emergent as secular—from religion. In the case of law, secularization is thought to entail the demarcation of a regime of positive law free from the control of or admixture with religion. A genealogical reconstruction of this process in colonial India reveals that such a definition is inadequate. Secularization in this context meant not merely a division of labor between law and religion, but the inauguration of a new spiritual economy in which there was little space left for ritual.[10] As Anidjar presciently suggested, colonial secularism patterned itself on Christian anti-Judaism.

This process of secularization also entailed the replacement of one soteriology—one economy of salvation, based on ritual practice—by another more conducive to colonial and modern modes of social organization and conduct. In *The Protestant Ethic*, Weber argued that capitalism had inherited its ethos and soteriology from the Reformation. The Protestant attack on the doctrine of salvation through works that underpinned the ritual economy of the medieval Christian Church paved the way for a new soteriology in which nonritual, utilitarian work and achievement could serve as substitute signs of grace.[11] The repudiation of ritual, meaning the rise of polemics against, if not an actual decline of ritual, has, as we saw, been recognized as characteristic of modernity by a number of other scholars, although not all have emphasized the connection of this development with Christianity to the same degree as Weber. Something analogous appears to have occurred in the transformation of the Hindu tradition under colonialism. There was, to borrow Weber's phrase, an "elective affinity" between Christianity and colonialism that reinforced their mutual hostility toward Hindu ritual. As Weber himself pointed out, the ritualistic Indian caste system was hardly fertile ground for the growth of modern-style capitalism: "A ritual law in which every change of occupation, every change of work technique, may result in ritual degradation is certainly not capable of giving birth to economic and technical revolutions from within itself, or even of facilitating the first germination of capitalism in its midst."[12]

Weber contended that the confounding of "legal prescriptions" in Hinduism, Judaism, and other Oriental religions with "ceremonial and ritual norms . . . constitute[d] one of the most significant limitations on the rationalization of the economy."[13] The development of capitalism in India therefore required both the intervention of colonialism and the displacement of the indigenous ritual tradition. Although South Asia had its own merchant classes, which Weber referred to as the "Jews of India," these were confined and ghettoized by ritual.[14] Weber drew an analogy between Indian caste and the ritual restrictions of the Jews opposed by St. Paul.[15] The elimination of ritual barriers was vital to the universal message of freedom that Paul articulated. Weber accordingly went so far as to suggest that this was the birth-hour of the Western notion of a citizenry.

As David Ellenson has pointed out,[16] Weber's analysis of ancient Judaism, as well as his attitude toward the role of Jews in modern society, echoed Paul's message that "there cannot be Greek and Jew, circumcised and uncircumcised,"[17] but only a single Christian identity in which such distinctions evaporate. This bears a striking resemblance to the modern ethos, in which "all specific identities are either subsumed under or dissolve into the universal. There is no tolerance for the particular." The terms on which modernity offered emancipation to the Jews were that they were to be granted everything as individuals and nothing as a people:[18] They could walk through the gates of modernity as long as they abandoned their identity as a nation—in part, by accepting that the formerly prescribed ritual laws were no longer binding on the whole (now Christian) community. Modern notions of religious freedom, especially as applied to the question of the emancipation of the Jews, represent a "secularization of Christian universalism."[19] Under this interpretation, the concept of religious freedom becomes little more than a pretext for the hegemony of one, particular tradition that styles itself as universal.

If Ellenson is correct, then Weber's theory of secularization represented a normative trope of Christian theology as objective history. Although this ought to make us suspicious, in itself it does not disprove the validity of secularization as an historical theory. Tropes, and particularly eschatological or soteriological tropes, can influence modes of social organization and behavior, as Weber demonstrated in *The Protestant Ethic*. Indeed, something of this sort seems to have happened in colonial India, where Christian attitudes toward Judaism served as a model for the interpretation of Hinduism and informed the marginalization of Hindu ritual laws, which, like the laws of Moses with which these were frequently compared, were relegated to a now superseded stage of human evolution. From this perspective, Christianity and colonial modernity are both marked by an eschatology or soteriology based on anti-ritualism and universalism. Genealogical analysis suggests that the freedom *of* religion we associate with secularism meant originally freedom *from* religion, meaning from the ritual dimensions of traditional religion in particular. Behind such a trajectory, as Anidjar, Ellenson, and some others have glimpsed, lay the self-definition of Christianity as against Judaism. The modern repudiation of ritual invoked and redeployed an originally anti-Jewish soteriology embodied in the opposition between the freedom of Christian grace and the boundedness of Jewish law.

The Disestablishment of Hindu Ritual by the Colonial Legal Administration

Prior histories have noted that the British colonial administration in India clearly demarcated those areas that were to be governed by universal laws from those areas reserved for the jurisdiction of indigenous religious laws. Based on a plan first drawn up in 1772 under then-Governor of India Warren Hastings,[20] Hindus and Muslims were ruled in certain matters such as family law, inheritance, and adoption by versions of their own traditional laws, as transformed—sometimes radically—through their incorporation into colonial common law and, later, statutory law. A number of scholars have pointed out that this division of labor paralleled the traditional British distinction between civil and ecclesiastical law.[21] However, not all of the laws found in Dharmaśāstra that we think of as religious were incorporated under this new scheme. For example, the rules relating to ceremonial observances (*ācāra*) and penances (*prāyaścitta*) were not incorporated as law. In other words, the transformation of Dharmaśāstra into colonial law involved not merely the diminution of its jurisdiction to private matters, but also the removal of many of its ritual elements. Bernard Cohn described this process of censorship or marginalization: "The portions of the texts dealing with what the British thought of as ethical and religious matters—instructions for rituals, incantations, speculative philosophy, and even rules of evidence—all had to be excised to produce what the British thought of as the rules determining 'contracts' and 'succession.'"[22]

Nathaniel Halhed's *Code of Gentoo Laws* (1776), the earliest translation into English of a compilation of Dharmaśāstra provisions, omitted the rituals, and incorporated only matters that we should regard as practical, and of immediate interest to the colonial administration.[23] The same was true of Colebrooke's *A Digest of Hindu Law on Contracts and Successions* (1797–1798) and many other early manuals.[24]

Reforms of the traditional curriculum in Dharmaśāstra similarly excluded ritual prescriptions. According to William Adam's report on indigenous education in Bengal in the 1830s, this had involved teaching a wide selection from among the entire set of twenty-eight *tattvas* or digests of dharma authored by the sixteenth-century Bengali scholar Raghunandana Bhattacharya on different topics ranging from inheritance to how to vivify the images of gods, perform ordeals and expiations, and celebrate the festival of the goddess Durga.[25] Raghunandana's text had long served as perhaps the highest authority on Dharmaśāstra in Bengal. Even at points after 1830, the curriculum in Hindu law (*smṛti*) at the government Sanskrit College in Calcutta included certain of Raghunandana's treatises dealing with ritual topics, in addition to more practical texts such as the treatises on succession (*dāya*) and procedure (*vyavahāra*).[26] During the 1850–1851 academic year, the entire complement of twenty-eight tattvas constituted part of the official curriculum.[27] In the same year, the reformer Isvaracandra Vidyasagar argued that the study of Raghunandana's text ought to be discontinued, as "with the exception of the Dāya and Vyavahāra Tattwas . . . the other 26 Tattwas are treatises on the forms of the religious ceremonies. . . . Though they are useful to the Brahmans as a class of priests, they are not at all fitted for an academical course." Vidyasagar did, however, recommend teaching the *Laws of Manu* as "an index of Hindu society in ancient times"—that is, a fossil.[28] Shortly thereafter the teaching of the other twenty-six tattvas was discontinued.[29] The *Dāya* and *Vyavahāra Tattvas* together constitute less than five percent of the total text.[30] This fact bears repeating: Fully 95 percent of Raghunandana's text—including all of the portions dealing with what we think of as ritual—was excised in the course of separating and preserving the remainder as sufficiently law-like and useful to the colonial state. Even before the Dharmaśāstra tradition was fossilized by its incorporation within the colonial Indian judicial system, and eventually replaced by case law and modern codes, there had occurred a radical abridgment of this tradition and especially its ritual dimensions.

Scholars are still debating to what extent the Dharmaśāstra was an effective source of law at the commencement of the colonial period. The

Dharmaśāstra was hardly the law of the land to the extent to which the British imagined when they elevated it to the status of "the" Hindu law. However, at the end of the eighteenth century and beginning of the nineteenth century, there were still courts that enforced, if only on occasion, the rituals of Dharmaśāstra.[31] In 1788, Ali Ibrahim Khan, Chief Magistrate at Benares, reported his eyewitness accounts of some Dharmaśāstra ordeals.[32] Early in the nineteenth century, Brian Houghton Hodgson described the existence in Nepal of a special judge, the *dharmādhikāri*, with jurisdiction over violations of the caste and purity regulations of the Dharmaśāstra.[33]

In addition to these examples of its real-world application, we see that, in the first half of the nineteenth century, Dharmaśāstra still constituted an important part of the traditional Sanskrit curriculum in certain areas of India, and continued to be a vital point of reference in Hindu religious life. Not all of these traditions were uprooted as a result of the partial incorporation of Dharmaśāstra into colonial law. Beyond the Sanskrit College in Calcutta, traditional pedagogy could still choose to study the entirety of Raghunandana's text. And the very idea of Dharmaśāstra as a unified tradition continued to shape private belief, and practice, to varying degrees. It would be more accurate, perhaps, to refer to these developments as a partial establishment and partial disestablishment of Dharmaśāstra, with the caveat that this language, too, only applies to the extent that these provisions were already established.

Even after the Dharmaśāstra, thus mutilated, was given limited jurisdiction over Hindu family law, the progressive disestablishment of its ritual elements continued. Hindu rituals that had formerly possessed legal efficacy as well as religious value—for example, rites of adoption, inheritance, and marriage—were marginalized through their incorporation within colonial law. Discussions of the case law by such nineteenth-century authorities as Sir Thomas Strange and Herbert Cowell suggest that, within the courts, the question of the proper performance of a ritual—a question of the utmost importance in traditional Hinduism— was reduced to a question of intent with which British lawyers were more comfortable. For example, colonial judges declared that, for an adoption to be valid, it must be manifested by some overt act of gift and acceptance. However, this overt act need not take any particular form, such as that prescribed by Hindu ritual, so long as it showed an intention to adopt. Such views had the natural consequence of denying special legal effect to ritual performance.[34]

Dharmaśāstra and Colonial Theories
of the Evolution of Secular from Religious Law

The excision of the ritual elements of Dharmaśāstra constituted a radical abridgement of the Hindu tradition, one that coordinated with its conversion into a form of philosophy, mythology, or mysticism. What motivated this transformation? In part, it was the practical interests of colonialism, as Cohn pointed out. However, the marginalization of Hindu ritual also coincided with an evolutionary scheme according to which primitive law was commingled with religion and, with the advance of society, would become separate from religion, secular, and positive. Hinduism violated this ideal division of labor between law and religion. Such evolutionary accounts became, to a significant extent, self-fulfilling prophecies with the rise of British power in the subcontinent: If such secularization had not happened yet, due to the immaturity or lack of development of the Hindus, then it could and should be helped along. As we shall see, such evolutionary accounts echoed an earlier Christian eschatological and soteriological scheme, according to which religion had transcended the law, meaning first and foremost the prescriptions of the Jewish ritual law.

In 1824, Francis Workman Macnaghten stated that for Hindus "their laws, and their religion are so blended together, that we cannot disturb the one, without doing violence to the other."[35] Dharmaśāstra was frequently described as containing both the "civil" and "religious" laws of the Hindus, by scholars from Sir William Jones, Colebrooke, and A. Loiseleur Deslongchamps in the late eighteenth and early nineteenth centuries to J. Duncan M. Derrett in the twentieth.[36] Jones's Preface to his 1794 translation of the *Laws of Manu* described the Dharmaśāstra as "a system of despotism and priestcraft . . . abound[ing] with minute and childish formalities, with ceremonies generally absurd and often ridiculous," yet nevertheless possessing "a spirit of sublime devotion."[37] This judgment echoed Deist attacks on priestcraft and on ritual, yet still acknowledged a glimmer of true religion in *Manu*.[38] Strange characterized the Dharmaśāstra as "the general body of ceremonial and religious observances, of moral duties, and of municipal law . . . of the Hindoos," among whom "law and religion are so intimately blended."[39] This statement from a practicing jurist invoked all three of the traditional categories Christians had used to categorize the Mosaic law, "municipal" being synonymous with "civil" law. However, none of these terms was indigenous to vernacular South Asian languages, so missionaries had to construct neologisms in these languages to represent the equivalent concepts, for example, by translating the phrase ceremonial law with cumbersome formulas.[40]

A classic evaluation of Hindu Dharmaśāstra as religious law can be seen in Henry Maine's 1883 essay "The Sacred Laws of the Hindus."[41] Maine compared *Manu* and other Hindu scriptures to Leviticus, as both combined law with "ritual, . . . priestly duty and religious observance."[42] Both books exemplified a general stage in legal evolution: "There is no system of recorded law, literally from China to Peru, which, when it first emerges into notice, is not seen to be entangled with religious ritual and observance."[43] In keeping with other systems of ancient law, the law books of the Hindus "contain much more ritual than law, a great deal more about the impurity caused by touching impure things than about crime, a great deal more about penances than about punishments." This emphasis of the Dharmaśāstra texts on ritual "only disappeared when they [became] mere law-books."[44]

The reason for these characterizations of Dharmaśāstra as religious was its prescription of a number of practices, including particularly rites of purification and expiation that supported the caste system, or the distinction of persons into four broad groups or *varṇas* and numerous smaller units or *jātis*.[45] Higher castes, and especially the Brahmins or priests, had to preserve their purity by avoiding contact with lower castes and with polluting substances. The occurrence of such taboos side-by-side with what was considered to be normal or secular law—such as laws against murder and theft, and the rules for contract—was what primarily marked Hindu law, as embodied in the Dharmaśāstra texts, as (at least in part) religious, and not (to this extent) civil or secular. The problem was the mixture of truly moral and practical laws with superstitious injunctions and prohibitions.

Before the British introduced it, the distinction between civil and religious (or ritual) laws did not exist in Hinduism in the same form or to the same extent. Traditional Hinduism did distinguish between laws with a seen (*dṛṣṭārtha*) and an unseen (*adṛṣṭārtha*) purpose. The former were rules that served a manifest, practical function accessible to reason. The latter were rules, such as especially certain injunctions for ritual practices, which had no obvious purpose but were obeyed because prescribed by the Vedas.[46] Another distinction, found also in *Manu*, was that between prescriptions for acts that promote happiness in mundane existence, and those that promote ultimate salvation.[47] However, as mundane existence could be improved through ritual practice, such a distinction scarcely coincided with the modern notion of secular law. Some, such as Herbert Cowell, argued that Hindu law had begun to distinguish between the *vinculum juris* and the *vinculum pudoris*—binding obligations of law and less obligatory norms of decency or morality—with the separation between law and religion that this implied.[48]

More importantly, Hindus also identified *vyavahāra*, the basic meaning of which is custom, as one of the main topics of Dharmaśāstra, together with *ācāra* or ritual practices and *prāyaścitta* or expiations. Vyavahāra comprised, among other things, the rules and procedures for settling civil disputes. A number of European scholars chose to translate vyavahāra as "litigation"[49] or even simply "law."[50] Whereas *Manu* was part law-book for the king's courts, part manual for priestly conduct, with accounts of the cosmogony and the afterlife to boot—a comprehensive rule for both religious and secular life, at least for Brahmins—some other texts focused on the topic of vyavahāra or avoided an emphasis on ritual. Among these was the *Arthaśāstra* (ca. 200–400 CE), a manual of politics and conduct for kings that reflected a separate, nonpriestly legal tradition from which *Manu* (ca. 200 BCE–200 CE) appears to have drawn some of its own provisions. Another was the *Nāradasmṛti*, a somewhat later Dharmaśāstra text that concentrated exclusively on vyavahāra. Some British praised this text as being much more recognizably law in the positive, secular sense.[51] In Maine's judgment, whereas *Manu* contained many sacerdotal rules, the *Nāradasmṛti* "is almost wholly a simple law-book . . . The ancient Brahmanical system has been toned down and tempered in all its parts by the good sense and equity" of its authors.[52]

Unlike many earlier scholars, J. Duncan M. Derrett in the twentieth century objected to Maine's evolutionary account of Hindu law as originally or fundamentally religious,[53] and called the view that religion and law are mixed up in the Dharmaśāstras both "naïve"[54] and an obstacle to reform.[55] Vyavahāra was followed by non-Hindus,[56] and was therefore a kind of civil or secular law contained within Dharmaśāstra as well as within the *Arthaśāstra*, which focused exclusively on vyavahāra:[57] "Religion is not the root of the rules which are comprised in the *vyavahāra* portions of the Dharmaśāstra, which are devoted to 'business,' litigation, law as we know it."[58] Religion elsewhere in Dharmaśāstra provided only a rhetorical justification, a religious sanction, for its rules. Where pragmatism demanded deviation from religion, the rules were changed or applied accordingly. All of this supposedly evidenced a secularism that was indigenous to Hindu law, albeit incipient.

There are some evident contradictions in these views of Hindu law as secular. If Dharmaśāstra embodied a recognition of the division between the religious and the secular, then why did it immediately proceed to violate this distinction by combining rules pertaining to the two domains within the same texts? Even a text such as the *Nāradasmṛti*, which at its beginning acknowledges the other topics of Dharmaśāstra as constituting part of dharma before limiting its own exposition to only the topic of vyava-hāra, is not devoid of what we should call religious law, including trials by ordeal that depend on a manifestly supernatural basis. Moreover, neither the *Arthaśāstra*'s nor the *Nāradasmṛti*'s ostensibly secularizing tendencies were representative of the broader Dharmaśāstra tradition. The *Arthaśāstra*, the sole text of its genre, was lost for centuries and rediscovered only in the first decade of the twentieth century. As Richard Lariviere states, the *Nāradasmṛti* was unique in concentrating solely on law (*vyavahāra*) to the exclusion of ritual.[59]

Despite such limited analogies between indigenous Hindu categories and the secular European distinction between law and religion, most British scholars evaluated Dharmaśāstra as representative of an early phase of legal evolution in which law and religion were originally confused, then began to be separated, for example, in such later texts as the *Nāradasmṛti*. Those who disputed the view that Dharmaśāstra was originally religious could also cite that tradition's incipient tendencies toward secularization in support of further reforms, as was done by such authorities as Cowell in the nineteenth and Derrett in the twentieth century.[60] In either case, the result was the same: The reform of Dharmaśāstra required the separation of its legal from its religious and especially its ritual elements.

Biblical Chronology and Historical Comparisons between Hindus and Jews

These ostensibly neutral historical accounts of legal evolution, which assigned Dharmaśāstra to the primitive phase of religious law, echoed and invoked an earlier evolutionary scheme according to which the Christian Gospel had replaced Jewish legalism. Often the comparisons between Hindus and Jews were indirect, being mediated through the application to each of these traditions of a common set of categories derived, at greater or lesser remove, from Christian theology. Sometimes—as in the case of Maine's analogy between *Manu* and Leviticus—the comparisons were more direct. When they were not simply categorized as idolaters, Hindus were often compared with Jews based upon the surface resemblances of certain of their ritual observances, each of which included dietary provisions and other rules alien to Christianity.[61] Both traditions supposedly exhibited a propensity for ceremonial minutiae, ridiculous distinctions, and superstitious observances. It was, more especially, the manner in which both traditions combined such rituals with both law and religion that reinforced the comparison. Alexander Duff argued that the incredible profuseness of Hinduism extended to its legal or ritual codes: "The Indian code does not, like the Christian, seize on great, fundamental, comprehensive principles, and illustrating these with the clearness of heaven's light . . . leave the practical application of them, through the varying changes of time and place, to the soul that is illumined with such divine knowledge. No, unlike Christianity, which is all *spirit* and *life*, Hinduism is all *letter* and *death*. The Indian codes deal comparatively little in general principles; they at once extend to all the *accessories* and *circumstantials* of conduct, with *a tenfold greater minuteness than Judaism ever knew*."[62]

The influence of the biblical model on the interpretation of Hinduism appeared already in one of the earliest accounts of Dharmaśāstra, in Lord's *A Display of Two Forraigne Sects* (1630), which described how God conveyed the laws to the Hindu god Brahma:

> Descending therefore on the Mountaine *Meropurbatee*, he called *Bremaw* to him, and out of a dark and duskie cloude, with certaine glimpses of his glory, . . . so delivering a booke out of the cloud into the hand of *Bremaw*, commanded him to acquaint the people with those things contained therein. So *Bremaw* made knowne the Sanctions and Laws unto the dispersed Generations. Of the contents thereof if any desire to be informed, the *Banians* [i.e., Hindus] deliver that this Booke by them called the SHASTER, or the book of their written Word, consisted of these three Tracts. The first whereof contained their morall Law, or their Booke of precepts . . . The second Tract unfolded their ceremoniall Law, shewing what ceremonyes they were to use in their worship. The third Tract distinguished them into certaine Casts or Tribes.[63]

Lord proceeded to enumerate the provisions of the "moral law," which consisted of eight "Commandements" made to resemble the Ten Commandments in form and, to some degree, in content.[64] However, in the

Hindu tradition, there was no such story of God handing down a book of laws from a cloud—a story clearly modeled on the episode at Mount Sinai; no such emphasis on written law, for, despite their possession of writing, Hindus still granted preeminence to the oral tradition; no such commandments, at least not presented in such form; and, above all, no division of the law into its moral and ceremonial components.

As we see, early European accounts of Hinduism were expressed within the framework of a Christian worldview. Europeans attempted to reconcile their growing knowledge of Hinduism with the biblical account of chronology or sacred history.[65] Resemblances between Hindus and Jews were frequently taken as evidence of diffusion, or of an historical connection between these peoples.[66] In some revisions of the biblical narrative, the practices of the Hindus were taken as evidence of a pure patriarchal tradition that had been adopted or inverted by the Jews, as mediated through their encounter with Egyptian idolatry.[67] Whereas the orthodox usually identified the Hebrews as the source and cradle of civilization and especially its laws, others gave priority to the Hindus. Such claims challenged the uniqueness and authority of biblical revelation, which is precisely why they were so persistently advanced by some Deists who wished to argue for the superiority of natural religion over revealed. Hananya Goodman notes that "comparisons between Judaism and Hinduism in the Enlightenment were instrumental in arguing for a deistic worldview in which the authority and centrality of biblical revelation and chronology were pitted against the claimed antiquity of the Vedas and the original religious practices of the Indians."[68]

An early entry in these debates, De la Créquinière's *The Agreement of the Customs of the East-Indians with those of the Jews*, translated into English in 1705,[69] pointed out a number of parallels between Hindu and Jewish customs, including the division into castes or, in the case of the Israelites, Twelve Tribes.[70] An important similarity between Indians and Jews was that "They practise very punctually all the Rules which their Religion they profess prescribes . . . and submit blindly to their Law."[71] While leaving unresolved the question of the ultimate source of such resemblances,[72] De la Créquinière noted the claim that the name of the "Brahmans" was taken from "Abraham."[73] After the appearance in 1760 of the *Ezourvedam*—which purported to be one of the most ancient scriptures of the Hindus, but was actually a Christian forgery—Voltaire argued that India was the cradle of civilization, and that Abraham and Brahmā were identical.[74]

Such comparisons continued even after Europeans came to possess more accurate knowledge of Dharmaśāstra. Halhed's *Code* compared Hindu law to Jewish, citing several points of resemblance, including their mutual employment of trials by ordeal[75] and severe punishments.[76] Halhed broached the possibility that, because of its great antiquity, the Hindu law might have been the source for Egyptian and, subsequently, Mosaic law.[77] Some estimates of the *Code* saw in it a pure religion devoid of priestcraft.[78] Other reviews of Halhed's work both questioned his orthodoxy and attacked Hinduism, in order to distinguish it from Judaism and Christianity. In 1790, confirming Halhed's tentative suggestion, Louis Langlès argued that Hinduism was the source of the religious ideas and customs of many other ancient peoples, including the Egyptians and Jews, who had merely "aped" (*singer*) the Hindus.[79] Members of the Asiatic Society joined in making comparisons and historical connections between Hinduism and Judaism,[80] although William Jones himself assimilated Hinduism to a generic category of idolatry in such a way as to preserve the integrity of sacred scripture.[81]

The scientist and theologian Joseph Priestley (1733–1804) rejected these comparisons between Hindus and Jews and defended the uniqueness of biblical revelation.[82] He allowed the resemblance of certain Hindu laws to the Mosaic, but emphasized "the unreasonable stress that . . . the Hindoos lay on mere external observances of various kinds."[83] Given the Indian predilection for idolatrous rituals, "it will hardly be pretended that the Hebrew institutions were copied from those of the Hindoos or the Egyptians."[84] Priestley's conclusion—a condemnation of Hindu ritualism—converged in some respects with that of some Deists, who upheld the analogy between Hinduism and Judaism in order to condemn the ritualistic nature of both traditions.

An especially late as well as extreme example of such comparisons is Louis Jacolliot's *The Bible in India: Hindoo Origin of Hebrew and Christian Revelation* (1870),[85] which argued, from certain similarities in their laws, that Hinduism was the source of Judaism. Only an historical connection could account for the occurrence in both legal systems of caste distinctions,[86] of Levirate marriage,[87] and of prohibitions against eating certain animals.[88] Etymology indicated the identity of Manu with Moses and Minos, the lawgivers of their respective peoples.[89] Jacolliot, echoing Deist arguments, deployed these comparisons in order to claim that the primitive truth of natural religion was soon corrupted by sacerdotalism, as exemplified by Hindu Brahminism and Levitical religion, finally reaching its apex in the Catholic Church.[90] His other goal, signaled in the subtitle of the original French edition (*La Bible dans l'Inde: Vie de Iezeus Christna*), was to show that Christianity too found its origin in Hinduism: Krishna or "Christna" was the prototype for Jesus Christ. Jacolliot was hardly an original thinker. Even the comparison between Christ and Krishna had been advanced by earlier thinkers.[91] Naturally, these comparisons were attacked vigorously by orthodox Christians.[92]

Comparisons between Hindus and Jews could be used strategically to elevate, or denigrate, either or both of these traditions, as well as to attack or promote Christianity itself. After the early nineteenth century, most accounts of Hinduism, even when these invoked the comparison with Judaism, moved away from the justification of biblical chronology, in part because this chronology could no longer be defended in literal terms. A major reason for this was the discovery of the Indo-European language family, which could not be reconciled with biblical history and seriously damaged the prestige of Hebrew in favor of other, non-Semitic languages such as Sanskrit. Despite abandoning an explicitly biblical historical framework, many later accounts of Hinduism retained the idea that both law and religion had evolved away from ritual and, in the process, become separate.

Echoes of Christian Soteriology in the Colonial Reception of Hindu Law

Like Judaism, supposedly, Hinduism had been transcended by the more spiritual religion of Christianity. The eighteenth-century German missionary Bartholomäus Ziegenbalg referred to the scriptures of the South Indians as *Gesetz*, meaning "law." This invoked the Lutheran and more broadly Christian opposition between the Gospel and the Law, meaning the Jewish law.[93] The same contrast between Hindu law and Christian Gospel can be found in a translation of a missionary tract originally written by Ram Ram Basu, an early convert who worked with William Carey in Bengal at the beginning of the nineteenth century. Basu said: "In other *sastras* [i.e., scriptures other than the Christian] there is not any account of salvation, and yet how many discourses there are upon the rites and ceremonies peculiar to the people of different countries. Both Hindoos and Mussulmans have many *sastras*, most of which we have examined. In none of them are to be found the principles of the true salvation ... Formerly we ourselves had only such *sastras*, but having obtained the great *sastra*, we flung those away."[94] Basu uses *sastra* as a general term for ritual law and says that such laws have been replaced by the "great *sastra*," meaning the Gospel.

One of the important sites for contestation over whether the character of Hindu law was civil or religious was the issue of caste, which was of special concern to Christian missionaries. Caste restrictions either prevented Hindus from converting or, when they continued even after conversion to divide the native members of the congregation, appeared to many British missionaries to be a direct violation of St. Paul's claim that under the Gospel "there is neither Greek nor Jew, circumcision nor uncircumcision . . . but Christ is all, and in all."[95] The story of these controversies can only be summarized here.[96] Different Christian sects pursued different policies at different times, ranging from an accommodation of existing Hindu caste prejudices to attempts to abolish all recognition of caste. Important for present purposes is that much of this debate focused on the question of whether caste was itself a religious or merely a civil distinction. If religious, it was tantamount to idolatry and need not be tolerated; if civil, like some European class and racial distinctions, it might be accommodated as not directly hostile to the church. Reginald Heber, Bishop of Calcutta (1823–1826), counseled toleration of the caste laws, arguing that this was no more than Paul had done for Jewish converts in the early Christian church.[97] However, his successor Daniel Wilson, who was consecrated as Bishop in 1832, took the opposite view.[98] These debates revealed that the categories of religious and civil law were not indigenous to Hinduism, as the missionaries themselves tended to recognize,[99] which reinforced the conclusion of many that caste was indisputably religious instead of, or as well as, civil, and therefore against the Gospel. Christian antinomianism and universalism were opposed to caste in the same way that they had opposed the Jewish ritual laws and the social distinctions that these enforced. The 1850 Madras Missionary Conference on the Subject of Caste concluded that Hindu caste was "*in its nature essentially a religious institution and not a mere civil distinction*. . . . If the ceremonial distinctions of the Jewish law—distinctions which separated man from man, though originally appointed by God—were done away at the introduction of the Christian dispensation, how diametrically opposed to the spirit of the New Testament must be the unnatural and anti-social usages of caste!"[100] The treatment of caste by the missionary church paralleled the treatment of Hindu law by the colonial state, which preserved a remnant of Hindu law as a limited concession to tribalism, and opposed the ritualism of the Hindu tradition to the universalism required by modern modes of exchange and governance.

The Christian opposition of law to grace or salvation—that is, to true religion—informed the British reception of Hindu law from the very beginning. William Jones's translation of *Manu* contains passages in which one may glimpse the translator's bias against ritual. Jones imported the distinction between civil and religious duties into the text where none existed.[101] Much more important, however, was his pejorative treatment of ceremony.[102] This appeared most revealingly in verse 4.204: "A wise man should constantly discharge all the moral duties, though he performs not constantly the ceremonies of religion; since he falls low, if, while he performs ceremonial acts only, he discharge not his moral duties." Jones opposed moral duties to ceremonial acts, to the disadvantage of the latter. In the original Sanskrit, the contrast is between *yama* and *niyama*. These two terms—which have the more neutral meaning of "greater" and "lesser," or "superior" and "inferior" rules—scarcely carry the contrast between inner, spiritual duty and mere outward performance that Jones imported into his translation.[103] Jones's translation encoded a hierarchical opposition between ritual observance and spiritual grace native to Christianity, but not necessarily to Hinduism, at least not in the same form. And to express this opposition, he used the very terminology that had been developed by Christian theologians to describe and denigrate Jewish law. Jones's translation of this verse was quoted by Priestley in one of his few complimentary estimations of Hinduism.[104]

As we saw, the usual Christian evaluation was that Hinduism is similar to Judaism, or even worse, because of its lack of revealed status: a religion of narrow law and empty ceremonial, requiring the sanctifying grace of the Gospel for redemption. Jones's translation at least discovered the possibility of transcendence within Hinduism itself, and in its own law books. In fact, the concept of liberation—in Sanskrit, *mokṣa* or *mukti*—was from the time of the early Upaniṣads (ca. 800–500 BCE) central to Hinduism as a religious tradition. Mokṣa meant freedom from worldly attachments, and from karma, meaning the performance and consequences of actions, especially ritual actions. *Manu*, like many other Hindu scriptures, at times expressed an ambivalent or even hostile attitude toward ritual. What many Christians did was to ignore selectively this transcendent dimension of Hindu religion in order to define a spiritual lack that could then be supplied by the Gospel. Even the largely sympathetic Jones, who perceived this transcendent dimension in Hinduism, could not avoid theological bias in his translation of *Manu*, which assimilated Hindu anti-ritualism to Christian categories. Another example is *Manu* 6.95, which Patrick Olivelle's recent translation renders as "casting off the inherent evil of rites by retiring from all ritual activities, being self-controlled, and reciting the Veda, he [the retiree] should live at ease under the care of his son." Two centuries earlier, Jones translated the beginning of this verse as "having abandoned all ceremonial acts." There is certainly a closer agreement here between the Hindu and Christian attitudes toward ritual. Yet, it is equally important to note the distinctions: This is a rule for the end of one's life, when one is approaching the goal of liberation, and not for all males, much less all humans, throughout life; and one doubts that reciting the Veda would count as an abandonment of all ceremonial for a Protestant who had embraced the attack on vain repetitions in prayer, which was applied to prohibit similar forms of chanting.

Masking Christianization: J. Duncan M. Derrett on Hindu and Ancient Jewish Law

A similar bias is evident in the work of John Duncan Martin Derrett, one of the leading scholars of Hindu law in our own times, whose work has been tremendously influential in both the interpretation of ancient Dharmaśāstra texts and the practical administration of law in independent India. As we have seen, he argued against the common view that Dharmaśāstra was essentially religious and recognized no distinction similar to our separation between law and religion. His point was that Hindu law was already in some sense secular, or had secular dimensions; therefore, to call it religious law was to mischaracterize it and to pose an unjustified obstacle to its reform. In an essay criticizing Weber's own mischaracterization of Hindu law as religious, Derrett reiterated arguments he had made elsewhere: that not all laws in Dharmaśāstra were religious;[105] that some texts, such as the *Arthaśāstra*, concerned themselves with purely practical goals;[106] and that Dharmaśāstra was aware of the practical as opposed to religious efficacy of some of its ordeals.[107] The fact that Dharmaśāstra combined practical with moral and ritual laws did not mean that its authors were unaware of the distinctions among these types of norms; ritual and legal judgments were clearly distinguished.[108] Derrett partly absolved Weber on the grounds that the latter's information was based on an inadequate knowledge of Hinduism received secondhand. He also attributed Weber's sharp distinction of and bias against religions based on ritual law to "the influence of contemporary Protestant conceptions of Christianity."[109] As noted earlier, others have made a similar point. Yet despite this, Derrett's own views of Dharmaśāstra, no less than Weber's, reflect a Christian bias against ritual law and a sharpened distinction among religion, law, and ritual alien to the Hindu tradition.[110]

Derrett's argument that Dharmaśāstra was already in some sense secular coordinated with his argument for further reform of the tradition. This can be seen in his contribution to the debate over the Hindu Code Bill in the 1950s, which concerned the statutory reform of those areas of law which had long been reserved for the jurisdiction of the religious laws of the Hindus. Some opponents of the Code voiced various religious objections against it—for example, that Hindu law is divine and shouldn't be changed, and that some of the provisions of the Code are against Hindu religion.[111] After acknowledging these objections, Derrett proceeded to counter that Dharmaśāstra recognized the authority of custom, and that vyavahāra was especially influenced by custom, and could therefore be altered.[112] His conclusion that Dharmaśāstra, being already amenable to secular reforms, could be further amended depended on a particular definition of religion as interior and spiritual, and of law as positive and secular, definitions which served to distinguish both of these categories from ritual:

> The proposed rules regarding divorce, adoption and succession . . . may be admitted at once to be contrary to religious doctrine. But this admission is of no value unless we agree upon a particular definition of "religion." . . . The relationship which an individual believes he bears to his Creator or the motive forces of the world, a relationship which inspires him with a supra-material regard for truth and good conduct, this is something which is much more intimate than a concept which, hiding under the name "religion," prescribes rules in minute detail concerning the order in which heirs ought to take the property of a deceased person, and the exact sorts of relations who ought not to be taken in adoption. Philosophy, reason, superstition or sheer love of regulations for their own sake, may justify such elaborations, but hardly religion in the usual sense of the word. If we were to agree with the point of view of those who say that the laws of marriage and succession, maintenance and

guardianship, are religious laws, we should be adhering to a sectarian and dogmatic standpoint. We should be taking part in a theological controversy, and this is a part which no Parliament in modern times will be content to play.[113]

Derrett inquired rhetorically whether, if we should retain these archaic provisions of Dharmaśāstra regarding the family, we ought not bring back other provisions, such as those prescribing ordeals or punishments for crimes, which had already been abrogated?[114]

Derrett's evaluations of Hindu law evidenced a manifest bias against ritual, which, in his view, constituted neither law, properly speaking, nor indeed religion, which he defined as a condition of belief, a personal relationship with one's Creator.[115] Of course, to engage in such a definition—or more accurately, a redefinition for the Hindu tradition—of religion is precisely to "take part in a theological controversy," as was understood by some of those who raised religious objections to the Hindu Code. Elsewhere, undermining his own claim that such a definition of religion is universal, and that the distinction of law from religion was already found in Hinduism, Derrett argued that it took colonialism to introduce such distinctions: "To sort legal from moral (i.e., not legally enforceable) commands was one of the more difficult tasks of European administrators of Asian laws."[116] In this context, he invoked Cornelius à Lapide's (1567–1637) theological division of law into its moral or natural, ceremonial, and judicial types.

If this were all the evidence we had to go on, we could conclude, at most, that Derrett's opinions of Hindu law reflected a bias against ritual common in modern culture. Yet there is more evidence. He has produced, in addition to a corpus of work on Hindu law ancient and modern, a second corpus of work on Christian theology and biblical interpretation. This second corpus sheds important light on his views of Hindu law. In his work on law and religion in the New Testament, Derrett's target was the Jews who opposed Jesus and Paul. He explained that the Pharisaic obsession with ritual is very difficult for us to understand, given that we value "conscientious belief" over the "exaltation of observance": "We know perfectly well that religion is an aspect of the healthy, mature personality, and that it does not suffer so much from a lack of organised observance as it does from an overemphasis upon demonstrations of piety."[117] Among the ancient Jews, however, although "the educated realised that observance has its uses and its value, the mass of the people were inclined to go much further and to suppose that observance was proof of belief; teachers who multiplied observances would tend to be the more beloved, rather than the reverse." A comparison with other ancient peoples showed that the fixation on observance was "a general oriental problem and not confined to the Jews."[118] In Hinduism, Islam, and other Asian traditions, as in ancient Judaism, law and lawyers enjoyed a quasi-divine status:[119] "As we have begun to realise, the Hebrews did not distinguish between religion and law: nor between religious and secular life. In this they resembled Asian nations with the limited exception of China."[120]

Significantly, Derrett distinguished the Hindus as the only Asian people to have grappled with this problem with any success. His basis for this claim was that they had a concept of a liberation that was purely spiritual: "In the short, ancient *smṛtis* such as *Manu* and *Yājñavalkya* and the *Bhagavad-Gītā* . . . is taught a peculiar doctrine: that a mental condition, be it described as knowledge or faith, alone ensures *mokṣa* ('release') while observances, especially those undertaken for reward (including spiritual reward) lead only to rebirth and continuation in the cycle of existences (which is an evil). Not that observances (*karma*) are evil—indeed they are prescribed, but their role is subordinate to that of true knowledge, and the renunciation of all desires."[121] Derrett quickly returned to his central theme: the condemnation of ancient Judaism.[122] Hinduism escaped the same evaluation—to the extent that it did—only because it, like Christianity (and unlike early Judaism), possessed a truly spiritual concept of salvation. In other words, Derrett endorsed Hinduism as a religion, not because of Dharmaśāstra, but in spite of it.

If we look more closely, we can divine the outlines of this theological bias in Derrett's scholarly work on Dharmaśāstra, which is, on the whole, a model of objectivity. As we saw, part of his argument for the secular nature of Dharmaśāstra depended on the existence and progressive increase in that tradition of texts, such as the *Nāradasmṛti*, concerned purely with law (*vyavahāra*). Derrett referred the gradual obsolescence of the ceremonial portions of the Dharmaśāstra to various causes. Only one of these was the sound practical sense of Hindu lawyers. Another was the ascendancy of a concept of salvation through faith in a personal savior, rather than through ritual performances.[123] Marking the rise of this new concept was the *Bhagavad Gītā* (ca. 200 BCE), which recognized multiple paths to salvation, including not only the performance of rituals and other prescribed duties (*karmayoga*[124]) and the cultivation of knowledge (*jñānayoga*), but also devotion to a personal god (*bhaktiyoga*):

The path of *bhakti*, devotion to the personal deity, is open to every-
one and is not less effective and worthy of recognition than the path
of "works." Performance of sacrifices, propitiation of ancestors and
devas, pilgrimages and other observances have not been discarded
or nullified by the growth of *bhakti* cults. But it is accepted that
those who prefer, because of their higher spiritual development, to
practise *bhakti* than to perform ceremonies . . . are entitled to . . .
pursue that path. The law must recognise the Hindu's acceptance
of the two main paths as equivalent in religious terms, namely the
karma and the *bhakti* paths to salvation (*mokṣa*). There can be no
presupposition that Hindu moral values require attention more to
rituals or duties of a ritual character than to the spiritual searchings
of the individual. . . . And a lessening interest in the traditional observances is not necessarily a sign of the decadence of Hinduism.[125]

What had been described, by Derrett and others, as the secularization of
Hindu law, was here evaluated by him as a spiritual transcendence of the
ritual dimensions of that tradition. Seizing on the existence of multiple
religious pathways in Hinduism, Derrett condemned ritualism as the path
of works, and declared a new freedom from such works in the name of both
modern, secular law and a more spiritual concept of religion. This represented an imposition of Christian categories on Hinduism. To translate
karmayoga as "the path of works," a religion of ceremony and ritual, as contrasted with the more spiritual path of *bhakti*, is to distort these Hindu concepts by assimilating them to centuries of intra-Christian debates over the
relative merits of works versus faith. Protestant polemics condemned both
Judaism and Roman Catholicism for elevating works, particularly ritual
works, over faith. Luther's famous dictum that salvation was by "faith alone"
(*sola fide*) signaled a radical devaluation of ritual practice. In Hinduism,
however, bhakti is scarcely opposed to ritual, as Derrett himself acknowledges, and the recognition of multiple paths to liberation is itself inconsis-
tent with the extreme devaluation of ritual practice evoked by the Protestant
contrast between faith and works. As we have seen, whereas some Hindu
texts deny that ritual practice may lead to ultimate liberation, other texts,
including *Manu*, also place great importance on the performance of ritual.
What Derrett proposed as a natural evolution of tendencies in Hinduism
would actually constitute a radical innovation in that tradition.

    To his credit, Derrett was forthright about his aims and motivations.
He acknowledged that what he proposed was a form of Christianization:

"What has actually occurred [in the evolution of *dharma*] is that much of the world, itself being educated by painfully slow steps in Christianity, or in Christianity masquerading as 'humanism,' anticipates what *dharma* would require from the alert Hindu, and masks, as if it were westernisation or 'cosmopolitanism,' a process which is fully compatible with the evolution of Hinduism."[126]

The problem with Derrett's view of Hinduism is that, despite its occasional pretensions to religious neutrality, it echoed and endorsed the Christian soteriological motif of true religion as freedom from the law. Behind his approval of a positive, that is nonreligious and de-ritualized, Hindu law lay Christian soteriology, as the "vanishing point" of religious law.[127] Given Derrett's authority as a scholar of Hindu law, and his long involvement in debates over its reform, his views can scarcely be dismissed as either marginal or irrelevant. His own characterization of how "westernisation" or secularization effectively masked a process of the Christianization of Hinduism is a judgment with which we must concur, at least as to the facts, even if we would place a different, more ambivalent value on these developments. Does it still appear to be a mere coincidence that scholars defined the ritualistic, Jewish tendencies of Hindu law at the same time that the colonial (and postcolonial) Indian state was forcibly secularizing this legal tradition by removing precisely its ritual elements?

Christianity and Colonial Universalism

We have seen how colonial accounts of Hindu law or Dharmaśāstra highlighted the manner in which that tradition confounded religion with law and especially with ritual. Many of these accounts drew upon a prior history of Christian interpretations of Judaism as the ritual tradition *par excellence*, the tradition that had been replaced and superseded by the Gospel, with its message of freedom from the law. Protestant presuppositions influenced supposedly neutral, objective accounts of Hindu law, and of its inevitable development toward secularization, facilitating the excision of precisely those ritual elements of the Dharmaśāstra tradition that were regarded as incompatible with law, properly speaking, that is, with secular, positive law, as well as with true, spiritual religion. Like Christianity, colonialism and the modernity that it ushered in deployed a teleological account of the triumph of reason over superstition to evaluate Hindu ritual as a fossilized relic of an age best left behind. This process was doubtless largely motivated by practical considerations of colonial rule: the need to establish secure property relations based on contract and inheritance, while conciliating native sentiment in those private areas where this could be done. However, there was more to these developments than utilitarian social policy and imperial exploitation. Such crasser aspects of colonialism were encouraged and given crucial ideological cover by a soteriological scheme that was only thinly disguised as secular. In nineteenth-century India, the modernizing influences of colonialism combined with Christian antinomianism to disestablish the ritual economy of traditional Hinduism. Both Christianity and colonialism aspired to be universal; both defined themselves against the rigid social boundaries described by ritual; both identified themselves as the fulfillment of an eschatological and soteriological scheme.

The British reform of the Hindu Dharmaśāstra tradition exemplified a number of tendencies shared with other colonial projects of secularization. The attack on the ritual dimensions of this tradition reinforces the nature of colonial modernity as a repudiation of ritual, observed earlier in the attack on Hindu mantras as vain repetitions. Like polemics against the figurative, fetishistic language of Hindu mythology, these attacks on ritual were leveled against symbolic modes of discourse.[128] The British disestablishment of Hindu ritual invoked Christian views of the analogous Jewish laws as empty ceremonies, mere types that were disposable following the emergence of the Gospel, which they prefigured. The attack on Hindu ritual laws followed a broader pattern of supersession: a replacement of past traditions in which colonial modernity modeled Christianity's replacement of Judaism and paganism. The designation of Hindu ritual laws as narrow and tribal—marks of separation, like the Jewish ritual laws with which they were frequently compared—echoed Christian universalism, which was evident also in the colonial insistence on the transcendent nature of the deity, the attack on any idolatrous representations, the insistence on the principle of one God for all nations and peoples, and the various proposals for a universal language that would reverse the curse of Babel. Finally, it was, as Derrett suggested, only by masking themselves as the agents of the ineluctable ascendancy of a globalizing reason, of which European colonialism was merely the vehicle, that Christians succeeded, to some degree, in converting other cultures.

Afterword

SECULARIZATION IS FREQUENTLY represented as the ascendance of rationality over superstition, and as the decline of religion, or at least of those aspects of it that have been safely relegated to a primitive past. What a careful study of British colonial projects for the reform of traditional Hindu culture has revealed, however, is the continuity between these projects and Christian messianism. Much of the discourse of British colonialism in India, including especially its aspirations to universalism, identify that discourse as a soteriology, a plan for salvation or transcendence. This is nowhere clearer than in the various reforms in favor of plain speech, which echoed the earlier trope of the Gospel as illuminating and replacing the obscure discourses of other religions. Like some forms of Christianity, colonialism affirmed its own mode of transcendence, as the banishing of a pagan, Jewish, or Hindu past replete with superstition, idolatry, and false knowledge. Such religious motivations inspired not merely missionary polemics, but also a number of ostensibly scientific and rational projects in colonial India, some of which stemmed from the Baconian tradition. As Weber already suggested, it was in terms of the continuity and transformation of soteriological motifs that we may observe the hidden religious dimensions of modernity, as revealed in those processes he referred to as "disenchantment."

Weber argued that this Western, Reformed Christian rationality was both unique and universal. Our investigation of British discourses of disenchantment in colonial India suggests a different interpretation. Universalism is a political strategy for the marginalization and replacement of competing systems denigrated as tribal, parochial, or limited. A tradition that aspires to be universal may be successful in advancing its claims only to the extent that it succeeds in erasing any traces of its own contingent origins. Hence Balagangadhara's claim that "Christianity could become universal only if it ceased being specifically Christian." What we call secularization appears in some cases to represent the process by which a particular religion has attempted to transcend its own past and limits. Despite this, the process of self-transcendence was gradual, and the echoes of Reformation theological debates can still clearly be heard in British colonial discourse in nineteenth-century India, at least once our ears have been trained a little.

Claims for the universality of Western reason are normative, teleological, even soteriological. My intent has been to expose a certain set of such claims, and the very contingent theological assumptions on which they depended, rather than to reinstate a narrative of the triumph of Christianity. Colonialism itself was neither monolithic nor omnipotent. British discourses of disenchantment were never as effective as promised; among other things, the efforts to replace South Asian scripts with the Roman alphabet were generally unsuccessful. However, the ascendance and widespread dissemination of a range of polemics against traditional Hindu culture, its mythology, rituals, languages, and laws, and especially against the cosmology expressed in these, was not without consequences, as the apparent decline of such large-scale cultural traditions as those embodied in the Tantra or Dharmaśāstra texts indicates. Even the utopian dream of a single language did not fail utterly, as, encouraged by such ideas, English ideas and practices of language were more widely disseminated in Indian culture. Colonialism in India was much more than its cosmologies or linguistic ideologies, and cannot be reduced to either Christianization or an event of discourse. Yet, in their own way, the theological and discursive dimensions of British colonialism that have been the focus of this book were just as important as the political, military, or economic dimensions.

Although this book has focused largely on colonial India, I would like to think that it also tells us something more general about modernity. The patterns of rhetoric, reason, and regimentation at work in colonial India resemble, in some cases closely, the ones we inhabit, and can serve us as a mirror, although not an especially flattering one. Perhaps this spur to self-recognition will inspire both more regard for other cultures and a deeper inquiry into the roots of modern exceptionalism and disenchantment.

Although disenchantment was and remains, in the first instance, a myth, the ascendance of this particular myth over others was an important moment in the religious history of humanity, and the consequences of this myth for those who inhabit it can be all too real, in conforming attitudes and modes of behavior. Indeed, it would not be too much of a stretch to call this myth our religion. The uncovering of the origins of this myth in Christianity undermines the pretensions of modernity to have accomplished any complete break with its religious past. The very exposure of the theological dimensions of what we call disenchantment only enhances our awareness of the importance of this trope and its contributions to the project of modernity. Less a reality than an ideology, disenchantment assumes its greatest salience in the moment of cultural conflict, as a polemical discourse or eristic directed against those thought to be primitive, superstitious, or unenlightened. The colonial encounter between British and Hindus illustrates a pattern recognizable from earlier polemics of Protestants against Catholics, Christians against Jews, or Jews against Gentiles. Disenchantment is a sign of both exclusion and inclusion, an attack on superstition and a mode of proselytizing that invites us to emerge from that condition.

In the end, the goal of this book has been less to prove that disenchantment happened than to point to the Christian genealogy of those processes we commonly refer to under this rubric; less to reaffirm the break with an enchanted past than to highlight the continuity between modernity and Christianity that this very idea of rupture suggests; less to argue for the reality of the historical event of secularization than to use the representations of this event to describe the contours of modern rationality, which is quite as constraining as any religion. This book has used the myth of disenchantment against itself, so as to call into question the religious neutrality and universality of a secular modernity that, having once been exposed as myth, may open to a different history or even a different future.

Notes

PREFACE

1. Max Weber, *The Protestant Ethic and the Spirit of Capitalism*, trans. Talcott Parsons (New York: Charles Scribner's Sons, 1958). See also Peter Berger, *The Sacred Canopy: Elements of a Sociological Theory of Religion* (New York: Doubleday, 1967), for a classic account of the concept of disenchantment.
2. Mark C. Taylor, *After God* (Chicago: University of Chicago Press, 2007), xiv.
3. For a discussion of such theories, see Robin Horton and Ruth Finnegan, eds., *Modes of Thought: Essays in Thinking in Western and Non-Western Societies* (London: Faber & Faber, 1973). Bruno Latour also comments on the Great Divide in *We Have Never Been Modern*, trans. Catherine Porter (Cambridge, MA: Harvard University Press, 1993), esp. 97–99. The claim that secularization instituted such a divide has resurfaced recently in Mark Lilla's argument upholding the "Great Separation" between politics and theology, in *The Stillborn God* (New York: Knopf, 2007), 55–103. As I argue in chapter 1 in this volume, a principal source for such ideas appears to be Christian supersessionism.
4. Dipesh Chakrabarty, *Provincializing Europe: Postcolonial Thought and Historical Difference* (Princeton, NJ: Princeton University Press, 2008). T. N. Madan, "Secularism in Its Place," in Rajeev Bhargava, *Secularism and Its Critics* (Delhi: Oxford University Press, 1998), 297–320 at 308, has formulated this in similar terms: "Paradoxically, the uniqueness of the history of modern Europe lies, we are asked to believe, in its generalizability."
5. Robert A. Yelle, *Explaining Mantras: Ritual, Rhetoric, and the Dream of a Natural Language in Hindu Tantra* (New York: Routledge, 2003).
6. Cf. Patton E. Burchett, "The 'Magical' Language of Mantra," *Journal of the American Academy of Religion* 76 (2008): 807–43. Burchett provides a critique of the view that mantras are magical while endorsing my view that they constitute a natural language, one in which words are believed to be inherently connected to

the physical reality they depict. My own view regarding the appropriateness of designating these formulas as magical has not changed. For a defense of the category of magic, see Robert A. Yelle, *Semiotics of Religion: Signs of the Sacred in History* (London: Bloomsbury, 2012), chapter 2.

7. Bronislaw Malinowksi, *Magic, Science and Religion and Other Essays* (Boston: Beacon Press, 1948).

8. See chapter 4 in this volume.

9. Matthew 6:7. Here and elsewhere, unless otherwise noted, all citations to the Bible are to the Revised Standard Version.

10. My study of the Protestant genealogy of Jeremy Bentham's legal reform proposals had also suggested this, outside of the context of colonial India. See Robert A. Yelle, "Bentham's Fictions: Canon and Idolatry in the Genealogy of Law," *Yale Journal of Law & the Humanities* 17 (2005): 151–79.

11. Karl Löwith, *Meaning in History: The Theological Implications of the Philosophy of History* (Chicago: University of Chicago Press, 1957). See the discussion of Gauchet's work in chapter 1 in this volume. Schmitt is discussed in Robert A. Yelle, "The Trouble with Transcendence: Carl Schmitt's 'Exception' as a Challenge for Religious Studies," *Method & Theory in the Study of Religion* 22 (2010): 189–206; and Yelle, "Moses' Veil: Secularization as Christian Myth," in Winnifred Fallers Sullivan, Robert A. Yelle, and Mateo Taussig-Rubbo, eds., *After Secular Law* (Stanford: Stanford University Press, 2011), 23–42.

12. Acts 2:1–13.

13. The intersection of the Protestant bias against certain forms of poetic language with print culture is addressed further in Yelle, *Semiotics of Religion*, chapter 5.

CHAPTER 1

1. Löwith, *Meaning in History*, 202.

2. Gil Anidjar, "Secularism," *Critical Inquiry* 33 (2006): 52–77 at 66.

3. Yelle, "Moses' Veil."

4. Anidjar, "Secularism," 60.

5. Id. at 62.

6. Edward Said, *Orientalism* (New York: Vintage, 1979).

7. Said himself drew on Raymond Schwab, *Oriental Renaissance: Europe's Rediscovery of India and the East, 1680–1880*, trans. Gene Patterson-Black and Victor Reinking (New York: Columbia University Press, 1987). Also in this category are Wilhelm Halbfass, *India and Europe: An Essay in Understanding* (Albany: SUNY Press, 1988); Ronald Inden, *Imagining India* (Cambridge, MA: Blackwell, 1990); Peter Marshall, *The British Discovery of Hinduism in the Eighteenth Century* (Cambridge: Cambridge University Press, 1970); Thomas Trautmann, *Aryans and British India* (Berkeley: University of California Press, 1997); Geoffrey Oddie, *Imagined Hinduism: British Protestant Missionary Constructions of*

Hinduism, 1793–1900 (London: Sage, 2006); Sharada Sugirtharajah, *Imagining Hinduism: A Postcolonial Perspective* (New York: Routledge, 2003); and Sharada Sugirtharajah, "Colonialism," in Gene Thursby and Sushil Mittal, eds., *Studying Hinduism: Key Concepts and Methods* (New York: Routledge, 2007), 73–85.

8. See esp. Brian Pennington, *Was Hinduism Invented?: Britons, Indians, and the Colonial Construction of Religion* (Oxford: Oxford University Press, 2005), who interrogates this thesis. An anthology of articles, some of which deal with these issues, is Jack Llewellyn, *Defining Hinduism: A Reader* (New York: Routledge, 2005). Works that examine the role of the British in shaping particular aspects of Indian traditions include Nicholas B. Dirks, *Castes of Mind: Colonialism and the Making of Modern India* (Princeton, NJ: Princeton University Press, 2001); Hugh Urban, *Tantra: Sex Secrecy, Politics and Power in the Study of Religion* (Berkeley: University of California Press, 2003); and Lata Mani, *Contentious Traditions: The Debate on Sati in Colonial India* (Berkeley: University of California Press, 1998). A work that focuses on Indian rationalist reform movements and their ties to European movements, and that unfortunately appeared too recently for me to consult, is Johannes Quack, *Disenchanting India: Organized Rationalism and Criticism of Religion in India* (New York: Oxford University Press, 2011).

9. E.g., Robert Eric Frykenberg, *Christians and Missionaries in India: Cross-Cultural Communication since 1500, with Special Reference to Caste, Conversion, and Colonialism* (Grand Rapids, MI: Eerdmans, 2003); Geoffrey Oddie, *Religious Traditions in South Asia: Interaction and Change* (Richmond, UK: Curzon, 1998); Daniel Potts, *British Baptist Missionaries in India, 1793–1837* (Cambridge: Cambridge University Press, 1967); Gerald Studdert-Kennedy, *British Christians, Indian Nationalists, and the Raj* (New York: Oxford University Press, 1991); Jeffrey Cox, *The British Missionary Enterprise since 1700* (London: Routledge, 2008).

10. Richard Fox Young, *Resistant Hinduism: Sanskrit Sources on Anti-Christian Apologetics in Early Nineteenth-Century India* (Leiden: Brill, 1981), is noteworthy for its study of the debates conducted in Sanskrit between Christian Orientalist missionaries and traditional Hindu pundits.

11. Peter van der Veer, *Imperial Encounters: Religion and Modernity in India and Britain* (Princeton, NJ: Princeton University Press, 2001), 66.

12. Another partial exception to this pattern of neglect was Eric Stokes, *The English Utilitarians and India* (Oxford: Clarendon Press, 1959), 54, who already noted that "certain broad similarities have often been detected in the thinking of Utilitarians and Evangelicals": "It was the special character of imperialism to be imbued with [a] profound religious sense, and yet to be, strictly speaking, non-Christian . . . The key then to the emotionalism of imperialism is the transposition of evangelicalism to wholly secular objects, or alternatively the translation of secular objects to a religious level. In a strict sense its creed was the consecration of force" (307–08).

13. Peter van der Veer, *Imperial Encounters*; van der Veer, ed., *Conversion to Modernities: The Globalization of Christianity* (London: Routledge, 1995).

14. Gauri Viswanathan, *Outside the Fold: Conversion, Modernity, and Belief* (Princeton, NJ: Princeton University Press, 1998); Viswanathan, *Masks of Conquest: Literary Study and British Rule in India* (New York: Columbia University Press, 1989); Viswanathan, "Colonialism and the Construction of Hinduism," in Gavin Flood, ed., *The Blackwell Companion to Hinduism* (Malden, MA: Blackwell, 2005), 23–44.

15. Rasiah S. Sugirtharajah, *The Bible and the Third World: Precolonial, Colonial, and Postcolonial Encounters* (Cambridge: Cambridge University Press, 2001); Rasiah S. Sugirtharajah, *The Bible and Empire: Postcolonial Explorations* (Cambridge: Cambridge University Press, 2005).

16. Richard King, *Orientalism and Religion: Postcolonial Theory, India and "The Mystic East"* (London: Routledge, 1999), 40, 42, 56, 101–05, 210.

17. Id. at 62–72. Other scholars who have pointed to the same pheonomenon are Gregory Schopen, "Archaeology and Protestant Presuppositions in the Study of Indian Buddhism," in *Bones, Stones, and Buddhist Monks* (Honolulu: University of Hawaii Press, 1997), 1–22; Charles Hallisey, "Roads Taken and Not Taken in the Study of Theravada Buddhism," in Donald S. Lopez, Jr., ed., *Curators of the Buddha: The Study of Buddhism under Colonialism* (Chicago: University of Chicago Press, 1995), 31–61. For a discussion of colonial codification, see chapter 3 in this volume.

18. S. N. Balagangadhara, *The Heathen in His Blindness: Asia, the West, and the Dynamic of Religion* (Leiden: Brill, 1994), esp. chapter 7; Balagangadhara, "Balagangadhara on the Biblical Underpinnings of 'Secular' Social Sciences," in Krishnan Ramaswamy, Antonio de Nicolas, and Aditi Banerjee, eds., *Invading the Sacred: An Analysis of Hinduism Studies in America* (New Delhi: Rupa and Co., 2007), 123–31.

19. Balagangadhara, "Biblical Underpinnings," 127–28.

20. Balagangadhara, *Heathen in His Blindness*, 221; cf. 294–95, 436–38.

21. Chakrabarty, *Provincializing Europe*, xiii.

22. Id. at 4.

23. Id. at 14. See also 11–16, 237–49. Chakrabarty specifically refers to the thesis of the "disenchantment of the world" at 16.

24. Id. at 16.

25. See esp. Weber, *The Protestant Ethic*, 105.

26. On what Weber meant by the terms "secularization" and "disenchantment," see Antônio Flávio Pierucci, "Secularization in Max Weber: On Current Usefulness of Re-Accessing That Old Meaning," *Brazilian Review of Social Sciences*, special issue no. 1 (2000): 129–58. As explained below, Weber took the terms "disenchantment" (*Entzauberung*) and the related adjective "dis-godded" (*entgöttete*) from Romanticism. Both terms had been used previously by the poet Friedrich

Schiller, the latter in the phrase "die entgöttete Natur." Pierucci, "Secularization," 136.

27. Weber, "Science As A Vocation," in H. H. Gerth and C. Wright Mills, eds., *From Max Weber: Essays in Sociology* (London: Routledge, 1991), 129–56 at 139.

28. See esp. Weber, *Protestant Ethic*, 105 and n. 19; cf. 165 and n. 58.

29. The literature regarding secularization is far too voluminous to cite. However, the reader is recommended to turn to the following works for an introduction and overview of contemporary discussions of secularization: José Casanova, *Public Religions in the Modern World* (Chicago: University of Chicago Press, 1994); Talal Asad, *Formations of the Secular: Christianity, Islam, Modernity* (Stanford: Stanford University Press, 2003); Charles Taylor, *A Secular Age* (Cambridge, MA: Harvard University Press, 2007).

30. As can be seen from Schwab, *Oriental Renaissance*; David Kopf, *British Orientalism and the Bengal Renaissance: The Dynamics of Indian Modernization, 1773–1835* (Berkeley: University of California Press, 1969).

31. Yelle, "Chanting the Cosmogony: Mantras as Diagrams of Creation," in *Explaining Mantras*, 23–48.

32. Peter Auksi, *Christian Plain Style: The Evolution of a Spiritual Ideal* (Montréal: McGill-Queen's University Press, 1995); Richard Bauman, *Let Your Words Be Few: Symbolism of Speaking and Silence among Seventeenth-Century Quakers* (Cambridge: Cambridge University Press, 1983).

33. Arvind-Pal S. Mandair, *Religion and the Specter of the West: Sikhism, Postcoloniality, and the Politics of Translation* (New York: Columbia University Press, 2009), 13.

34. Id. at 85–96.

35. Id. at 88.

36. See Yelle, "Moses' Veil."

37. Moshe Halbertal and Avishai Margalit, *Idolatry*, trans. Naomi Goldblum (Cambridge, MA: Harvard University Press, 1992), 112.

38. E.g., Andrew Dickson White, *A History of the Warfare of Science with Theology in Christendom* (New York: D. Appleton and Co., 1896).

39. One of the interesting questions raised by the following account is the extent to which Protestant iconoclasm is distinctive. However, the phenomenon of iconoclasm in other religious traditions is beyond the scope of this book.

40. Jan Assmann, *Moses the Egyptian: The Memory of Egypt in Western Monotheism* (Cambridge, MA: Harvard University Press, 1997); Assmann, *The Price of Monotheism*, trans. Robert Savage (Stanford: Stanford University Press, 2010).

41. Berger, *The Sacred Canopy*, 112.

42. Sudipta Kaviraj, "The Sudden Death of Sanskrit Knowledge," *Journal of Indian Philosophy* 33 (2005): 119–42 at 132. The question of the decline or, more broadly, development and transformation of the Sanskrit literary tradition before the advent of colonialism has been addressed by Sheldon Pollock, "The Death of Sanskrit," *Comparative Studies in Society and History* 43 (2001): 392–426.

Pollock describes several moments in the development of Sanskrit as a literary tradition; colonialism represents only one of these. At the time the British assumed dominance in India, and control over educational policy, internal transformations had already occurred in different branches of the Sanskrit tradition. Some of these were stagnant or moribund, while others were burgeoning and innovative. Pollock acknowledges the break that colonialism introduced into the Sanskrit knowledge tradition (394), but emphasizes the role of developments internal to the tradition. I am not concerned here with the internal developments, but with the ideology and, to a limited extent, the effects of colonialism.

43. Saurabh Dube, ed., "Modernity and its Enchantments: An Introduction," in *Enchantments of Modernity: Empire, Nation, Globalization* (New Delhi: Routledge, 2009), 1– 41 at 1. Cf. Peter Pels, "Introduction: Magic and Modernity," in Birgit Meyer and Peter Pels, eds., *Magic and Modernity: Interfaces of Revelation and Concealment* (Stanford: Stanford University Press, 2003), 1–38 at 30: "modernity . . . refer[s] to the . . . spread of a consciousness of radical temporal rupture"; Gustavo Benavides, "Modernity," in Mark C. Taylor, ed., *Critical Terms for Religious Studies* (Chicago: University of Chicago Press, 1998), 186–204 at 187: "modernity presupposes an act of self-conscious distancing from a past or situation regarded as naïve."

44. See esp. Michael Saler, "Modernity and Enchantment: A Historiographic Review," *American Historical Review* 111 (2006): 692–716. As valuable as Saler's review is, particularly in offering information regarding the recent history (eighteenth century onward) of the notion that modernity is disenchanted, and regarding the presence of magic in modernity, it neglects older, Christian versions of the concept of disenchantment that shaped these modern notions, and that are described below in this chapter. See also Joshua Landy and Michael Saler, eds., *The Re-enchantment of the World: Secular Magic in a Rational Age* (Stanford: Stanford University Press, 2009); Simon During, *Modern Enchantments: The Cultural Power of Secular Magic* (Cambridge, MA: Harvard University Press, 2002); James K. A. Smith, *After Modernity?: Secularity, Globalization, and the Re-enchantment of the World* (Waco, TX: Baylor University Press, 2008); Michael Taussig, *The Magic of the State* (New York: Routledge, 1997); Wouter Hanegraaff, "How Magic Survived the Disenchantment of the World," *Religion* 33 (2003): 357–80; Gustavo Benavides, "Magic," in Robert A. Segal, ed., *The Blackwell Companion to the Study of Religion* (Malden, MA: Blackwell, 2006), 295–308 at 299.

45. Gyan Prakash, *Another Reason: Science and the Imagination of Modern India* (Princeton, NJ: Princeton University Press, 1999); Akeel Bilgrami, "Occidentalism, the Very Idea: An Essay on the Enlightenment and Enchantment," *Critical Inquiry* 32 (2006): 381–411; and more recently Bilgrami, "What is Enchantment?", in Michael Warner, Jonathan VanAntwerpen, and Craig Calhoun, eds., *Varieties of Secularism in a Secular Age* (Cambridge, MA: Harvard University Press, 2010), 145–65.

46. Jonathan Z. Smith, *Imagining Religion: From Babylon to Jonestown* (Chicago: University of Chicago Press, 1982); Tomoko Masuzawa, *The Invention of World Religions, or, How European Universalism Was Preserved in the Language of Pluralism* (Chicago: University of Chicago Press, 2005).

47. See Bruce Lincoln, *Theorizing Myth: Narrative, Ideology, and Scholarship* (Chicago: University of Chicago Press, 1999).

48. The original source for this quote was Gertrude Stein's description of Oakland, California.

49. Asad, *Formations of the Secular*, 13–14.

50. Peter Burke, "The Repudiation of Ritual in Early Modern Europe," in *The Historical Anthropology of Early Modern Italy: Essays on Perception and Communication* (Cambridge: Cambridge University Press, 1987), 223–38. Cf. Jonathan Z. Smith, *To Take Place* (Chicago: University of Chicago Press, 1992), 99–103; Catherine Bell, "Ritual Reification," in Graham Harvey, ed., *Ritual and Religious Belief: A Reader* (New York: Routledge, 2005), 265–85; Talal Asad, "Toward a Genealogy of the Concept of Ritual," in *Genealogies of Religion* (Baltimore: Johns Hopkins University Press, 1993), 55–79. The condemnation of rhetoric in worship did not begin with Protestantism. John O. Ward, "Magic and Rhetoric from Antiquity to the Renaissance: Some Ruminations," *Rhetorica* 6 (1988): 57–118 at 70, notes that "the medieval church periodically proscribed not only sorcery, divination, and beneficial magic . . . but also other sources of irrational persuasion or power, such as art, rhetoric, and polyphony."

51. See, e.g., Carlos M. N. Eire, *War against the Idols: The Reformation of Worship from Erasmus to Calvin* (Cambridge: Cambridge University Press, 1986); Eamon Duffy, *The Stripping of the Altars: Traditional Religion in England c. 1400– c. 1580* (New Haven: Yale University Press, 1982); Margaret Aston, *England's Iconoclasts* (Oxford: Oxford University Press, 1988); and Jonathan Sheehan, ed., "Thinking about Idols in Early Modern Europe," special issue of the *Journal of the History of Ideas* 67, no. 4 (2006): 561–712.

52. Yelle, *Explaining Mantras*.

53. See Robert A. Yelle, "To Perform or Not to Perform?: A Theory of Ritual Performance versus Cognitive Theories of Religious Transmission," *Method & Theory in the Study of Religion* 18 (2006): 372–91; and Yelle, *Semiotics of Religion*, 56, 116.

54. Smith, *To Take Place*, 103. Indeed, the Protestant use of the word "vain" in the phrase "vain repetitions" expresses this sense of emptiness, already present in Calvin's Latin gloss of the word "battology" in Matthew 6:7 as "superfluous and unsaverie repetition [*supervacua est et putida repetitio*]."

55. Burke, "Repudiation of Ritual," 224.

56. The points at issue here were raised already during the debate between the anthropologist Hildred Geertz and the historian Keith Thomas concerning the latter's thesis that sixteenth- and seventeenth-century Britain witnessed a "decline of magic." See Keith Thomas, *Religion and the Decline of Magic* (New York:

Charles Scribner's Sons, 1971); and the exchange in Hildred Geertz, "An Anthropology of Religion and Magic, I," *Journal of Interdisciplinary History* 6 (1975): 71–89; and Keith Thomas, "An Anthropology of Religion and Magic, II," *Journal of Interdisciplinary History* 6 (1975): 91–109. Geertz emphasized that "magic" is a pejorative label, one applied by outsiders against the practices of others from whom they differ, and can never be assumed to be an adequate description of what the group so practicing actually believes itself to be doing. "Magic" is an etic (outsider's), rather than an emic (insider's) category, one with an especially checkered history in nineteenth- and twentieth-century anthropology, where it has been applied to label certain beliefs and practices as "primitive" and therefore functioned as one of the key concepts in evolutionary, ethnocentric accounts of the modern West's anthropological "others." Thomas rejected Geertz's contention that "magic" was a term used only by outsiders (see esp. 97–98). Magicians, too, used this and related terms to describe themselves, and believed in the efficacy of their practices (101). However, he agreed with her that the rise of a particular use of the term "magic," and its distinction from "religion," was a crucial issue:

> From the anthropologist's point of view, much of what historians call social change can be regarded as a process of mental reclassification, of redrawing conceptual lines and boundaries. My book was meant to demonstrate a hardening of mental divisions, between natural and supernatural, between the moral order and the natural order; which, I take it, is what Max Weber meant by the disenchantment of the world. I cannot, therefore, agree with Geertz in dismissing as a boring nonquestion the problem of how far the various practices which I identified as magical did in fact decline. On the contrary, I maintain that in England magic declined in a double sense: The clergy abandoned all claims to be able to achieve supernatural effects; and the practice of the various magical arts diminished in prestige and extent. I also think that this declining faith in the physical efficacy of religious ritual and in the power of the cunning men, poses some crucial historical issues. Despite the popular survival of many of the practices and attitudes which I discussed, I remain convinced that what I called the "decline of magic" has to be regarded as one of the great historical divides. (98; cf. 96–97.)

More anthropologists and scholars of religion probably now agree with Geertz that the designation magic—like myth or even religion itself—is useless as a category for describing historical reality. Yet, as mentioned previously, this leaves us with the problem of how to describe more adequately those beliefs that were formerly dismissed as magic, as well as the difference between such a worldview and our own, and the historical process that connects the two. Like Thomas, I am of the opinion that it is meaningful to refer to something like a decline of magic or disenchantment, although what, precisely, that means has yet to be worked out, and I will attempt to do so in relation to a different set of materials than he used.

It is important to note also that skepticism regarding the efficacy of magical practices is an ancient phenomenon, not confined to post-Reformation or Enlightenment culture. As Michael D. Bailey has argued, "processes identifiable as 'disenchantment'—notably the conceptualization of much magical and religious ritual as merely symbolic rather than directly effective—were evident already in the fifteenth century, and indeed earlier, and thus nothing like Weber's 'disenchantment of the world' or any concomitant lurch toward modernity should be bound exclusively to the impact of the Reformation." Bailey, "The Disenchantment of Magic: Spells, Charms, and Superstition in Early European Witchcraft Literature," *American Historical Review* 111 (2006): 383–404 at 387–88.

57. Mircea Eliade, *The Sacred and the Profane: The Nature of Religion*, trans. Willard Trask (New York: Harcourt, Brace, 1959); Eliade, *The Myth of the Eternal Return: or, Cosmos and History*, trans. Willard Trask (Princeton, NJ: Princeton University Press, 1954).

58. For a fuller account of the anti-Jewish versions and consequences of this myth, and their connections with secularism, see Yelle, "Moses' Veil."

59. Marcel Gauchet, *The Disenchantment of the World: A Political History of Religion* (Princeton, NJ: Princeton University Press, 1997).

60. Matthew 27:51.

61. 2 Corinthian 3:13, King James Version (see discussion below).

62. William Thompson, "The Magi," in *Poems on Several Occasions* (Oxford: printed at the theatre, 1757), 116–21 at 118.

63. *The Obsolescence of Oracles* (*De Defectu Oraculorum*), sec. 17. All of the translations of Plutarch used here are from Plutarch, *Moralia*, vol. 5, trans. Frank Cole Babbitt, Loeb Classical Library (Cambridge, MA: Harvard University Press, 1936). Plutarch also advanced an alternative, naturalistic interpretation of the agency behind the oracles: the oracles were literally "inspired" by fumes or exhalations coming out of caves and fissures in the ground (secs. 40–50). The decline of the oracles was the result of the cessation of such vapors, This explanation was, however, presented as consistent with a belief in the gods (secs. 47–48). Plutarch wrote another dialogue on the subject that considered a different aspect of the oracles' decline, why they were no longer written in verse, *The Oracles at Delphi No Longer Given in Verse*. This text (secs. 17–28) claimed a general process of the replacement of poetic language by prose. The more passionate nature of the men of former times predisposed them to poetry, which was more impressive than prose, and therefore suited to the communication of important subjects. Gradually, this changed, and history and philosophy began to be composed in plainer language. The oracles were affected as well:

When [the god] had taken away from the oracles epic versification, strange words, circumlocutions, and vagueness, he had thus made them ready to talk to his consultants as the laws talk to States, or as kings meet with common people, or as pupils listen to teachers, since he adapted the language to what was intelligible and convincing. . . . The introduction of clearness was attended also by a revolution in belief . . . And this was the result: in days of old what was not familiar or common, but was expressed altogether indirectly and through circumlocution, the mass of people imputed to an assumed manifestation of divine power, and held it in awe and reverence; but in later times, being well satisfied to apprehend all these various things clearly and easily without the attendant grandiloquence and artificiality, they blamed the poetic language with which the oracles were clothed, not only for obstructing the understanding of these in their true meaning and for combining vagueness and obscurity with the communication, but [also because] already they were coming to look with suspicion upon metaphors, riddles, and ambiguous statements, feeling that these were secluded nooks of refuge devised for furtive withdrawal and retreat for him that should err in his prophecy.

The interlocutors in Plutarch's dialogue noted that, although it may not be true that the oracles were always delivered in verse, it was indeed the case that philosophers since Empedocles and Thales had ceased to use metre. Poetry, suitable for matters of importance, had declined in an age in which the oracles were consulted only concerning mundane matters. Yet this did not signal a change for the worse. In fact, it was appropriate to the times and also reflected the discrediting of certain frauds and charlatans who dressed up their false oracles with poetic eloquence.

64. For an account of these interpretations, see Patricia Merivale, *Pan the Goat-God: His Myth in Modern Times* (Cambridge, MA: Harvard University Press, 1969), 13–16; C. A. Patrides, "The Cessation of the Oracles: The History of a Legend," *The Modern Language Review* 60 (1965): 500–07. Eusebius, *Praeparatio Evangelica*, trans. E. H. Gifford (Oxford: Clarendon Press, 1903), Book 5, said that "Pan" referred to a demon or the Devil. Cf. John Edwards, *A Discourse Concerning the Authority, Style, and Perfection of the Books of the Old and New Testament* (London: Richard Wilkin, 1693), 378–79. The fifteenth-century commentator Paulus Marsus and most others said that it referred to Christ himself, whose death on the cross, and subsequent harrowing of hell, brought an end to the reign of the demons on earth. *Commentary on Ovid's Fasti* (ca. 1482), I, 397, cited in Patrides, "Cessation," 13–14. Cf. George Hakewill, *An Apologie of the Power and Providence of God in the Government of the World* (Oxford: printed by John Lichfield and William Turner, 1627), 195; Peter Sterry, *A Discourse of the Freedom of the Will* (London: printed for John Starkey, 1675); Anthony Horneck, *The Crucified Jesus* (London: printed for Samuel Lowndes, 1695), 149–50; Benjamin Keach, *The Glorious Lover* (London: printed by J. D. for Christopher Hussey, 1679), 141–42; Nathanael Ingelo, *The Perfection, Authority, and Credibility of the Holy Scriptures*, 2nd ed. (London: printed by E. T. for Luke Fawn, 1659), 85–86; Philip of Mornay, Lord of Plessie Marlie, *A Woorke Concerning the Trewnesse of*

the Christian Religion (London: printed for Thomas Cadman, 1587), 604–05; Ralph Cudworth, *The True Intellectual System of the Universe* (London: printed for Richard Royston, 1678), 345–46; Peter Hausted, *Ten Sermons Preached upon Severall Sundayes and Saints Dayes* (London: printed for John Clark, 1636), 15–16. For some, it was the Messiah's incarnation and birth, rather than crucifixion, that led to the banishment of the demons, or the prediction of their demise: *A Compendious and Curious Miscellaneous History from the Creation to William the Conqueror* (London, 1754), 119; see also the quote referenced in note 62 from Thompson, *The Magi*, 18. Bernard Fontenelle, in his famous *Histoire des Oracles* (1687), summarized these views: "This great *Pan* . . . was the Master of the *Dæmons*, whose Empire was ruined by the Death of a God of such Salvation to the Universe: Or, if this Explanation do not please you, . . . this great *Pan* was *Jesus Christ* himself, whose Death caused so general a Grief and Consternation among the *Dæmons*, who from that Time could no more exercise their Tyranny over Mankind: Thus a Way has been found out to give two Faces very different to this great *Pan*." Bernard le Bovier de Fontenelle, *The History of Oracles*, trans. Stephen Whatley (London: printed for D. Browne and J. Whiston, 1750), 11–12. Cf. Edmund Spenser, *The Shepheardes Calendar* (London: printed for R. Dodsley, 1579), fol. 21; Lewes Lavaterus, *Of Ghostes and Spirites Walking by Nyght*, trans. R. H. (London: printed by H. Benneyman for Richard Watkyns, 1572), 95.

65. Samuel Mather, *The Figures or Types of the Old Testament* (London: printed for N. Hillier, 1705), 331.

66. See also the quote from Alexander Ross appended as an epigraph to this book. Alexander Ross, *Pansebeia: or, A View of All Religions in the World*, 2nd ed. (London: John Saywell, 1655), 181.

67. Hakewill, *An Apologie*, 195.

68. William Vaughan, *The Church Militant* (London: printed by Thomas Paine for Humfrey Blunden, 1640), 45. William Cave, *Apostolici, or, the History of the Lives, Acts, Death, and Martyrdom of Those Who Were Contemporary with, or Immediately Succeeded the Apostles*, 4th ed. (London: printed by W. D. for J. Walthoe and several others, 1716), vii, extended the metaphor: "The Shadows of Night do not more naturally vanish at the rising of the Sun, than the Darkness of Pagan Idolatry and Superstition fled before the Light of the Gospel; which the more it prevailed, the clearer it discovered the Folly and Impiety of their Worship: Their solemn Rites appeared more trifling and ridiculous, their Sacrifices more barbarous and inhumane; their Dæmons were expelled by the meanest Christian, their Oracles became mute and silent, and their very Priests began to be ashamed of their Magic Charms and Conjurations; and the more prudent and subtile Heads among them, who stood up for the Rites and Solemnities of their Religion, were forced to turn them into mystical and allegorical Meanings, far enough either from the Apprehension or Intention of the Vulgar."

69. Merivale, *Pan the Goat-God*, 239 n.34.

70. Reginald Scot, *Discovery of Witchcraft* (London: printed by Richard Gates, 1651 [1584]), 118. Scot (117) quoted Zechariah 13:1 for the idea of a disenchantment occurring through divine agency. Merivale, *Pan the Goat-God*, 15 and n.34, also identified Scot as a forerunner of eighteenth-century skepticism that interpreted the oracles as a hoax. However, she failed to note that Scot's "skepticism" was still distinctively Christian.

71. Thomas Ady, *A Candle in the Dark* (London: printed for Robert Ibbitson, 1655), 77–78.

72. Id. at 80–81.

73. John Webster, *The Displaying of Supposed Witchcraft* (London: printed by J. M., 1677), 37–43, esp. 41.

74. Id. at 40.

75. Cf. Joseph Glanvill, *Saducismus Triumphatus* (London: printed for J. Collins and S. Lownds, 1681).

76. See note 63 in this chapter.

77. Fontenelle, *History of Oracles*, 4.

78. Id. at 217–18.

79. Daniel Defoe, *The Political History of the Devil* (London: T. Warner, 1726), 252.

80. *Encyclopaedia Britannica*, 2nd ed. (Edinburgh, 1781), s.v. "Oracle," p. 5541.

81. M. W., *The Sacred Outcry, upon a View of the Principal Errors and Vices of Christendom, in the Eighteenth Century* (London: printed for W. Richardson and several others, 1788).

82. E.g., George Gordon, Lord Byron, "Aristomenes" (1823). Many other Romantics used the same line, e.g., Elizabeth Barrett Browning, "The Dead Pan" (1844). See Merivale, *Pan the Goat-God*, for references and discussion. Friedrich Nietzsche, who might be described as a "critical Romantic," used the line "Great Pan is dead" in *The Birth of Tragedy*, sec. 11, to describe the death of tragedy at the birth of Socratic rationalism. This may also foreshadow Nietzsche's later concept of the "death of God."

83. Friedrich Schlegel, "Talk on Mythology," trans. in Burton Feldman and Robert D. Richardson, *The Rise of Modern Mythology 1680–1860* (Bloomington: Indiana University Press, 1972), 309–13.

84. The term "linguistic ideology" or "language ideology" has become popular in linguistic anthropology and sociolinguistics to denote theories of the nature and functions of language held within particular cultures. See Bambi B. Schieffelin, Kathryn Ann Woolard, and Paul V. Kroskrity, *Language Ideologies: Practice and Theory* (New York: Oxford University Press, 1998); Paul V. Kroskrity, *Regimes of Language: Ideologies, Polities, and Identities* (Sante Fe, NM: School of American Research Press, 2000). Webb Keane, *Christian Moderns: Freedom and Fetish in the Mission Encounter* (Berkeley: University of California Press, 2007), 2, 16–18, uses the terms "semiotic ideology" and "language ideology."

85. Alexander Nowell, *A True Report of the Disputation or Rather Private Conference Had in the Tower of London, with Ed. Campion Jesuite* (London: printed by Christopher

Barker, 1583): "And yet in this plaine style, the Apostle [Paul in Corinthians] was of al others most mightie & most eloquent"; Anthony Burgess, *Spiritual Refining: Or a Treatise of Grace and Assurance* (London: printed by A. Miller for Thomas Underhill, 1652), 497: "The simple and plain stile of the Scripture . . . this plain way of Gods Word preached"; Thomas Fuller, *Abel Redevivus or, The Dead Yet Speaking* (London: printed by Thomas Brudnell for John Stafford, 1652), 444: "The plaine stile of the Scripture. . . ."; Joseph Glanvill, *A Seasonable Defence of Preaching and the Plain Way of It* (London: printed by M. Clarke for H. Brome, 1678).

86. The Revised Standard Version renders this "we are very bold," a formula which, if literally accurate, obscures the historical interpretation of this verse as an attack on the "shadows" or "hieroglyphs" of Jewish religion.

87. On Christian typology, see Eric Auerbach, "Figura," *Scenes from the Drama of European Literature* (Minneapolis: University of Minnesota Press, 1959), 11–78; Friedrich Ohly, "Typology as Historical Thought," in *Sensus Spiritualis: Studies in Medieval Significs and the Philology of Culture* (Chicago: University of Chicago Press, 2005), 31–67; Sacvan Bercovitch, *Typology and Early American Literature* (Amherst: University of Massachusetts Press, 1972); Paul Korshin, *Typologies in England 1650–1820* (Princeton, NJ: Princeton University Press, 1982).

88. The distinction between allegory and typology, though important, is not crucial for purposes of our discussion here.

89. John Weemes, *An Explanation of the Ceremoniall Lawes of Moses, As They Are Annexed to the Tenne Commandements* (London: printed by T. Cotes for John Bellamie, 1632), 176.

90. Cf. John Lightfoot, *The Works of the Reverend and Learned John Lightfoot* (London: printed by W. R. for Robert Scot, Thomas Basset, and Richard Chiswell, 1684), 1187: "Hereupon the Gospel is called *the Truth*, because it unridled those mysterious Hieroglyphicks, unveiled the face of *Moses*, and shewed the substance and body, which those vails and shadows did infold."

91. Johannes Cocceius (1603–1669) even argued that the ceremonial law was a punishment to the Jews for worshiping the Golden Calf. See John Weemes, *An Explanation of the Ceremoniall Lawes*, 76; William Warburton, *The Divine Legation of Moses Demonstrated*, 2 vols. (London: printed for the executor of the late Mr. Fletcher Gyles, 1742–1758), 2: 390; Hugo Grotius, *On the Truth of Christianity* (London: printed for J. Dodsley, 1782), 101, 249, 253–54, 258; Richard Watson, *A Collection of Theological Tracts* (Cambridge: printed by J. Archdeacon for J. & J. Merrill, T. Evans, and J. Fletcher, 1785), 1: 318; Stephen D. Benin, "The 'Cunning of God' and Divine Accommodation," *Journal of the History of Ideas* 45 (1984): 179–91; Guy Stroumsa, "John Spencer and the Roots of Idolatry," *History of Religions* (2001): 1–23; Amos Funkenstein, "Accommodation and the Divine Law," in *Theology and the Scientific Imagination: From the Middle Ages to the Seventeenth Century* (Princeton, NJ: Princeton University Press, 1986), 222–43.

92. John Toland, *Christianity Not Mysterious* (London: printed for Samuel Buckley, 1696), 115.

93. See chapter 4 in this volume.

94. Peter Harrison, *The Bible, Protestantism, and the Rise of Natural Science* (Cambridge: Cambridge University Press, 1998), 116.

95. For the concept of ritual as a mode of rhetorical performance, see Yelle, "To Perform or Not to Perform?" and Yelle, *Semiotics of Religion*, chapters 2 and 5.

96. Michael Foucault, "The Order of Discourse," in Robert Young, ed., *Untying the Text: A Post-Structuralist Reader* (London: Routledge & Kegan Paul, 1981), 48–78 at 52.

97. Id. at 73.

98. Id. at 70.

99. See esp. Webb Keane, "From Fetishism to Sincerity: Agency, the Speaking Subject, and their Historicity in the Context of Religious Conversion," *Comparative Studies in Society and History* 39 (1997): 674–93; "Religious Language," *Annual Review of Anthropology* 26 (1997): 47–71; "Sincerity, Modernity, and the Protestants," *Cultural Anthropology* 17 (2002): 65–92. See also Keane, *Christian Moderns*. Keane uses the term "representational economy" at "Sincerity" 65, as a synonym of "language ideology," which he uses, e.g., at "Fetishism," 680 and "Sincerity," 66. In addition to Keane, see also Joel Robbins, "Ritual Communication and Linguistic Ideology," *Current Anthropology* 42 (2001): 591–614 at 598; and esp. Robbins, "God Is Nothing But Talk: Modernity, Language, and Prayer in a Papua New Guinea Society," *American Anthropologist* 103 (2001): 901–12, which shows that the Urapmin tribe has converged with Protestantism in its focus on the linguistic dimensions of worship. The phrase "God is nothing but talk," which can be a derogatory reference to this Christian focus, for some Urapmin resonates with John 1:1, "In the beginning was the Word" (904–05). See also Joel Robbins, *Becoming Sinners: Christianity and Moral Torment in a Papua New Guinea Society* (Berkeley: University of California Press, 2004). Richard Bauman and Charles L. Briggs, *Voices of Modernity: Language Ideologies and the Politics of Inequality* (Cambridge: Cambridge University Press, 2003), provides an account of the the development of the modern idea of a universal, perfectly rational language, beginning with such figures as Locke and other members of the Royal Society. With a nod to Chakrabarty's call to "provincialize Europe" (3–4, 318–21), Bauman and Briggs show how Western projects of anthropology and colonialism exerted their transforming powers of definition, representation, and control on other cultures through the development and propagation of the idea of language as a neutral, purely objective and descriptive medium of communication and the critique of traditional language.

100. Keane, "Fetishism," 679.

101. Id. at 681.
102. Id. at 680.
103. Keane, "Sincerity," 74.
104. Keane, "Religious Language," 63.
105. Id. at 65.
106. Id. at 55–56. Interpreting one missionary's complaint that the Sumbanese believe their prayers can coerce even God, Keane, "Fetishism," 681, states that this "prayer tempts mere humans to lèse-majesté with respect to the spirit world and, by implication, divinity." Although Keane does not note this, such missionary complaints echo the earlier Puritan critique of "vain repetitions" in prayer.
107. Keane, "Sincerity," 67. Keane, "Fetishism," 685 refers to this as a process of "secularization."
108. Keane, "Sincerity," 66.
109. Id. at 83–84. Cf. 67.
110. Ady, *Candle in the Dark*, 77–78.
111. Id. at 80–81.
112. The *Compact Oxford English Dictionary*, 2nd edition (Oxford: Clarendon Press, 1991), quoting Ady, defines "harr" as "To snarl as a dog; to make a rough guttural trill."
113. Ady, *Candle in the Dark*, 78.
114. Jeremy Bentham, "Book of Fallacies," *The Works of Jeremy Bentham*, ed. John Bowring, 11 volumes (Edinburgh: William Tait, 1843), 2: 448.
115. Taylor, *A Secular Age*, 37–42, 134–42.
116. Lilla, *The Stillborn God*. See also Yelle, "Moses' Veil."
117. Talal Asad has questioned the validity or interest of such theological readings of modernity: "I take the view, as others have done, that the 'religious' and the 'secular' are not essentially fixed categories. However, I do not claim that if one stripped appearances one would see that some apparently secular institutions were *really* religious. I assume, on the contrary, that there is nothing *essentially* religious, nor any universal essence that defines 'sacred language' or 'sacred experience.' . . . Here, as in the other cases I deal with, I simply want to get away from the idea that the secular is a mask for religion, that secular political practices often simulate religious ones." *Formations of the Secular*, 25–26; cf. 61. I take a more pragmatic view: to the extent that a religious genealogy of modernity proves illuminating, it should be undertaken.
118. Löwith, *Meaning in History*.
119. Asad, *Formations of the Secular*, 13.
120. For further discussion of the theological dimensions of Weber's thought, see Yelle, "The Trouble with Transcendence."
121. Balagangadhara, "Biblical Underpinnings," 131.
122. Chakrabarty, *Provincializing Europe*, 16.

CHAPTER 2

1. Cf. Viswanathan, *Masks of Conquest*, 81–82.

2. *Primitiae Orientales: Essays by the Students of the College of Fort William in Bengal,* vol. 1 (Calcutta: [College of Fort William], 1802), 73. In the same volume (81), C. T. Metcalfe argued that Oriental languages themselves exhibited both despotism and servility, and that British rule would change the language of Indians along with their mode of government. Cf. John Borthwick Gilchrist, *Strangers East Indian Guide to the Hindoostanee*, 2nd ed. (Calcutta, 1808), 111.

3. Lynn Zastoupil and Martin Moir, *The Great Indian Education Debate: Documents Relating to the Orientalist-Anglicist Controversy, 1781–1843* (Richmond, UK: Curzon, 1999), 165.

4. Thomas B. Macaulay, "Essay on Bacon," in *Critical and Historical Essays*, vol. 3 (London: Longman, Brown, Green, and Longmans, 1848), 280–429 at 383. Quoted in Kopf, *British Orientalism*, 249.

5. Quoted in Zastoupil and Moir, *Great Indian Education Debate*, 298.

6. Quoted in id. at 295–96.

7. Alexander Duff [Eis Eclectikon, pseud.], *Language in Relation to Commerce, Missions, and Government: England's Ascendancy and the World's Destiny* (Manchester, 1846), 11; an almost identical passage is found in Alexander Duff, *New Era of the English Language and English Literature in India* (Edinburgh: Johnstone, 1837), 37.

8. Monier Monier-Williams, *The Study of Sanskrit in Relation to Missionary Work in India* (London: Williams and Norgate, 1861), 53.

9. Hans Aarsleff, *The Study of Language in England, 1780–1860* (Princeton, NJ: Princeton University Press, 1967), 122.

10. Ibid., quoting Jones, "Preliminary Discourse," in *The Works of Sir William Jones, with the life of the author*, ed. Lord Teignmouth [John Shore], 13 vols. (London: John Stockdale, 1807), 3: 1–9 at 7.

11. Ibid.

12. India Office Records V/ 24/ 954, "Report by Isvar Chandra Sharma transmitted with letter dated December 16, 1850, to F. J. Mouat," in *General Report on Public Instruction in the Lower Provinces of the Bengal Presidency from 1st October 1850 to 30th September 1851* (Calcutta: Bengal Military Orphan Press, 1852), 39–40. Reproduced in Indramitra, *Karunasagar Vidyasagar* (Kolkata: Ananda Publishers, 2006), 641–50 at 647.

13. Viswanathan, *Masks of Conquest*, 54, 138.

14. James Long, *Handbook of Bengal Missions* (London: J. F. Shaw, 1848), 472–73.

15. James Robert Ballantyne, *An Explanatory Version of Bacon's Novum Organum, Printed for the Use of the Benares Sanskrit College* (Mirzapore: Orphan School Press, 1852), 37.

16. *Novum Organum*, Book 1, chap. 59–60. Unless otherwise indicated, citations to Bacon are to the edition of *The Works of Francis Bacon* edited by James Spedding,

Robert Leslie Ellis, and Douglas Denon Heath (Cambridge: Riverside Press and New York: Hurd and Houghton, 1869) (hereinafter "Bacon, *Works*").

17. Ibid.

18. See the discussion of Hobbes below in this chapter.

19. John Locke, *An Essay Concerning Human Understanding*, ed. Alexander Campbell Fraser, 2 vols. (New York: Dover, 1959 [1690]), 2: 132 (Book 3, chap. 10, sec. 14). Similarly, John Wilkins argued that "Words being but the images of matter, and to be wholly given up to the study of these, what is it but *Pygmalions* phrenzy, to fall in love with a picture or image. . . ." John Wilkins, *Sermons Preached upon Several Occasions* (London: printed for Thomas Basset, Richard Chiswell, and William Rogers, 1682), 184. Cf. Thomas Gustafson, *Representative Words: Politics, Literature, and the American Language, 1776–1865* (New York: Cambridge University Press, 1992), 142, who attributes the phrase "Pygmalion's frenzy" to Bacon.

20. John Horne Tooke, *Epea Pteroenta, or The Diversions of Purley*, 2nd ed., 2 vols. (London, 1798 and 1805).

21. Yelle, "Bentham's Fictions." Later in the nineteenth century, another utilitarian philosopher, John Stuart Mill, is quoted as having said that "The tendency has always been strong to believe that whatever received a name must be an entity or being, having an independent existence of its own, and if no real entity answering to the name could be found, men did not for that reason suppose that none existed, but imagined that it was something particularly abstruse and mysterious." Quoted in Stephen Jay Gould, *The Mismeasure of Man*, revised ed. (London: Penguin, 1997), 350, 378. This quote is commonly attributed to Mill, although I have been unable to locate its source.

22. Bernard Cohn, "The Command of Language," in *Colonialism and its Forms of Knowledge: The British in India* (Princeton, NJ: Princeton University Press, 1996), 16–56 at 18–19.

23. Charles Morris, *Signs, Language, and Behavior* (New York: Prentice-Hall, 1950), 217–20.

24. Mandair, *Religion and the Specter of the West*, 85–86 makes a similar point.

25. This does not mean that language did not also serve other referential and communicative functions. Indeed, it is impossible to imagine any culture in which these functions are not served, either by spoken language or by some analogue of speech. For most everyday purposes, then, language can be presumed to have functioned largely as it has done and continues to do in most cultures. Thus, the differences among British and Indian views of language were operationalized in a relatively delimited sphere—that of ritual—and did not affect ordinary, mundane activity. The sphere of ritual may have, as Cohn suggests, been larger in traditional India; and the linguistic cosmology that was operative in ritual also had influence outside of that domain, in defining a certain worldview and locating and reinforcing a system of norms. However, we must beware

of drawing too rigid a distinction between British and Indian mentalities, lest we should caricature the latter as exotic and primitive. Moreover, as Maurice Bloch has emphasized, views of time in ritual versus mundane activity may differ within the same society. Data that appear to confirm Benjamin Lee Whorf's hypothesis of radical linguistic relativity may actually reflect such intra-cultural, rather than crosscultural, differences. For example, although Hindus may have viewed time as cyclical for ritual purposes, they treated it as linear on other occasions. See Maurice Bloch, "The Past and the Present in the Present," in *Ritual, History, and Power: Selected Papers in Anthropology* (London: Athlone Press, 1989), 1–18 at 10–11.

26. Sheldon Pollock, "Introduction: Forms of Knowledge in Early Modern South Asia," *Comparative Studies of South Asia, Africa and the Middle East* 24 (2004): 19–21 at 19.

27. *Rig Veda* 10.125.

28. Yelle, *Explaining Mantras*, chapter 2.

29. The idea that language may not only say, but also do something—may bring about some state of affairs and not only describe it—has been developed especially by J. L. Austin, *How to Do Things with Words* (Cambridge, MA: Harvard University Press, 1962); and John Searle, *Speech Acts: An Essay in the Philosophy of Language* (London: Cambridge University Press, 1969).

30. On these rites, see Teun Goudriaan, *Maya: Divine and Human* (Delhi: Motilal Banarsidass, 1978).

31. Arthur Avalon [John Woodroffe], *The Garland of Letters: Studies in the Mantra Sastra* (Madras: Ganesh and Co., 1998), 70–81, 90–91.

32. Thus *Śāktānandataraṅgiṇī* 9: "devatāyāḥ śarīran tu bījād utpadyate dhruvam." In *Śāktānandataraṅgiṇī*, ed. Ram Kumar Rai (Benares: Prachya Prakashan, 1993).

Cf. *Bṛhadgandharva Tantra* 5, quoted in Avalon, *Garland of Letters*, 261: "śṛṇu devi pravakṣyāmi bījānāṃ devarūpatām/ mantroccāraṇamātrena devarūpatāṃ prajāyate."

33. The Vedas and, later, the Tantras reflected influential or even normative views regarding the power of certain forms of sacred or ritual speech. However, not all Hindus accepted the theory of natural name. The minority opinions of materialists and nonbelievers were noted already in Vedic times (e.g., a certain Kautsa, mentioned in *Nirukta*). See Lakshman Sarup, trans., *The Nighaṇṭu and the Nirukta* (Delhi: Motilal Banarsidass, 1998). The canonical or orthodox system of Vedic interpretation known as *Mīmāṃsā* denied the view that the gods referred to in Vedic mantras had corporeal existence, and argued that "divinity is only sound." See Richard Davis, *The Lives of Indian Images* (Princeton, NJ: Princeton University Press, 1997), 46. Mīmāṃsā also denied the view that sound and substance were the same, so that uttering the word would supposedly produce that to which it referred. However, Mīmāṃsā retained a belief in the authority of the language of the revealed Vedas. Śabara explained that

(the) language (of the Vedas), or more specifically the relation between word (*śabda*) and meaning (*artha*), is eternal or originary (*autpattika*) (*Mīmāṃsāsūtra* 1.5, in Ganganath Jha, *Shabara-Bhāṣya*, 3 vols. (Baroda: Oriental Institute, 1933), 1: 8, 18). The following saying is put into the mouth of an opponent as an argument against this claim: "If the relation between the word and the thing denoted by it were held to be of the nature of Contact (Conjunction), then on the utterance of the word 'razor,' the mouth (of the speaker) would be ripped open, and similarly on the utterance of the word 'sweets,' his mouth would become filled with sweets." The authoritative view expressed by Śabara does not dispute this argument, but maintains that the relation between word and meaning is original in a different sense. Whether Śabara—or the opposing viewpoint (*pūrvapakṣa*) that he quotes—was criticizing an actual, existing theory of natural name, such as was later elaborated in the Tantras, is unclear. However, the *Mṛgendrāgama*, a Tantra of the southern school, later specifically rejected the Mīmāṃsā doctrine that "divinity is only sound": "Words as signifiers must refer to real things, they aver, for 'the word "pot" does not hold water and the word "moon" does not shine.' So too, they go on, with a word like Indra: it is the deity and not the word that carries out Indra's divine activities" (quoted in Davis, *Lives*, 46).

34. Brian Vickers, "Analogy Versus Identity: The Rejection of Occult Symbolism, 1580–1680," in *Occult and Scientific Mentalities in the Renaissance* (Cambridge: Cambridge University Press, 1984), 95–163 at 95. Taylor, *A Secular Age* 37–42, 134–42, 300–07, has also referred to this distinction as a key component of secularism and the construction of a "buffered self."

35. Vickers, "Analogy Versus Identity," 102–03, 113, 133; cf. 121.

36. Id. at 97.

37. Ernst Cassirer, *Language and Myth* (New York: Harper, 1946), 49.

38. See Benjamin Colby and Michael Cole, "Culture, Memory and Narrative," in Horton and Finnegan, *Modes of Thought*, 63–91 at 67; Ernest Gellner, "The Savage and the Modern Mind," in id. at 162–81 at 174.

39. The term is from Jacques Derrida, "White Mythology: Metaphor in the Text of Philosophy," in *Margins of Philosophy*, trans. Alan Bass (Chicago: University of Chicago Press, 1982), 207–72.

40. W. P. Stephens, *The Theology of Huldrych Zwingli* (Oxford: Clarendon Press, 1986), 218–50.

41. Bacon returned to this image again and again. The image first appears in *Temporis Partus Masculus* (Bacon, *Works*, 3: 520–40), where the idols are only three in number. See also *Valerius Terminus* (id. at 3: 215–52); *Great Instauration*, Plan of the Work (id. at 8:45); *Novum Organum*, Book I, chap. 39–65 (id. at 8: 76–93); *De Augmentis*, Book 5 (id. at 9: 97–101). See Paolo Rossi, *Francis Bacon: From Magic to Science* (Chicago: University of Chicago Press, 1968), 160–72, for a discussion. The editors of the authoritative edition of

Bacon's *Works* rejected the religious dimensions of this aspect of his philosophy, specifically disputing the translation of *idola* as "false gods" and substituting the neutral sense of "image." (Bacon, *Works*, 1: 157–58; cf. *Bacon's Novum Organum*, ed. Thomas Fowler, 2nd ed. (Oxford: Clarendon Press, 1889), 204 n.28). However, Charles Whitney, *Francis Bacon and Modernity* (New Haven: Yale University Press, 1986), 4–7, 37–39, claims that the concept of idols was more than mere rhetorical window-dressing for Bacon. Scholarly dismissals of the significance of Bacon's deployment of religious and prophetic language serve a primarily defensive purpose of insulating modernity from the taint of irrationality associated with religion. Whitney has argued convincingly that Bacon's use of this word must be understood "in its biblical sense also, not literally, but metaphorically, as a displacement from the religious to the secular world" (38). As a mode of prophecy, as well as science, Bacon's philosophy set as its first task to oppose the false gods of ignorance. James Stephens, *Francis Bacon and the Style of Science* (Chicago: University of Chicago Press, 1975), 85, argued that Bacon "formulates a composite image of himself which combines th[e] role as messenger with the more meaningful Mosaic function as a destroyer of idols." This is in accord with Reinhard Brandt, "Über die vielfältige Bedeutung der Baconschen Idole," *Philosophisches Jahrbuch* 83 (1976): 42–70, at 51–52, who argues that Bacon's attack on the *idola* had religious resonances. Contra Ellis, although Bacon "strebt eine strikte Trennung seines Idolenbegriffs von dem christlichen Religionskritik an. . . . Diese Trennung besagt nicht, daß beide Idolenbegriffe nichts miteinander zu tun hätten; Bacon transformiert deutlich den religiösen Inhalt ins Profane, so z. B. bei der Bezeichnung der Idole als Objekte des Aberglaubens . . . und der Anbetung. . . . Auch bei Bacon sind die Idole also Götzen; sie sind wie die alten Idole ein Machwerk des Menschen, eine Ausgeburt des Wahns, die doch eigenes Leben gewinnt und die Herrschaft erringt über den Erzeuger." Further supporting this conclusion is a passage in *Valerius Terminus* ("On the Interpretation of Nature," chapter 11, in Bacon, *Works*, 3: 241), where Bacon begins a brief exposition of the four idols by referring to the idea of false gods: "The opinion of Epicurus that the gods were of human shape, was rather justly derided than seriously confuted by the other sects, demanding whether every kind of sensible creatures did not think their own figure fairest, as the horse, the bull, and the like, which found no beauty but in their own forms, as in appetite of lust appeared. And the heresy of the Anthropomorphites was ever censured for a gross conceit bred in the obscure cells of solitary monks that never looked abroad." In this passage, Bacon locates the cause of idolatry in anthropomorphism, and identifies this as a prototype for a range of cognitive errors. This strongly suggests that the religious meaning of idolatry was at least one of the meanings invoked by his use of *idolum*.

42. Sprat's criticisms of linguistic idolatry, as described below, most closely resemble Hobbes's, although Barbara J. Shapiro, *John Wilkins, 1614–1672: An Intellectual*

Biography (Berkeley: University of California Press, 1969), 206, claims that "the History's famous comments on proper language and style should almost certainly be attributed to Wilkins rather than Sprat."

43. Thomas Sprat, *History of the Royal Society* (London: printed by T. R. for J. Martyn and J. Allestry, 1667), 434.

44. Id. at 105.

45. Id., Dedicatory Poem.

46. Comenius had also employed the image of the scarecrow for epistemological fictions. *Joh. Amos Comenius's Visible World: Or, a Picture and Nomenclature of all the Chief Things that are in the World* (London, 1659), quoted in G. A. Padley, *Grammatical Theory in Western Europe 1500–1700: The Latin Tradition* (Cambridge: Cambridge University Press, 1976), 147.

47. Sprat, *History of the Royal Society*, 5.

48. Id. at 11–12.

49. Id. at 12.

50. Id. at 16.

51. Id. at 29, 35.

52. Id. at 51.

53. Thomas Hobbes, *Leviathan*, chap. 12, "Of Religion," sec. 16. All citations to the *Leviathan* are to Thomas Hobbes, *Leviathan*, ed. Edwin Curley (Indianapolis: Hackett, 1994) (hereinafter "*Lev.*").

54. *Lev.* chap. 44, sec. 3; chap. 45, sec. 4; cf. chap. 12, secs. 13–18. See also chap. 45, "Of Demonology and Other Relics of the Religion of the Gentiles," for an extended discussion of idolatry.

55. *Lev.* chap. 45, sec. 14: "And these are the images which are originally and most properly called *ideas* and *idols*, and derived from the language of the Grecians, with whom the word *eido* signifieth to *see*."

56. *Lev.* chap. 45, sec. 16.

57. *Lev.* chap. 4, sec. 21.

58. *Lev.* chap. 8, sec. 27; chap. 44, sec. 11.

59. *Lev.* chap. 34, "Of the Signification of Spirit, Angel, and Inspiration in the Books of Holy Scripture."

60. *Lev.* chap. 38, sec. 12.

61. Thomas Hobbes, "Of Religion," *Philosophical Rudiments concerning Government and Society*, in *The English Works of Thomas Hobbes of Malmesbury*, ed. William Molesworth, 11 vols. (London: J. Bohn, 1839–45) (hereinafter "Hobbes, *Works*"), 2: 249.

62. *Lev.* chap. 45, sec. 16. Echoing the rendering of *ecclesia* as "congregation" rather than "church" in William Tyndale's earlier translation of the Bible, Hobbes applied the nominalist argument that all class terms are fictions or abstractions to the word "church" itself. He argued that this word could be taken legitimately to mean one body or person only if there were a company of members united

under one sovereign. As there was no universal sovereign, there could be no single, universal Church, as the Catholics claimed. *Lev.* chap. 39.

63. See Eldon J. Eisenach, "Hobbes on Church, State and Religion," in Preston King, ed., *Thomas Hobbes: Critical Assessments*, (London: Routledge, 1993), 4: 290–316 at 296; Frank Coleman, "Thomas Hobbes and the Hebraic Bible," *History of Political Thought* 25 (2004): 642–69 at 642–49, 660, 666–69; Paul J. Johnson, "Hobbes's Anglican Doctrine of Salvation," in Ralph Ross, Herbert W. Schneider, and Theodore Waldman, eds., *Thomas Hobbes in His Time* (Minneapolis: University of Minnesota Press, 1974), 102–25 at 114–15; Mark Whitaker, "Hobbes's View of the Reformation," in King, *Thomas Hobbes*, 1: 473. Cf. Richard Tuck, "The 'Christian Atheism' of Thomas Hobbes," in Michael Hunter and David Wootton, eds., *Atheism from the Reformation to the Enlightenment* (Oxford: Clarendon Press, 1992), 111–30; Willis B. Glover, "Human Nature and the State in Hobbes," in King, *Thomas Hobbes*, 4: 50–72 at 52; Patricia Springborg, "Leviathan and the Problem of Ecclesiastical Authority," in King, *Thomas Hobbes*, 4: 136–48 at 144; Shirley R. Letwin, "Hobbes and Christianity," in King, *Thomas Hobbes*, 4: 149–73.

64. Locke, *Essay*, 2: 132.

65. Locke, *Essay*, 2: 5 (Book 3, chap. 1, sec. 5).

66. In his most extended discussion of idolatry, Locke explained "how . . . it comes to pass that men worship the idols that have been set up in their minds." Through the force of tradition and human laziness especially, a man comes "to take monsters lodged in his own brain for the images of the Deity, and the workmanship of his hands." Locke, *Essay*, 1: 89 (Book 1, chap. 2, sec. 26). Later, Locke rejected the explanation of heathen polytheism as only the employment of "figurative ways of expressing the several attributes of that [one] incomprehensible Being." Id. at 1: 104 (Book 1, chap. 3, sec. 15). The defense of polytheism as a conscious and possibly innocent fiction, rather than a real delusion, was a thesis of several Cambridge Platonists and presented a more benign linguistic interpretation of pagan mythology, as described below in this chapter. In the earliest version of his *Essay*, Locke criticized the tautological reasoning of the schoolmen, who say that "What is a soule is a soule or a soule is a soule, a Spirit is a Spirit, a Fetiche is a Fetiche & c." R. I. Aaron and Jocelyn Gibb, eds., *An Early Draft of Locke's Essay* (Oxford: Clarendon Press, 1936), 49. As Frank Manuel noted, in his early manuscripts on religion Locke "explained idol- and saint-worship as a result of the almost ineradicable tendency of common people to concretize. Savages knew the names of objects, not of abstract qualities, and for ordinary people God had to be portrayed in a manner comprehensible to the senses." Manuel, *The Changing of the Gods* (Hanover, NH: University Press of New England, 1983), 64. This idea does not occur in the discussions of idolatry in Locke's journal from 1676, which present a more orthodox interpretation of this concept. See John Locke, *Essays on the Law of Nature*, trans. W. Von Leyden

(Oxford: Clarendon Press, 1954), 259–62. When Locke later discussed idolatry in his *Letters on Toleration*, it was in defense of the religious liberty of such forms of heterodoxy.

67. Tooke, *Diversions of Purley*, 1: 31–32, note.
68. Id. at 1: 54–55. Tooke cites Gerard Vossius at 1: 55, note.
69. Id. at 2: 18; cf. 2: 20.
70. Another example is Isaac Newton, who served as the Royal Society's President from 1703–1727. Newton was deeply concerned with the origins of idolatry, which he attributed partly to the influence of Egyptian hieroglyphs, anticipating William Warburton's later account. Newton, like Hobbes, attributed idolatry and the belief in spirits to a misplaced literalism in interpretation. See esp. *The Chronology of Ancient Kingdoms Amended* (London: printed for J. Tonson, 1728), 160–62, 225–28; *Theologiae gentilis origines philosophicae* ("The Philosophical Origins of Gentile Theology"), discussed in Robert Charles Iliffe, "The Idols of the Temple: Isaac Newton and the Private Life of Anti-Idolatry," unpublished Cambridge University Ph.D. Thesis (1989), 154; Bodmer MS 5A. fol. 8v., quoted in Stephen D. Snobelen, "'God of Gods, and Lord of Lords': The Theology of Isaac Newton's General Scholium to the *Principia*," *Osiris*, 2nd series, 16 (2001): 169–208 at 183; *Observations upon the Prophecies*, quoted in Frank Manuel, *Isaac Newton, Historian* (Cambridge, MA: Harvard University Press, 1963), 149. For additional discussion, see Frank Manuel, *The Religion of Isaac Newton* (Oxford: Clarendon Press, 1974), 46–47, 69; Manuel, *Isaac Newton, Historian*, 112–13, 180–81; Manuel, *The Eighteenth Century Confronts the Gods* (Cambridge, MA: Harvard University Press, 1959), 117–18, 122–23; Richard S. Westfall, *The Life of Isaac Newton* (Cambridge: Cambridge University Press, 1993), 138–39; Westfall, *Never at Rest: A Biography of Isaac Newton* (Cambridge: Cambridge University Press, 1980), 351–56; Westfall, "Isaac Newton's *Theologiae gentilis origines philosophicae*," in Warren Wagar, ed., *The Secular Mind: Tranformations of Faith in Modern Europe* (New York: Holmes and Meier, 1982), 15–34; Westfall, "Newton's Theological Manuscripts," in Zev Bechler, ed., *Contemporary Newtonian Research* (Dordrecht: D. Reidel, 1982), 129–43; John Hedley Brooke, "The God of Isaac Newton," in John Fauvel, ed., *Let Newton Be!* (Oxford: Oxford University Press, 1988), 169–83 at 174–77; Karen Figala, "Newton's Alchemy," in I. Bernard Cohen and George E. Smith, eds., *The Cambridge Companion to Newton* (Cambridge: Cambridge University Press, 2002), 370–86 at 375–76.

The sources for Newton's ideas of pagan mythology are uncertain, although Hobbes, Selden, Gerard Vossius, and Ralph Cudworth have been named as influences. Manuel, *Religion of Newton*, 84, 86, names the first three; Iliffe, "The Idols of the Temple," 63, 67, adds Spencer and Cudworth to this list; Westfall, "Isaac Newton's *Theologiae gentilis*," 20–21, names Vossius, John Marsham, and Samuel Bochart. J. E. McGuire and P. M. Rattansi, "Newton and the 'Pipes of Pan,'" *Notes and Records of the Royal Society* 21 (1966): 108–43 at 134, trace Newton's debt to the Cambridge Platonists, especially Cudworth's *True Intellectual System*, on which Newton took notes. The annotated work is in the William Andrews Clark Memorial Library at UCLA. Westfall, *Never at Rest*, 353, says that the notes indicate Newton read Cudworth after he composed the *Theologiae gentilis*. However, Iliffe, "The Idols of the Temple," 62, claims that the notes for Yahuda MS 41 show that Newton read Cudworth before composing "The original of Religions." See also Richard H. Popkin, "The Crisis of Polytheism and the Answers of Vossius, Cudworth, and Newton," in James E. Force and Richard H. Popkin, eds., *Essays on the Context, Nature, and Influence of Isaac Newton's Theology* (Dordrecht: Kluwer, 1990), 9–26. A perusal of the catalogues of Newton's personal library reveals relevant works by Hobbes, Selden, and Vossius. British Library MS Add. 25424, Catalogue of Sir Isaac Newton's Library, is a list of the contents of Newton's Library purchased after his death in 1727 by John Huggins. This includes the following works, among many others (I have filled out the names and titles for better identification):

> Cicero, *Opera*, Gruteri ed. (Hamburg, 1618)
> Diodorus Siculus (Hanover, 1604)
> Diodorus Siculus, English trans. (1706)
> Schedius, *De diis germanis* (Amsterdam, 1648)
> John Selden, *De diis syris* (Amsterdam, 1681)
> John Spencer, *De legibus hebraeorum* (Cambridge, 1685)
> Thomas Sprat, *History of the Royal Society* (London, 1677)
> Anthony Van Dale, *De origine et progressu idolatriae* (Amsterdam, 1696)
> Vossius, *De idolatria* [i.e., Gerard Vossius, *De theologia gentili*]
>   (Amsterdam, 1641)

As this list refers also to "waste books," it may not be comprehensive. Richard de Villamil, *Newton: The Man* (London: Gordon D. Knox, 1931), reproduces the catalogue of the library of James Musgrave, who acquired Newton's library from Huggins's heirs in 1750. The lists do not coincide in every detail, as Musgrave's library presumably contained some books that never belonged to Newton, and some of the books passing from Newton's estate to Huggins may not have been enumerated in the British Library list. However, all of the above works are found in Musgrave's catalogue as well. The work listed as "Vossius, *de Idolatria* (Amsterdam, 1641)" in the British Library list appears in the Musgrave list as "Gerard Vossius, *de Theologia Gentili* (1641)," and there is also a separate entry for "Maimonides *de Idolatria* per Vossium (1642)," i.e., the translation of Maimonides's treatise on idolatry done by Gerard's son Isaac. The Musgrave catalogue also lists Edward Stillingfleet's *Origines Sacræ* (1702), which is not found on the British Library list. For additional information, see John R. Harrison, *The Library of Isaac Newton* (Cambridge: Cambridge University Press, 1978).

71. Sprat, *History of the Royal Society*, 377.
72. Id. at 362–63.
73. The most famous, scholarly version of this thesis is that of Robert K. Merton, who noted the high concentration of Puritans among the Royal Society's early membership. See Merton, *Science, Technology & Society in Seventeenth Century England* (New York: Harper Torchbooks, 1970); originally published in 1938 as Volume IV, Part Two of *Osiris: Studies on the History and Philosophy of Science, and on the History of Learning and Culture*. See also Dorothy Stimson, "Puritanism and the New Philosophy in 17th century England," *Bulletin of the Institute of the History of Medicine* 3 (1935): 321–34. Borrowing and extending Weber's account of the Protestant work ethic, Merton argued that there was a correlation of ascetic practices, a convergence of interests, between Puritanism and science that encouraged the development of the latter in post-Restoration England: "Puritanism transfused ascetic vigor into activities which, in their own right, could not as yet achieve self-sufficiency. It so redefined the relations between the divine and the mundane as to move science to the front rank of social values." (86–87). Merton's argument, first advanced in the 1930s, has attracted many followers and critics. Among the more trenchant critiques of the Merton thesis are Theodore K. Rabb, "Puritanism and the Rise of Experimental Science in England," *Journal of World History* 7 (1962): 46–67, and Rabb, "Religion and the Rise of Modern Science," *Past & Present* 31 (1965): 111–26. Supporters include Christopher Hill, *Intellectual Origins of the English Revolution* (Oxford: Clarendon Press, 1965), 22–26. For discussions of this debate, see Harrison, *The Bible*, 5–8; Richard L. Greaves, "Puritanism and Science: The Anatomy of a Controversy," *Journal of the History of Ideas* 30 (1969): 345–68; Lotte Mulligan, "Civil War Politics, Religion and the Royal Society," *Past & Present* 59 (1973): 92–116; G. A. Abraham, "Misunderstanding the Merton Thesis: A Boundary Dispute between History and Sociology," *Isis* 74 (1983): 368–87. For a bibliography of works debating the relationship of Protestantism to the rise of science, see S. N. Eisenstadt, *The Protestant Ethic and Modernization: A Comparative View* (New York: Basic Books, 1968), 395–97. For a general bibliography on science and religion in the seventeenth century, see Richard S. Westfall, *Science and Religion in Seventeenth-Century England* (Hamden, CT: Archon Books, 1970), 221–28.
74. Sprat, *History of the Royal Society*, 366.
75. Id. at 367.
76. Id. at 372–73.
77. Id. at 372.
78. Id. at 377.
79. See, however, Rodney Stark, *The Victory of Reason: How Christianity Led to Freedom, Capitalism, and Western Success* (New York: Random House, 2005).
80. Merton, *Science, Technology & Society*, 87.

81. John Smith, *Select Discourses* (London: printed by J. Flesher for W. Morden, 1660), 264–65.
82. Merton, *Science, Technology & Society*, 17–18.
83. Id. at 114.
84. Richard Foster Jones recognized some of the same affinities, yet stressed the overriding importance of the scientific movement to the birth of the plain style. Jones agreed with Merton in recognizing a close connection between Puritanism and the Royal Society. However he invoked this connection for a nearly opposite end, to assert the influence of science on religion. Richard Foster Jones, *The Seventeenth Century: Studies in the History of English Thought and Literature from Bacon to Pope* (Stanford: Stanford University Press, 1951). According to Jones, where contemporaneous movements for linguistic reform in religious discourse, such as the attack on eloquence in preaching, paralleled those in scientific discourse, they were an import from the latter, a case of a "new standard of prose . . . invad[ing] an alien field" (112). This required Jones to posit "a possible channel through which the scientific spirit could have reached the pulpit" (125), a conduit of influence in which the Royal Society figured prominently. Jones's thesis has been criticized from a number of perspectives for decades, and it is now clear that, among other things, he underestimated the role of religion in these developments. From this perspective, the most important criticism of Jones's thesis is that the plain style appears to have originated not in science, but in Puritanism itself. Jones may have reversed the chronological priority and possibly even the direction of influence between these two movements. He apparently felt that such movements for language reform must necessarily be associated with reason and, therefore, with science, as opposed to religion. In fact, the movements for a plain style of preaching were as old as Protestantism, if not Christianity itself, where in the course of history they were repeated, often in association with a more general iconoclasm. Attacks on pulpit eloquence were not an alien importation into religion, but part of the main tradition of Protestantism. The phrases "plain style" (114, n.8) and "plain way" (124) that Jones used to describe the new literary model appear to have been used first to refer to the style of the Gospels or of Protestant preaching, as noted in chapter 1 of this volume. As early as 1578, Laurence Chaderton—later one of the translators of the King James Bible—was calling for simplicity in preaching. Vivian Salmon states that "thereafter, one Puritan preacher after another proclaims the necessity of simplicity of speech." Salmon, *The Works of Francis Lodwick* (London: Longman, 1972), 73. C. John Sommerville has also emphasized the contribution of Puritanism to the "secularization of language," stating that Keith Thomas was "surprise[d], in studying the decline of a mystic faith in words, that it was caused more by Protestantism than by science. Protestant writers associated 'magical' philosophies and technologies with the Catholic Church and disparaged them at a time when scientists were still maintaining

open minds." Sommerville, "The Secularization of Language," in *The Seculari-*
zation of Early Modern England (New York: Oxford University Press, 1992),
44–54 at 50. Margreta de Grazia, "The Secularization of Language in the Seventeenth Century," *Journal of the History of Ideas* 41 (1980): 319–29, argues that a
breakdown of confidence in the interpretation of the Book of Scripture led to a
corresponding increase in the authority of the Book of Nature. The Protestant
critique of vain repetitions in prayer, described in chapter 4 of this volume, reinforces the importance and historical priority of theological critiques of rhetoric. See esp. Harold Fisch, "Puritanism and the Reform of Prose Style,"
English Literary History 19 (1952): 229–48; W. Fraser Mitchell, *English Pulpit Ora-*
tory from Andrewes to Tillotson (London: Society for Promoting Christian
Knowledge, 1932), esp. 337; Robert Adolph, *The Rise of Modern Prose Style* (Cambridge, MA: The MIT Press, 1968), esp. 97, 162–64, 190–91, 195, 208, 210–11;
Auksi, *Christian Plain Style*, 27, 268–69 (although he also acknowledges the
importance of the scientific tradition: see 308); Hill, *Intellectual Origins*, 129–30,
113; Brian Vickers, "The Royal Society and English Prose Style: A Reassess-
ment," in *Rhetoric and the Pursuit of Truth: Language Change in the Seventeenth*
and Eighteenth Centuries (Los Angeles: William Andrews Clark Memorial Library, 1985), 17 (arguing that the two movements were simultaneous). Michael
Clark, "The Word of God and the Language of Man: Puritan Semiotics and the
Theological and Scientific 'Plain Styles' of the Seventeenth Century," *Semiotic*
Scene 2 (1978): 61–90, defends Jones's thesis of a connection between religious
and scientific discourse (71), although he notes that the Puritan plain style predated the Royal Society (61) and tries to distinguish between the scientific and
theological plain styles.

85. Christopher Hill, *The English Bible and the Seventeenth-Century Revolution* (New
York: Penguin, 1993), 34, has stated the problem clearly: "We must differentiate
between the Biblical idiom in which men expressed themselves [in the seventeenth century], and their actions which we should today describe in secular
terms. But at the same time we must avoid the opposite trap of supposing that
'religion' was used as a 'cloak' to cover 'real' secular interests."

86. *Chips* 1:354.

87. *SR* 203–04.

88. Lourens P. van den Bosch, *Friedrich Max Müller: A Life Devoted to the Human-*
ities (Leiden: Brill, 2002), 517. This nearly six hundred page volume is now the
finest analysis of Müller available. Still useful as a brief introduction to Müller
is Joseph M. Kitagawa and John S. Strong, "Friedrich Max Müller and the Comparative Study of Religion," in Ninian Smart, John Clayton, Steven Katz, and
Patrick Sherry, eds., *Nineteenth Century Religious Thought in the West* (Cambridge:
Cambridge University Press, 1985), 3: 179–213.

89. For the definition of mythology as a "disease of language," see *SL* 1: 12–13; *Intro*
ST 7; *Intro SR* 41 n.1, 101; cf. *Intro SR* 252.

90. Delta [pseud.], *The Oxford Solar Myth: A Contribution to Comparative Mythology* (n.p., 1870).

91. In recent decades, however, Giuseppe Tucci, the scholar of Tantric Buddhism, applied a Müllerian analysis to the Buddhist formulas called *vidyā* and *dhāraṇī*: "Names and abstractions became gods. . . . Thus Buddhism is always open to a never-ceasing introduction of new gods who have no relation at all to any presences believed to exist in the actual experience of people, but are rather the transfiguration into supposed entities of mere names." Giuseppe Tucci, "Nomina Numina," in Joseph Kitagawa and Charles Long, eds., *Myths and Symbols* (Chicago: University of Chicago Press, 1969), 3–7 at 3, 7.

92. Müller's claimed role as disciplinary progenitor is well known. The interpretations of Müller as theologian and scientist are discussed in note 29. Brahm Datt Bharti wrote a scurrilous polemic against Müller as a missionary against Hinduism entitled *Max Müller: A Lifelong Masquerade (the inside story of a secular Christian missionary who masqueraded all his lifetime from behind the mask of literature and philology and mortgaged his pen, intellect and scholarship to wreck Hinduism)* (New Delhi: Erabooks, 1992). For Müller as colonialist, see Martin Maw, *Visions of India: Fulfilment Theology, the Aryan Race Theory, and the Work of British Protestant Missionaries in Victorian India* (New York: Peter Lang, 1990); David Chidester, "'Classify and Conquer: Friedrich Max Müller, Indigenous Religious Traditions, and Imperial Comparative Religion," in Jacob K. Olupona, *Beyond Primitivism: Indigenous Religious Traditions and Modernity* (New York: Routledge, 2004), 71–88.

93. See, e.g., Eric J. Sharpe, *Comparative Religion: A History* (La Salle, IL: Open Court, 1986), 35–46; Johannes H. Voigt, *F. Max Müller: The Man and His Ideas* (Calcutta: K. L. Mukhopadhyay, 1967), 27–34.

94. Donald Wiebe stated that Müller's "proposed science of religion . . . rest[s] wholly upon a scientific rather than a religio-theological foundation." Wiebe, "Religion and the Scientific Impulse in the Nineteenth Century: Friedrich Max Müller and the Birth of the Science of Religion," in *The Politics of Religious Studies: The Continuing Conflict with Theology in the Academy* (New York: St. Martin's Press, 1998), 9–30 at 11. Tomoko Masuzawa argued that Müller's primary concerns were with philology, rather than mythology and religion. Tomoko Masuzawa, "Accidental Mythology," in *In Search of Dreamtime: The Quest for the Origin of Religion* (Chicago: University of Chicago Press, 1993), 58–75. In part to contest van den Bosch's opposite view, Masuzawa reiterated her earlier position in a stronger form by stating that "Müller was generally indifferent to theology . . . he saw religious concerns and worries more as a propensity of other people around him that continually came to disturb his scholarship from without, rather than as something that motivated his own work from within." Masuzawa, "Our Master's Voice: F. Max Müller

after a Hundred Years of Solitude," *Method & Theory in the Study of Religion* 15
(2003): 305–28. Masuzawa's earlier analysis prompted a scathing review from
Ivan Strenski, in which he asserted that there was no disjunction between
Müller's philological studies and his religious presuppositions. Strenski,
"Misreading Max Müller," *Method & Theory in the Study of Religion* 8 (1996): 291–96
at 294–95. In a later article, Strenski stated: "Other founders [of religious
studies] like Friedrich Max Müller . . . never abandoned their theological and
ideological ambitions, even though they contributed greatly to the study of religion as a scientific endeavor." Strenski, "The Proper Object of the Study of Religion," in Slavica Jakelic and Lori Pearson, eds., *The Future of the Study of Religion*
(Leiden: Brill, 2004), 145–72 at 155. Timothy Fitzgerald, *The Ideology of Religious
Studies* (New York: Oxford University Press, 2000), 35, states that "Müller's
theory of the origin of natural religion . . . is surely a theological theory." Maurice
Olender argued similarly that "[Müller's] theological presuppositions determined his approach to linguistics and religious history. . . . Programmatically as
well as practically, some of the 19th-century 'sciences of religion' were thus
sacred sciences." Maurice Olender, *The Languages of Paradise: Race, Religion,
and Philology in the Nineteenth Century*, trans. Arthur Goldhammer (Cambridge,
MA: Harvard University Press, 1992), 87, 92. Van den Bosch, *Friedrich Max
Müller*, 517, argues that "from the very beginning, Müller's whole approach to
the study of religion had been determined by the problem of how to redefine
divine revelation in the presence of various forms of Higher Criticism of religion. . . . As such, Müller was a proponent of a theological view of the science of
religion . . . In contemporary terms, Müller's position may be described as that of
a religionist." Van den Bosch further argued that Müller's "linguistic investiga-
tions . . . reveal[ed] . . . [his] deeper religious inclinations," especially as exemplified in his concept of the Logos" (241–42). Cf. Maw, *Visions of India*, 32: "Expressed
in Christian terminology, [Müller's] was a quest for the Logos." As will be seen
from my analysis, I am largely in agreement with van den Bosch on these
points.

95. Franz Felix Adalbert Kuhn, *Über Entwicklungsstufen der Mythenbildung* (Berlin:
Vogt, 1874); Michel Bréal, *Mélanges de mythologie et de linguistique* (Paris:
Hachette, 1882), 9–10.

96. The resemblance of Müller's theory of myth to earlier theological attacks on
idolatry has been suggested before. Halbertal and Margalit noted the parallel
between religious iconoclasm and various Enlightenment critical projects, including the project of modern Anglophone philosophers to demythicize language
by exposing dead metaphors: "The idea that myth is a 'sickness of language' is
not new. Max Müller, in his study of myth . . . was perhaps the first to use the
expression though not the idea." Halbertal and Margalit, *Idolatry*, 267 (n.15 to p. 77).
Jan Assmann stated that "[William] Warburton explains [Egyptian] idolatry as a sickness of [hieroglyphic picture] writing, in the same way as more than 100 years

later Friedrich Max Müller explains myth as a sickness of language. Both idolatry
and mythology result from a literalistic misunderstanding of metaphor." Jan Assmann, "Pictures versus Letters: William Warburton's Theory of Grammatological Iconoclasm," in Jan Assmann and Albert I. Baumgarten, eds., *Representation
in Religion: Studies in Honor of Moshe Barasch* (Leiden: Brill, 2001), 297– 312 at
308. Assmann didn't note that Isaac Newton had argued for a similar connection
between hieroglyphs and idolatry long before Warburton. Perhaps more than any
other scholar, Peter Harrison, *Religion and the Religions in the English Enlightenment* (Cambridge: Cambridge University Press, 1990), has traced some of the
classical and early modern roots of the linguistic interpretation of polytheism.
Harrison noted the revival of such ideas, which sometimes drew explicitly on
classical authors, especially among the Cambridge Platonists, including Henry
More and Ralph Cudworth (56–57, 102), and among early comparative my-
thologist such as Samuel Shuckford and Jacob Bryant (142, 143, 146, 157). He
identified these thinkers, as well as Bacon and the deist John Toland, as possible
influences on Müller's later linguistic interpretation of mythology. The present
chapter will more fully develop and demonstrate such influences.

97. Müller affirmed: "I have the highest regard for Nominalism. I believe it has
purified the philosophical atmosphere of Europe more effectually than any
other system." *ST* 1: x. In *SL* 1: 12–13, following a passage that outlined how "Mythology . . . is in truth a disease of language," Müller shifted to a discussion of
the controversy between nominalism and realism and how this prepared the
way for the Reformation. However, Müller chose a new name for his theory—
Nominism—to distinguish it from earlier theories (ibid.). Müller was familiar
not only with Hobbes's, but also with older, medieval forms of nominalism,
including those of Roscelin, Abelard (*Intro ST* 51), and William of Ockham (*ST*
1: x). Müller also employed such nominalist technical terms as *flatus vocis*—that
words are mere sounds or puffs of breath—although he rejected the contention
that there could ever be such a thing as "mere words" (*ST* 2: 555).

98. *Chips* 4: 29ff. similarly complains compares the belief in infinitives to the belief
in ghosts and witches.

99. *SL* 2: 633.

100. *Into ST* 89.

101. *Chips* 5: 79; *OGR* 196; *NR* 313; *ALS* 2: 172 gives still another mechanism of personification: the fact that the Vedic hymns refer to the deities in the second
person.

102. *Chips* 2: 70: "It is the essential character of a true myth that it should no longer
be intelligible by a reference to the spoken language."

103. *SR* 203; cf. *CSM* 1: 296: "It is well known that the ancient gods were very polyonymous"; "Comparative Mythology," *Chips* 2: 71.

104. *SL* 2: 390–91: "One and the same object would receive many names, or would
become, as the Stoics called it, *polyonymous*, many-named having many *alias's*."

105. *SL* 2: 372; *ST* 2: 501: "Every word, without a single exception, which has an im-material meaning had originally a material meaning." His key examples in this passage are angel and spirit. *BW* 17: "Every word expressed in the beginning something that could be handled or smelt or seen or heard." *SR* 198: "The first materials of language supply expressions for such impressions only as are received through the senses." *Intro ST* 86: "Matter is all that is given us to know."

106. *PR* 296–97.

107. At the same time, contradicting his own announced empiricism, Müller insisted that language was also fundamentally conceptual: "Of course we begin with our senses, and with the percepts or intuitions with which they supply us. On them all our knowledge and language are founded, but they by themselves are neither knowledge nor language. Our percepts become knowledge by being named, and they become named by being conceived" (*ST* 2: 557). The ultimate illustration of this was the roots, elementary forms of language that had recently been discovered by philologists as the basis of all language. The linguistic fact of roots presented some further complications for Müller's crudely nominalist theory of myth. Before the names of deities—which which originally constituted appellatives, adjectives, or predicates—could exist, there was first a stage when language consisted entirely of roots, such as the root "to shine" (*div*). Then, by metaphorical extension, the sun was referred to as a "shiner." This naturally suggested that there was an agency underlying the activity of the sun. Cf. *SS* 35: "What can be simpler than the simple conviction that the regularly occurring events of nature require certain agents? Animated by this conviction the Vedic poets spoke not only of rain (Indu), but of a rainer (Indra), not only of fire and light as a fact, but of a lighter and burner, an agent of fire and light, a Dyaus (Zeus) and an Agni (ignis)." Müller referred to this as the "dynamic" stage of language (*NR* 390), to indicate that it was not yet the stage of myth. Myth came later, after the names thus given to the sun and other phenomena were fossilized into proper names. Müller's insistence on the conceptual nature of language may have reflected the philosophy of Kant, whose *Critique of Pure Reason* he translated into English. However, Müller's Kantianism never overcame the basic empiricism and nominalism that he inherited from the British tradition.

108. *NR* 127: "It is with percepts that all our knowledge, even the most abstract, ought to begin. We cannot perceive supernatural beings, or living agencies, but we can perceive the sky."

109. *Chips* 3: 222; cf. *SL* 2: 622.

110. *BW* 17; *SL* 1: 15, 32; *SL* 2: 368–74, 622. Müller on several occasions used Locke's famous example of how we know the meaning of the word "gold": *Intro ST* 70; *ST* 2: 556–57.

111. *SL* 1: 290–91; *SL* 2: 372–74; *SR* 147. Cf. Locke, *Essay*, 2: 57 (Book 3, chap. 6).

112. Hobbes may have proved the greatest influence on Müller's nominalism. Müller seconded John Stuart Mill's judgment that Hobbes was "one of the clearest and most consecutive thinkers whom this country or the world has produced." *ST* 2: 528; cf. 1: 74. The motto for Müller's *Science of Thought*—"No reason without language, . . . No language without reason" (*ST* xi)—was partly an *homage* to, and partly a criticism of Hobbes's statement that "The Greeks have but one word, logos, for both speech and reason; not that they thought there was no speech without reason, but no reasoning without speech." *Lev.* chap. 4, sec. 14. The same idea was also summed up in Hobbes's Latin pun: "Homo animal rationale, quia orationale," quoted in *Chips* 4: 222.

113. *SL* 2: 373–74, 380, 387; *SL* 1: 434; *ST* 2: 501; *SR* 196; *NR* 162; *AR* 205–06, 208–20. Cf. *Chips* 5: 69, 72–73; *ST* 2: 454 (deriving *anima* and animal from *AN*, to breathe). Hobbes's conclusion that "incorporeal substance" is an oxymoron is recalled by the following statement made by Müller in *ALS* 2: 2: "I have never been a very superstitious man, and have never believed in ghosts or spirits . . . in fact, in any-thing that can strike the material senses, and yet pretend to be immaterial, and has nothing to strike with. This is the whole problem of ghosts in a nutshell. If ghosts are immaterial, they cannot strike our eyes, or tickle our ears. . . . If, on the contrary, they are material, they are not ghosts." Cf. *Chips* 2: 157–58: "The name of Pan is connected with the Sanskrit name for wind, namely, 'pavana.' The root from which it is derived means, in Sanskrit, to purify . . . we have from 'pû,' to purify, the Greek 'Pân,' 'Pânos,' the purifying or sweeping wind, strictly corre-sponding to a possible Sanskrit form 'pav-an.' . . . It is thus that mythology arose."

114. *Intro ST* 86–87; cf. *LE* 2: 359–60: "Words for *soul* mostly turn out to have been at first words for the visible or tangible wind, or the breath issuing from the mouth. They became gradually divested of their material and visible attributes till they were brought to mean the vital breath or something stirring and striving within us, something of which breath was the visible sign."

115. *Chips* 1: 352, 355; 2: 52, 71, 75.

116. *Chips* 2: 54, 56.

117. *Chips* 2: 71; *SL* 2: 580; *SR* 199.

118. Tooke, *Diversions of Purley*, 2: 18; cf. 2: 20.

119. *Chips* 2: 76; cf. *SR* 266: "Are there any who still believe in the actual existence of false gods, or of gods not quite true? Do they believe that Bel, or Jupiter, or Varuna, or Shang-ti were so many individual beings existing by the side of Jeho-vah? They were, if you like, false, or, at least, imperfect names of God; but never the names of false or imperfect gods."

120. Bacon, *Temporis Partus Masculus*, in *Works*, 3: 520–40. See Rossi, *Francis Bacon*, 39.

121. *Chips* 5: 73.

122. Müller also glossed took the word *eidos* as synonymous with species, and attacked Charles Darwin for fetishizing the concept of species: see *ST* 1: 92, 108; 2: 568, 571.

123. E.g., the epigraph to this section. See also *SL* 2: 633: "The mischief begins when language forgets itself, and when we mistake the Word for the Thing, the Quality for the Substance, the *Nomen* for the *Numen*"; *Chips* 2: 76.

124. *SL* 2: 490.

125. *SL* 2: 613–14. Cf. *Chips* 2: 54; the discussion of "virtus" and "fortuna" in *BW* 9; *OGR* 120–21: "It may have seemed strange to many of us, that among the Ten Commandments which were to set forth, in the shortest possible form, the highest, the most essential duties of man, the second place should be assigned to a prohibition of any kind of images. [quotes Exodus 20:3–5] . . . Let those who wish to understand the hidden wisdom of these words, study the history of ancient religions. . . . Let them witness also the pomp and display in some of our own Christian churches and cathedrals. . . . One of the lessons which the history of religions certainly teaches is this, that the curse pronounced against those who would change the invisible into the visible, the spiritual into the material, the divine into the human, the infinite into the finite, has come true in every nation on earth. We may consider ourselves safe against the fetish-worship of the poor negro; but there are few of us, if any, who have not their own fetishes, or their own idols, whether in their churches, or in their hearts." See also Müller's Letter to the Duke of Argyll dated February 22, 1880, in *LL* 2: 85: "It always struck me as a wonderful guess at the Divine, when in the *Bhagavat Gita* the Supreme spirit is made to say: 'Even those who worship idols, worship me.' Paul's 'unknown God' springs from the same source. It was because I wanted a Substance for all Divine ideas that I traced the presence of the Infinite, or the Nameless, or the Unknown, as the antecedent though unconscious *sine qua non* of all later assertions about it; and I still think that unless we hold to that, we worship eidola which will be broken some day or other, but that which never can be broken, is that of which the eidolon is but the eidolon—the name but a name—and for which I find no better name than the Infinite, the Indefinite, or the Indefinable."

126. *Intro ST* 90–91; cf. *OGR* 24; *NR* 162–63; *ST* 1: 71–72.

127. *SL* 2: 573–74.

128. Masuzawa, *In Search of Dreamtime*, 74–75.

129. A number of scholars have noted that the French Orientalist Eugène Burnouf, with whom Müller worked briefly in Paris during 1845–1846, before proceeding to London, was the source both for Müller's Nomina-Numina formula and for the idea that it expressed, namely, that myth originates in a disease of language. Kitagawa and Strong, "Friedrich Max Müller," 201, stated that the formula "was most likely borrowed from Burnouf"; and that "it was also Burnouf who first suggested the theory of the origins of deities in a disease or confusion of language: what was a *nomen* became a *numen*, a view Müller was to argue for at great length" (183). Cf. Masuzawa, "Our Master's Voice," 314, n.14; Schwab, *Oriental Renaissance*, 478; Ernest Renan, *Nouvelles considérations sur le caractere*

général des peuples sémitiques et en particulier sur leur tendance au monothéisme (Paris: Imprimerie Impériale, 1859), 83; Pinard de la Boullaye, *L'Étude comparée des religions*, 2 vols. (Paris: Gabriel Beauchesne, 1922), 1: 346, n.2. Burnouf did use the formula on several occasions. I owe the first reference to Tomoko Masuzawa, personal communication. In his *Introduction à l'histoire du Buddhisme Indien*, Vol. 1 (Paris: Imprimerie Royale, 1844), 19–20, Burnouf argues for the importance of understanding the original meaning of the words used in ancient religions, such as the Buddhist term *nirvāṇa*: "Cela est d'autant plus nécessaire que les systèmes sont plus antiques et plus originaux, car il y a une époque où l'on peut dire de la théologie: *nomina numina*." Eugène Burnouf, *Le Bhâgavata Purâna*, vol. 3 (Paris: Imprimerie Royale, 1847), uses the formula (though not quite where Kitagawa and Strong say he does) even more directly to express the personification of language that occurs in myth. The Preface to this work, xcii, expresses something resembling the idea of a personification of language in mythology: "On sait par le Nirukta de Yâska, . . . quand il s'agit d'expliquer les noms les plus révérés des Vêdas, un double système d'interprétation qu'on pourrait nommer l'un direct, l'autre figuré. Le second de ses systèmes s'appuie sur les Itihâsas ou légendes fréquemment entremêlées aux Brâhmanas des Vêdas; ce système consiste à personnifier des mots, qui pris au propre désignent les grands corps ou les forces élémentaires de la nature, ou seulement les qualités qu'on leur attribue. L'autre acceptant, en général, le sens direct des mots, repose sur d'anciennes gloses des Vêdas, dont la tradition a été conservée par les scoliastes qui se sont appliqués à commenter ces livres." The formula itself appears at p. xciv: the Vedic commentators "nous signalent les textes qui ont servi de base aux conceptions de la mythologie populaire; ils nous donnes les preuves palpables de la marche et des procédés qu'a suivis l'esprit indien, quand il a personnifié les noms sacrés qu'on adressait comme des titres d'honneur aux forces physiques pur célébrer leur puissance et implorer leur secours. Si j'ai pu ailleurs, par un rapprochement de mots qui exprime une vérité historique, avancer que les Dieux et leur histoire ne sont d'ordinaire, aux plus anciennes époques du polythéisme, que la personnification des noms mêmes par lesquels on les invite au sacrifice, cela est vrai surtout des origines de la religion indienne; cela s'applique surtout à la transformation qu'ont subie les textes du Vêda, où tant de noms sont devenus des Dieux, *nomina numina*." It is highly likely that Müller knew of Burnouf's use of the formula, which may have served as the most proximate source for Müller's own theory of myth. However, there were numerous other, especially older sources in Christian comparative mythology that expressed the same idea, often in the same formula. These older sources would appear to have influenced both Burnouf and Müller, including the latter's identification of "polyonymy" as the cause of pagan polytheism. Perhaps Burnouf inspired Müller to explore the same tradition of comparative mythology from which he himself took the idea. To my knowledge, Müller's earliest use of the Nomina-Numina formula occurred in his winning 1849 essay for the Prix Volney, "Comparative Philology of the Indo-European Languages in its Bearing on the Early Civilisation of Mankind." See Joan Leopold, ed., *The Prix Volney*, 3 vols. in 4 parts (Dordrecht: Kluwer, 1999), vol. 3, *Contributions to Comparative Indo-European, African and Chinese Linguistics: Max Müller and Steinthal*. Although Leopold (37) says that Müller's theory of myth as a disease of language does not appear in this 1849 essay, that essay does include possibly his earliest use of the Nomina-Numina formula. While identifying traces of the Indo-European god Dyaus in the Vedas, Müller says (144 [ms. 67]): "For the names of gods are so intimately connected & grown together with the origin, the character, & history of the ancient gods, that a different name (nomen) would constitute an originally different god (numen)." On the origin of polytheism he adds (147 [ms. 73]): "Another consideration also is this, that, while at first they called god, Dyaus, they afterwards called Dyaus, god . . . This wrong conclusion I consider from a linguistic point of view, as one of the principal roots of polytheism in its usual contradictory sense."

130. Patricia Springborg argues that Hobbes's attack on the belief in incorporeal substances was influenced by the accounts of ancient paganism advanced by his acquaintances John Selden and Edward Lord Herbert of Cherbury as well as by Gerard Vossius. "Thomas Hobbes and Cardinal Bellarmine: Leviathan and 'The Ghost of the Roman Empire'," *History of Political Thought* 16 (1995): 503–31 at 510; Springborg, "Hobbes, Heresy, and the *Historia Ecclesiastica*," *Journal of the History of Ideas* 55 (1994): 553–71 at 563–65. Springborg names Vossius's *De theologia gentili*. Although Richard Tuck's connection of Hobbes with Selden has been disputed by Perez Zagorin, both note that Selden's *Titles of Honor* is mentioned favorably in *Leviathan*. Richard Tuck, *Natural Rights Theories: Their Origin and Development* (Cambridge: Cambridge University Press, 1979), 119; Perez Zagorin, "Clarendon and Hobbes," in King, *Thomas Hobbes*, 1: 430–52 at 434–35. In *De diis syris syntagmata* (London: printed by William Stansby, 1617), Selden claimed that the pagans' Jove or Jupiter is none other than a corrupt form of Jehovah. See the partial English translation in *The Fabulous Gods Denounced in the Bible*, trans. W. A. Hauser (Philadelphia: J. B. Lippincott & Co., 1880), 77–78. In *Titles of Honor* (London: printed by William Stansby for John Helme, 1614), 3, Selden presented an interpretation of pagan polytheism that closely resembled Hobbes's:

> Hardly was any [pagan] so Idolatrous that could not upon mature consideration (as *Orpheus* did in his last Will and Testament) confesse a unitie of Nature in that multiplicitie of Names, which fabulously they applied to the Deitie . . . Hence they could not but thinke, that the imperfections of the giddie-headed multitudes government would be much repaired, if they subjected themselves to some eminent *One*, as they saw themselves, and what els was to be in regard of the unseen Creator.

Selden, like Hobbes after him, raised the linguistic interpretation of polytheism in connection with a theory of political sovereignty: monotheism is a logical corollary of monarchy. Selden later explained that idolatry proper—the worship of statues called by the names of gods—was the result of first memorializing dead men in statues, then worshipping these statues, and, finally, transferring the names of gods to them (9). It was this progression or sleight-of-hand that led to error. The name Bel or Baal, meaning "Lord," was the title given to the greatest god of the pagans, and subsequently transferred to human kings and their images. Selden made the same claim in *De diis syris*, his main work on the pagan gods, where he quoted Hosea 2:16, where the Lord says that he will prohibit both the name and the memory of the "Baalim," the plural of "Baal," a name that "had been too often used for designating that of the fabulous gods" (Selden, *Fabulous Gods*, 74). Selden's concern was with the abuse of titles that, in some sense, constituted the heart of the offense of idolatry. Hobbes, as we saw, gave a similarly political interpretation of idolatry in his definition of that crime. Hobbes, "Of Religion," *Works*, 2: 249. Idolatry is indeed a linguistic offense, but also a misattribution or misappropriation of the titles properly belonging to the divinity: at once a form of sacrilege and *lèse-majesté* or treason against the Divine Majesty.

131. Stroumsa, "John Spencer," 3, n.9, suggests that Selden was one of the first to use the term "polytheism" (in Greek), in his *De diis syris*.

132. The nineteenth-century French historian of religions Pinard de la Boullaye, *L'Étude comparée*, 161–62, already pointed out that this formula had been used by John Selden and Ralph Cudworth (1617–1688) to explain the origins of pagan idolatry. De la Boullaye's discussion of Selden and Cudworth appeared under the heading of "The Origin of Idolatry" (*Origine de l'idolatrie*). Kitagawa and Strong, "Friedrich Max Müller," 183, 201, also noted de la Boullaye's attribution of the Nomina-Numina formula to Selden. H. Clavier, perhaps following de la Boullaye, also connected Selden and Cudworth with Müller's use of this formula. See H. Clavier, "Résurgences d'un Problème de Méthode en Histoire des Religions," *Numen* 15 (1968): 94–118 at 102, n.33. See also Stroumsa, "John Spencer," 10–11, 14, citing Selden as a major influence on both Ralph Cudworth and Gerard Vossius. Selden's "nomina/numina" formula was cited in Frodhi Ari Thorgilsson, *Aræ multiscii schedæ de islandia*, ed. Arni Magnusson and Christen Worm (Oxford, 1716), 81; and a similar formula appears also in William King, *Opera* (London, 1754), 91. Cudworth, *True Intellectual System*, 2: 526, quotes at length Vossius's version of the Nomina/Numina formula. Cf. Johannes Tarnovius (Johann Tarnow, 1586–1629), comm. on Hosea 13, quoted in Thomas Hall, *Samaria's Downfall* (London: printed by R. I. for Jo. Cranford, 1660), 53: "Reliqua numina sunt tantum nomina, nihil sunt, nihil possunt, nihil prosunt."

133. Quoted in de la Boullaye, *L'Étude comparée*, 1: 161. Translated in Kitagawa and Strong, "Friedrich Max Müller," 201.

134. Selden, *Titles of Honour*, 9. Cf. Selden, *Fabulous Gods*, 75, 135–40.

135. Müller cites (*AR* 74) the Greek Epicharmos (5th c. BCE) as precedent. See the discussion of Joseph Spence below in this chapter.

136. See Stroumsa, "John Spencer," 11–12, noting Vossius's influence on Herbert.

137. Edward Herbert, *Pagan Religion: A Translation of* De religione gentilium, ed. and trans. John Anthony Butler (Ottawa: Dovehouse Editions, 1996).

138. Id. at 300.

139. John Tillotson, *A Sermon Concerning the Unity of the Divine Nature and the B[lessed] Trinity* (London: printed for B. Aylmer and W. Rogers, 1693), 6–7.

140. John Turner, *Attempt towards an Explanation of the Theology and Mythology of the Antient Pagans, First Part* (London: printed by H. Hills for Walter Kettleby, 1687), notes, 162; cf. 165, 199.

141. Joseph Spence, *Polymetis* (London, 1747), 47.

142. See Stroumsa, "John Spencer," for an account of the centrality of the category of "idolatry" to early comparative religion in seventeenth-century Europe.

143. D. P. Walker, *Ancient Theology: Studies in Christian Platonism from the Fifteenth to the Eighteenth Century* (Ithaca: Cornell University Press, 1972); Frances W. Yates, *Giordano Bruno and the Hermetic Tradition* (Chicago: University of Chicago Press, 1964); Don Cameron Allen, *Mysteriously Meant: The Rediscovery of Pagan Symbolism and Allegorical Interpretation in the Renaissance* (Baltimore: Johns Hopkins University Press, 1970), esp. chapter 3, "The Renaissance Search for Christian Origins: Sacred History," 53–82, which deals with the period in question here.

144. On the two basic theories of the relation of polytheism to monotheism, as either anticipation or degeneration, see Stroumsa, "John Spencer," 9.

145. Ross, *Pansebeia*, 516. Ross further claimed that the deity so worshipped was the Sun (139–40, 516).

146. Thomas Fuller, *A Pisgah-Sight of Palestine* (London: printed by J. F. for John Williams, 1650), 126.

147. Id. at 127.

148. Randle Holme, *The Academy of Armory, or, A Storehouse of Armory and Blazon* (Chester, 1688), 222–23. Archbishop of Canterbury John Tillotson, *A Sermon*, 4-6, similarly maintained that the "greatest and wisest" had always affirmed the unity of the deity. But just as an ocean is given different names by the different countries that border it "so [the ancients] gave several *Names* to this *One Deity* . . . Or else, they adored the several Perfections and Powers of the *One Supreme God* under several *Names* and *Titles*." However, he allowed that the pagans also regarded the subordinate deities as really distinct (3).

149. Warburton, *Divine Legation*, 2: x (there are two pages in the preface with this number; this is the second such).

150. Cudworth, *True Intellectual System*, vol. 2, table of contents to p. 477: "For they supposing God to pervade all things, and to be all things, did therefore look

upon every thing as sacred or divine; and theologize the parts of the world and natures of things; titularly making them gods and goddesses" (table of contents to pp. 507, 510). "The Pagans did thus verbally personate and deify the things of nature," but without the intention of worshipping them separately from the One Creator (table of contents to pp. 513, 515).

151. Id. at table of contents to p. 477.

152. Id. at 526.

153. Edward Stillingfleet, *Origines Sacræ, or, A Rational Account of the Grounds of Christian Faith* (London: printed by R. W. for Henry Mortlock, 1662), 587 (Book 3, chap. 5).

154. Id. at 577 (Book 3, chap. 5). See also Robert Boyle, *Some Considerations Touching the Style of the Holy Scriptures* (London: printed for Henry Herringman, 1661), 158–59.

155. Stillingfleet, *Origines Sacræ*, 577–78 (Book 3, chap. 5).

156. John Edwards, *Theologia Reformata* (London: printed for John Lawrence, John Wyat, and Ranew Robinson, 1713), 343–44.

157. Edwards, *A Discourse*, 224.

158. Id. at 224–30. See Selden, *Fabulous Gods*, 77–78: "For even the name Jove became also corrupted in the pronunciation of the Europeans by the use of the tetragrammaton, or four mystic Hebrew letters, J, H, V, H. Thus, Jupiter is none other than Jovispeter, that is, Iao pater or Jaou pater, which means the same, Jehovah, father. . . . Zeus, Jupiter, and Dios are names which signify not so much this or that idol as they fitly designate the Mighty and Everlasting Creator of the world." Müller later used the same process of etymological analysis for the same purpose, to assert the unity underlying the different names of God. Yet with advances in philology, he no longer assimilated the Indo-European names for their chief god to the Hebrew.

159. Edwards, *Discourse*, 252.

160. Edwards, *Theologia*, 344. Richard Brocklesby, *An Explication of the Gospel-Theism and the Divinity of the Christian Religion* (London: printed by J. Heptinstall, 1706), 159–60, also criticized the "polyonymy" thesis, which he attributed to "Some unwise Theologers," including Kircher. Brocklesby contended that "the Philosophic-Pagan Theology," exemplified by the Stoics, was "really . . . a pompous futility," and that the idea "that the Pagans Polytheism was in part not *real*, but *apparent* only," was a fiction. The pagans populated the world with divinities, whom they worshipped: such behavior was idolatry, no matter what interpretation one placed upon it.

161. Warburton, *Divine Legation*, 2: 185.

162. Warburton also affirmed a version of the linguistic interpretation of pagan polytheism and idolatry that resembled Selden's. Warburton, *Divine Legation*, 2: 286–87, referred to Egyptian religion as a "religion of Names," the result of a propensity to "decorate their Gods with distinguished Titles" The Jews had

inherited this tendency, as evidenced by Moses's inquiry after God's name, which He answered by "I AM" (Exodus 3:14). In a later version of the book included in his *Works*, Warburton added that this episode proved the Jews were "a people not only lost to all knowledge of the UNITY (for the asking for a *name* necessarily implied their opinion of a plurality), but likewise possessed with the very spirit of Egyptian idolatry." *The Works of the Right Reverend William Warburton* (London: printed by J. Nichols for T. Cadell, 1788), 2: 567. He found the divine rejection of the religion of names in Zechariah 14:9: "*In that day shall there be one Lord, and* HIS NAME ONE" (id. at 568).

163. Warburton, *Divine Legation*, 2: 66, 96.

164. Id. at 2: 151–52.

165. Ibid.

166. Id. at 2: 154.

167. Id. at 2: 166, 172.

168. Id. at 2: 141; cf. 170–71.

169. Warburton's emphasis on the connection between hieroglyphics and idolatry recalled some earlier proposals for a universal language (described in chapter 3 in this volume) that took hieroglyphics as a precedent, and Isaac Newton's earlier argument that hieroglyphs were a principal cause of idolatry. See James E. Force, "Biblical Interpretation," in Richard H. Popkin and Arjo Vanderjagt, ed., *Scepticism and Irreligion in the Seventeenth and Eighteenth Centuries* (Leiden: Brill, 1993), 282–305 at 290–91. On the connection between Newton's views on idolatry and those of Cudworth, see note 70 in this chapter.

170. Moses Mendelssohn, *Jerusalem, oder über religiöse Macht und Judentum* (Berlin: Friedrich Maurer, 1783), presents a similar theory of hieroglyphs which he may have taken from Warburton.

171. *PR* 387.

172. *India* 18.

173. Hobbes, *Works*, 2: 227: "*Idolatry* therefore did easily fasten upon the greatest part of men; and almost all the nations did worship God in images and resemblances of finite things; and they worshipped spirits or vain visions, perhaps out of fear calling them devils."

174. David Hume, *The Natural History of Religion* (London: A. Millar, 1757), secs. 1–3.

175. *SR* 251: "To maintain that all religion begins with fetishism . . . is simply untrue. . . ."; *LE* 1: 168: "It is a fact . . . that fetishism represents a secondary stage in the growth of religion, and that it presupposes an earlier stage, in which the name and the concept of something divine, the predicate of every fetish, was formed." Müller devoted an entire lecture of *OGR* to the question "Is Fetishism a Primitive Form of Religion?" See Müller's distinction of "fetish" from "idol" at *OGR* 57–58. On most other occasions (e.g., *OGR* 120–21), he did not keep these categories rigorously separate.

176. *SL* 2: 449.

177. *SL* 2: 450; *Chips* 5: 102–03.

178. Jones, *Works*, 3: 319–97 at 321–22.

179. William Westall, *The Hindoos: Including a General Description of India, its Government, Religion, Manners and Customs*, 2 vols. (London: M. A. Nattali, 1847), 1: 143–44.

180. Id. at 144; quoting H. T. Colebrooke, "On the Vedas," in *Asiatic Researches* 8 (London, 1808 [1805]): 377–498 at 395. Foreshadowing another of Müller's ideas, he added that among ancient peoples it was the Sun that held "the most distinguished place" of worship "as the great pervading soul of the universe." Westall, *The Hindoos*, 154.

181. Robert Chatfield, *An Historical Review of the Commercial, Political, and Moral State of Hindoostan, from the Earliest Period to the Present Time: The Rise and Progress of Christianity in the East* (London: J. M. Richardson, 1808), 211.

182. Id. at 215–16.

183. *Chips* 1: 351–52, 361; cf. *NR* 314: "Words which display their radical elements retain a certain perspicuity, and are less liable therefore to mythological misunderstandings. Thus the Semitic languages in which the triliteral skeleton is generally clearly discernible in every word have produced less of poetical mythology than the Aryan languages."

184. Thomas Hobbes, "On the Nicene Creed," trans. in *Lev.*, pp. 498–521 at p. 499.

185. *Chips* 1: 348–49 (emphasis added).

186. Cf. *SR* 251; *SL* 2: 455–56: "Before the Greeks could call the sky, or the sun, or the moon *gods*, it was absolutely necessary that they should have framed to themselves some idea of the godhead. We cannot speak of King Solomon unless we first know what, in a general way, is meant by King, nor could a Greek speak of gods in the plural before he had realized, in some way or other, the general predicate of the godhead."

187. *Chips* 1: 27ff., 347; *PR* 180–81.

188. *Chips* 1: 27–28. Müller also referred to the religion of the Vedas as "henotheism, a worship of single gods, which must be carefully distinguished both from monotheism, or the worship of one god, involving a distinct denial of all other gods, and from polytheism, the worship of many deities which together form one divine polity, under the control of one supreme god," *OGR* 295; cf. 277: "*Henotheism* [is] . . . a successive belief in single supreme gods. . . ."; *Chips* 1: 350: "The belief in One God, is properly called monotheism, whereas the term of henotheism would best express the faith in a single god."; *SR* 80–81: "Henotheistic religions differ from polytheistic because, although they recognize the existence of various deities, or names of deities, they represent each deity as independent of all the rest, as the only deity present in the mind of the worshipper at the time of his worship and prayer."; *OGR* 266: "Henotheism [is] . . . a belief and worship of those single objects, whether semi-tangible or intangible, in which man first suspected the presence of the invisible and the infinite."

189. *CSM* 1: 139; *OGR* 277; *PR* 180.
190. *Chips* 1: 347.
191. *Chips* 1: 27; cf. 2: 75; *SL* 2: 453; *VP* 25–26; *SS* 36. Other divine names, such as Mitra and Indra, had already become proper names, or were on the point of doing so, and could no longer be recognized as referring to natural phenomena. *Chips* 1: 27.
192. *Chips* 2: 70.
193. *SL* 2: 414–15.
194. *CSM* 2: 429; *HS* 511.
195. *Chips* 1: 37; 4: 258; *PR* 201: "In the ancient Vedic religion there is no sign as yet of graven images." *CSM* 1: 148: "Another important feature, which shows how far the Greek gods have advanced beyond their Vedic relatives, is the pronounced human form of the Greek gods. . . . Here again we find the germs only in the Veda, far removed as yet from the perfection of Greek mythology. . . . But the creation of a Zeus or Athene by Phidias, of a Hermes by Praxiteles, of an Artemis or an Aphrodite, like those seen in the Louvre, was beyond the Vedic horizon."
196. *SBE*, vol. 32, *Vedic Hymns*, Part I, trans. Max Müller, p. 1. Müller translates all or part of this hymn also in *HS* 521–23; *ALS* 232; *SS* 42, 46–48. Another hymn, *Rig Veda* 1.164, has often been singled out as philosophical and monotheistic. John Muir stated that this hymn "may . . . be held to convey the more general idea that all the gods, though differently named and represented, are in reality one—*pollon onomaton morphe mia* [in Greek]." See Muir, "Progress of the Vedic Religion towards Abstract Conceptions of the Deity," in *Original Sanskrit Texts on the Origin and History of the People of India*, vol. 5 (London: Trübner & Co., 1870), 350–420 at 353.
197. Müller acknowledged that the hymn was relatively recent, but as a *Mantra* (hymn) text it still predated the *Brāhmaṇas*, which were responsible for the decline of Vedic religion into mythology. *SBE* 32: 3–6; *HS* 523. Moreover, he sharply interrogated the prejudice that would ascribe such a hymn to a recent date simply on the basis of its monotheistic tendencies. *SBE* 32: 3; *HS* 512.
198. *HS* 433; *SBE* 32: 12; *RV*, 3: viii; *PR* 197.
199. *SBE* 32: 1; *SS* 46.
200. Müller used this line on other occasions: *Intro SR* 81; "Semitic Monotheism," *Chips* 1: 373; *SL* 2: 438–39.
201. Acts 17:23.
202. *HS* 512.
203. This line from the Vedas is often quoted (like the following quote from the *Bhagavad Gītā*) as evidence of the ecumenical nature of Hinduism.
204. *AR* 112.
205. Van den Bosch, *Friedrich Max Müller*, 152. Cf. *TPR* x; *ST* 1: 74.
206. *TPR* 361.
207. *TPR* ix.
208. *TPR* x–xi.

209. In Müller's manuscripts there is an undated passage that makes these connections even more explicit. The "Mantissa to Lev[iticus] I," in Bodleian MS Eng. 2357, pp. 130–37, returned again to the linguistic and religious differences between Jews and Greeks, and explained the motivation for the creation of mythological entities as stemming from the desire on the part of human beings to communicate with the divine. In the first chapter of Leviticus, God provides Moses with instructions for various types of burnt offerings, the smoke from which may reach to the heavens as "a pleasing odor to the Lord." As such, it already proposes one solution to the perennial problem of communication between humans and God. In his "mantissa" or brief commentary, Müller stressed that once the idea of a transcendent deity arises, this problem is sharpened. Aryans and Semites have grappled with this problem in different ways. The key distinction concerned the existence and nature of intermediate beings capable of bridging the gap between human and divine:

> If once the idea of the Godhead is so conceived that the divine nature is totally separated from human nature, then, unless all religion becomes extinct, nothing remains for a time but the admission of intermediate beings. . . . In all parts of the world, where living beings are separated by a river, human ingenuity will devise means of communication: and among all races of men where reason has created an impassable gulf between the Divine and the Human, faith will throw its bridges, or strive to soar across on angels' wings.

Müller went on to explain how this dynamic, shared by all religions, had led to different yet parallel results in Greek and Jewish religion. The Greeks invented the ideas of lesser gods and goddesses, subsidiary to Zeus, as well as of *daimones* and angels or messengers. Later these "assumed a definite office, both in the mythology and in the philosophy of the Greek nation, and their name in the later language of Greece, conveyed the idea of real beings, if not of individual persons" (134). Something similar happened in Judaism, where the idea of a personal God speaking with Moses face-to-face gave way to the idea of a transcendent deity of whom it is said "no man can see His face & live" (136). This distancing of God from man led to the admission of messengers or angels, as in Greece, although among Jews "a deeper assurance of the divine majesty" prevented the development of "rank mythology." Müller added that "Hebrew scholars have pointed out long ago that the word which in the Old Testament is translated by angels, meant originally no more than messenger." This point had been made also by Hobbes. In all of this, there is no mention of what Müller clearly regarded as the best solution to the problem posed by the idea of a transcendent God: the Christian concept of the Incarnation, or Logos, the linguistic dimensions of which Müller consistently emphasized in his writings on the subject, just as he emphasized the linguistic dimensions of the inferior solutions to this problem posed by the mythological traditions.

210. *Chips* 1: 351.
211. *SL* 1: 391.
212. *SL* 1: 143.
213. For William Jones's efforts along these lines, see Thomas Trautmann, "The Mosaic Ethnology of Asiatick Jones," in *Aryans and British India*, 28–61.

CHAPTER 3

1. Matthew Henry, *Commentary on the Whole Bible* (London: printed for J. and B. Sprint, 1706–1721), on Genesis 11.
2. Brian Houghton Hodgson, *Preeminence of the Vernaculars; or the Anglicists Answered* (Serampore: Serampore Press, 1837), 46.
3. George Grierson, *The Bible in India* (London: British and Foreign Bible Society, 1904), 4, refers to "the Indian Babel" as a challenge for Christianity.
4. Indeed, in England the legal reformer and utilitarian philosopher Jeremy Bentham, who invented the word "codification" to describe his proposal to replace the common law with statutes, explicitly identified codification with the work of Reformation and the attack on linguistic idols. See Yelle, "Bentham's Fictions."
5. R. V. De Smet, "Categories of Indian Philosophy and Communication of the Gospel," *Religion and Society* 10 (1963): 20–26 at 20.
6. Cohn, "Command of Language," in *Colonialism and its Forms of Knowledge*, 16-56; Sugirtharajah, *Imagining Hinduism*, 73: "Both orientalists and missionaries aimed at bringing about a separation between the written and the oral, privileging the written. The outcome of such an exercise resulted in the production of textual knowledge about Hinduism that had little relevance to the vast majority of Hindus whose lives were not directly informed by written texts." Philip C. Almond, *The British Discovery of Buddhism* (Cambridge: Cambridge University Press, 1988), 139: "Buddhism was reified as a textual object. By the middle of the Victorian period, Buddhism was seen as essentially constructed by its textuality." The bias toward locating "authentic" Indian religion in written texts began early. In the National Library in Kolkata, there is an unpublished manuscript on Hindu religion in South India authored in 1786 by David Simpson, a servant of the Company in the area of Trichinopoly. This book provided a systematic account, in two parts, of Brahmanical religion. Part I, pp. 10–13, treats "Of the Vedam, Shastrums, and the Sanscrit Language": "The Vedam, Bedam or Beids is a Book containing the System of Religion of the Brahmins, as transmitted to them by Brimhah [Brahmā]. My Shastree [Brahmin priest] gives me but an indistinct account of the time when the Vedam was committed to writing; but says, that it is divided into four Books or Parts— . . . The Shastrums were also written Books . . . Both the Vedam & the Shastrums are written in the Sanscrit Language, but in the Character which is common in the different countries where they are used . . . My Shastree assures me, there is no

Sanscrit Character now existing. I show'd him Mr. Halhed's Book with the Sanscrit alphabet & extracts from the Shastrums [Nathaniel Brassey Halhed, *A
Code of Gentoo Laws* (London, 1776)], which I told him were the proper Sanscrit
Characters, in which the Vedam & Shastrums were originally written.—He
replied, that he knew not, nor does he think any man knows the Character, in
which their sacred Books were first written; but, that the Characters I had
shown him he knew, were the Nagarum [Devanāgarī] Characters in common
use in the Northern districts in Bengal at this day." Simpson assumes that the
Hindu scriptures were "originally written."

7. See references in chapter 1, note 18, in this volume. However, Sheldon Pollock,
   "Deep Orientalism? Notes on Sanskrit and Power beyond the Raj," in Carol
   Breckenridge and Peter van der Veer, eds., *Orientalism and the Postcolonial Predicament* (Philadelphia: University of Pennsylvania Press, 1993), 76–133, has
   rightly pointed out that the privileging of texts was an important phenomenon
   also in precolonial India. As the very longevity and authority of the Veda in
   India shows, the difference between precolonial Indian and colonial British attitudes toward language cannot be attributed exclusively to an emphasis on
   texts, especially if this term is extended to include oral compositions and
   manuscripts.

8. This policy change appears to have had some immediate effects. India Office
   Records V/ 24/ 946, *Report of the General Committee of Public Instruction of the
   Presidency of Fort William in Bengal for the year 1836* (Calcutta: Baptist Mission
   Press, 1837), 2, shows that the number of students studying English nearly dou-
   bled in the year following the Committee's decision, while there was a slight
   decrease in the number of students studying Sanskrit during the same period.

9. Quoted in Zastoupil and Moir, *The Great Indian Education Debate*, 165–66.

10. Charles Trevelyan, *The English Instructor* (Calcutta: Baptist Mission Press, 1834),
    4–5. Cf. Macaulay in Zastoupil and Moir, *The Great Indian Education Debate*,
    291: "You will now ask, Where is this great and wonderful knowledge to be
    found?—and how may we obtain it, and so become as wise and great as the
    English are? All this knowledge is to be found in the English language. And if
    you learn this language, it will be the key by which you may unlock the treasury
    of all knowledge."

11. Bacon, *Novum Organum*, Book 1, chap. 129.

12. Mullens is probably referring to a member of one of the Hindu reformist
    groups such as the Brahmo Samaj founded by Rammohun Roy earlier in the
    nineteenth century.

13. Joseph Mullens, *Vedantism, Brahmism, and Christianity Examined and Com-
    pared* (Calcutta: Baptist Mission Press for the Calcutta Christian Tract and Book
    Society, 1852), 236.

14. John Aubrey, *Remaines of Gentilisme and Judaisme* (London, 1686–1687); reprint
    ed. (London: W. Satchell, Peyton, and Co., 1881), 68.

15. Cf. "On the Origins of Printing," 206, in the Hindu reformist paper Dig Darshan 5 (August, 1818), cited in Kopf, *British Orientalism*, 158. Charles Grant expressed clearly the relation between printing and Christianity: "With our language, much of our useful literature might, and would, in time, be communicated. The art of Printing, would enable us to disseminate our writings in a way the Persians could never have done . . . Hence the Hindoos would see the great use we make of reason on all subjects, and in all affairs; they also would learn to reason . . . Except a few Brahmins, who consider the concealment of their learning as part of their religion, the people are totally misled as to the system and phenomena of nature; and their errors of this branch of science, . . . may be more easily demonstrated to them, than the absurdity and falsehood of their mythological legends. . . . But undoubtedly the most important communication which the Hindoos could receive through the medium of our language, would be the knowledge of our religion, the principles of which are explained in a clear, easy way, in various tracts circulating among us, and are completely contained in the inestimable volume of Scripture. . . . Wherever this knowledge should be received, idolatry, with all the rabble of its impure deities, its monsters of wood and stone, its false principles and corrupt practices, its delusive hopes and vain fears, its ridiculous ceremonies and degrading superstitions, its lying legends and fraudulent impositions, would fall." Grant, "Observations on the State of Society among the Asiatic Subjects of Great Britain, particularly with Respect to Morals; and on the Means of Improving it Written Chiefly in the Year 1792," in *General Appendix to the Report from the Select Committee on the Affairs of the East India Company*, No. 1 (1831–1832), 61; reprinted in *British Parliamentary Papers, Colonies: East India*, volume 5 (Shannon: Irish University Press, 1977).

16. "On the Effect of the Native Press in India," *Friend of India*, Quarterly Series 1, No. 1 (Serampore, 1820): 119–40 at 135–36.

17. J. S. M. Hooper, *Bible Translation in India, Pakistan and Ceylon*, 2nd ed. (Oxford: Oxford University Press, 1963), 33. Episode cited in Swapan Chakravorty and Abhijit Gupta, eds., *Print Areas: Book History in India* (Delhi: Permanent Black, 2004), 11. As Martha Kaplan has pointed out in a different context, printing was a "key aspect[ ] . . . of the magic of the colonial state," or what she refers to as a "state familiar." Kaplan, "The Magical Power of the Printed Word," in Meyer and Pels, *Magic and Modernity*, 183–99 at 184, 186. If so, this "familiar" proved to be a jealous god.

18. *NR* 550–51; *PR* 216.

19. *ASL* 457.

20. *RR* 75; *ALS* 2: 97–98. Cf. *ALS* 2: 42: "When Luther was translating the Bible in the castle of the Wartburg, he little dreamt that he was laying the foundation of a new Church in Germany and in all Teutonic countries, nor did Rammohun Roy on his death-bed at Bristol foresee what would grow up from the few hints

he had thrown out as to the possibility of a reform and revival of the ancient national religion of his country."

21. ALS 2: 41: "For years, for centuries, nay for thousands of years, this Veda on which their whole religion was founded had been to them a kind of invisible power, much as the Bible was in the early centuries of the Papacy, when the privileged only were supposed to know it and were allowed to interpret it. In discussions between Brahmans and Christian missionaries, . . . [the] Veda itself was never produced when they were asked to point out chapter and verse." See also "On encouraging the cultivation of the Sungskrit Language among the Natives," *Friend of India*, Monthly Series 2, No. 5 (1822): 131–[147] at 133: "The language which most resembles the Sungskrit in imparting power to the sacerdotal tribe, is the Latin as used in the Romish church. This indeed, in the dark ages, acquired a kind of sacred character, being thus regarded by the vulgar throughout Europe for the space of at least nine centuries." See the translation of C. Gowan's Sanskrit declamation, in *Primitiae Orientales*, vol. 3 (Calcutta: [College of Fort William], 1804), 84: "The progressive improvement of literature in the East has at length unfolded to us a language, long hidden under the Veil of Mystery. The Shanscrit, for Ages supposed to be known only to the Brahmans, who considered it too sacred to be imparted to an alien, is now open to our researches."

22. *LE* 2: 126, 220. Cf. Letters to Olcott cited in Sugirtharajah, *Imagining Hinduism*, 46.

23. *LL* 2: 350ff.; cited in van den Bosch, *Friedrich Max Müller*, 161.

24. Sugirtharajah, *Imagining Hinduism*, 67. See also Müller's letter noting his intent to help missionaries, cited in ibid. Indeed, in his preface to the *SBE*, Müller noted the distasteful aspect of many of these texts. Cf. the thesis that "the translation of the best works extant in the Shanscrit into the popular languages of India, would promote the extension of science and civilization," trans. by A. B. Tod, in *Primitiae Orientales*, vol. 3, pp. 60–61: "If we view the present manners and habits of European nations, and reflect upon the comparative state of backwardness they were in at former periods, which might in some measure be ascribed to the ignorance of the times, and the influence the monks and priests in those days possessed over the people; when we come to consider that the acquisition of knowledge and the more extensive enquiries into literature and science gradually occasioned the diminution of confidence placed in the monks, and ultimately brought the people to their present state of perfection; we may confidently hope that the same happy consequences would be the result arising from the translation of the Shanscrit works; particularly as it is supposed that they contain many contradictions concerning their Deities and Devotions. When these circumstances shall have been made manifest to the people, it is not impossible that they might forsake and relinquish many of their foolish and idolatrous prejudices."

25. Friedrich Max Müller, Letter to Baron Christian Bunsen, cited in Sugirtharajah, *Imagining Hinduism*, 64–65: "After the last annexation the territorial conquest of India ceases—what follows next is the struggle in the realm of religion and of spirit, in which, of course, centres the interests of the nations. India is much riper for Christianity than Rome or Greece were at the time of St. Paul."

26. Quoted in Eric J. Ziolkowski, *A Museum of Faiths: Histories and Legacies of the 1893 World's Parliament of Religions* (Atlanta: Scholars Press, 1993), 157–58.

27. *Chips* 4: 301–02. Cf. *Chips* 5: 62; SBE 1: xv: "Nor must we forget that though oral tradition, when once brought under proper discipline, is a most faithful guardian, it is not without its dangers in its incipient stages. Many a word may have been misunderstood, many a sentence confused, as it was told by father and son, before it became fixed in the tradition of a village community, and then resisted by its very sacredness all attempts at emendation." Elsewhere, perhaps in a rare moment of self-reflection, Müller acknowledged that books were apt also to become a "fetish" (*NR* 564).

28. "Letters on the State of Christianity in India, in which the Conversion of the Hindoos is considered as impracticable, &c.&c.—By the Abbé J. A. Dubois, Missionary in Mysore," *Friend of India*, Quarterly Series 3, No. 10 (Serampore, 1825): 187–392 at 238, 240–41.

29. Sugirtharajah, *Imagining Hinduism*, 47.

30. See Halbfass, "Neo-Hinduism, Modern Indian Traditionalism, and the Presence of Europe," in *India and Europe*, 217–46.

31. Some examples of the influence of Protestant literalism on Rammohan's thinking are discussed in chapter 4 in this volume. For Dayananda's concept of the Vedas as a canon, see Jack E. Llewellyn, "From Interpretation to Reform: Dayanand's Reading of the Vedas," in Laurie Patton, ed., *Authority, Anxiety, and Canon* (Albany: SUNY Press, 1994), 235–51. On Dayananda more generally, see J. T. F. Jordens, *Dayananda Sarasvati: His Life and Ideas* (Oxford: Oxford University Press, 1978) and Kenneth W. Jones, *Arya Dharm: Hindu Consciousness in 19th-Century Punjab* (Berkeley: University of California Press, 1976).

32. A number of Rammohun's published writings consist of translations of Upaniṣads into English and Bengali. For Dayananda's role as vernacular expositor, see Llewellyn, "From Interpretation to Reform," 245.

33. See, however, the discussion in chapter 4 in this volume regarding indigenous influences on each of these individuals' critiques of chanting, and Noel Salmond, *Hindu Iconoclasts: Rammohun Roy, Dayananda Sarasvati, and Nineteenth-Century Polemics against Idolatry* (Waterloo, ON: Wilfred Laurier University Press, 2004), which points out that Rammohun and Dayananda were not merely passive conduits for Protestantism.

34. Dayananda Sarasvati, *The Light of Truth* [Satyartha Prakasha], trans. Ganga Prasad Upadhyaya, revised ed. (Allahabad: Kala Press, 1960 [1908]), 394. Jones, *Arya Dharm*, 110, has noted other uses by the Arya Samaj of "pope" as "an

epitaph [sic: epithet] of condemnation assimilated from the Protestant missionaries."

35. Llewellyn, "From Interpretation to Reform," 239–40.

36. Sarasvati, *Light of Truth*, 445.

37. Gyan Prakash, "Between Science and Superstition: Religion and the Modern Subject of the Nation in Colonial India," in Meyer and Pels, *Magic and Modernity*, 39–60, describes similar processes of rationalization and reform of Hindu traditions, including those involving Dayananda and the Arya Samaj.

38. Inden, *Imagining India*, 86.

39. In the sixteenth century, Richard Eden had called Native Americans "a smooth and bare table unpainted . . . upon the which you may at the first paint or write what you list, as you cannot upon tables already painted." Quoted in Robert A. Williams, *The American Indian in Western Legal Thought* (New York: Oxford University Press, 1990), 130–31.

40. Alexander Duff, *India and Indian Missions: Including Sketches of the Gigantic System of Hinduism Both in Theory and Practice* (Edinburgh: John Johnstone, 1839); reprint ed. (New York: AMS Press, 1988), 246–55. Cf. Horace Hayman Wilson, *Essays and Lectures Chiefly on the Religion of the Hindus*, vol. 2 (London: Trübner and Co., 1862), 79: "The practical religion of the Hindus is by no means a concentrated and compact system, but a heterogeneous compound, made up of various and not unfrequently incompatible ingredients, and that to a few ancient fragments it has made large and unauthorized additions, most of which are of an exceedingly mischievous and disgraceful nature."

41. See full title of Duff, *India*, in preceding note.

42. Id. at 204.

43. Id. at 65–66.

44. Id. at 75–76.

45. Id. at 79.

46. Id. at 212.

47. John Muir, *The Course of Divine Revelation* (Calcutta: Baptist Mission Press, 1846), 6–7.

48. "On the Cultivation of Sungskrita by Native Youth," *Friend of India*, Monthly Series 2 (Serampore, 1819): 426–42. Quoted in Anand Amaladass and Richard Fox Young, *The Indian Christiad: A Concise Anthology of Didactic and Devotional Literature in Early Church Sanskrit* (Anand, Gujarat: Gujarat Sahitya Prakash, 1995), 34–35. Cf. the comparable sentiments of the Rev. R. Caldwell, *The Languages of India in their Relation to Missionary Work* (London: R. Clay, Sons, and Taylor, 1875), 13: "The people by whom these languages are spoken, however cultured or however rude, belong to the same great family to which we ourselves belong . . . And it is not too much, I think, to assert respecting the various languages they speak, that they are as suitable as our own for being used as vehicles of Christian teaching."

49. "On the Cultivation of Sungskrita," 426–42.

50. Id. at 536.

51. Duff, *India*, 345, 347–48; cf. Homi Bhabha, *The Location of Culture* (New York: Routledge, 1994), 33, 101. "On encouraging the cultivation of the Sungskrit Language," 131, notes the earlier query by "A Friend of India" (who may be either Duff or Trevelyan) "whether, since the Sungskrit language has been the grand medium through which the Hindoo system of idolatry has been propagated and supported, to encourage the cultivation of it among the natives be not incompatible with seeking the improvement and welfare of India."

52. Viswanathan, *Masks of Conquest*, 113.

53. Duff, *India*, 378.

54. Id. at 404–06.

55. Id. at 406.

56. Id. at 708.

57. Id. at 543–44.

58. Duff, *New Era*, 38–42.

59. Cf. Sugirtharajah, *Bible and the Third World*, 58–59, describing analogous developments in Africa: "In translating biblical truths into vernacular languages, the [missionary] Reports made clear the inadequacy of local languages to convey the truth of God. . . . [One] report comments: 'Not only the heathen, but the speech of the heathen, must be Christianized. Their language itself needs to be born again. Their very words have to be converted from foul meanings and base uses and baptized into a Christian sense, before those words can convey the great truths and ideas of the Bible.'"

60. David Allen, *India: Ancient and Modern*, 2nd ed. (Boston: John P. Jewett and Co., 1856), 560.

61. See also "Remarks on the Various Modes of Translating Scriptural Phrases in the Languages of India" (Madras, 1838; originally printed in the *South India Christian Repository* for April, 1838), s.v. "God." *A Dictionary of the Bengalee Language* (Calcutta, 1856) translated *deva* as "a god, a demon or heathen god." *Papers Concerning the Bengali Version of the Scriptures* (Calcutta: Calcutta Auxiliary Bible Society, 1867), contain a debate over the propriety of using the term *devatā*, which had already been used to translate "God," to translate "idol" in 1 Corinthians 8.

62. W. Morton, *Biblical and Theological Vocabulary, English and Bengali* (Calcutta, 1845), translates "God" as "īśvara, parameśvara" while "idolater" is rendered "devapūjaka."

63. William Hodge Mill, *Proposed Version of Theological Terms, with a view to uniformity in translations of the holy scriptures, etc., into the various languages of India. Part the first—Sanscrit. With remarks upon the rendering proposed by Dr. Mill by Horace Hayman Wilson, Esq.* (Calcutta: Bishop's College Press, 1828). Vans Kennedy, "Remarks on Dr. Mill's Renderings of Scripture Terms," *The Oriental*

Christian Spectator 2 (Bombay: American Mission Press, 1831): 200–07 at 200, rejected Mill's choice of deva and recommended īśvara. "On the Sanscrit Renderings of Scripture Terms," pp. 319–20 in the same volume, rejected this and affirmed Mill's choice. For an account of this debate, see Young, *Resistant Hinduism,* 40–42 and esp. Amaladass and Young, *Indian Christiad,* 47–56.

64. Mill, *Proposed Version of Theological Terms,* 1. Cf. Horace Hayman Wilson's comments approving of this usage, id. at 25–26.

65. Young, *Resistant Hinduism,* 42.

66. *List of Proper Names Occurring in the Sacred Scriptures, Designed to Form the Basis of a Uniform Method of Spelling the Proper Names of Scripture in the Languages of India* (Calcutta: Baptist Mission Press, 1840), viii.

67. William Carey, Joshua Marshman, and William Ward, *Hints Relative to Native Schools: Together with the Outline of an Institution for Their Extension and Management* (London: Black, Parbury and Allen, 1817), 8. Complaints of this nature were common. See H. P. Forster, *Vocabulary, in two parts, English and Bongalee, and vice versa,* 2 vols. (Calcutta: Ferris and Co., 1799), Introduction, ii: "There never having been a Bongalee Grammarian . . . the orthography has, consequently, never been fixed: and amongst an illiterate people, almost every word has been, and continues in one district or another, to be variously spelt, and not infrequently is so disguised, as to render it difficult to recognize it, when met in its genuine form in the Songskrit." Nathaniel Halhed, *Bengali Grammar* (Hooghly: [Charles Wilkins], 1778), 3, already complained of the corruption and variability of the Bengali alphabet. The same author's earlier *A Code of Gentoo Laws, or Ordinations of the Pundits* (London, 1776) represented one of the first attempts to print Devanāgarī and Bengali characters.

68. Carey, Marshman, and Ward, *Hints Relative to Native Schools,* 11.

69. Monier Monier-Williams, ed., *Original Papers Illustrating the History of the Application of the Roman Alphabet to the Languages of India* (London: Longman, Brown, Green, Longmans, and Roberts, 1859) (hereinafter "*MW*").

70. See note 76 in this chapter for discussion and citations.

71. Another example of the two groups' overlap is the citation of William Jones's system of Roman transliteration, described below, by one of the major proponents of English spelling reform, Alexander John Ellis, *Essentials of Phonetics* (London: Fred Pitman, 1848), 232.

72. *MW* 12; cf. 132.

73. *MW* 257.

74. William Jones, "On the Orthography of Asiatick Words," *Asiatic Researches* 1 (1788), 1–56. A proposal for another scheme of transliteration was made by the French Orientalist Constantin-François de Chassebœuf, Comte de Volney (1757–1820), in a work presented to Jones's Asiatic Society on August 17, 1797: *Simplification des langues orientales ou methode nouvelle et facile d'apprendre les langues arabe, persane et turque, avec des caracteres* [sic] *européens.* Volney was

elected an Honorary Member of the Asiatic Society at the next meeting on September 28, 1797. Sibadas Chaudhuri, ed., *Proceedings of the Asiatic Society, Vol. 1: 1784–1800* (Calcutta: Asiatic Society, 1980), 273–75. Müller later won the Prix Volney for his linguistic efforts.

75. See esp. John Borthwick Gilchrist, *The Hindee-Roman Orthoepigraphical Ultimatum*, 2nd ed. (London: Kingsbury, Parbury, and Allen, 1820).

76. Christian Bunsen, *Christianity and Mankind, their Beginnings and Prospects*, 7 vols., vol. 4 (London: Longman, Brown, Green, and Longmans, 1854), Appendix D, "The Universal Alphabet, and the conferences regarding it held at the residence of Chevalier Bunsen, in January, 1854." The first conference was held on January 25, 1854. Attendees included Charles Trevelyan, Friedrich Max Müller, the missionary Henry Venn, and other missionaries. Bunsen stated (379–80): "Two great phenomena have occurred in the course of this century to urge upon Europe the importance and necessity of a universal alphabet, so powerfully called forth by Volney: the rise and wonderful advance of the science of languages, and of comparative philology, combined with universal ethnology, and the great Protestant missionary movement all over the globe. As to the first, it was particularly the British sway in India which opened the way. The study of Sanskrit . . . gave the enlightened statesmen and scholars employed in the administration of that vast empire a basis for a uniform Indian alphabet in Roman characters." Lepsius and H. H. Wilson attended the second conference on January 30. See id. at 399–435, "Lepsius' Succinct Exposition of his Universal Standard Alphabet." Bunsen, Part III, pp. 437–88, is Müller's *Proposal for a Missionary Alphabet*. See also Müller, *Proposals for a Missionary Alphabet* (London: A. and G. A. Spottiswoode, 1854); Müller, *The Languages of the Seat of War in the East* (London: Williams and Norgate, 1855); and Richard Lepsius, *Standard Alphabet for Reducing Unwritten Languages and Foreign Graphic Systems to a Uniform Ethnography in European Letters*, 2nd rev. ed. (London: Williams and Norgate, 1863); reprinted with an introduction by J. Alan Kemp (Amsterdam: John Benjamins, 1981), 28–32 and 43–45, describing the conferences. Lepsius stated that Venn announced his and the Church Missionary Society's preference for the Standard Alphabet, which was used in Africa, but rejected for India by Trevelyan and Monier-Williams. Lepsius's list (2–6, 309–13) of those using his system reads like a "Who's Who" of missionary societies.

77. See Lepsius, *Standard Alphabet*, 23: "The endeavor to establish a uniform orthography for writing foreign languages in English characters has both a scientific and a practical aim. The scientific aim is to bring these languages with their literature more completely within our reach, and to increase our knowledge of the nations to which they belong. The practical aim is to facilitate the propagation of the Christian faith and the introduction of Christian civilisation among heathen nations." Similarly, Robert Hunt, *Natural and Simple Symbolization of the Organic Facts of Universal Speech, with a Prefatory Statement on the*

Necessity for a Promptly Completed Protestant Reformation (London: William Hunt and Co., 1873), 26, reported the use of his Universal Syllabic Gospel in Santhalistan. Hunt sent his scheme to Müller, who responded, "I can see your views, and quite enter into them." Hunt, *The Ministration of the Spirit and Life of our Lord and Saviour, Jesus Christ, in all the Languages of the Illiterate Heathen World, by the Instrumentality of the Universal Syllabic Gospel*, 2nd ed. (London: Gilbert and Rivington, 1870), 23. Hunt's proposals for a universal language are discussed in note 109 in this chapter.

78. *MW* 37.
79. *Friend of India* 100 (24 November 1836): 370. See M. A. Laird, "The Contribution of the Serampore Missionaries to Education in Bengal, 1793–1837," *Bulletin of the School of Oriental and African Studies* 31 (1968): 92–112 at 108.
80. *MW* 164.
81. Douglas C. McMurtrie, *Early Mission Printing Presses in India* (Rajkot, 1933), 1.
82. *MW* ix. Duff's list of works in preparation in Roman type commences with the New Testament in Bengali and Hindustani (*MW* 126, note).
83. *MW* 166.
84. *MW* 238–39. Volney's proposal for the transliteration of Asiatic languages had printed the Lord's Prayer in Romanized Hebrew and different dialects of Arabic. Constantin-François de Chasseboeuf, Comte de Volney, *L'Alfabet européen appliqué aux langues asiatiques* (Paris: Didot, 1818), 198–201, 208–09.
85. *MW* 203, 231.
86. *MW* 231. *Devanāgarī* in Sanskrit means literally the "abode of the gods."
87. See the discussion of the Bunsen conferences and of Lepsius's system in note 76 in this chapter.
88. *MW* 241.
89. See Duff in *MW* 125. Cf. *A Letter from Alexander Murray to Charles Stuart on the Tendency of the Translation of the Scriptures into the Indian Languages, to Promote Science, Civilization, and the Commercial Interest of Great Britain* (Edinburgh: J. Ritchie, 1813); Duff, *Language in Relation to Commerce*, 5.
90. *MW* 264.
91. *MW* 275.
92. Quoted in Rasiah S. Sugirtharajah, *Postcolonial Criticism and Biblical Interpretation* (New York: Oxford University Press, 2002), 159.
93. *MW* 159.
94. *MW* 128. Cf. id. at 230; Duff, *New Era*, 27: "When the Romans conquered a province, they forthwith set themselves to the task of 'Romanizing' it . . . And has Rome not succeeded? Has she not saturated every vernacular dialect with which she came in contact, with terms copiously drawn from her own? Has she not thus perpetuated for ages, after her sceptre moulders in the dust, the magic influence of her character and name?"
95. *Chips* 5: 157.

96. "Lord Bacon's superficial objection to phonetic spelling answered": Lincoln-shire Herald notice of a specimen sheet of the Phonotype Bible, 1845. Tract No. 328 in Isaac Pitman, ed., *A Plea for Spelling Reform* (London: Fred Pitman, 1878), 2–3.

97. Good general accounts of some of the universal language projects, and of simi-lar ideas going back to Plato's *Cratylus* that anticipated these, may be found in Umberto Eco, *The Search for the Perfect Language*, trans. James Fentress (Oxford: Blackwell, 1995); Gérard Genette, *Mimologics*, trans. Thaïs Morgan (Lincoln: University of Nebraska Press, 1995); Louis Couturat and Léopold Léau, *Histoire de la langue universelle* (Paris: Librairie Hachette, 1903); Vivian Salmon, *Lodwick*; Salmon, "Language-Planning in Seventeenth-Century England; its Context and Aims," in *The Study of Language in Seventeenth-Century England*, 2nd ed. (Amsterdam: John Benjamins, 1988), 129–56; John Webster, *Academiarum Exa-men, or The Examination of Academies* (London: printed for Giles Calvert, 1654); Seth Ward, *Vindiciæ Academiarum* (Oxford: printed by J. Lichfield, 1654). Web-ster's and Ward's works are reproduced, with an introduction, in Allen G. Debus, *Science and Education in the Seventeenth Century: The Webster-Ward Debate* (London: MacDonald and Co., 1970). See also Thomas C. Singer, "Hiero-glyphs, Real Characters, and the Idea of Natural Language in English Seven-teenth-Century Thought," *Journal of the History of Ideas* 50 (1989): 49–70; James Knowlson, *Universal Language Schemes in England and France 1600–1800* (Toronto: University of Toronto Press, 1975), 14–15, 86–87; and Rhodri Lewis, *Language, Mind and Nature: Artificial Languages in England from Bacon to Locke* (Cambridge: Cambridge University Press, 2007), which offers an excellent overview of the early phase of development of universal language schemes in the Baconian tradition.

98. Salmon, *Lodwick*, 43–71.

99. Paolo Rossi, *Logic and the Art of Memory: The Quest for a Universal Language*, trans. Stephen Clucas (Chicago: University of Chicago Press, 2000), 155–56; cf. Clark, "The Word of God," 66: "Despite the generally secular motivations behind the search for a universal scientific language, the proposed model was designed to do no less than compensate for the epistemological power lost in Adam's fall." On the background of these projects, see also Sidonie Clauss, "John Wilkins' Essay toward a Real Character: Its Place in the Seventeenth-Century Episteme," *Journal of the History of Ideas* 43 (1982): 531–53; Benjamin DeMott, "Comenius and the Real Character in England," *PMLA* 70 (1955): 1068–81 at 1073–74.

100. See Harrison, *The Bible*, 225: "Many seventeenth-century thinkers believed that Babel had spelt the end of a simple and unaffected monotheism. From this time on, different nations had professed belief in different gods, on account of the various names for God which followed the fall of language."

101. Francis Bacon, *De Augmentis*, Book 6 (Bacon, *Works*, 9: 109–10). For references to Bacon's discussions of the real character, see Salmon, *Lodwick*, 14.

102. Erik Iversen, *The Myth of Egypt and its Hieroglyphs in European Tradition* (Princeton, NJ: Princeton University Press, 1993). John Wilkins, *Mercury, or the Secret and Swift Messenger* (London: printed by I. Norton for Iohn Maynard and Timothy Wilkins, 1641), 101, argued that hieroglyphs, such as animal figures, "did beare in them some naturall resemblance to the thing intended."

103. Cf. Padley, *Grammatical Theory*, 139.

104. John Bulwer's *Chirologia and Chironomia*, which attempted to reconstruct the "natural" language of gesture as an "universal character," was one such work. *Chirologia: or the Natural Language of the Hand and Chirologia: or the Art of Manual Rhetoric* (London: printed by Thomas Harper, 1644); reprint ed., ed. James W. Cleary (Carbondale: Southern Illinois University Press, 1974). See Jeffrey Wollock, "John Bulwer (1606–1656) and the Significance of Gesture in seventeenth-century Theories of Language and Cognition," *Gesture* 2 (2002): 227–58; Robert A. Yelle, "The Rhetoric of Gesture in Cross-Cultural Perspective," *Gesture* 6 (2006): 223–40.

105. John Wilkins, *An Essay towards a Real Character, and a Philosophical Language* (London: printed for Samuel Gellibrand, 1668), 13; cf. 21.

106. Id. at 385–86.

107. Ibid.

108. Mary M. Slaughter, *Universal Languages and Scientific Taxonomy in the Seventeenth Century* (Cambridge: Cambridge University Press, 1982), 205, argues that "the feature that distinguishes Locke's linguistic theory from his predecessors like Bacon and Wilkins" is his affirmation that "there is no tie between language and the real nature of objects." Cf. Singer, "Hieroglyphs," 65; Hans Aarsleff, *From Locke to Saussure: Essays on the Study of Language and Intellectual History* (Minneapolis: University of Minnesota Press, 1982), 62. Aarsleff (24–26) argues that Locke made the arbitrariness of language the central tenet of his linguistic doctrine, in direct response to the countervailing project of the alchemists and other magicians to recover an "Adamic language" that reflected nature perfectly. Some alchemists contended that knowledge of the essential nature of substances could be achieved through the linguistic and other symbols that represented them, and that, through the manipulation of such symbols, the substances themselves could be produced. Locke's nominalist account of the how the word "gold" is understood and used aimed at a refutation of such mysticism. Locke, *Essay*, 2: 57 (Book 3, chap. 6).

109. In the 1760s, Rowland Jones set out to demolish Locke's thesis of arbitrariness, and defend the idea of a natural, Adamic language. For Jones, the sounds of the English language and the letters of its alphabet held natural or "hieroglyfic" and, indeed, divine significance: "The character and letter O, being the alpha and omega, and as the indefinite circle of time and space, comprehending all nature, as well as all characters and letters, stands foremost in my alphabet." Rowland Jones, *The Origin of Language and Nations* (London: printed by

J. Hughes, 1764), preface. Cf. Jones, *Hieroglyfic* (London: printed by J. Hughes, 1768), 11–12. For a discussion of Jones, see Murray Cohen, *Sensible Words: Linguistic Practice in England, 1640–1785* (Baltimore: Johns Hopkins University Press, 1977), 135. A later text, the anonymous *Description and Explanation of a Universal Character or Manner of Writing* (Bath: J. Hollway, 1830), developed a set of new hieroglyphic signs, representing "man" by a stick figure and "spirit" by a one-legged stick figure with a slash mark through it. Alexander Melville Bell, *Visible Speech: The Science of Universal Alphabetics; or Self-Interpreting Physiological Letters, for the Writing of All Languages in One Alphabet* (London: Simpkin, Marshall and Co., 1867), 35, created an alphabet where each letter iconically represented the shape of the organs of speech when pronouncing it, or what Wilkins had called "apertion" (i.e., aperture). George Edmonds, *A Universal Alphabet, Grammar, and Language* (London: Richard Griffin and Co., 1856), which was explicitly based on Wilkins, similarly proposed "an Alphabet of Characters, which should, by their very forms, indicate the natural relation and circumstances of the organs of speech, in the production of the sounds they denoted" (v) and, moreover, "all the words . . . are arranged according to the nature of the things which those words represent" (23). Some of the most extreme and outlandish proposals came from Robert Hunt in a series of books, apocalyptic in tone, that sought to introduce a "Universal Syllabic Alphabet" capable of reversing the curse of Babel. Hunt, *The Ministration; Natural and Simple Symbolization; The Universal Syllabic Gospel: with English Key and Specimens in other Tongues* (London: William Hunt and Co., 1873); which is substantially the same as *The Universal Syllabic Gospel: The English of the Gospel According to St. John, with English key, and specimens in other tongues* (London: William Hunt and Co., 1873). According to Hunt, *The Ministration*, 22, this alphabet, which imitated both physiological reality and the nature of the world, would be based on English: "The English language retains the simple, three-fold, Pre-Babel conformations of 'place and instrument' for consonant vocalization . . . Its Vowel Scheme, like the Vocal Syllabarium of the whole world is but an interior modification, in place and action, of this simple Pre-babel vocalization."

110. Clauss, "John Wilkins' Essay," 533.
111. On the magical dimensions of some of these proposals, see esp. Wilkins, *Mercury*, 98, invoking as precedent for the idea of a real character both Egyptian hieroglyphs and "the characters that are used in Magick, which are mayntained to have, not only a secret signification, but likewise a naturall efficacie."
112. Salmon, *Lodwick*, 150–51; Slaughter, *Universal Languages*, 10–11, 86–87; David Heckel, "Francis Bacon's New Science: Print and the Transformation of Rhetoric," in Bruce Gronbeck, Thomas Farrell, and Paula Soukup, eds., *Media, Consciousness, and Culture: Explorations of Walter Ong's Thought* (Newbury Park, CA: Sage, 1991), 64–76.

113. On the currency of the Babel theme and its relation to seventeenth-century linguistic thought, see Eco, *Perfect Language, 238*; Salmon, *Lodwick*, 82–83; Margreta de Grazia, "Shakespeare's View of Language: An Historical Perspective," *Shakespeare Quarterly* 29 (1978): 374–88 at 377–81; Knowlson, *Universal Language Schemes*, 10. References to the curse of Babel and its reversal appear in connection with the idea of a universal language in: Thomas Urquhart, *Logopandecteision, or An Introduction to the Universal Language* (London, 1653), 4; Elias Ashmole, *Prolegomena to Fasciculus Chemicus* (1650), A7r–v, quoted in Salmon, *Lodwick*, 91–92; the dedicatory poems by Nathaniel Smart and Jos. Waite in Cave Beck, *The Universal Character* (London: printed by Thomas Maxey for William Weekly, 1657); Robert Boyle, regarding Lodwick, as noted in Slaughter, *Universal Languages*, 119 and Salmon, *Lodwick*, 17; John Webb, regarding Wilkins, as noted in Slaughter, *Universal Languages*, 174; Bulwer, *Chirologia*, 10, 18-19; Benajah J. Antrim, *Pantography, or Universal Drawings, in the Comparison of their Natural and Arbitrary Laws, with the Nature and Importance of Pasigraphy, as the Science of Letters* (Philadelphia, 1843), 161. For Wilkins's invocation of the Babel theme, see below in this chapter.

114. Locke, *Essay*, Book 3, chap. 6, esp. secs. 44–51.

115. Eco, *Perfect Language*, 8; Russell Fraser, *The Language of Adam: On the Limits and Systems of Discourse* (New York: Columbia University Press, 1977).

116. Bulwer, *Chirologia*, 18–19.

117. De Grazia, "Shakespeare's View of Language," 378.

118. Wilkins explicitly invoked Pentecost (see p. 91 in this chapter), as did Cave Beck, as noted in Harrison, *Religion and the Religions*, 149.

119. Several works affirmed the utility of these schemes for missionary work or the propagation of the Gospel: see Beck, *Universal Character*, preface; George Dalgarno, *Ars Signorum* (London: J. Hayes, 1661) and advertisements therefore, as noted in Salmon, *Lodwick*, 50; Antrim, *Pantography*, 160.

120. Salmon, *Lodwick*, 48.

121. Genesis 1 highlighted the cosmogonic power of the divine word—its ability to create and transform physical nature. John 1 identified Christ as the divine Word (*logos*) incarnate. Here are some examples of universal language proposals that invoked biblical texts that highlight the power of language: Beck, *Universal Character* (the Fifth Commandment); Dalgarno, *Ars Signorum*, 118–19 (Genesis 1); Francis Lodwick, *A Common Writing* (London, 1647), 27–30 (John 1), 137 (the Lord's Prayer) (regarding Lodwick, Salmon, *Lodwick*, 48 also notes that "one of his discourses deals with 'Converting infidels,' and among his manuscripts was one in Chinese containing the Creed, the Ten Commandments and several questions and answers on the principles of Christianity, which he lent to Wilkins for consultation in preparing the Essay"); Wilkins, *Essay*, 395, 421 (the Lord's Prayer); *The Description and Explanation of a Universal Character* (Genesis 1, Lord's Prayer, Apostle's Creed); George Edmonds, *The Philosophic Alphabet*

(London: Simpkin and Marshall, 1832), 63 (Genesis 1, Lord's Prayer); Edmonds, *A Universal Alphabet*, preface (John 1, selections from Genesis, Matthew, Psalms, etc.); Ellis, *Essentials of Phonetics*, 204 (Lord's Prayer).

122. Robert E. Stillman, *The New Philosophy and Universal Language Schemes in Seventeenth-Century England: Bacon, Hobbes, and Wilkins* (Lewisburg, PA: Bucknell University Press, 1995), 15–16, 266.

123. The Latin version had been published in 1638.

124. *New Atlantis* (Bacon, *Works*, 5: 372–73). See Lewis, *Language, Mind and Nature*, 19, for a discussion of this passage.

125. Only one year after the publication of Wilkins's Essay, Theophilus Gale's *The Court of the Gentiles* (Oxford: printed by Henry Hall for Thomas Gilbert, 1669), "Upon this Elaborate Work," sec. 1, 7, illustrated the convergence of the "scientific" idea of a universal language with the Christian project of a sacred history that would reconcile pagan mythologies with the Bible. Gale traced pagan ideas and institutions to Jewish originals, and identified Hebrew as the primeval language. The reconstruction of these relationships would succeed to some extent in restoring the unity of religions and languages. The dedicatory poem claimed that the Bible is

> *Wrot in an Universal Character . . .*
> *And if we scan their letters All,*
> *Some are Rough Guttural,*
> *Some Dentals hissing far,*
> *Some Palatins [i.e., palatals], and Linguals are,*
> *And Others they are murmuring Labial. . . .*
> *This Holy Language [i.e., Hebrew] was for Natures Empire fit,*
> *But Sin and Babel ruin'd it. . . .*

Of course, the idea that Hebrew was the original language was not new. What is noteworthy is the connection of this idea with both phonetic analysis and the specific notion of a "universal character." Whereas Wilkins and other universal-language schemers wanted to write the Bible in a universal language, so as to preserve it from the corruption of linguistic decay, Gale argued that the Bible was *already* written in such a character, if we could only learn to read it and recover its true sense.

126. Wilkins, *Mercury*, 109–10; cf. 106. Over a decade later, Webster, *Academiarum Examen*, 24–25, called for a "universal Character" modeled on "*Hieroglyphical, Emblematical, Symbolical* and *Cryptological* learning" and capable of "repair[ing] the ruines of *Babell*."

127. Wilkins, *Essay*, Epistle Dedicatory. For further references to Babel, see id. at 2, 13, 20.

128. Ibid.

129. Id. at 7.

130. Id. at 421–22.

131. Id. at 435.
132. Id. at 17.
133. Id. at 20.
134. Cf. Slaughter, *Universal Languages*, 88–89. These ideas continued into the nineteenth century. George Edmonds, *A Universal Alphabet*, 22, stated: "One grand principle of the Philosophic Language is, that every word shall be strictly univocal:— rigidly confined to one meaning only."
135. Bentham, *Works*, 8: 315; cf. 3: 260, 10: 561.
136. Edward Groves, *Pasilogia: An Essay towards the Formation of a System of Universal Language, Both Written and Vocal* (Dublin: James McGlashan, 1846), 87: "Each word should be expressed by a single character. The characters should be arbitrary; neither hieroglyphical nor emblematical . . . Every written character should be expressed by a distinct monosyllabic sound. There should be a separate sound for every written character; as many sounds as characters."
137. Hunt, *The Universal Syllabic Gospel: with English Key*, preface, iv.
138. Jones, "Orthography," 12.
139. Id. at 13.
140. Ibid.
141. *MW* 67.
142. *ST* 2: 610; *SL* 2: 50–51, 622–23; *Chips* 4: 65; Müller, *Missionary Alphabet*, liii.
143. *The Methodist*, 22–23.
144. Id., preface, i–iii.
145. Id. at iv.
146. Pennington, *Was Hinduism Invented?*, 121.
147. *MW* 26 (Trevelyan); *MW* 254 (Monier-Williams).
148. *MW* 8–9.
149. *MW* 153. Cf. 168: "We need not say that, next to a universal *language*, a universal *character*, by removing nearly one half the difficulties of his task, promises to a philanthropist the most glorious results."
150. *MW* 34.
151. Duff, *Language in Relation to Commerce*, 5–6.
152. Id. at 9.
153. Id. at 10.
154. G[eorge] U[glow] Pope, *One Alphabet for All India* (Madras: Gantz Bros., 1859).
155. Id. at 6. Bunsen's 1854 conference for "a Universal Missionary Alphabet" is cited at 2.
156. Id. at 10–11. Even some opponents of Roman transliteration acknowledged the desirability of a "universal language" that would reverse Babel. See Captain W. Nassau Lees, "Review of *On the Application of the Characters of the Roman Alphabet to Oriental Languages*," *Journal of the Asiatic Society* 4 (1864): 345–59 at 347.

157. Jones, "Orthography," iii. *The Methodist* stated that "*All such* Sounds *as are the same (or very nearly the same) may be signify'd by the* same Characters."

158. *LE* 55. Cf. Müller, *Missionary Alphabet*, liii; Pope, *One Alphabet*, 22.

159. Hodgson, *Preeminence of the Vernaculars*, 19.

160. Id. at 36.

161. Id. at 30–32, 39.

162. Id. at 39. W. H. Macnaghten also reminded the Anglicists that "Our object is to impart ideas, not words." W. H. Macnaghten, *Minute* (March 24, 1835), quoted in Kopf, *British Orientalism*, 250–51.

163. Hodgson, *Preeminence of the Vernaculars*, 64.

164. *SL* 2: 65 illustrated Wilkins's philosophical language with the following example: "if *Da* is once known to signify God, then *ida* must signify that which is opposed to God, namely, idol."

165. Müller, *Missionary Alphabet*, 53.

166. Müller also contributed to the preparation of an *Outline Dictionary for the Use of Missionaries, Explorers and Students of Language with an Introduction on the Proper Use of the Ordinary English Alphabet in Transcribing Foreign Languages* (Calcutta: George Wyman and Co., 1867). This was a dictionary of basic English words with blank ruled lines on which the missionary could write native equivalents in a kind of modified phonetic English. Specimens of such transliteration included Genesis 1:1 (ix) and *Rig Veda* 1.1 (x). In the same work, Müller (xv) referred approvingly to A. M. Bell's *Visible Speech*.

167. *MW* 257.

168. Müller, *Missionary Alphabet*, 49.

169. Id. at 33–34.

170. See Yigal Bronner, *Extreme Poetry: The South Asian Movement of Simultaneous Narration* (New York: Columbia University Press, 2010).

171. It is not entirely clear who introduced these changes first. Mofakhkhar Hussain Khan, *The Bengali Book: History of Printing and Bookmaking 1667–1866*, 2 vols. (Dhaka: Bangla Academy, 2001), 1: 232, states: "Before the introduction of printing, Bengali had no punctuation mark except *purnaccheda* or full stop (I), double *purnaccheda* or double full stop (II), dash (-), or full stop plus a dash (I-) at the end of a sentence. It was Serampore which for the first time introduced all of the punctuation marks in practice in Western languages but retaining full stop (I) instead of a *dot* of an English full stop." However, *Primitiae Orientales*, vol. 3, xxxviii, states that Gilchrist improved Charles Wilkins's Persian type by adding "Marks of Punctuation, never before introduced into Oriental Writing." It claims also (xxxix) that similar marks were introduced into Devanāgarī. Kopf, *British Orientalism*, 82 dates Gilchrist's report on the introduction of punctuation into Urdu at June 27, 1803.

172. Gilchrist referred to this as a "typographic reformation" of Urdu. *Papers of the College of Fort William*, June 27, 1803, quoted in Kopf, *British Orientalism*, 82.

173. Monier-Williams, *Study of Sanskrit*, esp. 50–54.

174. Id. at 54.

175. *MW* 120–21.

176. Pope, *One Alphabet*, 6–7.

177. *Letters of Indophilus* [Trevelyan] *to* "the Times," 3rd ed. (London: Longman, Brown, Green, Longmans, and Roberts, 1858), No. 5, "Causes of the Mutiny," dated London, Oct. 20, 1857, argues that it was the greased cartridges and insensitivity to native religious sentiment.

178. *Correspondence Relating to the Establishment of an Oriental College in London, Reprinted from the Times, with Notes and Additions* (London: Williams and Norgate, 1858). Letters of Philindus (Müller) and Indophilus (Trevelyan). Philindus, Letter no. 1, "The Neglect of the Study of Indian Languages as a Cause of the Indian Rebellion," dated Oxford, Dec. 30, 1857. Cf. *LL* 1: 204.

179. *Correspondence Relating to an Oriental College*, Letters of Philindus and Indophilus, No. 2, from Indophilus dated London, Dec. 30, 1857, "On the Establishment of an Oriental College," called for exactly that in London. No. 3, from Philindus dated Oxford, Jan. 4, 1858, "On the Proper Mode of Teaching the Language of India," seconded the plan for the establishment of a college and called for every civil servant to have an elementary knowledge of Sanskrit. No. 4, from Trevelyan (as himself) dated Jan. 7, 1858, "On the Relative Importance of Sanskrit," called for vernaculars to be taught first and rejected the idea that all need study Sanskrit. No. 5, from Philindus, dated Oxford, Jan. 10, 1858, "On the Practical Advantages of Sanskrit in Teaching the Languages of India," rejoined (25): "I do not wish to deny that India may be conquered by the sword, and governed by the sword; that Hindu religion may be exterminated, Hindu literature destroyed—nay, that the English alphabet and the English language may be introduced by force, and take the place of Sanskrit and its living dialects. The same policy was followed by the Romans." No. 6, by Monier-Williams dated Haileybury, Jan. 16, 1858, chimed in in support of Sanskrit.

180. "The English Alphabet Applied to the Languages of India," *The Saturday Review* (Dec. 5, 1857), No. 110, Vol. 4, 515–17.

181. Id. at 517.

182. Cohn, "Command of Language," in *Colonialism and its Forms of Knowledge*.

183. Williams, *American Indian*, 74.

184. *TLSL* 50–51.

185. Müller, *Seat of War*, ix.

186. William Ward, *A View of the History, Literature, and Mythology of the Hindoos* (London: Kingsbury, Parbury, and Allen, 1822), vol. 1, Introductory Remarks, clxix [*sic*: cxlix].

187. *SM* 1: 139.

188. *OGR* 292.

189. *OGR* 298.

CHAPTER 4

1. John Calvin, *A Harmonie upon the Three Evangelists* (London: George Bishop, 1584), 189.

2. John Wilson, *An Exposure of the Hindu Religion* (Bombay: American Mission Press, 1832), 88.

3. Zastoupil and Moir, *The Great Indian Education Debate*, 165.

4. Samuel Purchas, *Purchas His Pilgrimes in Five Bookes* (London: printed by William Stansby for Henrie Fetherstone, 1625), vol. 2 of 4, Part 2, Book 9, chap. 6, sec. 3, pp. 1476–77. The identical passage appears in *The Travels of Sig. Pietro della Valle, a Noble Roman, into East-India, . . . Whereunto is Added a Relation of Sir Thomas Roe's Voyage into the East-Indies* (London: printed by J. Macock for Henry Herringman, 1665), 423. Terry (in id. at 422) compares the daily prayer of the Muslims, "La alla illa alla, Mahomet Resul-alla," with the Ephesians' continual cry, "Great is Diana of the Ephesians" in Acts 19:24. This was one of the standard illustrations of "vain repetitions." Cf. Thomas Herbert, *Some Years Travels into Divers Parts of Africa and Asia* (London: printed by R. Everingham for R. Scot, T. Basset, J. Wright, and R. Chiswell, 1677), 191: "Battologizing the names Allough Whoddaw and Mohumet very often."

5. Cf. Jamieson, Fausset, and Brown, quoted in Joseph F. Sheahan, *Vain Repetitions, or The Protestant Meaning of Batta* (New York: Cathedral Library Association, 1901), 80: "This method of *heathen* devotion is still observed by Hindoo and Mohamedan devotees . . . In the Church of Rome not only is it carried to a shameless extent, but . . . the very prayer which our Lord gave as an antidote to vain repetition [i.e., the Lord's Prayer] is the most abused to this *superstitious* end . . . Is not this just that characteristic *feature of heathen devotion* which our Lord here condemns?"

6. Edward Stillingfleet noted the "strange resemblance between the Roman religion" and Oriental practices. *A Defence of the Discourse Concerning the Idolatry Practised in the Church of Rome, the two first parts* (London: printed by Robert White for Henry Mortlock, 1676), 117; cf. 119: "[Japanese Buddhists] say their prayers exactly with their Beads, of which they have 180 on a string; . . . they understand not one word of their prayers, and yet they hope for forgiveness of their sins for saying them. They have a kind of Ave-Mary Bell for the times of their prayers." Stillingfleet's sources were Trigautius and Bartoli, the Catholic missionaries. But the English Bishop converted these observations into an indictment of both Papistry and its pagan parallels. See also "Heathenism of Popery," *The Oriental Christian Spectator* 2 (Bombay: American Mission Press, 1831): 409–12 at 410: "The Romanist must repeat 'Ave Maria' and 'Credo' & c. The Hindooo [sic] in like manner must perform *Jup* and *Namochurun*." "Remarks on the State of the Roman Catholic Church in India, with reference to the Instruction of the Heathen," *Friend of India*, Quarterly Series 2, No. 6 (Serampore,

1822): 237–53 at 249: "Nor did the Romish church obtain from the Sacred Scriptures the idea that certain formulas have the property of charms by which evil spirits, diseases, and even moral offences, may be removed. The sentiment is wholly heathen. With these views a Romish christian repeats certain Ave Marias; the common Hindoo repeats the name of his deity, and the brahmun, his gayutree, for the very same purpose. The former repeats the name of his guardian saint to ward off evil spirits, and the Hindoo, to obtain the same end, repeats that of his guardian deity. Both use the bead-roll under one impression, that there is in these a virtue, a merit, some propitiatory or atoning quality; and that the merit is proportioned to the number of repetitions. While these ceremonies have not the slightest countenance from the Holy Scriptures, they are identically the same with those used among the heathens."

7. Henry Lord, *A Display of Two Forraigne Sects* (London: printed for Francis Constable, 1630), 59, 72–73. This account is reproduced in Bernard Picart, *The Ceremonies and Religious Customs of the Various Nations of the Known World; Together with Historical Annotations and Several Curious Discourses Equally Instructive and Entertaining*, Vol. 3, *Concerning the Ceremonies of the Idolatrous Nations* (London: William Jackson, 1734), 327, 332. Picart compiled accounts from a number of travellers, including Lord. The electronic copy of Picart's work I consulted bears the handwritten name of Warren Hastings, one-time governor of British India, on its title page.

8. Richard Baxter, *A Christian Directory* (London: printed by Robert White for Nevill Simmons, 1673), 179.

9. See 1 Corinthians 3.

10. Authorized (King James) Version (1611).

11. See Thomas, *Religion and the Decline of Magic*, 61. Stanley Tambiah, *Magic, Science, Religion, and the Scope of Rationality* (Cambridge: Cambridge University Press, 1990), 19, similarly attributes the distinction between prayers and spells to Protestantism, although he does not discuss the critique of vain repetitions.

12. Apart from the Protestant polemics analyzed below, there is remarkably little secondary literature on this important chapter in the "repudiation of ritual." Joseph Sheahan's is one of the few modern works on the subject, and it is still implicated in these polemics, coming as it does in the form of a defense of repetitive prayers written by a Catholic priest. See also Wilhard Becker, *Nicht plappern wie die Heiden* (Hannover-Kirchrode: Die Rufer Buch- und Schriftenverlag, 1980). Susannah Brietz Monta's 2011–2012 ACLS project, "Sacred Echoes: Repetitive Prayer and Reformation-Era Poetics in Early Modern England," may offer some new insights.

13. Some possible parallels for this injunction appear at Ecclesiastes 5:2 ("let your words be few") and Ecclesiasticus (Sirach) 7:14 ("Do not prattle in the assembly of the elders, nor repeat yourself in your prayer"). See Sheahan, *Vain Repetitions*, 58–60.

14. Bauman, *Let Your Words Be Few.* John Vicars, *The Opinion of the Roman Judges Touching upon Imprisonment and the Liberty of the Subject* ([London,] 1643), 4, quoted this verse against "such as abused the saying of Saint *Paul*, *Pray continually*, to vaine babling, and thinke that God is perswaded by Battalogies and Tautologies."

15. Cf. Sheahan, *Vain Repetitions*, 30.

16. John Calvin, *Institutes of the Christian Religion*, chap. 20, sec. 29; trans. John Allen, 7th ed., 2 vols. (Philadelphia: Presbyterian Board of Christian Education, 1936), 138.

17. John Calvin, *Harmonie*, 189. Of course, Calvin was writing in Latin. This language is taken from the 1584 English translation. As previously mentioned, the English phrase "vain repetitions" was first used to translate Matthew 6:7 in the second edition of the Geneva Bible (1560).

18. Id. at 189. I cite this translation rather than a modern one as it illustrates the form in which Calvin's concept of vain repetitions was received by British Protestants.

19. The word appears in two forms, as "batto-" and "batta-." See Sheahan, *Vain Repetitions*, 67.

20. E. Jacquier states that this is a *hapax legomenon.* Jacquier, "Matthew, Saint, Gospel of," in Charles G. Herbermann et al., eds., *The Catholic Encyclopedia,* volume 10 (New York: Robert Appleton Co., 1911), 57–65.

21. Thomas Wilson, *The Arte of Rhetorique* (London: printed by Richard Grafton, 1553), fol. 810.

22. Hill, *The English Bible*, 336, citing Wilson, *The Arte of Rhetorique* (1560), no page.

23. Wilson, *Arte of Rhetorique* (1553 ed.), fol. 109.

24. Sheahan, *Vain Repetitions*, 5.

25. See chapter 1 in this volume.

26. Sheahan, *Vain Repetitions*, 62–65, denies this. He states that the fifth-century Greek lexicographer Hesychius, on whom others have relied for this interpretation, suggested instead that a different word—*batta-ridzein*—was an onomatopoetic term meaning "to stammer"; and this has falsely been extended to *battalogein.*

27. William Annand, *Pater Noster* (Edinburgh: printed by George Swinton and James Glen, 1670), 35.

28. Thomas Manton, *A Practical Exposition of the Lord's Prayer* (London: printed by J. D. for Jonathan Robinson, 1684), 41. George Downame, *The Doctrine of Practicall Praying* (London: printed by W. H. for Nicolas Bourne, 1656), 128–29, attributes this explanation to "the Etymologist," meaning probably Hesychius or perhaps the tenth century Byzantine *Suda* attributed erroneously to "Suidas." Sheahan regarded this identification of Ovid's Battus as erroneous for two reasons: it did not appear in Suidas, and Ovid's Battus was not a poet. He also argued (*Vain Repetitions*, 71) that the second, tautological line was really a comment by Ovid, and not by Battus at all.

29. Offspring Blackall, *Practical Discourses on the Lord's Prayer* (London: printed by W. B. for Thomas Ward, 1717). Blackall mentions a number of different Battuses to whom this word might refer.

30. Sheahan also rejected this interpretation, which he attributed to Suidas. For some King Battuses who stammered, see Plutarch, *The Oracles at Delphi No Longer Given in Verse*, sec. 22, in *Moralia*, 5: 319: "Battus had a lisp and a shrill thin voice."

31. John Whitgift, "The Defence of the Answer to the Admonition, against the Reply of Thomas Cartwright," in *The Works of John Whitgift*, ed. John Ayre, 3 vols. (Cambridge: Cambridge University Press, 1853), 3: 513–17.

32. Sheahan, *Vain Repetitions*, 83 pointed out that in "several of the psalms . . . *number and length* and even the *letters of the alphabet* numbered in order . . . are a prominent *point of observance.* Eight of the psalms are alphabetical; the first verse begins with A, the second with B, and so on until the alphabet is exhausted."

33. John Fisher, *The Answere unto the Nine Points of Controversy* (Saint-Omer: English College Press, 1626), 241–42. Cf. Francis White, *A Replie to Iesuit Fishers Answere to Certain Questions* (London: printed by Adam Islip, 1624), which quotes Fisher's earlier citation of various examples.

34. Matthew Poole, *Annotations upon the Holy Bible* (London: printed by John Richardson for Thomas Parkhurst, 1685), re: Matthew 6:7.

35. Cf. Sheahan, *Vain Repetitions*, 81: "Protestant scholars find it very difficult to agree in specifying exactly what is condemned by these words. Some seem to think that repetition itself is vain; others think the text is denouncing unmeaning irrelevant repetitions; others see superstitious repetition in it. Some can even see a sin in the use of synonyms, others in making number and length the point of observance."

36. Samuel Mather, *The Lord's Prayer* (Boston: printed by Kneeland and Adams, 1766), 4.

37. Manton, *A Practical Exposition*, 50, cites both of these illustrations. See also Blackall, *Practical Discourses*, 150. Sheahan, *Vain Repetitions*, 74, argued that repetition was not characteristic of pagan prayers, yet "Protestant scholars found it necessary to prove that it was, in order to defend their new translation and interpretation of *Batta* in Matt. vi–7." He gives Hugo Grotius as one example. As should be obvious from the discussion of ritual earlier in this chapter, this claim of Sheahan's, which partly contradicts his statement quoted above that "until the sixteenth century neither Jews, Christians, Mohammedans nor Pagans ever saw any harm in repetition," is not especially convincing to me. Repetition has been characteristic of the prayers of many cultures, Christian as well as non-Christian. See Yelle, *Explaining Mantras*; Yelle, *Semiotics of Religion*, chapter 2.

38. Manton, *A Practical Exposition*, 61; Downame, *Practicall Praying*, 100, 131; Blackall, *Practical Discourses*, 150–51; Francis Howgill, *The Rock of Ages* (London: printed for G. C., 1662), 44–45.

39. Henry Burton, *Christ on his Throne* (London, 1640), 26 (litany); Jeremy Taylor, *A Dissuasive from Popery* (London: printed by J. G. for Richard Royston, 1664), 206 (Jesus Psalter); John Anderson, *The Answer to the Dialogue between the Curat and the Countrey-man* ([Edinburgh], 1712), 35; Edward Leigh, *A Systeme or Body of Divinity Consisting of Ten Books* (London: printed by A. M. for William Lee, 1654), 407 (Jesus Psalter). Zachary Grey, *A Caveat against the Dissenters* (London: printed for J. Roberts, 1736), 37–38, quotes an attack on the Anglican Litany as "a very *fascinating Fardel of Tautologies* and *Battalogies.*"

40. Taylor, *A Dissuasive*, 205.

41. Fisher, *The Answere*, 242.

42. John Rawlet, *A Dialogue betwixt Two Protestants* (London: printed for Samuel Tidmarsh, 1685), 144–45.

43. Robert Calder, *An Answer to a Pamphlet Called, A Dialogue betwixt a Curat and a Country-man, concerning the English-service, or Common-prayer-book of England* ([Edinburgh,] 1711) (the Litany).

44. Lightfoot, *Works*, 157.

45. James Blair, *Our Saviour's Divine Sermon* (London: printed for J. Brotherton, 1722), 368, 370.

46. Annand, *Pater Noster*, 100.

47. Downame, *Practicall Praying*, 100.

48. Id. at 101. Elsewhere the same author says to Catholics: "Thou, if unlearned, as the most are, thou prayest in an unknowne language, speaking like a Par-rat thou knowest not what, thy prayer is a meere lip-labour, thou hopest by the multitude of thy words, and the often repetitions of thy Ave-maries, thy Pater-nosters and thy Creeds, most ridiculously and odiously reiterated upon thy Beads by most superstitious Battology." George Downame, *A Trea-tise of Iustification* (London: printed by Felix Kyngston for Nicolas Bourne, 1633), 144.

49. John Downe, *Certaine Treatises of the Late Reverend and Learned Divine, Mr. Iohne Downe* (London: printed by John Lichfield for Edward Forrest, 1633), 68.

50. Rawlet, *A Dialogue*, 147.

51. Blackall, *Practical Discourses*, 126; Samuel Walker, *Divine Essays* (Cambridge: printed at the university press for R. Thurlbourne, 1709), 136.

52. Manton, *A Practical Exposition*, 42. Robert Ferguson, *A Sober Enquiry into the Nature, Measure, and Principle of Moral Virtue* (London: printed for D. Newman, 1673), 181: "Amongst those I reckon first their *battologies* and reiterated repeti-tions of the Names and Titles of their Deities, as if by Elogies they had a mind to wheadle them."

53. Blackall, *Practical Discourses*, 34; Richard Baxter, *An Accompt of All the Proceed-ings* (London: printed for R. H., 1661), 62. This appears to be what Sheahan, *Vain Repetitions*, 82–83, meant by ridiculing the Protestant conviction in the "sin of synonyms."

54. See Richard A. Lanham, *A Handlist of Rhetorical Terms*, 2nd ed. (Berkeley: University of California Press, 1991), s.v. "tautologia."

55. Walker, *Divine Essays*, 136.

56. Thomas Hobbes, *The Art of Rhetorick* (London: printed for William Crooke, 1681), 163–64. Richard Sherry, *A Treatise of Schemes and Tropes* (London: printed by John Day, 1550), a translation of a treatise on rhetoric by Erasmus, already identified (at C.i) "a vayne repeting agayn of one word or moe" with tautology.

57. John Webster, *Academiarum Examen*, 35, used "battology" and "tautology" interchangeably to describe the tedious wordplay of the Scholastics: "That which might be concluded in a plain, and short proposition, must be drawn into mood, and figure, and after the framing, repeating, and answering some scores of Syllogisms, the matter is further off from a certain and *Apodictical* conclusion than in the beginning, and so most extremely becomes guilty of *Battology*, and *Tautologie*." Wilkins, *Essay*, 346, employed both terms as synonyms and intensified forms of the word "repetition." The theologian Daniel Featley used the two words battology and tautology as synonyms in his attack on the Catholic doctrine of transubstantiation. If the words "This is my body" were taken to refer to Christ's actual body, then they constituted a logical truism, a tautology in our modern sense, meaning a form of circular reasoning. Therefore, these words must refer to the bread, but only, of course, symbolically. Featley, *Transubstantiation Exploded* (London: printed by G. M[iller] for Nicolas Bourne, 1638), 179; Featley, *The Grand Sacrilege of the Church of Rome* (London: printed by Felix Kyngston for Robert Milbourne, 1630), 300.

58. Robert Lowth, *On the Sacred Poetry of the Hebrews* (London: printed for J. Johnson, 1787).

59. Blair, *Our Saviour's Divine Sermon*, 369 (Psalms).

60. Manton, *A Practical Exposition*, 41 (Eccles. 10:14); Matthew Henry, *The Psalms of David* (Philadelphia: printed by R. Aitken, 1783), 362; Zedekiah Sanger, *A Sermon Preached, March 12, 1794, at the Ordination of the Rev. Hezekiah Hooper* (Worcester, MA: printed by Isaiah Thomas, 1795), 8.

61. Lightfoot, *Works*, 157. Cf. Isaac de Beausobre and Jacques Lenfant, *A New Version of the Gospel* (Cambridge: printed by J. Archdeacon, 1779), 305, re: Matthew 6:7: "The *Jews* were also guilty of the same faults [as the heathens], (*viz.* repetitions and immoderate length) reckoning that they were very prevailing, as appears from their writings and forms of prayer."

62. Richard Baxter, *The Saints Everlasting Rest* (London: printed by Robert White for Thomas Underhill and Francis Tyton, 1650), 511, compared the "vain repetitions" used by some ministers with the "vain Rhetorick" used by actors on the stage. Walker, *Divine Essays*, 135, associated them with "*Mock-formalities*, empty *Pageantry*, [and] *Hypocritical Cringes*." A popular late-eighteenth-century American handbook of rhetoric directed that in prayer there should be "nothing of

vain repetition, haranguing, flowers of rhetorick, or affected figures of speech."
The Art of Speaking, 4th ed. (Philadelphia: R. Aitken, 1775), 22. Also in *Elements
of Gesture*, prefixed to William Scott, *Lessons in Elocution*, 2nd American ed.
(Philadelphia: printed by William Young, 1790), 45.

63. Blair, *Our Saviour's Divine Sermon*, 368.
64. Id. at 374.
65. Blackall, *Practical Discourses*, 148.
66. Id. at 132.
67. Manton, *A Practical Exposition*, 58–59.
68. Thomas Cartwright, *A Confutation of the Rhemists Translation* (n.p., 1618), 29;
reprint ed. (Amsterdam and New York: Da Capo Press, 1971).
69. Ibid.
70. William Annand, *Fides Catholica* (London: printed by T. R. for Edward Brewster,
1661), 531.
71. Blair, *Our Saviour's Divine Sermon*, 368–69, 373, stated that "The Heathens had
really no better Notions of their Gods; but thought they might be harangued
and persuaded, like Men, by human Eloquence; or even wearied out by Dun-
ning and Importunity. . . . The erroneous Notion of Almighty God, this Practice
of much speaking in Prayer is built upon is, that he is like unto us weak Men;
unknowing in many Things, till we inform him; averse to some Things, till we
persuade him; forgetful, till we remind him; and wavering and unresolved, till
we fix him by our Arguments and Importunity." Downame, *Practicall Praying*,
129, asked, "Why must not Christians be like the heathen? Because the God on
whom we call is most unlike. The heathen might well imagine concerning their
gods (the best whereof were men deceased) that by multitude of words they
might be perswaded." Blackall, *Practical Discourses*, 149–50, put it this way: "To
think to move God by verbal and studied Eloquence, is to think him like a weak
and shallow Man, who sees not fully into the Truth of things, and so by an eloquent Speech or Address may be moved to do that, which if it had been propos'd
to him in plain Expressions, and nakedly represented, he would have discern'd
was not fit for him to do." Cf. David Dickson, *A Brief Exposition of the Evangel of
Jesus Christ According to Matthew* (London: printed for Ralph Smith, 1651), 62:
"Idle repetitions of words presupposeth and proceedeth from a base miscon-
ception of God, as if he could be moved by multitude of words, as men are
moved"; Poole, *Annotations*, re: Matthew 6:7: "Repetitions after the manner of
Heathens, are Condemned as proceeding from irreverent thoughts of God, as if
he did not know what things we have need of, or were like a Man to be prevail'd
upon by a multitude of Words"; Walker, *Divine Essays*, 137: "And the Expectation
of Success upon this account arises from the Principle of thinking God to be
altogether such a one as themselves"; Calder, *An Answer*, 23; *Catena Aurea* l. c.,
quoted in Sheahan, *Vain Repetitions*, 25: "A multitude of words was necessary
for the Gentiles, on account of the demons, who did not know what was wanted

until they were informed by their words; hence it is added: 'For they think that they will be heard on account of their much speaking.'"

72. Manton, *A Practical Exposition*, 50. Id. at 49 cites the scriptural account of the origin of idolatry appearing at Romans 1:21 as an explanation.

73. Richard Greenham, *The Works of the Reverend and Faithfull Servant of Jesus Christ M. Richard Greenham* (London: printed by Felix Kyngston, 1599), 411.

74. Mather, *Lord's Prayer*, 3, stated that "The *Heathen* . . . used such *vain Repetitions, from an Opinion of a certain Power, like a Charm, in them.*" In addition to the citations here, see Thomas, *Religion and the Decline of Magic*, 62.

75. Baxter, *Christian Directory*, 858.

76. *A Whip for the Devil, or the Roman Conjurer* (London: printed for Thomas Malthus, 1683), 52.

77. Taylor, *A Dissuasive*, 198–99 (italics deleted).

78. See pp. 103–04 in this chapter. William Bedwell, *Mohammedis Imposturae* (London: printed by Richard Field, 1615), epistle to the reader, quoted the famed Hebraist and Arabist Guillaume Postel as applying the term battology to the Islamic *shahada* or daily prayer, "Alhamdu lillah, hamdu lillah, hamdu lillah, & caetera."

79. Ward, *A View of the History*, vol. 1, Introductory Remarks, clxx [*sic*: cl] (emphasis original).

80. Id. at 1: Introductory Remarks, cxvii.

81. Id. at 1: 211–12. Cf. George Mundy, *Christianity and Hinduism Contrasted*, 2nd enlarged ed., 2 vols. (Serampore: Serampore Press, 1834), 1: 215: "To suppose that calling on the name of God, that is, merely pronouncing his name over and over, will atone for the transgression of his laws, is likewise equally fallacious."

82. Ward, *A View of the History*, 2: 506–36.

83. Id. at 2: 527.

84. The American missionary David Allen (1800–1863) similarly invoked Matthew 6:7 to explain the common Hindu practice of repeating the names of the gods using a string of beads: "In view of this practice and the belief in which it originates, we see the propriety of what our Saviour said to his disciples, 'When ye pray, use not vain repetitions as the heathens do; for they think that they shall be heard for their much speaking.'" Allen, *India*, 403. Joseph Roberts, *Oriental Illustrations of the Sacred Scriptures*, 2nd ed. (London: printed for Thomas Tegg, 1844), 432, likewise found parallels between the heathens depicted in the Bible and the practices of contemporary Hindus. Although he did not gloss Matthew 6:7 directly, a reference to this passage appeared in his illustration of Isaiah 45:20, "Thou pray unto a god that cannot save": "Most of the prayers of the Hindoos consist in vain repetitions." Similarly, in applying Exodus 23:13, "Make not mention of the name of other gods, neither let it be heard out of thy mouth," he stated (76–77): "The Heathen attach great importance to the mentioning of the names of their gods. They do not generally pray as we do; but in time of difficulty or danger, repeat the name of their deity,

which is believed to have great power, carrying with it the nature of a charm which nothing can resist."

85. Ram Comul Sen, *A Dictionary of English and Bengalee, translated from Todd's edition of Johnson's English Dictionary*, 2 vols. (Serampore: Serampore Press, 1834), uses "mantra" as a translation of each of these English words, but not of "prayer." "Mantramaya" glosses English "magick."

86. *A Dictionary of the Bengalee Language, Volume 1, Bengalee and English, Abridged from Dr. Carey's Quarto Dictionary*, 2nd ed. (Serampore, 1856).

87. Abbé Dubois, *Hindu Manners, Customs, and Ceremonies*, trans. Henry K. Beauchamp, 3rd ed. (Oxford: Clarendon Press, 1906), chap. 12, pp. 142, 384–85.

88. Bror Tiliander, *Christian and Hindu Terminology* (Uppsala: Almqvist & Wiksell, 1974), 281–83.

89. I consulted the 1801 first edition of Carey's New Testament at the Boston Athenaeum.

90. Samuel Tobias Lachs, Review of Louis H. Feldman, *Jew and Gentile in the Ancient World*, in *Bryn Mawr Classical Review* 94.05.06.

91. Bible, New Testament, Bengali [a.k.a. *Mangala Samacara* or *Dharmapustaka*.], trans. Serampore Baptist Missionaries (Serampore: Mission Press, 1801):
    kintu jakhan tomrā kāmanā kara takhan anarthaka vākyavyāya kario nā je mata pratimāpūjakerā [i.e., the idolaters] kare ekāraṇa tāhārā bhāve tāhārder aneka kahaner [kathaner] kāraṇa śunā jāve

92. A perusal of some standard reference works available at the time confirms these connotations. Forster, *Vocabulary*, translates *pratimā* as "cut-picture, idol, image" and *mūrti* as "puppet, scarecrow, statue, toy, picture." "Idol" is rendered by "moorti" and "protima," while God is rendered by "eeshwor [*īśvara*], bhogwan [*bhagavān*], debta [*devatā*]." Sen, *A Dictionary of English and Bengalee*, glosses "idol" with, inter alia, *devamūrtti, pratimā*, and *devapratimā*; and "idolater" with *devapūjaka* and *pratimāpūjaka*. Rammohun Roy, who frequently used the word "idolatry," also employed this as a translation of the Bengali *pratimāpūjā*. Dermot Killingley, *Rammohun Roy in Hindu and Christian Tradition: The Teape Lectures 1990* (Newcastle upon Tyne: Grevatt & Grevatt, 1993), 76, n.28.

93. Bible, New Testament, Bengali, trans. Serampore Baptist Missionaries (Serampore: Mission Press, 1803):
    Kintu tomār kāmanā karaṇa kāle devapūjakerder [i.e., the idolaters] mata nirarthaka vākyavyāya kario nā kenana taharder aneka kahaner [kathaner] kāraṇa je tāhārder kathā śunā jābe ei tāhārā bhāve
    The same term *devapūjaka* is used to translate "Gentile" in both the 1832 Bengali edition and the 1808 Sanskrit first edition.

94. Cf. *A Dictionary of the Bengalee Language*, which renders *devapūjaka* as "worshipping heathen gods . . . an idolater." Morton, *Biblical and Theological Vocabulary*, renders "Idolatry" with *devapūjā*, "Idolater" with *devapūjaka*, and "Gentiles" with *devapūjakgaṇa*, as well as the more neutral *yihūdībhinna anyajātīya sakala*,

which means simply "peoples other than the Jews" (see below). Amaladass and Young, *Indian Christiad*, 38–39 confirm that, although the Bible uses *theos* to refer to both true and false gods, Carey in this verse and throughout the rest of his translation always used *deva* to denote false gods or idols and reserved other terms, such as *īśvara* ("lord"), to denote the one true God.

95. Michael Bergunder, "The 'Pure Tamil Movement' and Bible Translation," in Judith M. Brown and Robert Eric Frykenberg, eds., *Christians, Cultural Interactions, and India's Religious Traditions* (London: RoutledgeCurzon), 212–31 at 225, states that "*tevan* [Tamil *deva*] has strong polytheistic connotations." Cf. Amaladass and Young, *Indian Christiad*, 48, n.38. Tiliander, *Christian and Hindu Terminology*, 83–85, says that the use of *deva* for God was rejected in the Hindi-speaking areas of India, and was used with reservation in Tamil-speaking areas, in recognition of its polytheistic connotations.

96. *The New Testament of our Lord and Saviour Jesus Christ, in the Bengallee Language* (Calcutta: Baptist Mission Press, 1833): "*apara prārthanā kāle devapūjakader nyāya vṛthā punarukti kario nā, kaenonā tāhārā bodh kore, anek kathā kahile āmāder prārthanā grāhya hoibe.*" The 1845 edition is the same up to *kaenonā*. A translation with only the most minor variations from this one appears in *The New Testament of our Lord and Savior Jesus Christ, in Bengali and English*, vol. 1, *Matthew to John* (London: Richard Watts for the British and Foreign Bible Society, 1839). The 1844 and 1851 Sanskrit editions by the Calcutta Baptist Missionaries have: *aparaṃ prārthanākāle devapūjakā iva mudhā punaruktiṃ ma kuru, yasmāt te bodhante, bahuvāraṃ kathāyāṃ kathitāyām teṣāṃ prārthanā grāhiṣyate.*

97. The 1886 Sanskrit edition by the Calcutta Baptist Missionaries has: *prārthanākāle ca yūyaṃ parajātīyajanavad vṛthā punaruktiṃ mā kuruta, te hi svavākyabāhulyād uttaralābhaḥ sambhaviṣyatīti manyante.*

98. A translation of the Gospels in Bengali in the Serampore College Library, supposedly by John Ellerton and dated 1817, translates Gentile as *bhinnadeśi varga* (peoples of other lands). Mill's term is *anyajāḥ*. William Hodge Mill, *Christa-Sangītā, Or The Sacred History of Our Lord Jesus Christ in Sanskrit Verse*, 4 vols. (Calcutta: Bishop's College Press, 1831–37). The relevant verse is reproduced in Amaladass and Young, *Indian Christiad*, 268. "Remarks on the Various Modes of Translating Scriptural Phrases" renders "Gentile" with *anyadeśi* and similar terms meaning simply "foreigner," and "Heathen" (Greek *ethne*) with *prajā* or *kula*, meaning the same as "people." Cf. *Yiśucaritam*, trans. Vaneśvarapāṭhaka (Ranci: Satya Bharati, 1989): "*yūyañ ca prārthanākāle yahūdītarajātivat/ uccairāratane naiva pravarttadhvaṃ kadācana// manyante kila te sarve yahūdītaramānavāḥ prārthanayā mahatyaiva teṣu santuṣyati prabhuḥ.*"

99. John Wilson, *An Exposure of the Hindu Religion* (Bombay: American Mission Press, 1832), 13.

100. Id. at 15.

101. Id. at 75, quoting the *Tantrasāra's* statement that "He will inevitably be punished in hell who considers the image of the Deity as a simple stone."

102. Id. at 87–88.

103. Ibid.

104. *Detached Thoughts on Vedantism: Or a Few Pages of Advice to a Member of the Tutobodheenee Sobha, by a Native Friend* (Calcutta, 1845), 9–11.

105. An example is Horace Hayman Wilson, *Essays and Lectures*, 2: 48–49, arguing that Vedic prayers "are used as little else than unmeaning sounds . . . and when they are studied it is merely for the sake of repeating the words; the sense is regarded as a matter of no importance, and is not understood even by the Brahman who recites or chants the expressions." Cf. id. at 2: 78. Friedrich Max Müller rarely attacked repetitive chants, as opposed to mythological language, his favorite target. However, in his manuscripts there is a passage on "Religious Differences" where he contends that, although all higher religions, including Brahmanism, affirm monotheism, two other commandments of the Decalogue are more contentious: the prohibitions against worshipping graven images or taking the Lord's name in vain: "In some religions . . . the repetition of a divine name a hundred and a thousand times is actually looked upon as something meritorious." It is very likely that Müller was thinking of Hinduism. See Bodleian MS Eng. 2357, pp. 122–23.

106. Colebrooke, "On the Vedas," 389–90.

107. Id. at 390.

108. Monier Monier-Williams, *A Dictionary, English and Sanskrit* (London: William H. Allen and Co., 1851), s.v. "battology."

109. Monier Monier-Williams, *Modern India and the Indians*, 3rd ed. (London: Trübner and Co., 1879), 108–15. The phrase "vain repetitions" appears at 108.

110. Id. at 111.

111. Id. at 108.

112. Id. at 109.

113. Monier Monier-Williams, *Religious Thought and Life in India: Vedism, Brahmanism and Hinduism* (London: J. Murray, 1885); reprint ed. (New Delhi: Oriental Books Reprint Corp., 1979), 197, 199–201. An abbreviated version in almost the same words appears in Monier-Williams, *Hinduism* (Delhi: Rare Books, 1971), 128–29.

114. Monier-Williams, *Religious Thought*, 198. See discussion of this concept in chapter 2, note 33 in this volume.

115. Cf. Monier Monier-Williams, *Buddhism, in its Connection with Brahmanism and Hinduism* (London: Macmillan, 1889), 338, 540; Monier-Williams, *Modern India*, 112, 256.

116. Monier-Williams, *Buddhism*, 541.

117. Rupert Gethin, "The Mātikās: Memorization, Mindfulness, and the List," in Janet Gyatso, ed., *In the Mirror of Memory: Reflections on Mindfulness and Remembrance in Indian and Tibetan Buddhism* (Albany: SUNY Press, 1992), 149–72.

118. Monier-Williams, *Buddhism*, 557–58. In a separate address contrasting *The Holy Bible and the Sacred Books of the East* (London: Society for the Promotion of Christian Knowledge, 1900), Address III, Monier-Williams further emphasized the primacy of sound over sense in Hinduism and Islam: "It is the sound and intonation of the sacred Sanskrit and of the sacred Arabic which is of primary importance and primary efficacy; the sense is merely secondary" (33). By contrast, Christianity emphasized the sense of its scriptures and accordingly encouraged their translation. The Sikhs also came in for criticism (41, 44) for "idolizing" their holy book, the Grantha, the incessant repetition of which in a little-known language was thought to be most efficacious. Monier-Williams distinguished such "Bibliolatry" from the English Christian practice of reading the Bible in the vernacular: another swipe at Catholicism.

119. John Robson, *Hinduism and Christianity Contrasted*, 3rd ed. (Edinburgh: Oliphant Anderson & Ferrier, 1905 [1893]), 20, 100, 102–03.

120. Ibid.

121. See the discussion of John Duncan Martin Derrett's application of this distinction between faith and works in chapter 5, page 158 in this volume.

122. Rammohan Roy, *The English Works of Raja Rammohun Roy*, ed. Kalidas Nag and Debajyoti Burman (Calcutta: Sadharana Brahmo Samaj, 1945), 2: 106–08. A note to the first part of this passage reads: "As instances of the erroneous confidence which is placed in the repetition of the name of a god to effect purification from sins . . . I may quote the following passages. 'He who pronounces "Doorga" (the name of the goddess), though he constantly practice adultery, plunder others of their property, or commit the most heinous crimes, is freed from all sins.' etc." (2: 117).

123. Id. at 6: 53.

124. Id. at 2: 45.

125. Rammohun Roy has also been identified as the possible author of Brajamohan Debashya, *A Tract against the Prevailing System of Hindu Idolatry* (Calcutta: Baptist Mission Press, 1821). This essay has been edited and republished, with an English translation, by Stephen Hay as *Dialogue between a Theist and an Idolater* (Calcutta: Firma KLM, 1963). See Hay's Introduction for his identification of Rammohun as the likely author. Page references below are to the original 1821 ed. This text denied (5) that mantras have the power to animate images of the gods, and condemned (66) the "parrot-like" teaching of the mythical *Purāṇas*. The tract recommended worship by "repeating the Pranab [*praṇava*, i.e., the syllable *om*] and Gaytree, or by hearing and meditating on the Oopanishads and other Shasters . . . By doing so, all ceremonies which must be practised daily or on certain occasions are virtually performed" (57). In this way, an interior or mental form of worship was substituted for external rites and ceremonies. Accordingly, the tract ridiculed worship by "moving [one's] hands and feet, and [one's] whole body, and by dancing, singing and jumping in honour of images"

(35–36). Although the tract appears to reflect Protestant criticism of external ceremony, it preserved the use of a few mantras and followed ancient precedent in allowing the substitution of such chanting, as well as meditation, for other rituals. The original model for such ritual substitution is the "(internal) fire-sacrifice (conducted by means) of breath" (*prāṇāgnihotra*) announced in the Upaniṣads.

126. Dayananda, *Light of Truth*, 439–40.

127. See chapter 2, note 31, in this volume.

128. See chapter 3, pages 77–78 in this volume.

129. Cf. Nilakantha Goreh's claim that "by repeating the names of *Bhagavan* incessantly [sic], consciousness enters into God time and again. Now, it is false to say that [repetition] of the name of God is tantamount to a son making his father weary, saying 'Father! Father!'" Quoted in Young, *Resistant Hinduism*, 127.

130. For a more extended comparative argument concerning the role of printing in transformations in attitudes toward poetic, ritual language, see Yelle, *Semiotics of Religion*, chapter 5.

131. Romila Thapar, "The Oral and the Written in Early India," in *Cultural Pasts: Essays in Early Indian History* (New Delhi: Oxford University Press, 2000), 195–212; Shlomo Biderman, "Dharma and the Limits of Interpretation," in Shlomo Biderman and Ben-Ami Scharfstein, eds., *Interpretation in Religion* (Leiden: Brill, 1992), 111–28 at 117. Sheldon Pollock, *The Language of the Gods in the World of Men: Sanskrit, Culture, and Power in Premodern India* (Berkeley: University of California Press, 2006), argues that Sanskrit literature and poetry are incomprehensible except as a written tradition. However, the Vedas, as appropriate to a tradition of sacred literature, conserved the older, oral modes of transmission for centuries. It would be interesting to consider the implications of Pollock's argument for our understanding of the later Tantric tradition, which does, in some of its forms, depend on writing. The references to drawing or writing mantras; the *yantras*, *maṇḍalas*, and other mystical diagrams; the incredibly elaborate patterns employed in some mantras, which defy comprehension as strictly oral forms; and the later dissemination, outside of the initiatory context, of manuals or compendia of mantras in which one could look up a particular mantra for a particular occasion: all of these features indicate the importance of writing in Tantra. However, colonial attacks on mantrajapa appear to have focused on the oral dimensions of Hindu ritual.

132. Charles Malamoud, *Le Svadhyaya: récitation personnelle du Veda* (Paris: Editions de Boccard, 1977).

133. See J. R. Ballantyne, "The Pandits and Their Manner of Teaching," in Vijaya Narayana Misra, ed., *Pandit Revisited* (Varanasi: Sampurnanand Sanskrit University, 1991), 45–46, quoted in Nita Kumar, "Sanskrit Pandits and the Modernisation of Sanskrit Education in the Nineteenth to Twentieth Centuries," in William Radice, ed., *Swami Vivekananda and the Modernization of Hinduism*

(Delhi: Oxford University Press, 1998), 36–60 at 42. Cf. K. Parameswara Aithal and Axel Michaels, eds., *The Pandit: Traditional Scholarship in India* (New Delhi: Manohar, 2001).

134. See Yelle, *Explaining Mantras*, 142–43.

135. *Tantrarāja Tantra* 1.75. In *Tantrarāja Tantra*, ed. Arthur Avalon and Lakshmana Shastri (Delhi: Motilal Banarsidass, 1997).

136. Cohn, "Command of Language," in *Colonialism and its Forms of Knowledge*, 51–53.

137. A. D. Campbell, quoted in id. at 51–52. Campbell's 1823 report is quoted in Bureau of Education, India, *Selections from Educational Records, Part I: 1781–1839* (Calcutta: Superintendent of Government Printing, 1920), 68, as follows: "Few teachers can explain, and still fewer scholars understand, the purport of the numerous books which they thus learn to repeat from memory. Every schoolboy can repeat verbatim a vast number of verses, of the meaning of which he knows no more than the parrot that has been taught to utter certain words." The entire report is reproduced as "Collector, Bellary to Board of Revenue: 17 August 1823," in Dharampal, *The Beautiful Tree: Indigenous Indian Education in the Eighteenth Century* (New Delhi: Biblia Impex Private Ltd.), 178–87.

138. Minute of June 8, 1833 meeting of the General Committee of Public Instruction, in *General Committee of Public Instruction, Correspondence and Proceedings*, vol. 2, February 17, 1830 to April 20, 1839, at the West Bengal State Archives. Similar complaints can of course be found in the British context, often associated with movements for the standardization of language made possible by print culture. Alexander John Ellis, one of the main supporters of English spelling reform in the nineteenth century, contrasted the benefits of such reforms with the present system of instruction in terms that echoed the Protestant attack on vain repetitions: "At present, a child's intellectual acquirements, when he leaves school, are very small, and his moral and religious attainments are but too frequently limited to a parrot-like power of repeating certain prayers and catechisms—religion being degraded to a mere exercise of memory." Ellis associated orality, mnemotechnics, and irregular spelling with traditional Christianity, and a reformed system of writing with the religion of the Reformation. "A Plain Statement of the Objects and Advantages of the Spelling Reform," appended as a preface to Ellis, *Essentials of Phonetics*.

139. Debashya, *Tract*, 66.

140. William Adam, *Reports on the State of Education in Bengal (1835 and 1838)*, ed. Anathnath Basu (Calcutta: University of Calcutta, 1941), 152. See also Joseph DiBona, ed., *One Teacher, One School: The Adam Reports on Indigenous Education in 19th Century India* (New Delhi: Biblia Impex Private Ltd., 1983). Similar is the following account of Sanskrit pedagogy in India Office Records V/ 24/ 905, *General Report on Public Instruction in the North Western Provinces, of the Bengal Presidency, for 1844–45* (Agra: Secundra Orphan Press, 1846), Appendix I,

Mr. Fink's Report, to J. Middleton, Esq. (xlviii–xc), "General Remarks on Sanscrit Instruction" (lxvii–lxix): "They first commit to memory either the whole book or a lesson every day, and then proceed to learn the meaning of it from the mouth of the teacher, without enquiring into the grammatical construction of each of the sentences which it contains. The consequence of this is, that they are unable to explain any book which they have not read" (lxvii). The cause of this decline is that "the path to eminence no longer lies through Sanskrit learning" (ibid.). However, Brahmins "continue to preside at religious ceremonies, to cast nativities, explain omens, point out auspicious moments . . . and give moral, religious, and historical instruction by the recitation of Puranas. The object of Sanskrit studies in general is . . . to qualify them for these duties. . . . It is a fact, that some priests learn no more than 2 or 3 Shlokas from the Shigrabadha, and make use of them at *all* religious ceremonies" (lxviii). Cf. the rather more positive view of low-level instruction in the Koran by rote memorization in G. W. Leitner, *History of Indigenous Education in the Panjab Since Annexation and in 1882* ([Patiala:] Languages Department Punjab, 1971), 67.

141. Frances Robinson, "Islam and the Impact of Print in South Asia," in Nigel Crook, ed., *The Transmission of Knowledge in South Asia* (Delhi: Oxford University Press, 1996), 62–97.

142. Gethin, "The *Matikas*."

143. "On the Progress and Present State of the Native Press in India," *Friend of India*, Quarterly Series 4, No. 12 (1825): 138–56 at 150–52. See H. H. Wilson, "Remarks on the Character and Labours of Dr. Carey, as an Oriental Scholar and Translator," in Eustace Carey, *Memoir of William Carey* (London: Jackson and Walford, 1836), 596: "The printing-press brought literature within the reach of a large public and enabled it to develop in many ways hitherto impossible. It finally destroyed the oral tradition which Bengali, in common with other Indian literature, had retained from its origin, and facilitated, really necessitated, the growth of prose." Halhed's Bengali grammar also noted that Bengali compositions were almost entirely in poetry or verse.

144. India Office Records V/ 24/ 947, *Report of the General Committee of Public Instruction of the Presidency of Fort William in Bengal, for the year 1835* (Calcutta: G. H. Huttmann, Bengal Military Orphan Press, 1836), Hindu College Essay, "On Printing," by Kylas Chunder Dutt, February 16, 1836, pp. 77–82 at 77–78. For an earlier use of the phrase "Divine Art of Printing," see Aubrey, *Remaines of Gentilisme*, 68.

145. Mandair, *Religion and the Specter of the West*, 313–78.

146. Id. at 325–28.

147. Id. at 319–20, 354.

148. Id. at 330–31.

149. James Hastings, *Encyclopaedia of Religion and Ethics* (Edinburgh: T & T Clark, 1908–1927), 204.

150. Although originally published in 1921, Heiler's book remained on the reading lists of the Ph.D. program in the History of Religions at the University of Chicago Divinity School into the 1990s. My source for this is Winnifred Fallers Sullivan, oral communication. I graduated from the same program in 2002, having passed my exams in 1999, by which time Heiler was no longer required reading.

151. Friedrich Heiler, *Prayer: A Study in the History and Psychology of Religion*, trans. Samuel McComb (Oxford: Oxford University Press, 1932), 65.

152. Id. at 71.

153. Id. at 72.

154. Id. at 71.

155. Id. at 68–69.

156. Another example is the general article on "Prayer" in Hastings's *Encyclopaedia*, which identifies primitive prayer with magic spells.

157. Paul VI, *Sacrosanctum Concilium* (Constitution on the Sacred Liturgy), December 4, 1963, secs. 33–34 (my emphasis).

158. Paul VI, *Marialis Cultus* (Apostolic Exhortation of his Holiness Pope Paul VI for the Right Ordering and Development of Devotion to the Blessed Virgin Mary), February 2, 1974, sec. 47 (my emphasis).

159. John Paul II, *Rosarium Virginis Mariae* (Apostolic Letter of the Supreme Pontiff John Paul II to the Bishops, Clergy, and Faithful on the Most Holy Rosary), October 16, 2002, sec. 12.

160. Id. at sec. 26 (emphasis original).

161. Id. at sec. 43.

162. Philip Zaleski and Carol Zaleski, *Prayer: A History* (Boston: Houghton Mifflin, 2005).

163. Id. at 5.

164. Id. at 150.

165. Id. at 24–32. Heiler appears at 29–30.

166. Id. at 41–41.

167. Id. at 260–61.

168. Id. at 71.

169. *Encyclopaedia Britannica*, 6th ed. (Edinburgh, 1822), s.v. "Prayer."

170. Zaleski and Zaleski, *Prayer*, 338–46.

171. "Long-Awaited Medical Study Questions the Power of Prayer," *New York Times*, March 31, 2006. See also the op-ed by Raymond J. Lawrence, "Faith-Based Medicine," *New York Times*, April 11, 2006.

172. Cf. Ramie Targoff, *Common Prayer: The Language of Public Devotion in Early Modern England* (Chicago: University of Chicago Press, 2001), 26.

173. Weber, *Protestant Ethic*, 157–58.

174. For an additional discussion of these points, see Yelle, *Semiotics of Religion*, chapter 5.

175. Stanley Tambiah, "A Performative Approach to Ritual," in *Culture, Thought, and Social Action: An Anthropological Perspective* (Cambridge, MA: Harvard University Press, 1995), 123-66, esp. 128.

176. See Smith, *To Take Place*, 103 and the discussion in chapter 1, page 16 of this volume.

CHAPTER 5

1. E.g., J. Duncan M. Derrett, "The Administration of Hindu Law by the British," *Comparative Studies in Society and History* 4 (1961): 10–52; Marc Galanter, "The Displacement of Traditional Law in Modern India," *Journal of Social Issues* 24 (1968): 65–90.

2. See, however, Rajeev Dhavan, "Dharmaśāstra and Modern Indian Society," *Journal of the Indian Law Institute* 34 (1992): 515–40 at 519, which gestures at these developments.

3. As many scholars have pointed out, Dharmaśāstra was only one tradition of law indigenous to India. In their quest for an authoritative source of law, British elevated this older, textual tradition, represented by such texts as the *Laws of Manu*, to the status of "Hindu law," in the process displacing a variety of other, especially customary and local traditions. Scholars have questioned also the normative status and real-world enforcement of the Dharmaśāstra tradition. See, e.g., Don Davis, "*Dharma, Maryāda*, and Law in Early British Malabar: Remarks on Words for 'Law' in the Tellicherry Records," *Studien zur Indologie und Iranistik* 23 (2002): 51–70.

4. Romans 6:14.

5. See Yelle, "Moses' Veil."

6. See, e.g., *Westminster Confession of Faith* (1646) (moral, civil, ceremonial); John Maynard, *The Law of God Ratified, by the Gospel of Christ* (London: printed for Francis Tyton, 1674), 75; John Edwards, *A Compleat History or Survey of All the Dispensations and Methods of Religion* (London: printed for Daniel Brown, 1699), 148.

7. Cf. Romans 1.

8. See chapter 1 in this volume.

9. This figure is illustrated by the etymological identification, described below, between "Moses" and "Manu," the Hindu law giver. It is also an homage to the title of Jan Assmann's excellent book, *Moses the Egyptian*.

10. This analysis complements, to some degree, Richard King's contention, discussed in chapter 1 in this volume, that the British defined Hinduism as a form of mysticism centered on subjective experiences or spiritual or psychological states, and thus, by implication, unconcerned with worldly conduct such as that defined by law; as well as Donald Davis's recent observation that Western scholars have neglected the legal (including ritual), as opposed to, say, the mythological and philosophical dimensions of traditional Hinduism, a neglect that would be

partly explained (though not excused) by the present analysis. Donald R. Davis, Jr., "Hinduism as a Legal Tradition," *Journal of the American Academy of Religion* 75 (2007): 241–67.

11. Weber, *Protestant Ethic*, esp. chapter 4, "The Religious Foundations of Worldly Asceticism."

12. Max Weber, *The Religion of India: The Sociology of Hinduism and Buddhism*, trans. H. H. Gerth and Don Martindale (New York: Free Press, 1958), 112.

13. Max Weber, *The Sociology of Religion*, trans. Ephraim Fischoff (Boston: Beacon Press, 1964), 207–08.

14. Weber, *The Religion of India*, 112.

15. Id. at 37–38.

16. David Ellenson, "Max Weber on Judaism and the Jews," in *After Emancipation: Jewish Religious Responses to Modernity* (Cincinnati: Hebrew Union College Press, 2004), 80–95. See also Gary Abraham, *Max Weber and the Jewish Question: A Study of the Social Outlook of His Sociology* (Urbana and Chicago: University of Illinois Press, 1992), 67–68.

17. Colossians 3:11. Cf. Galatians 3:28.

18. In the famous formula appearing during the French Revolution in Stanislas-Marie-Adélaide, Comte de Clermont-Tonnerre, "Speech on Religious Minorities and Questionable Professions" (December 23, 1789) (accessed April 15, 2012 at http://chnm.gmu.edu/revolution/d/284/).

19. Ellenson, "Max Weber," 94.

20. India Office Records, Home Misc/420, pp. 31–55: *Extract of a Letter from the Governor and Council at Fort William to the Court of Directors, dated 3d November 1772, Transmitting a Letter from the Committee of Circuit, at Cossimbuzar, and a Plan, Framed by that Committee, for the Administration of Justice, in Bengal*, 4.

21. J. Duncan M. Derrett, "Sanskrit Legal Treatises Compiled at the Instance of the British," *Zeitschrift für vergleichende Rechtswissenschaft* 63 (1961): 72–117 at 81; Richard Lariviere, "Justices and *Panditas*: Some Ironies in Contemporary Readings of the Hindu Legal Past," *Journal of Asian Studies* 48 (1989): 757–69 at 759; Lauren Benton, "Colonial Law and Cultural Difference: Jurisdictional Politics and the Formation of the Colonial State," *Comparative Studies in Society and History* 41 (1999): 563–88 at 567.

22. Bernard Cohn, "Law and the Colonial State," in *Colonialism and its Forms of Knowledge*, 57–75 at 71. In addition to the examples below, see Sir Thomas Strange, Hindu Law, 2 vols. (London: Parbury, Allen, and Co., 1830), Preface, xi. Charles Hamilton, *The Hedaya, or Guide: A Commentary on the Mussulman Laws*, 2nd ed. (London: Wm. H. Allen & Co., 1870), similarly expurgated almost all of the ritual portions of this work of Muslim law.

23. Derrett, "Sanskrit Legal Treatises," 86.

24. Henry T. Colebrooke, *A Digest of Hindu Law on Contracts and Successions*, 4 vols. (Calcutta, 1797–1798), vol. 1, Preface, ix–x. Edward Röer and W. A. Montriou,

Hindu Law and Judicature from the Dharma-sastra of Yajnavalkya in English (Calcutta: R. C. Lepage and Co., 1859), severely abridged the first book, on "Ritual and Moral Conduct," so as to introduce the topics of "civil and municipal law" (1) addressed in the second book on "Law and Judicature" (9–80). Whereas all of the verses in the second book are translated, only 28 out of more than 367 in the first book are.

25. Adam, *Reports*, 179: "The compilation of Raghunandana on every branch of Hindu law, comprised in twenty-eight books, is almost exclusively studied in this district. . . . Of the twenty-eight books those are almost exclusively read which prescribe and explain the ritual of Hinduism. The first book invariably read is that on lunar days [i.e., the *Tithitattva*]; and this is followed by the others without any fixed order of succession, such as those on marriage, on penance, on purification, on obsequies, on the intercalary month of the Hindu calendar, &c.; but the number of books read is seldom more than ten and never exceeds twelve, and is sometimes not more than four, three, and even two."

26. India Office Records V/ 24/ 946, *Report on the Colleges and Schools for Native Education, under the superintendence of the General Committee of Public Instruction in Bengal for 1831* (Calcutta: Bengal Military Orphan Press, 1832): the *Śuddhitattva* ("Treatise on Purifications") and *Prāyaścittatattva* ("Treatise on Expiations") were taught in the Calcutta Sanskrit College (9–10), while the *Prāyaścittanirṇaya* and *Prāyaścittaviveka* (other works on expiations) were taught at the Benares College (19–20). India Office Records V/ 24/ 946, *Report of the General Committee of Public Instruction of the Presidency of Fort William in Bengal for the Year 1836* (Calcutta: Baptist Mission Press, 1837), 95, states that the *Tithitattva* ("Treatise on Lunar Rites") was used at the Calcutta Sanskrit College.

27. India Office Records V/ 24/ 905, *Annual Reports of the Calcutta Mudrissa, . . . Hindu College, Sanscrit College, . . . [etc.], for 1850–51* (Calcutta: Military Orphan Press, 1851), 9. This appears to represent a deviation, so far unexplained, from earlier practice. Duff, *New Era*, 15, provides a list of books printed for the government Oriental schools between 1824 and 1831. Listed are the *Dāyatattva* and the *Vyavāharatattva*, but not the *Aṣṭaviṃśatitattva* ("the Twenty-eight Treatises").

28. "Report by Isvar Chandra Sharma transmitted with letter dated December 16, 1850, to F. J. Mouat." The recommendations contained therein are reproduced in the above-mentioned Report for 1850–1851, as well as in India Office Records V/ 24/ 954, *General Report on Public Instruction in the Lower Provinces of the Bengal Presidency from 1st October 1850 to 30th September 1851* (Calcutta: Bengal Military Orphan Press, 1852), 39–40, which adds (34) that "The suggestions contained therein were approved by the Council, and ordered to be adopted in the next session of 1851–52."

29. Later volumes up through 1857 in the India Office Records did not reveal any evidence that the ritual texts were reinstated in the curriculum.

30. In Jivananda Vidyasagara's edition of the *Smṛtitattva*, there are 1,631 pages. The *Dāyatattva* and the *Vyavahāratattva* together add up to 74 pages, or just over four and one-half percent of the total. *Smṛtitattva*, ed. Jivananda Vidyasagara (Calcutta: Siddhesvara Press, 1895).

31. J. Duncan M. Derrett, *Religion, Law and the State in India* (New York: Free Press, 1968), 83, argued that caste tribunals effectively enforced caste restrictions or rules of a noncriminal nature into the early British period.

32. Ali Ibrahim Khan, "On the Trial by Ordeal among the Hindus," *Asiatic Researches* 1 (London, 1806 [1788]), 389–404.

33. This court had the power to censure and levy fines, as well as to impose penance (*prāyaścitta*) for such offences as "eating with those with whom you ought not to eat; sexual commerce with those between whom it is forbidden; drinking water from the hands of those not entitled to offer it;—in a word, doing any thing from negligence, inadvertence, or licentiousness, by which loss of caste is incurred." Brian Houghton Hodgson, "Some Account of the Systems of Law and Police as Recognised in the State of Nepal," *Journal of the Royal Asiatic Society* 1 (1834): 258–79 at 260. See Leonhard Adam, "Criminal Law and Procedure in Nepal a Century Ago: Notes Left by Brian H. Hodgson," *Far Eastern Quarterly* 9 (1950): 146–68 at 149; and Axel Michaels, *The Price of Purity: The Religious Judge in 19th Century Nepal, containing the edition and translation of the chapters on the Dharmadhikarin* (Torino: CESMEO, 2006), which I have not been able to consult.

34. See, e.g., the following treatises and the cases referred to therein: Strange, *Hindu Law*, 1: 95–97, 2: 140–47, 154–58, 164–73, 218–20; Herbert Cowell, *The Hindu Law: Being a Treatise on the Law Administered Exclusively to Hindus by the British Courts in India* (Calcutta: Thacker, Spink and Co., 1870), 59–60, 241, and esp. 227–30; Ernest John Trevelyan, *Hindu Family Law As Administered in British India* (London: W. Thacker and Co., 1908), 154–56.

35. Francis Workman Macnaghten, *Considerations on the Hindoo Law, as it is current in Bengal* (Serampore: Mission Press, 1824), vi.

36. As can be seen already in the titles of some of the following works: William Jones, *Institutes of Hindu Law: or, the Ordinances of Menu, According to the Gloss of Culluca, Comprising the Indian System of Duties, Religious and Civil* (Calcutta, 1794); Colebrooke, *Digest*, volume 1, preface; Auguste Loiseleur Deslongchamps, *Lois de Manou, comprenant les institutions religieuses et civiles des Indiens* (Paris: Crapelet, 1833); E. Gibelin, *Études sur le droit civil des Hindous; Recherches de législation comparée sur les lois de l'Inde, les lois d'Athènes et de Rome, et les coutumes des Germains*, 2 vols. (Pondichéry: A. Toutin, 1846), 1: xvi: *Manu* "est le recueil de toutes les règles qui concernent la conduite civile et religieuse de l'homme"; Derrett, *Religion, Law and the State*, 103.

37. Jones, *Works*, 3: 62.

38. See the discussion of Jones's translation below in this chapter.

39. Strange, *Hindu Law*, preface, xi, 93. Cf. Arthur J. Patterson, *Caste Considered under its Moral, Social, and Religious Aspects: The Le Bas Prize Essay in the University of Cambridge for the Year 1860* (London: Smith, Elder & Co., 1861), 20: "Its title in the original Sanskrit is *Manava-dharma-sastra*, generally translated Menu's Code, but its sense would be more perfectly expressed by the paraphrase, 'the treatise on what is just, right, and according to good custom in things civil, religious, moral and ceremonial, according to the teaching and traditions of the disciples or descendants of Menu.'" Debashya, *Tract*, 40, also used the term "ceremonial law" in pejorative reference to Hindu ritual.

40. Morton, *Biblical and Theological Vocabulary*, renders "law" as "vyavasthā, vidhāna," "moral law" as "pāpapuṇya viṣayak vyavasthā, nītir vidhāna," "judicial law" as "nyāyānyāyer vidhāna, danta kanta," and "ceremonial law" as "dhārāvāhika rītir vidhāna, āhnikādi nitya kriyār vidhāna." See note 99 below in this chapter for H. Bower's evaluation of various attempts to translate the term "civil law" into vernacular South Asian languages.

41. Henry Sumner Maine, "The Sacred Laws of the Hindus," in *Dissertations on Early Law and Custom* (London: John Murray, 1883), 1–25.

42. Id. at 5.

43. Ibid. Substantially in agreement with this judgment, at least as to the religiosity of *Manu* and the Dharmaśāstra tradition, were Julius Jolly, *Recht und Sitte* (Strassburg: Karl J. Trübner, 1896), 1; Deslongchamps, *Lois de Manou*, préface, i–ii.

44. Maine, "The Sacred Laws," 18–19.

45. Hodgson, *The Preeminence of the Vernaculars*, 47, stated that Hinduism was distinguished by "the universal precurrency of its divine sanctions through all the effects of life, so as to leave no corner of the field of human action as neutral ground." Some Hindus also registered the complaint against the excessive ritualism of Dharmaśāstra. Ganganath Jha, *Manusmrti: With the Manubhasya of Medhatithi*, 10 vols. (Delhi: Motilal Banarsidass, 1999), 10: xxiii–xxix, quoted Govindasa's evaluation that in the Dharmaśāstra "Vyavahara occupies but a small fragment of their energies, which are all spent on Achara and Prayashchitta," and argued that the reason was that Brahmins, having lost temporal power to Muslims and others, turned away from mundane matters.

46. J. Duncan M. Derrett, "The Concept of Law according to Medhātithi, A Pre-Islamic Indian Jurist," in Wilhelm Hönerbach, ed., *Der Orient in der Forschung* (Wiesbaden: Otto Harrassowitz, 1967), 18–41 at 31–36.

47. The former were *pravṛtta*; the latter *nivṛtta*. *Manu* 12.88–90. Unless otherwise specified, all references to and translations of *Manu* are from Patrick Olivelle, *Manu's Code of Law* (New York: Oxford University Press, 2005). See also Johannes Laping, "Pragmatism and Transcendence: Aspects of Pragmatic Soteriology ('Heilspragmatik') in Indian Tradition," in Detlef Kantowsky, ed., *Recent Research on Max Weber's Studies of Hinduism* (München: Weltforum Verlag, 1986), 199–207 at 202.

48. Cowell, *Hindu Law*, 18.

49. Derrett, "The Concept of Law," 26; Derrett, *Religion, Law and the State*, 99.

50. E.g., at Jolly, *Recht und Sitte*, 1 (*das Recht*).

51. The *Arthaśāstra*, discussed below, did not figure in these nineteenth-century evolutionary accounts of Hindu law, as the text itself was not discovered until the early twentieth century.

52. Maine, "Religion and Law," in *Dissertations*, 26–49 at 41.

53. J. Duncan M. Derrett, "Sir Henry Maine and Law in India, 1858–1958," *Juridical Review* 4 (1959): 40–55 at 48–49; reprinted in *Essays in Classical and Modern Hindu Law*, 4 vols. (Leiden: Brill, 1976–78), 3: 260–76. Arthur S. Diamond, *Primitive Law, Past and Present* (London: Methuen and Co., 1971), vii, 47–52, and esp. 104–13, also disputed Maine's thesis as to ancient law, including Hindu, and argued that the conflation of law with religion in *Manu* and Leviticus, etc., belonged to a phase of later codes developed under the influence of priesthoods. An early view counter to Maine's was J. D. Mayne, *A Treatise on Hindu Law and Usage* (Madras: Higginbotham and Co., 1878), 4, which—like Diamond in the next century—applied to Hindu law an earlier Protestant and Deist narrative of the corruption of law by priesthoods.

54. Derrett, *Religion, Law and the State*, 97. See also chapter 3, "Religious Commands and Legal Commands," in id. at 75–96. Cf. Werner Menski's argument that the term "religious legal system" as applied to Hindu law is misleading and ideologically driven. "Hindu Law as a 'Religious' System," in Andrew Huxley, ed., *Religion, Law and Tradition: Comparative Studies in Religious Law* (London: RoutledgeCurzon, 2002), 108–26.

55. Derrett, "Religion and Law in Hindu Jurisprudence," *Proceedings of the 23rd International Congress of Orientalists* (London: The Royal Asiatic Society, 1957), 225–26. Cf. Derrett, "Religion and the Making of Hindu Law," in *Religion, Law and the State*, 97–121.

56. Derrett, *Religion, Law and the State*, 102.

57. Cf. Derrett, *Hindu Law, Past and Present* (Calcutta: A. Mukherjee, 1957), 45.

58. Derrett, *Religion, Law and the State*, 98–99.

59. Richard Lariviere, *The Naradasmṛti* (Delhi: Motilal Banarsidass, 2003), 1.

60. Cowell, *Hindu Law*, 18–19, 26. See discussion of Derrett below in this chapter.

61. See, e.g., George Crawshay, *The Immediate Cause of the Indian Mutiny, as Set Forth in the Official Correspondence* (London: Effingham Wilson, 1857), 2, distinguishing between "moral" and "ceremonial" offences in Hindu and ancient Jewish law.

62. Duff, *India*, 153. The statement in Allen, *India*, 366, 401, is also representative: "As these laws [of Manu] profess to be of divine origin, kings had no authority to change them . . . In these respects they resembled the laws given by Moses and contained in the Old Testament. In no nation were ever civil and religious matters more closely united than among the Hindus. . . . Many of the Hindu rites [regarding impurity] . . . resemble the laws of the Jews contained in the Pentateuch."

63. Lord, *Display*, 40.

64. See also *A Seasonable Prospect for the View and Consideration of Christians* (London: printed by J. L. for Luke Meredith, 1691), 5–6, which copied Lord's earlier account of the commandments.

65. For a particularly late and extravagant example, see Alexander Hamilton, *A Key to the Chronology of the Hindus*, 2 vols. (Cambridge: printed by J. Smith for F. and C. Rivington, 1820). Such comparisons were applied not only to Hinduism; they were part of a more general effort to reconcile sacred history with ethnographic knowledge. For references to texts comparing Native Americans to the Jews, see David Chidester, *Savage Systems: Colonialism and Comparative Religion in Southern Africa* (Charlottesville: University of Virginia Press, 1996), 17.

66. See, in addition to those cited below, M. [Maturin] Veyssière La Croze, *Histoire du Christianisme des Indes*, 2 vols. (La Haye: aux dépens de la Compagnie, 1758); Constantin-François de Chassebœuf, Comte de Volney, *Les Ruines, ou, Méditation sur les révolutions des empires* (Paris: Desenne, 1791).

67. The main source for this tradition was the seventeenth-century Hebraist John Spencer's explanation, in *De legibus hebraeorum ritualibus et earum rationibus libri tres* (Cambridge: Richard Chiswel, 1685), that Mosaic laws were designed in opposition to, and as an inversion of, Egyptian idolatry. For a discussion, see Stroumsa, "John Spencer."

68. Hananya Goodman, "Introduction: Judaism and Hinduism: Cultural Resonances," in *Between Jerusalem and Benares: Comparative Studies in Judaism and Hinduism* (Albany: SUNY Press, 1994), 1–14 at 3.

69. M. De la Créquinière, *The Agreement of the Customs of the East-Indians with those of the Jews* (London: printed for W. Davis, 1705). This work, attributed by some to John Toland, was a translation of De la Créquinière's own *Conformité des coutumes des Indiens orientaux avec celles des Juifs et des autres peuples de l'antiquité* (Brussels, 1704).

70. Id. at 70.

71. Id. at 136–37, 139.

72. Id. at vi–vii.

73. Id. at 100.

74. See Goodman, "Introduction." This argument, based on a superficial resemblance in the names of these legendary ancestors, had been made earlier by Guillaume Postel. On the *Ezourvedam*, see Ludo Rocher, *Ezourvedam: A French Veda of the Eighteenth Century* (Amsterdam: John Benjamins, 1984).

75. Halhed, *Code*, lviii.

76. Id. at lxv, lxii–lxiii.

77. Id. at xliv.

78. See the Abbé Raynal, *Histoire philosophique et politique des établissements et du commerce des Européens dans les deux Indes* (Génève, 1780), cited in Michael John Franklin's introduction to Halhed, *Code*.

79. Louis Langlès, *Fables et contes Indiens* (Paris: Royez, 1790), Discours prélimi-naire, xi. Langlès argued, *inter alia*, that the five Vedas (one now being lost) were the prototype for the five books of Moses (xxii).

80. Chaudhuri, *Proceedings*, 63, quoting a letter from R. Landaff to William Jones dated Feb. 19, 1785: "Another subject of inquiry is, whether there are any marks of Judaism among any of these castes. It has often been said that the Brahmins are descended from Abraham."

81. See esp. Jones, "On the Gods of Greece, Italy, and India," in *Works*, 3: 319-97.

82. Joseph Priestley, *A Comparison of the Institutions of Moses with Those of the Hindoos and Other Ancient Nations* (Northumberland: printed by A. Kennedy, 1799). On Priestley's contribution to this debate, see Martin Priestman, *Romantic Atheism: Poetry and Freethought 1780–1830* (Cambridge: Cambridge University Press, 1999), 25. For John Adams's reading of Priestley, see Manuel, *The Eighteenth Century*, 272. Cf. John Mitchell, *An Essay on the Best Means of Civilising the Subjects of the British Empire in India, and of Diffusing the Light of the Christian Religion Throughout the Eastern World* (Edinburgh: W. Blackwood, 1805), which endorsed Priestley's "The Comparison betwixt the Jewish and Hindoo Codes."

83. Priestley, *Comparison*, 47.

84. Id. at 85.

85. Louis Jacolliot, *The Bible in India: Hindoo Origin of Hebrew and Christian Revelation* (London: John Camden Hotten, 1870). This was a translation of the author's *La Bible dans l'Inde: Vie de Iezeus Christna* (Paris, 1868).

86. Id. at 118.

87. Id. at 131–32.

88. Id. at 133–34.

89. Id. at 55.

90. Id. at 56, 61, 63–64, 97–176.

91. Volney, *Les Ruines*, 297.

92. George Stanley Faber, *The Origins of Pagan Idolatry*, 3 vols. (London: F. and C. Rivingtons, 1816), 3:661; Thomas Maurice, *Brahminical Fraud Detected; or The Attempts of the Sacerdotal Tribe of India to Invest Their Fabulous Deities and Heroes with the Honours and Attributes of the Christian Messiah, Examined, Exposed, and Defeated* (London: W. Bulmer and Co., 1812).

93. Daniel Jeyaraj, *Genealogy of the South Indian Deities: An English Translation of Bartholomäus Ziegenbalg's Original German Manuscript with a Textual Analysis and Glossary* (London: RoutledgeCurzon, 2005), 4.

94. This translation of a tract by Ram Boshoo appears in Major John Scott-Waring's *Vindication of the Hindoos, Part the Second* (London: R. & J. Rodwell, 1808), 184–94 at 187.

95. Colossians 3:11, quoted in Joseph Roberts, *Caste in its Religious and Civil Character Opposed to Christianity* (London: Longman, Brown, Green, and Longmans, 1847), 4–5, 19.

96. See Duncan B. Forrester, *Caste and Christianity: Attitudes and Policies on Caste of Anglo-Saxon Protestant Missions in India* (London: Curzon, 1979); H. Bower, *Essay on Hindu Caste* (Calcutta: Baptist Mission Press, 1851); *Minute of the Madras Missionary Conference and other Documents on the Subject of Caste* (Madras: American Mission Press, 1850).

97. Letter dated March 21, 1826, from Bishop Reginald Heber to Reverend Mr. Schreyvogel [D. Schrievogel], in Bower, *Essay on Hindu Caste*, 103, and Roberts, *Caste in its Religious and Civil Character*, 1–3.

98. Wilson rejected both the comparison of caste to Mosaic law and the use of this comparison to uphold caste as a civil distinction. Circular dated July 5, 1833, in Bower, *Essay on Hindu Caste*, 113.

99. Bower, *Essay on Hindu Caste*, 14, points out that such terms as *deśācāra* used to describe caste as a civil or local institution were not native, and moreover, should really be translated as "the religious usage of the land" rather than "the civil custom of the country."

100. *Minute of the Madras Missionary Conference on the Subject of Caste*, February, 1850, in Bower, *Essay on Hindu Caste*, 120–21.

101. See Jones's translation of *Manu* 4.155.

102. See, in addition to Jones's translations of *Manu* 4.204 and 6.95 discussed here, verses 12.88 and 6.82: "No man, who is ignorant of the supreme spirit, can gather the fruit of mere ceremonial acts."

103. Patrick Olivelle translates the first half of 4.204 as follows: "A wise man should always practice the central virtues and not busy himself constantly with the secondary observances." His note to this verse argues that "the terms here refer to two sets of observances, *yama* being central virtues such as non-injury and *niyama* being outward religious rites such as twilight-worship." This distinction, however, may not be as clear as Olivelle suggests. *Manu* does not even specify what are *yamas* and what *niyamas*. Subsequently, *yama* was sometimes interpreted as a prohibition, a restraint on activity (e.g., an abstention from sexual activity or violence), and *niyama* as a positively enjoined performance. The distinction was not simply that between inward, "moral" and external, "ritual" conduct. Whether a rule enjoins one to refrain from or to perform an activity, the reference point of the rule remains a physical act. Moreover, some lists of *niyamas* included inner, subjective moral conditions such as contentment or devotion to God. See P. V. Kane, *History of Dharmaśāstra*, 2nd ed. (Poona: Bhandarkar Oriental Research Institute, 1977), vol. 5, pt. 2, pp. 946 n., 1419–22.

104. Priestley, *Comparison*, 48.

105. J. Duncan M. Derrett, "Die Entwicklung des indischen Rechts," in Wolfgang Schluchter, ed., *Max Webers Studie über Hinduismus und Buddhismus: Interpretation und Kritik* (Frankfurt: Suhrkamp, 1984), 178–201 at 190.

106. Id. at 189.

107. Ibid. Derrett elsewhere advanced a (dubious) "scientific" explanation for some Hindu ordeals, which coordinated with his attempt to downplay the religious element in Dharmaśāstra. See J. Duncan M. Derrett, "Ancient Indian 'Nonsense' Vindicated," *Journal of the American Oriental Society* 98 (1978): 100–06; and the critique in Robert A. Yelle, "Hindu Law as Performance: Ritual and Poetic Elements in *Dharmaśāstra*," in *Hinduism and Law: An Introduction*, ed. Timothy Lubin, Donald R. Davis, Jr., and Jayanth K. Krishnan (Cambridge: Cambridge University Press, 2010), 183–192 at 185.

108. Derrett, "Die Entwicklung des indischen Rechts," 193.

109. Id. at 181 (my trans.).

110. The question of Christian bias in Derrett's interpretation of Hindu law is a sensitive and important one, given his status in the field and vast accomplishments, and requires a careful investigation. It should be cautioned in advance that I am in no way accusing Derrett, whose work I greatly admire, of anti-Semitism. Rather, I am contending that his Christian theological views, to which he is perfectly entitled, and concerning which he has been quite explicit on numerous occasions, have in some instances influenced his positive and especially normative judgments of Hindu law.

111. Derrett, *Hindu Law*, 38.

112. Id. at 42–43.

113. Id. at 44–45.

114. Id. at 46–47.

115. Elsewhere, Derrett defined law, morality, and religion—not to mention superstition—as separate categories. J. Duncan M. Derrett, *Law and Morality* (Northamptonshire, UK: Pilkington Press, 1998), 15. Cf. the definitions of "Religion," "Recht," and "Gesetz," and his statement that "'Religiöses Gesetz' ist eine irreführende Bezeichnung," in J. Duncan M. Derrett, "Recht und Religion im Neuen Testament," in Wolfgang Schluchter, ed., *Max Webers Sicht des antiken Christentums: Interpretation und Kritik* (Frankfurt: Suhrkamp, 1985), 317–62 at 317–18.

116. Derrett, *Law and Morality*, 105.

117. J. Duncan M. Derrett, *Law in the New Testament* (London: Darton, Longman & Todd, 1970), xxvii.

118. Ibid.

119. Id. at xxx–xxxi.

120. J. Duncan M. Derrett, *Jesus's Audience: The Social and Psychological Environment in which He Worked* (London: Darton, Longman & Todd, 1973), 97.

121. Derrett, *Law in the New Testament*, xxvii, n.1. Cf. J. Duncan M. Derrett, *Two Masters: The Buddha and Jesus* (Northamptonshire, UK: Pilkington Press, 1995), 123, arguing for the inferiority of religious observances and claiming that *Manu* 6.66–67 "is sceptical of observances."

122. Derrett, *Law in the New Testament*, xxviii: "There was a great deal from which they needed to be liberated ('redeemed' if you like to adopt their emotionally overcharged vocabulary): we should say that they all needed to *grow up*."

123. Derrett, *Religion, Law and the State*, 81–82.

124. This phrase translates literally as "the discipline of action." While it is true that karma also meant ritual action, its primary meaning in the context of the Gītā is following one's assigned dharmic duties in life. This underscores the tendentiousness of Derrett's assimilation of these two paths to the Protestant contrast between works and faith.

125. J. Duncan M. Derrett, *A Critique of Modern Hindu Law* (Bombay: N. M Tripathi, 1970), 36–37.

126. Id. at 3.

127. Cf. J. Duncan M. Derrett, *Studies in the New Testament*, vol. 1 (Leiden: Brill, 1977), Preface, xvii, regarding Jesus's conflict with (some) Jews; "the not infrequent, continual conversions of thinking Jews to Christianity even to this day testify to the fact that no amount of *odium theologicum* can conceal Jesus's being, in an entirely constructive sense, the 'end' of the Law."

128. For an examination of the semiotic dimensions of British Protestant attacks on Jewish ceremonial law, see further Yelle, *Semiotics of Religion*, chapter 6.

Bibliography

PRIMARY SOURCES
Manuscripts and Archival Materials

Bodleian Library MS Eng. 2357. Papers of Friedrich Max Müller.

British Library MS Add. 25424. Catalogue of Sir Isaac Newton's Library.

India Office Records, Home Misc/420. *Extract of a Letter from the Governor and Council at Fort William to the Court of Directors, dated 3d November 1772, Transmitting a Letter from the Committee of Circuit, at Cossimbuzar, and a Plan, Framed by that Committee, for the Administration of Justice, in Bengal.*

India Office Records V/ 24/ 905. *Annual Reports of the Calcutta Mudrissa, . . . Hindu College, Sanscrit College, . . . [etc.], for 1850–51.* Calcutta: Military Orphan Press, 1851.

India Office Records V/ 24/ 905. *General Report on Public Instruction in the North Western Provinces, of the Bengal Presidency, for 1844–45.* Agra: Secundra Orphan Press, 1846.

India Office Records V/ 24/ 946. *Report on the Colleges and Schools for Native Education, under the superintendence of the General Committee of Public Instruction in Bengal for 1831.* Calcutta: Bengal Military Orphan Press, 1832.

India Office Records V/ 24/ 946. *Report of the General Committee of Public Instruction of the Presidency of Fort William in Bengal for the Year 1836.* Calcutta: Baptist Mission Press, 1837.

India Office Records V/ 24/ 947. *Report of the General Committee of Public Instruction of the Presidency of Fort William in Bengal, for the year 1835.* Calcutta: G. H. Huttmann, Bengal Military Orphan Press, 1836.

India Office Records V/ 24/ 954. Report by Isvar Chandra Sharma transmitted with letter dated December 16, 1850, to F. J. Mouat. In *General Report on Public Instruction in the Lower Provinces of the Bengal Presidency from 1st October 1850 to 30th September 1851,* 39–40. Calcutta: Bengal Military Orphan Press, 1852.

National Library, Kolkata. Simpson, David. Unpublished manuscript on Hindu religion in South India. In two parts. Trichonopoly, June 1, 1786.

West Bengal State Archives. *General Committee of Public Instruction, Correspondence and Proceedings.* Vol. 2. February 17, 1830 to April 20, 1839.

Papal Documents

John Paul II. *Rosarium Virginis Mariae.* Apostolic Letter of the Supreme Pontiff John Paul II to the Bishops, Clergy, and Faithful on the Most Holy Rosary. October 16, 2002.

Paul VI. *Marialis Cultus.* Apostolic Exhortation of his Holiness Pope Paul VI for the Right Ordering and Development of Devotion to the Blessed Virgin Mary. February 2, 1974.

Paul VI. *Sacrosanctum Concilium.* Constitution on the Sacred Liturgy. December 4, 1963.

Bibles in Sanskrit and Bengali

Bible. Gospels. Bengali. Trans. John Ellerton. [Calcutta: Calcutta Auxiliary Bible Society, 1819.]

Bible. New Testament. Bengali. [A.k.a. *Maṅgala Samācāra* or *Dharmapustaka.*] Trans. Serampore Baptist Missionaries. Serampore: Mission Press, 1801.

Bible. New Testament. Bengali. Trans. Serampore Baptist Missionaries. Serampore: Mission Press, 1803.

Bible. New Testament. Sanskrit. Trans. Serampore Baptist Missionaries. Serampore: Mission Press, 1808.

Bible. New Testament. Bengali. Trans. Serampore Baptist Missionaries. Serampore: Mission Press, 1833.

Christa-Saṅgītā, Or The Sacred History of Our Lord Jesus Christ in Sanskrit Verse. Trans. William Hodge Mill. 4 vols. Calcutta: Bishop's College Press, 1831–37.

The Four Gospels with the Acts of the Apostles, in Sanscrit. Calcutta: Baptist Mission Press, 1844.

The New Testament of our Lord and Savior Jesus Christ, in Bengali and English. Vol. I. Matthew to John. London: Richard Watts for the British and Foreign Bible Society, 1839.

The New Testament of our Lord and Saviour Jesus Christ, in the Bengallee Language. Calcutta: Baptist Mission Press, 1833.

The New Testament of our Lord and Saviour Jesus Christ, in the Bengallee Language. Calcutta: Baptist Mission Press, 1845.

The New Testament of our Lord and Saviour Jesus Christ, in Sanscrit. 2nd ed. Calcutta: Baptist Mission Press, 1851.

The New Testament of our Lord and Saviour Jesus Christ, in Sanscrit. 3rd ed. Calcutta: Baptist Mission Press, 1886.

Yiśucaritam. Trans. Vaneśvarapāṭhaka. Ranci: Satya Bharati, 1989.

Other Books and Articles

Aaron, R. I., and Jocelyn Gibb, eds. *An Early Draft of Locke's Essay.* Oxford: Clarendon Press, 1936.

Adam, William. *Reports on the State of Education in Bengal (1835 and 1838).* Ed. Anathnath Basu. University of Calcutta, 1941.

Ady, Thomas. *A Candle in the Dark.* London: printed for Robert Ibbitson, 1655.

Allen, David. *India: Ancient and Modern.* 2nd ed. Boston: John P. Jewett and Co., 1856.

Amaladass, Anand, and Richard Fox Young. *The Indian Christiad: A Concise Anthology of Didactic and Devotional Literature in Early Church Sanskrit.* Anand, Gujarat: Gujarat Sahitya Prakash, 1995.

Anderson, John. *The Answer to the Dialogue between the Curat and the Countrey-man,* [Edinburgh], 1712.

Annand, William. *Fides Catholica.* London: printed by T. R. for Edward Brewster, 1661.

———. *Pater Noster.* Edinburgh: printed by George Swinton and James Glen, 1670.

Antrim, Benajah J. *Pantography, or Universal Drawings, in the Comparison of their Natural and Arbitrary Laws, with the Nature and Importance of Pasigraphy, as the Science of Letters.* Philadelphia, 1843.

The Art of Speaking. 4th ed. Philadelphia: R. Aitken, 1775.

Aubrey, John. *Remaines of Gentilisme and Judaisme.* London, 1686–87. Reprint ed. London: W. Satchell, Peyton, and Co., 1881.

Bacon, Francis. *The Works of Francis Bacon.* Ed. James Spedding, Robert Leslie Ellis, and Douglas Denon Heath. 15 vols. Cambridge: Riverside Press and New York: Hurd and Houghton, 1869–72.

———. *Bacon's Novum Organum.* Ed. Thomas Fowler. 2nd ed. Oxford: Clarendon Press, 1889.

Ballantyne, James Robert. *An Explanatory Version of Bacon's Novum Organum, Printed for the Use of the Benares Sanskrit College.* Mirzapore: Orphan School Press, 1852.

Baxter, Richard. *An Accompt of All the Proceedings.* London: printed for R. H., 1661.

———. *A Christian Directory.* London: printed by Robert White for Nevill Simmons, 1673.

———. *The Saints Everlasting Rest.* London: printed by Robert White for Thomas Underhill and Francis Tyton, 1650.

Beausobre, Isaac de, and Jacques Lenfant. *A New Version of the Gospel.* Cambridge: printed by J. Archdeacon, 1779.

Beck, Cave. *The Universal Character.* London: printed by Thomas Maxey for William Weekly, 1657.

Bedwell, William. *Mohammedis Imposturae.* London: printed by Richard Field, 1615.

Bell, Alexander Melville. *Visible Speech: The Science of Universal Alphabetics; or Self-Interpreting Physiological Letters, for the Writing of All Languages in One Alphabet.* London: Simpkin, Marshall and Co., 1867.

Bentham, Jeremy. *The Works of Jeremy Bentham.* 11 vols. Ed. John Bowring. Edinburgh: William Tait, 1843.

Blackall, Offspring. *Practical Discourses on the Lord's Prayer.* London: printed by W. B. for Thomas Ward, 1717.

Blair, James. *Our Saviour's Divine Sermon.* London: printed for J. Brotherton, 1722.

Bower, H. *Essay on Hindu Caste.* Calcutta: Baptist Mission Press, 1851.

Boyle, Robert. *Some Considerations Touching the Style of the Holy Scriptures.* London: printed for Henry Herringman, 1661.

Bréal, Michel. *Mélanges de mythologie et de linguistique.* Paris: Hachette, 1882.

Brocklesby, Richard. *An Explication of the Gospel-Theism and the Divinity of the Christian Religion.* London: printed by J. Heptinstall, 1706.

Bulwer, John. *Chirologia: or the Natural Language of the Hand* and *Chirologia: or the Art of Manual Rhetoric.* London: printed by Thomas Harper, 1644. Reprint ed. Ed. James W. Cleary. Carbondale: Southern Illinois University Press, 1974.

Bunsen, Christian. *Christianity and Mankind, their Beginnings and Prospects.* 7 vols. London: Longman, Brown, Green, and Longmans, 1854.

Bureau of Education, India. *Selections from Educational Records, Part I: 1781–1839.* Calcutta: Superintendent of Government Printing, 1920.

Burgess, Anthony. *Spiritual Refining: Or a Treatise of Grace and Assurance.* London: printed by A. Miller for Thomas Underhill, 1652.

Burnouf, Eugène. *Le Bhâgavata Purâna.* Vol. 3. Paris: Imprimerie Royale, 1847.

———. *Introduction à l'histoire du Buddhisme Indien.* Vol. 1. Paris: Imprimerie Royale, 1844.

Burton, Henry. *Christ on his Throne.* London, 1640.

Calder, Robert. *An Answer to a Pamphlet Called, A Dialogue betwixt a Curat and a Country-man, concerning the English-service, or Common-prayer-book of England.* [Edinburgh], 1711.

Caldwell, R. *The Languages of India in their Relation to Missionary Work.* London: R. Clay, Sons, and Taylor, 1875.

Calvin, John. *A Harmonie upon the Three Evangelists.* London: George Bishop, 1584.

———. *Institutes of the Christian Religion.* Trans. John Allen. 7th ed. 2 vols. Philadelphia: Presbyterian Board of Christian Education, 1936.

Carey, Eustace. *Memoir of William Carey.* London: Jackson and Walford, 1836.

Carey, William, Joshua Marshman, and William Ward. *Hints Relative to Native Schools: Together with the Outline of an Institution for Their Extension and Management.* London: Black, Parbury, and Allen, 1817.

Cartwright, Thomas. *A Confutation of the Rhemists Translation.* N.p., 1618. Reprint ed. Amsterdam and New York: Da Capo Press, 1971.

Cave, William. *Apostolici, or, the History of the Lives, Acts, Death, and Martyrdom of Those Who Were Contemporary with, or Immediately Succeeded the Apostles.* 4th ed. London: printed by W. D. for J. Walthoe and several others, 1716.

Chatfield, Robert. *An Historical Review of the Commercial, Political, and Moral State of Hindoostan, from the Earliest Period to the Present Time: The Rise and Progress of Christianity in the East.* London: J. M. Richardson, 1808.

Chaudhuri, Sibadas, ed. *Proceedings of the Asiatic Society. Vol. 1. 1784–1800.* Calcutta: Asiatic Society, 1980.

Clermont-Tonnerre, Stanislas-Marie-Adélaide, Comte de. "Speech on Religious Minorities and Questionable Professions." December 23, 1789. Accessed April 15, 2012 at http://chnm.gmu.edu/revolution/d/284/.

Colebrooke, Henry T. *A Digest of Hindu Law on Contracts and Successions.* 4 vols. Calcutta, 1797–98.

———. "On the Vedas, Or Sacred Writings of the Hindus." *Asiatic Researches* 8 (London, 1808): 377–498.

A Compendious and Curious Miscellaneous History from the Creation to William the Conqueror. London, 1754.

Correspondence Relating to the Establishment of an Oriental College in London, Reprinted from the Times, with Notes and Additions. London: Williams and Norgate, 1858.

Cowell, Herbert. *The Hindu Law: Being a Treatise on the Law Administered Exclusively to Hindus by the British Courts in India.* Calcutta: Thacker, Spink and Co., 1870.

Crawshay, George. *The Immediate Cause of the Indian Mutiny, as Set Forth in the Official Correspondence.* London: Effingham Wilson, 1857.

Créquinière, M. De la. *The Agreement of the Customs of the East-Indians with Those of the Jews.* London: printed for W. Davis, 1705.

Croze, Maturin Veyssière La. *Histoire du Christianisme des Indes.* 2 vols. La Haye: aux dépens de la Compagnie, 1758.

Cudworth, Ralph. *The True Intellectual System of the Universe.* London: printed for Richard Royston, 1678.

Dalgarno, George. *Ars Signorum.* London: J. Hayes, 1661.

Debashya, Brajamohan. *A Tract against the Prevailing System of Hindu Idolatry.* Calcutta: Baptist Mission Press, 1821.

Defoe, Daniel. *The Political History of the Devil.* London: T. Warner, 1726.

Delta [pseud.]. *The Oxford Solar Myth: A Contribution to Comparative Mythology.* N.p., 1870.

Description and Explanation of a Universal Character or Manner of Writing. Bath: J. Hollway, 1830.

Deslongchamps, Auguste Loiseleur. *Lois de Manou, comprenant les institutions religieuses et civiles des Indiens.* Paris: Crapelet, 1833.

Detached Thoughts on Vedantism: Or a Few Pages of Advice to a Member of the Tutobodheenee Sobha, by a Native Friend. Calcutta, 1845.

Dialogue between a Theist and an Idolater. Ed. Stephen Hay. Calcutta: Firma KLM, 1963.

DiBona, Joseph. *One Teacher, One School: The Adam Reports on Indigenous Education in 19th Century India.* New Delhi: Biblia Impex Private Ltd., 1983.

Dickson, David. *A Brief Exposition of the Evangel of Jesus Christ According to Matthew.* London: printed for Ralph Smith, 1651.

A Dictionary of the Bengalee Language. Calcutta, 1856.

A Dictionary of the Bengalee Language. Volume 1, Bengalee and English. Abridged from Dr. Carey's Quarto Dictionary. 2nd ed. Serampore, 1856.

Downe, John. *Certaine Treatises of the Late Reverend and Learned Divine, Mr. Iohne Downe.* London: printed by John Lichfield for Edward Forrest, 1633.

Downame, George. *The Doctrine of Practicall Praying.* London: printed by W. H. for Nicolas Bourne, 1656.

———. *A Treatise of Iustification.* London: printed by Felix Kyngston for Nicolas Bourne, 1633.

Dubois, Abbé. *Hindu Manners, Customs, and Ceremonies.* Trans. Henry K. Beauchamp. 3rd ed. Oxford: Clarendon Press, 1906.

Duff, Alexander. *India and Indian Missions: Including Sketches of the Gigantic System of Hinduism Both in Theory and Practice.* Edinburgh: John Johnstone, 1839. Reprint ed. New York: AMS Press, 1988.

——— [Eis Eclectikon, pseud.]. *Language in Relation to Commerce, Missions, and Government: England's Ascendancy and the World's Destiny.* Manchester: A. Burgess & Co., 1846.

———. *New Era of the English Language and English Literature in India.* Edinburgh: Johnstone, 1837.

Edwards, John. *A Compleat History or Survey of All the Dispensations and Methods of Religion.* London: printed for Daniel Brown, 1699.

———. *A Discourse Concerning the Authority, Style, and Perfection of the Books of the Old and New Testament.* London: Richard Wilkin, 1693.

———. *Theologia Reformata.* London: printed for John Lawrence, John Wyat, and Ranew Robinson, 1713.

Edmonds, George. *The Philosophic Alphabet.* London: Simpkin and Marshall, 1832.

———. *A Universal Alphabet, Grammar, and Language.* London: Richard Griffin and Co., 1856.

Ellis, Alexander John. *Essentials of Phonetics.* London: Fred Pitman, 1848.

Eusebius. *Praeparatio Evangelica.* Trans. E. H. Gifford. Oxford: Clarendon Press, 1903.

Faber, George Stanley. *The Origins of Pagan Idolatry.* 3 vols. London: F. and C. Rivingtons, 1816.

Featley, Daniel. *The Grand Sacrilege of the Church of Rome.* London: printed by Felix Kyngston for Robert Milbourne, 1630.

————. *Transubstantiation Exploded*. London: printed by G. M[iller] for Nicolas Bourne, 1638.

Ferguson, Robert. *A Sober Enquiry into the Nature, Measure, and Principle of Moral Virtue*. London: printed for D. Newman, 1673.

Fisher, John. *The Answere unto the Nine Points of Controversy*. Saint-Omer: English College Press, 1626.

Fontenelle, Bernard le Bovier de. *The History of Oracles*. Trans. Stephen Whatley. London: printed for D. Browne and J. Whiston, 1750.

Forster, H. P. *Vocabulary, in two parts, English and Bongalee, and vice versa*. 2 vols. Calcutta: Ferris and Co., 1799.

Fuller, Thomas. *Abel Redevivus or, The Dead Yet Speaking*. London: printed by Thomas Brudnell for John Stafford, 1652.

————. *A Pisgah-Sight of Palestine*. London: printed by J. F. for John Williams, 1650.

Gale, Theophilus. *The Court of the Gentiles*. Oxford: printed by Henry Hall for Thomas Gilbert, 1669.

Gibelin, E. *Études sur le droit civil des Hindous; Recherches de législation comparée sur les lois de l'Inde, les lois d'Athènes et de Rome, et les coutumes des Germains*. 2 vols. Pondichéry: A. Toutin, 1846.

Gilchrist, John Borthwick. *The Hindee-Roman Orthoepigraphical Ultimatum*. 2nd ed. London: Kingsbury, Parbury, and Allen, 1820.

————. *Strangers East Indian Guide to the Hindoostanee*. 2nd ed. Calcutta, 1808.

Glanvill, Joseph. *Saducismus Triumphatus*. London: printed for J. Collins and S. Lownds, 1681.

————. *A Seasonable Defence of Preaching and the Plain Way of It*. London: printed by M. Clarke for H. Brome, 1678.

Grant, Charles. "Observations on the State of Society among the Asiatic Subjects of Great Britain, particularly with Respect to Morals; and on the Means of Improving it Written Chiefly in the Year 1792." In *General Appendix to the Report from the Select Committee on the Affairs of the East India Company*, No. 1 (1831–32). Reprinted in *British Parliamentary Papers, Colonies: East India*. Vol. 5. Shannon: Irish University Press, 1977.

Greenham, Richard. *The Works of the Reverend and Faithfull Servant of Jesus Christ M. Richard Greenham*. London: printed by Felix Kyngston, 1599.

Grey, Zachary. *A Caveat against the Dissenters*. London: printed for J. Roberts, 1736.

Grierson, George. *The Bible in India*. London: British and Foreign Bible Society, 1904.

Grotius, Hugo. *On the Truth of Christianity*. London: printed for J. Dodsley, 1782.

Groves, Edward. *Pasilogia: An Essay towards the Formation of a System of Universal Language, Both Written and Vocal*. Dublin: James McGlashan, 1846.

Hakewill, George. *An Apologie of the Power and Providence of God in the Government of the World*. Oxford: printed by John Lichfield and William Turner, 1627.

Halhed, Nathaniel Brassey. *Bengali Grammar.* Hooghly: [Charles Wilkins], 1778.

———. *A Code of Gentoo Laws, or, Ordinations of the Pundits.* London, 1776. Reprint ed. Ed. Michael John Franklin. London: Routledge, 2000.

Hall, Thomas. *Samaria's Downfall.* London: printed by R. I. for Jo. Cranford, 1660.

Hamilton, Alexander. *A Key to the Chronology of the Hindus.* 2 vols. Cambridge: printed by J. Smith for F. and C. Rivington, 1820.

Hamilton, Charles. *The Hedaya, or Guide: A Commentary on the Mussulman Laws.* 2nd ed. London: Wm. H. Allen & Co., 1870.

Hausted, Peter. *Ten Sermons Preached upon Severall Sundayes and Saints Dayes.* London: printed for John Clark, 1636.

"Heathenism of Popery." *The Oriental Christian Spectator* 2 (Bombay: American Mission Press, 1831): 409–12.

Henry, Matthew. *Commentary on the Whole Bible.* London: printed for J. and B. Sprint, 1706–1721.

———. *The Psalms of David.* Philadelphia: printed by R. Aitken, 1783.

Herbert, Edward, of Cherbury. *Pagan Religion: A Translation of* De religione gentilium. Ed. and trans. John Anthony Butler. Ottawa: Dovehouse Editions, 1996.

Herbert, Thomas. *Some Years Travels into Divers Parts of Africa and Asia.* London: printed by R. Everingham for R. Scot, T. Basset, J. Wright, and R. Chiswell, 1677.

Hobbes, Thomas. *The English Works of Thomas Hobbes of Malmesbury.* Ed. William Molesworth. 11 vols. London: J. Bohn, 1839–45.

———. *Leviathan.* Ed. Edwin Curley. Indianapolis: Hackett, 1994.

———. *The Art of Rhetorick.* London: printed for William Crooke, 1681.

Hodgson, Brian Houghton. *Preeminence of the Vernaculars; or the Anglicists Answered.* Serampore: Serampore Press, 1837.

———. "Some Account of the Systems of Law and Police as Recognised in the State of Nepal." *Journal of the Royal Asiatic Society* 1 (1834): 258–79.

Holme, Randle. *The Academy of Armory, or, A Storehouse of Armory and Blazon.* Chester, 1688.

Horneck, Anthony. *The Crucified Jesus.* London: printed for Samuel Lowndes, 1695.

Howgill, Francis. *The Rock of Ages.* London: printed for G. C., 1662.

Hume, David. *The Natural History of Religion.* London: A. Millar, 1757.

Hunt, Robert. *The Ministration of the Spirit and Life of our Lord and Saviour, Jesus Christ, in all the Languages of the Illiterate Heathen World, by the Instrumentality of the Universal Syllabic Gospel.* 2nd ed. London: Gilbert and Rivington, 1870.

———. *Natural and Simple Symbolization of the Organic Facts of Universal Speech, with a Prefatory Statement on the Necessity for a Promptly Completed Protestant Reformation.* London: William Hunt and Co., 1873.

———. *The Universal Syllabic Gospel: The English of the Gospel According to St. John, with English Key, and Specimens in Other Tongues.* London: William Hunt and Co., 1873.

Ingelo, Nathanael. *The Perfection, Authority, and Credibility of the Holy Scriptures.* 2nd ed. London: printed by E. T. for Luke Fawn, 1659.

Jacolliot, Louis. *The Bible in India: Hindoo Origin of Hebrew and Christian Revelation.* London: John Camden Hotten, 1870.

Jeyaraj, Daniel. *Genealogy of the South Indian Deities: An English Translation of Bartholomäus Ziegenbalg's Original German Manuscript with a Textual Analysis and Glossary.* London: RoutledgeCurzon, 2005.

Jha, Ganganath. *Manusmṛti: With the Manubhāṣya of Medhātithi.* 10 vols. Delhi: Motilal Banarsidass, 1999.

———. *Shabara-Bhāṣya.* 3 vols. Baroda: Oriental Institute, 1933.

Jolly, Julius. *Recht und Sitte.* Strassburg: Karl J. Trübner, 1896.

Jones, Rowland. *Hieroglyfic.* London: printed by J. Hughes, 1768.

———. *The Origin of Language and Nations.* London: printed by J. Hughes, 1764.

Jones, William. *Institutes of Hindu Law: or, the Ordinances of Menu, According to the Gloss of Culluca, Comprising the Indian System of Duties, Religious and Civil.* Calcutta, 1794.

———. "On the Orthography of Asiatick Words." *Asiatic Researches* 1 (1788): 1–56.

———. *The Works of Sir William Jones, with the life of the author.* Ed. Lord Teignmouth [John Shore]. 13 vols. London: John Stockdale, 1807.

Keach, Benjamin. *The Glorious Lover.* London: printed by J. D. for Christopher Hussey, 1679.

Kennedy, Vans. "Remarks on Dr. Mill's Renderings of Scripture Terms." *The Oriental Christian Spectator* 2 (Bombay: American Mission Press, 1831): 200–07.

Khan, Ali Ibrahim. "On the Trial by Ordeal among the Hindus." *Asiatic Researches* 1 (1806 [1788]): 389–404.

King, William. *Opera.* London, 1754.

Kuhn, Franz Felix Adalbert. *Über Entwicklungsstufen der Mythenbildung.* Berlin: Vogt, 1874.

Langlès, Louis. *Fables et contes Indiens.* Paris: Royez, 1790.

Lariviere, Richard, ed. *The Nāradasmṛti.* Delhi: Motilal Banarsidass, 2003.

Lavaterus, Lewes. *Of Ghostes and Spirites Walking by Nyght.* Trans. R. H. London: printed by H. Benneyman for Richard Watkyns, 1572.

Lees, W. Nassau. "Review of *On the Application of the Characters of the Roman Alphabet to Oriental Languages.*" *Journal of the Asiatic Society* 4 (1864): 345–59.

Leigh, Edward, *A Systeme or Body of Divinity Consisting of Ten Books.* London: printed by A. M. for William Lee, 1654.

Leitner, G[ottlieb] W[ilhelm]. *History of Indigenous Education in the Panjab Since Annexation and in 1882.* [Patiala]: Languages Department Punjab, 1971 [1882].

Lepsius, Richard. *Standard Alphabet for Reducing Unwritten Languages and Foreign Graphic Systems to a Uniform Ethnography in European Letters.* 2nd revised ed. London: Williams and Norgate, 1863. Reprinted with an introduction by J. Alan Kemp. Amsterdam: John Benjamins, 1981.

"Letters on the State of Christianity in India, in which the Conversion of the Hindoos is considered as impracticable. By the Abbé J. A. Dubois, Missionary in Mysore." *Friend of India,* Quarterly Series 3, No. 10 (Serampore, 1825): 187–392.

Lightfoot, John. *The Works of the Reverend and Learned John Lightfoot*. London: printed by W. R. for Robert Scot, Thomas Basset, and Richard Chiswell, 1684.

List of Proper Names Occurring in the Sacred Scriptures, Designed to Form the Basis of a Uniform Method of Spelling the Proper Names of Scripture in the Languages of India. Calcutta: Baptist Mission Press, 1840.

Locke, John. *An Essay Concerning Human Understanding*. Ed. Alexander Campbell Fraser. 2 vols. New York: Dover, 1959.

———. *Essays on the Law of Nature*. Trans. W. Von Leyden. Oxford: Clarendon Press, 1954.

Lodwick, Francis. *A Common Writing*. London, 1647.

Long, James. *Handbook of Bengal Missions*. London: J. F. Shaw, 1848.

Lord, Henry. *A Display of Two Forraigne Sects*. London: printed for Francis Constable, 1630.

Lowth, Robert. *On the Sacred Poetry of the Hebrews*. London: printed for J. Johnson, 1787.

Macaulay, Thomas B. *Critical and Historical Essays*. London: Longman, Brown, Green, and Longmans, 1848.

Macnaghten, Francis Workman. *Considerations on the Hindoo Law, as it is current in Bengal*. Serampore: Mission Press, 1824.

Maine, Henry Sumner. "The Sacred Laws of the Hindus." In *Dissertations on Early Law and Custom*, 1–25. London: John Murray, 1883.

Manton, Thomas. *A Practical Exposition of the Lord's Prayer*. London: printed by J. D. for Jonathan Robinson, 1684.

Mather, Samuel. *The Figures or Types of the Old Testament*. London: printed for N. Hillier, 1705.

———. *The Lord's Prayer*. Boston: printed by Kneeland and Adams, 1766.

Maurice, Thomas. *Brahminical Fraud Detected; or The Attempts of the Sacerdotal Tribe of India to Invest Their Fabulous Deities and Heroes with the Honours and Attributes of the Christian Messiah, Examined, Exposed, and Defeated*. London: W. Bulmer and Co., 1812.

Maynard, John. *The Law of God Ratified, by the Gospel of Christ*. London: printed for Francis Tyton, 1674.

Mayne, J. D. *A Treatise on Hindu Law and Usage*. Madras: Higginbotham and Co., 1878.

Mendelssohn, Moses. *Jerusalem, oder über religiöse Macht und Judentum*. Berlin: Friedrich Maurer, 1783.

The Methodist: or, A New Method of Reading, Writing, and Printing, all Languages in Short-Hand, by a New and Universal Alphabet; and of Learning All Arts and Sciences, by a Real Character and Philosophical Language. London, 1741.

Mill, William Hodge. *Proposed Version of Theological Terms, with a view to uniformity in translations of the holy scriptures, etc., into the various languages of India. Part the first—Sanscrit. With remarks upon the rendering proposed by Dr. Mill by Horace Hayman Wilson, Esq.* Calcutta: Bishop's College Press, 1828.

Minute of the Madras Missionary Conference and other Documents on the Subject of Caste. Madras: American Mission Press, 1850.

Mitchell, John. *An Essay on the Best Means of Civilising the Subjects of the British Empire in India, and of Diffusing the Light of the Christian Religion Throughout the Eastern World.* Edinburgh: W. Blackwood, 1805.

Monier-Williams, Monier. *Buddhism, in its Connection with Brahmanism and Hinduism.* London: Macmillan, 1889.

———. *A Dictionary, English and Sanskrit.* London: William H. Allen and Co., 1851.

———. *The Holy Bible and the Sacred Books of the East.* London: Society for the Promotion of Christian Knowledge, 1900.

———. *Modern India and the Indians.* 3rd ed. London: Trübner and Co., 1879.

———, ed. *Original Papers Illustrating the History of the Application of the Roman Alphabet to the Languages of India.* London: Longman, Brown, Green, Longmans, and Roberts, 1859.

———. *The Study of Sanskrit in Relation to Missionary Work in India.* London: Williams and Norgate, 1861.

———. *Religious Thought and Life in India: Vedism, Brahmanism and Hinduism.* London: J. Murray, 1885. Reprint ed. New Delhi: Oriental Books Reprint Corp., 1979.

Mornay, Philip of, Lord of Plessie Marlie. *A Woorke Concerning the Trewnesse of the Christian Religion.* London: printed for Thomas Cadman, 1587.

Morton, W. *Biblical and Theological Vocabulary, English and Bengali.* Calcutta, 1845.

Muir, John. *The Course of Divine Revelation.* Calcutta: Baptist Mission Press, 1846.

———. "Progress of the Vedic Religion towards Abstract Conceptions of the Deity." In *Original Sanskrit Texts on the Origin and History of the People of India*, vol. 5, 350–420. London: Trübner & Co., 1870.

Mullens, Joseph. *Vedantism, Brahmism, and Christianity Examined and Compared.* Calcutta: Baptist Mission Press for the Calcutta Christian Tract and Book Society, 1852.

Müller, Friedrich Max. *Anthropological Religion.* London: Longmans, Green and Co., 1892.

———. *Auld Lang Syne.* Second series. London: Longmans, Green and Co., 1899.

———. *Biographies of Words and the Home of the Aryas.* London: Longmans, Green and Co., 1912.

———. *Chips from a German Workshop.* 5 vols. New York: Charles Scribner's Sons, 1895–98.

———. *Contributions to the Science of Mythology.* 2 vols. London: Longmans, Green and Co., 1897.

———. "The English Alphabet Applied to the Languages of India." *The Saturday Review*, Number 110, Vol. 4 (Dec. 5, 1857): 515–17.

———. *A History of Ancient Sanskrit Literature so far as It Illustrates the Primitive Religion of the Brahmans.* London: Williams and Norgate, 1859.

———. *India: What Can It Teach Us?* London: Longmans, Green and Co., 1892.

———. *Introduction to the Science of Religion.* London: Longmans, Green and Co., 1882.

———. *The Languages of the Seat of War in the East.* London: Williams and Norgate, 1855.

———. *Last Essays.* First series. *Essays on Language, Folklore and Other Subjects.* London: Longmans, Green and Co., 1901.

———. *Last Essays.* Second series. *Essays on the Science of Religion.* London: Longmans, Green and Co., 1901.

———. *Lectures on the Origin and Growth of Religion.* London: Longmans, Green and Co., 1901.

———. *Lectures on the Science of Language.* 2 vols. London: Longmans, Green and Co., 1874.

———. *Lectures on the Science of Religion, with a Paper on Buddhist Nihilism, and a Translation of the Dhammapada or "Path of Virtue."* New York: Charles Scribner's Sons, 1872.

———. *The Life and Letters of the Right Honourable Friedrich Max Müller.* Ed. Georgina Adelaide Müller. 2 vols. London: Longmans, Green and Co., 1902.

———. *Natural Religion.* London: Longmans, Green and Co., 1889.

———. *Outline Dictionary for the Use of Missionaries, Explorers and Students of Language with an Introduction on the Proper Use of the Ordinary English Alphabet in Transcribing Foreign Languages.* Calcutta: George Wyman & Co., 1867.

———. *Physical Religion.* London: Longmans, Green and Co., 1891.

———. *Proposals for a Missionary Alphabet.* London: A. and G. A. Spottiswoode, 1854.

———. *Rammohun to Ramakrishna.* Calcutta: Susil Gupta, 1952.

———. *Rig-Veda-Sanhita: The Sacred Hymns of the Brahmans, together with the Commentary of Sayanacharya.* 6 vols. London: W. H. Allen, 1849–74.

———. *The Science of Thought.* 2 vols. New York: Charles Scribner's Sons, 1887.

———. *The Six Systems of Indian Philosophy.* London: Longmans, Green and Co., 1899.

———. *Theosophy or Psychological Religion.* London: Longmans, Green and Co., 1903.

———. *Three Introductory Lectures on the Science of Thought.* Chicago: Open Court, 1898.

———. *Three Lectures on the Science of Language.* London: Longmans, Green and Co., 1889. Reprint ed. Varanasi: Indological Book House, 1961.

———. *Three Lectures on the Vedanta Philosophy.* London: Longmans, Green and Co., 1904.

———, ed. *The Sacred Books of the East.* 50 vols. Oxford: Clarendon Press, 1879–1910. Reprint ed. Delhi: Motilal Banarsidass, 1962–66.

Mundy, George. *Christianity and Hinduism Contrasted.* 2nd ed. 2 vols. Serampore: Serampore Press, 1834.

Murray, Alexander. *A Letter from Alexander Murray to Charles Stuart on the Tendency of the Translation of the Scriptures into the Indian Languages, to Promote Science, Civilization, and the Commercial Interest of Great Britain.* Edinburgh: J. Ritchie, 1813.

Newton, Isaac. *The Chronology of Ancient Kingdoms Amended.* London: printed for J. Tonson, 1728.

Nietzsche, Friedrich. "The Birth of Tragedy." In Walter Kaufmann, ed., *Basic Writings of Nietzsche,* 15–144. New York: Modern Library, 1968.

Nowell, Alexander. *A True Report of the Disputation or Rather Private Conference Had in the Tower of London, with Ed. Campion Jesuite.* London: printed by Christopher Barker, 1583.

Olivelle, Patrick. *Manu's Code of Law.* New York: Oxford University Press, 2005.

"On the Cultivation of Sungskrita by Native Youth." *Friend of India,* Monthly Series 2 (Serampore, 1819): 426–42.

"On the Effect of the Native Press in India." *Friend of India,* Quarterly Series 1, No. 1 (Serampore, 1820): 119–40.

"On Encouraging the Cultivation of the Sungskrit Language among the Natives." *Friend of India,* Monthly Series 2, No. 5 (Serampore, 1822): 131–[47].

"On the Progress and Present State of the Native Press in India." *Friend of India,* Quarterly Series 4, No. 12 (Serampore, 1825): 138–56.

"On the Sanscrit Renderings of Scripture Terms." *The Oriental Christian Spectator* 2 (Bombay: American Mission Press, 1831): 319–20.

Papers Concerning the Bengali Version of the Scriptures. Calcutta: Calcutta Auxiliary Bible Society, 1867.

Patterson, Arthur J. *Caste Considered under its Moral, Social, and Religious Aspects: The Le Bas Prize Essay in the University of Cambridge for the Year 1860.* London: Smith, Elder and Co., 1861.

Picart, Bernard. *The Ceremonies and Religious Customs of the Various Nations of the Known World; Together with Historical Annotations and Several Curious Discourses Equally Instructive and Entertaining.* Vol. 3. *Concerning the Ceremonies of the Idolatrous Nations.* London: William Jackson, 1734.

Pitman, Isaac, ed. *A Plea for Spelling Reform.* London: Fred Pitman, 1878.

Plutarch. *Moralia.* Vol. 5. Trans. Frank Cole Babbitt. Loeb Classical Library. Cambridge, MA: Harvard University Press, 1936.

Poole, Matthew. *Annotations upon the Holy Bible.* London: printed by John Richardson for Thomas Parkhurst, 1685.

Pope, G[eorge] U[glow]. *One Alphabet for All India.* Madras: Gantz Bros., 1859.

Priestley, Joseph. *A Comparison of the Institutions of Moses with Those of the Hindoos and Other Ancient Nations.* Northumberland: printed by A. Kennedy, 1799.

Primitiae Orientales. Essays by the Students of the College of Fort William in Bengal. Vol. 1. Calcutta: [College of Fort William], 1802.

———. Vol. 3. Calcutta: [College of Fort William], 1804.

Purchas, Samuel. *Purchas His Pilgrimes in Five Bookes*. London: printed by William Stansby for Henrie Fetherstone, 1625.

Rawlet, John. *A Dialogue betwixt Two Protestants*. London: printed for Samuel Tidmarsh, 1685.

"Remarks on the State of the Roman Catholic Church in India, with reference to the Instruction of the Heathen." *Friend of India*, Quarterly Series 2, No. 6 (Serampore, 1822): 237–53.

"Remarks on the Various Modes of Translating Scriptural Phrases in the Languages of India." Madras, 1838. Originally printed in the *South India Christian Repository* for April, 1838.

Renan, Ernest. *Nouvelles considérations sur le caractere général des peuples sémitiques et en particulier sur leur tendance au monothéisme*. Paris: Imprimerie Impériale, 1859.

Roberts, Joseph. *Oriental Illustrations of the Sacred Scriptures*. 2nd ed. London: printed for Thomas Tegg, 1844.

———. *Caste in its Religious and Civil Character Opposed to Christianity*. London: Longman, Brown, Green, and Longmans, 1847.

Robson, John. *Hinduism and Christianity Contrasted*. 3rd ed. Edinburgh: Oliphant, Anderson & Ferrier, 1905.

Röer, Edward, and W. A. Montriou. *Hindu Law and Judicature from the Dharma-sastra of Yajnavalkya in English*. Calcutta: R. C. Lepage and Co., 1859.

Ross, Alexander. *Pansebeia: or, A View of All Religions in the World*. 2nd ed. London: John Saywell, 1655.

Roy, Rammohan. *The English Works of Raja Rammohun Roy*. Ed. Kalidas Nag and Debajyoti Burman. Calcutta: Sadharana Brahmo Samaj, 1945.

Śāktānandataraṅginī. Ed. Ram Kumar Rai. Benares: Prachya Prakashan, 1993.

Sanger, Zedekiah. *A Sermon Preached, March 12, 1794, at the Ordination of the Rev. Hezekiah Hooper*. Worcester, MA: printed by Isaiah Thomas, 1795.

Sarasvati, Dayananda. *The Light of Truth* [Satyartha Prakasha]. Trans. Ganga Prasad Upadhyaya. Revised ed. Allahabad: Kala Press, 1960 [1908].

Sarup, Lakshman, trans. *The Nighaṇṭu and the Nirukta*. Delhi: Motilal Banarsidass, 1998.

Schlegel, Friedrich. "Talk on Mythology." In Burton Feldman and Robert D. Richardson, *The Rise of Modern Mythology 1680–1860*, 309–13. Bloomington: Indiana University Press, 1972.

Scot, Reginald. *Discovery of Witchcraft*. London: printed by Richard Gates, 1651 [1584].

Scott, William. *Lessons in Elocution*. 2nd American ed. Philadelphia: printed by William Young, 1790.

Scott-Waring, John. *Vindication of the Hindoos. Part the Second*. London: R. & J. Rodwell, 1808.

A Seasonable Prospect for the View and Consideration of Christians. London: printed by J. L. for Luke Meredith, 1691.

Selden, John. *De diis syris syntagmata.* London: printed by William Stansby, 1617.

———. *The Fabulous Gods Denounced in the Bible.* Trans. W. A. Hauser. Philadelphia: J. B. Lippincott & Co., 1880.

———. *Titles of Honor.* London: printed by William Stansby for John Helme, 1614.

Sen, Ram Comul. *A Dictionary of English and Bengalee, translated from Todd's edition of Johnsons English Dictionary.* 2 vols. Serampore: Serampore Press, 1834.

Sherry, Richard. *A Treatise of Schemes and Tropes.* London: printed by John Day, 1550.

Smith, John. *Select Discourses.* London: printed by J. Flesher for W. Morden, 1660.

Smṛtitattva. Ed. Jivananda Vidyasagara. Calcutta: Siddhesvara Press, 1895.

Spence, Joseph. *Polymetis.* London: printed for R. Dodsley, 1747.

Spenser, Edmund. *The Shepheardes Calendar.* London, 1579.

Spencer, John. *De legibus hebraeorum ritualibus et earum rationibus libri tres.* Cambridge: Richard Chiswel, 1685.

Sprat, Thomas. *History of the Royal Society.* London: printed by T. R. for J. Martyn and J. Allestry, 1667.

Sterry, Peter. *A Discourse of the Freedom of the Will.* London: printed for John Starkey, 1675.

Stillingfleet, Edward. *A Defence of the Discourse Concerning the Idolatry Practised in the Church of Rome, the two first parts.* London: printed by Robert White for Henry Mortlock, 1676.

———. *Origines Sacræ, or, A Rational Account of the Grounds of Christian Faith.* London: printed by R. W. for Henry Mortlock, 1662.

Strange, Sir Thomas. *Hindu Law.* 2 vols. London: Parbury, Allen, and Co., 1830.

Tantrarāja Tantra. Ed. Arthur Avalon and Lakshmana Shastri. Delhi: Motilal Banarsidass, 1997.

Taylor, Jeremy. *A Dissuasive from Popery.* London: printed by J. G. for Richard Royston, 1664.

Thompson, William. *Poems on Several Occasions.* Oxford: printed at the theatre, 1757.

Thorgilsson, Frodhi Ari. *Aræ multiscii schedæ de islandia.* Ed. Arni Magnusson and Christen Worm. Oxford, 1716.

Tillotson, John. *A Sermon Concerning the Unity of the Divine Nature and the B[lessed] Trinity.* London: printed for B. Aylmer and W. Rogers, 1693.

Toland, John. *Christianity Not Mysterious.* London: printed for Samuel Buckley, 1696.

Tooke, John Horne. *Epea Pteroenta, or The Diversions of Purley.* 2nd ed. 2 vols. London, 1798 and 1805.

The Travels of Sig. Pietro della Valle, a Noble Roman, into East-India, . . . Whereunto is Added a Relation of Sir Thomas Roe's Voyage into the East-Indies. London: printed by J. Macock for Henry Herringman, 1665.

Trevelyan, Charles. *The English Instructor.* Calcutta: Baptist Mission Press, 1834.

———. *Letters of Indophilus to "the Times."* 3rd ed. London: Longman, Brown, Green, Longmans, and Roberts, 1858.

Trevelyan, Ernest John. *Hindu Family Law As Administered in British India.* London: W. Thacker and Co., 1908.

Turner, John. *Attempt towards an Explanation of the Theology and Mythology of the Antient Pagans. First Part.* London: printed by H. Hills for Walter Kettleby, 1687.

Urquhart, Thomas. *Logopandecteision, or An Introduction to the Universal Language.* London, 1653.

Vaughan, William. *The Church Militant.* London: printed by Thomas Paine for Humfrey Blunden, 1640.

Vicars, John. *The Opinion of the Roman Judges Touching upon Imprisonment and the Liberty of the Subject.* [London], 1643.

Volney, Constantin-François de Chassebœuf, Comte de. *L'Alfabet européen appliqué aux langues asiatiques.* Paris: Didot, 1818.

———. *Les Ruines, ou, Méditation sur les révolutions des empires.* Paris: Desenne, 1791.

W., M. *The Sacred Outcry, upon a View of the Principal Errors and Vices of Christendom, in the Eighteenth Century.* London: printed for W. Richardson and several others, 1788.

Walker, Samuel. *Divine Essays.* Cambridge: printed at the university press for R. Thurlbourne, 1709.

Warburton, William. *The Divine Legation of Moses Demonstrated.* 2 vols. London: printed for the executor of the late Mr. Fletcher Gyles, 1742–58.

———. *The Works of the Right Reverend William Warburton.* 7 volumes. London: printed by J. Nichols for T. Cadell, 1788.

Ward, Seth. *Vindiciæ Academiarum.* Oxford: printed by J. Lichfield, 1654.

Ward, William. *A View of the History, Literature, and Mythology of the Hindoos.* London: Kingsbury, Parbury, and Allen, 1822.

Watson, Richard. *A Collection of Theological Tracts.* Cambridge: printed by J. Archdeacon for J. & J. Merrill, T. Evans, and J. Fletcher, 1785.

Webster, John. *Academiarum Examen, or The Examination of Academies.* London: printed for Giles Calvert, 1654.

———. *The Displaying of Supposed Witchcraft.* London: printed by J. M., 1677.

Weemes, John. *An Explanation of the Ceremoniall Lawes of Moses, As They Are Annexed to the Tenne Commandements.* London: printed by T. Cotes for John Bellamie, 1632.

Westall, William. *The Hindoos: Including a General Description of India, its Government, Religion, Manners and Customs.* 2 vols. London: M. A. Nattali, 1847.

Westminster Confession of Faith (1646). Accessed April 15, 2012, at http://www.reformed.org/documents/index.html?mainframe=http://www.reformed.org/documents/westminster_conf_of_faith.html.

A Whip for the Devil, or the Roman Conjurer. London: printed for Thomas Malthus, 1683.

White, Andrew Dickson. *A History of the Warfare of Science with Theology in Christendom*. New York: D. Appleton and Co., 1896.

Whitgift, John. *The Works of John Whitgift*. Ed. John Ayre. 3 vols. Cambridge: Cambridge University Press, 1853.

White, Francis. *A Replie to Iesuit Fishers Answere to Certain Questions*. London: printed by Adam Islip, 1624.

Wilkins, John. *An Essay towards a Real Character, and a Philosophical Language*. London: printed for Samuel Gellibrand, 1668.

———. *Mercury, or the Secret and Swift Messenger*. London: printed by I. Norton for Iohn Maynard and Timothy Wilkins, 1641.

———. *Sermons Preached upon Several Occasions*. London: printed for Thomas Basset, Richard Chiswell, and William Rogers, 1682.

Wilson, Horace Hayman. *Essays and Lectures Chiefly on the Religion of the Hindus*. Vol. 2. London: Trübner and Co., 1862.

Wilson, John. *An Exposure of the Hindu Religion*. Bombay: American Mission Press, 1832.

Wilson, Thomas. *The Arte of Rhetorique*. London: printed by Richard Grafton, 1553.

Zastoupil, Lynn, and Martin Moir. *The Great Indian Education Debate: Documents Relating to the Orientalist-Anglicist Controversy, 1781–1843*. Richmond, UK: Curzon, 1999.

SECONDARY SOURCES

Aarsleff, Hans. *From Locke to Saussure: Essays on the Study of Language and Intellectual History*. Minneapolis: University of Minnesota Press, 1982.

———. *The Study of Language in England, 1780–1860*. Princeton, NJ: Princeton University Press, 1967.

Abraham, Gary A. *Max Weber and the Jewish Question: A Study of the Social Outlook of His Sociology*. Urbana: University of Illinois Press, 1992.

———. "Misunderstanding the Merton Thesis: A Boundary Dispute between History and Sociology." *Isis* 74 (1983): 368–87.

Adam, Leonhard. "Criminal Law and Procedure in Nepal a Century Ago: Notes Left by Brian H. Hodgson." *Far Eastern Quarterly* 9 (1950): 146–68.

Adolph, Robert. *The Rise of Modern Prose Style*. Cambridge, MA: The MIT Press, 1968.

Aithal, Parameswara, and Axel Michaels, eds. *The Pandit: Traditional Scholarship in India*. New Delhi: Manohar, 2001.

Allen, Don Cameron. *Mysteriously Meant: The Rediscovery of Pagan Symbolism and Allegorical Interpretation in the Renaissance*. Baltimore: Johns Hopkins University Press, 1970.

Almond, Philip C. *The British Discovery of Buddhism*. Cambridge: Cambridge University Press, 1988.

Anidjar, Gil. "Secularism." *Critical Inquiry* 33 (2006): 52–77.

Asad, Talal. *Formations of the Secular: Christianity, Islam, Modernity.* Stanford: Stanford University Press, 2003.

―――. *Genealogies of Religion.* Baltimore: Johns Hopkins University Press, 1993.

Assmann, Jan. *Moses the Egyptian: The Memory of Egypt in Western Monotheism.* Cambridge, MA: Harvard University Press, 1997.

―――. *The Price of Monotheism.* Trans. Robert Savage. Stanford: Stanford University Press, 2010.

―――. "Pictures versus Letters: William Warburton's Theory of Grammatological Iconoclasm." In Jan Assmann and Albert I. Baumgarten, eds., *Representation in Religion: Studies in Honor of Moshe Barasch,* 297–312. Leiden: Brill, 2001.

Aston, Margaret. *England's Iconoclasts.* Oxford: Oxford University Press, 1988.

Auerbach, Eric. "Figura." In *Scenes from the Drama of European Literature,* 11–78. Minneapolis: University of Minnesota Press, 1959.

Auksi, Peter. *Christian Plain Style: The Evolution of a Spiritual Ideal.* Montréal: McGill-Queen's University Press, 1995.

Austin, J. L. *How to Do Things with Words.* Cambridge, MA: Harvard University Press, 1962.

Avalon, Arthur [John Woodroffe]. *The Garland of Letters: Studies in the Mantra Sastra.* Madras: Ganesh and Co., 1998.

Bailey, Michael D. "The Disenchantment of Magic: Spells, Charms, and Superstition in Early European Witchcraft Literature." *American Historical Review* 111 (2006): 383–404.

Balagangadhara, S. N. "Balagangadhara on the Biblical Underpinnings of 'Secular' Social Sciences." In Krishnan Ramaswamy, Antonio de Nicolas, and Aditi Banerjee, eds., *Invading the Sacred: An Analysis of Hinduism Studies in America,* 123–31. New Delhi: Rupa and Co., 2007.

―――. *The Heathen in His Blindness: Asia, the West, and the Dynamic of Religion.* Leiden: Brill, 1994.

Bauman, Richard. *Let Your Words Be Few: Symbolism of Speaking and Silence among Seventeenth-Century Quakers.* Cambridge: Cambridge University Press, 1983.

Bauman, Richard, and Charles L. Briggs. *Voices of Modernity: Language Ideologies and the Politics of Inequality.* Cambridge: Cambridge University Press, 2003.

Becker, Wilhard. *Nicht plappern wie die Heiden.* Hannover-Kirchrode: Die Rufer Buch- und Schriftenverlag, 1980.

Bell, Catherine. "Ritual Reification." In Graham Harvey, ed., *Ritual and Religious Belief: A Reader,* 265–85. New York: Routledge, 2005.

Benavides, Gustavo. "Magic." In Robert A. Segal, ed., *The Blackwell Companion to the Study of Religion,* 295–308. Malden, MA: Blackwell, 2006.

―――. "Modernity." In Mark C. Taylor, ed., *Critical Terms for Religious Studies,* 186–204. Chicago: University of Chicago Press, 1998.

Benin, Stephen D. "The 'Cunning of God' and Divine Accommodation." *Journal of the History of Ideas* 45 (1984): 179–91.

Benton, Lauren. "Colonial Law and Cultural Difference: Jurisdictional Politics and the Formation of the Colonial State." *Comparative Studies in Society and History* 41 (1999): 563–88.

Bercovitch, Sacvan. *Typology and Early American Literature*. Amherst: University of Massachusetts Press, 1972.

Berger, Peter. *The Sacred Canopy: Elements of a Sociological Theory of Religion*. New York: Doubleday, 1967.

Bergunder, Michael. "The Pure Tamil Movement and Bible Translation." In Judith M. Brown and Robert Eric Frykenberg, eds., *Christians, Cultural Interactions, and India's Religious Traditions*, 212–31. London: RoutledgeCurzon, 2002.

Bhabha, Homi. *The Location of Culture*. New York: Routledge, 1994.

Bharti, Brahm Datt. *Max Müller: A Lifelong Masquerade (the inside story of a secular Christian missionary who masqueraded all his lifetime from behind the mask of literature and philology and mortgaged his pen, intellect and scholarship to wreck Hinduism)*. New Delhi: Erabooks, 1992.

Biderman, Shlomo. "Dharma and the Limits of Interpretation." In Shlomo Biderman and Ben-Ami Scharfstein, eds., *Interpretation in Religion*, 111–28. Leiden: Brill, 1992.

Bilgrami, Akeel. "Occidentalism, the Very Idea: An Essay on the Enlightenment and Enchantment." *Critical Inquiry* 32 (2006): 381–411.

———. "What is Enchantment?" In Michael Warner, Jonathan VanAntwerpen, and Craig Calhoun, eds., *Varieties of Secularism in a Secular Age*, 145–65. Cambridge, MA: Harvard University Press, 2010.

Bloch, Maurice. *Ritual, History, and Power: Selected Papers in Anthropology*. London: Athlone Press, 1989.

Bosch, Lourens P. van den. *Friedrich Max Müller: A Life Devoted to the Humanities*. Leiden: Brill, 2002.

Boullaye, Pinard de la. *L'Étude comparée des religions*. 2 vols. Paris: Gabriel Beauchesne, 1922.

Brandt, Reinhard. "Über die vielfältige Bedeutung der Baconschen Idole." *Philosophisches Jahrbuch* 83 (1976): 42–70.

Brooke, John Hedley. "The God of Isaac Newton." In John Fauvel, ed., *Let Newton Be!*, 169–83. Oxford: Oxford University Press, 1988.

Bronner, Yigal. *Extreme Poetry: The South Asian Movement of Simultaneous Narration*. New York: Columbia University Press, 2010.

Burchett, Patton E. "The 'Magical' Language of Mantra." *Journal of the American Academy of Religion* 76 (2008): 807–43.

Burke, Peter. "The Repudiation of Ritual in Early Modern Europe." In *The Historical Anthropology of Early Modern Italy: Essays on Perception and Communication*, 223–38. Cambridge: Cambridge University Press, 1987.

Casanova, José. *Public Religions in the Modern World*. Chicago: University of Chicago Press, 1994.

Cassirer, Ernst. *Language and Myth*. New York: Harper, 1946.

Chakrabarty, Dipesh. *Provincializing Europe: Postcolonial Thought and Historical Difference*. Princeton, NJ: Princeton University Press, 2008.

Chakravorty, Swapan, and Abhijit Gupta, eds. *Print Areas: Book History in India*. Delhi: Permanent Black, 2004.

Chidester, David. "Classify and Conquer: Friedrich Max Müller, Indigenous Religious Traditions, and Imperial Comparative Religion." In Jacob K. Olupona, ed., *Beyond Primitivism: Indigenous Religious Traditions and Modernity*, 71–88. New York: Routledge, 2004.

———. *Savage Systems: Colonialism and Comparative Religion in Southern Africa.* Charlottesville: University of Virginia Press, 1996.

Clark, Michael. "The Word of God and the Language of Man: Puritan Semiotics and the Theological and Scientific Plain Styles of the Seventeenth Century." *Semiotic Scene* 2 (1978): 61–90.

Clauss, Sidonie. "John Wilkins' Essay toward a Real Character: Its Place in the Seventeenth-Century Episteme." *Journal of the History of Ideas* 43 (1982): 531–53.

Clavier, H. "Résurgences d'un problème de méthode en histoire des religions." *Numen* 15 (1968): 94–118.

Cohen, Murray. *Sensible Words: Linguistic Practice in England, 1640–1785.* Baltimore: Johns Hopkins University Press, 1977.

Cohn, Bernard. *Colonialism and its Forms of Knowledge: The British in India.* Princeton, NJ: Princeton University Press, 1996.

Coleman, Frank. "Thomas Hobbes and the Hebraic Bible." *History of Political Thought* 25 (2004): 642–69.

Couturat, Louis, and Léopold Léau. *Histoire de la langue universelle.* Paris: Librairie Hachette, 1903.

Cox, Jeffrey. *The British Missionary Enterprise since 1700.* London: Routledge, 2008.

Crook, Nigel, ed. *The Transmission of Knowledge in South Asia.* Delhi: Oxford University Press, 1996.

Davis, Donald R., Jr. "*Dharma, Maryāda*, and Law in Early British Malabar: Remarks on Words for 'Law' in the Tellicherry Records." *Studien zur Indologie und Iranistik* 23 (2002): 51–70.

———. "Hinduism as a Legal Tradition." *Journal of the American Academy of Religion* 75 (2007): 241–67.

Davis, Richard. *The Lives of Indian Images.* Princeton, NJ: Princeton University Press, 1997.

Debus, Allen G. *Science and Education in the Seventeenth Century: The Webster-Ward Debate.* London: MacDonald and Co., 1970.

DeMott, Benjamin. "Comenius and the Real Character in England." *PMLA* 70 (1955): 1068–81.

Derrett, J[ohn] Duncan M[artin]. "The Administration of Hindu Law by the British." *Comparative Studies in Society and History* 4 (1961): 10–52.

———. "Ancient Indian 'Nonsense' Vindicated." *Journal of the American Oriental Society* 98 (1978): 100–06.

———. "The Concept of Law according to Medhātithi, A Pre-Islamic Indian Jurist." In Wilhelm Hönerbach, ed., *Der Orient in der Forschung*, 18–41. Wiesbaden: Otto Harrassowitz, 1967.

———. *A Critique of Modern Hindu Law.* Bombay: N. M Tripathi, 1970.

———. "Die Entwicklung des indischen Rechts." In Wolfgang Schluchter, ed., *Max Webers Studie über Hinduismus und Buddhismus: Interpretation und Kritik*, 178–201. Frankfurt: Suhrkamp, 1984.

———. *Hindu Law, Past and Present.* Calcutta: A. Mukherjee, 1957.

———. *Jesus's Audience: The Social and Psychological Environment in Which He Worked.* London: Darton, Longman & Todd, 1973.

———. *Law and Morality.* Northamptonshire, UK: Pilkington Press, 1998.

———. *Law in the New Testament.* London: Darton, Longman & Todd, 1970.

———. "Recht und Religion im Neuen Testament." In Wolfgang Schluchter, ed., *Max Webers Sicht des antiken Christentums: Interpretation und Kritik*, 317–62. Frankfurt: Suhrkamp, 1985.

———. "Religion and Law in Hindu Jurisprudence." *Proceedings of the 23rd International Congress of Orientalists*, 225–26. London: The Royal Asiatic Society, 1957.

———. *Religion, Law and the State in India.* New York: Free Press, 1968.

———. "Sanskrit Legal Treatises Compiled at the Instance of the British." *Zeitschrift für vergleichende Rechtswissenschaft* 63 (1961): 72–117.

———. "Sir Henry Maine and Law in India, 1858–1958." *Juridical Review* 4 (1959): 40–55.

———. *Studies in the New Testament.* Vol. 1. Leiden: Brill, 1977.

———. *Two Masters: The Buddha and Jesus.* Northamptonshire, UK: Pilkington Press, 1995.

Derrida, Jacques. "White Mythology: Metaphor in the Text of Philosophy." In *Margins of Philosophy*, 207–72. Trans. Alan Bass. Chicago: University of Chicago Press, 1982.

De Smet, R[ichard] V. "Categories of Indian Philosophy and Communication of the Gospel." *Religion and Society* 10 (1963): 20–26.

Dhavan, Rajeev. "Dharmaśāstra and Modern Indian Society." *Journal of the Indian Law Institute* 34 (1992): 65–91.

Diamond, Arthur S. *Primitive Law, Past and Present.* London: Methuen and Co., 1971.

Dirks, Nicholas B. *Castes of Mind: Colonialism and the Making of Modern India.* Princeton, NJ: Princeton University Press, 2001.

Dube, Saurabh, ed. *Enchantments of Modernity: Empire, Nation, Globalization.* New Delhi: Routledge, 2009.

Duffy, Eamon. *The Stripping of the Altars: Traditional Religion in England c. 1400– c. 1580.* New Haven: Yale University Press, 1982.

During, Simon. *Modern Enchantments: The Cultural Power of Secular Magic.* Cambridge, MA: Harvard University Press, 2002.

Eco, Umberto. *The Search for the Perfect Language.* Trans. James Fentress. Oxford: Blackwell, 1995.

Eire, Carlos M. N. *War against the Idols: The Reformation of Worship from Erasmus to Calvin.* Cambridge: Cambridge University Press, 1986.

Eisenstadt, S. N. *The Protestant Ethic and Modernization: A Comparative View*. New York: Basic Books, 1968.

Eliade, Mircea. *The Myth of the Eternal Return: or, Cosmos and History*. Trans. Willard Trask. Princeton, NJ: Princeton University Press, 1954.

———. *The Sacred and the Profane: The Nature of Religion*. Trans. Willard Trask. New York: Harcourt, Brace, 1959.

Ellenson, David. "Max Weber on Judaism and the Jews." In *After Emancipation: Jewish Religious Responses to Modernity*, 80–95. Cincinnati: Hebrew Union College Press, 2004.

Figala, Karen. "Newton's Alchemy." In I. Bernard Cohen and George E. Smith, eds., *The Cambridge Companion to Newton*, 370–86. Cambridge: Cambridge University Press, 2002.

Fisch, Harold. "Puritanism and the Reform of Prose Style." *English Literary History* 19 (1952): 229–48.

Fitzgerald, Timothy. *The Ideology of Religious Studies*. New York: Oxford University Press, 2000.

Force, James E. "Biblical Interpretation." In Richard H. Popkin and Arjo Vanderjagt, *Scepticism and Irreligion in the Seventeenth and Eighteenth Centuries*, 282–305. Leiden: Brill, 1993.

Forrester, Duncan B. *Caste and Christianity: Attitudes and Policies on Caste of Anglo-Saxon Protestant Missions in India*. London: Curzon, 1979.

Foucault, Michel. "The Order of Discourse." In Robert Young, ed., *Untying the Text: A Post-Structuralist Reader*, 48–78. London: Routledge & Kegan Paul, 1981.

Fraser, Russell. *The Language of Adam: On the Limits and Systems of Discourse*. New York: Columbia University Press, 1977.

Frykenberg, Robert Eric, ed. *Christians and Missionaries in India: Cross-Cultural Communication since 1500, with Special Reference to Caste, Conversion, and Colonialism*. Grand Rapids, MI: Eerdmans, 2003.

Funkenstein, Amos. *Theology and the Scientific Imagination: From the Middle Ages to the Seventeenth Century*. Princeton, NJ: Princeton University Press, 1986.

Galanter, Marc. "The Displacement of Traditional Law in Modern India." *Journal of Social Issues* 24 (1968): 65–90.

Gauchet, Marcel. *The Disenchantment of the World: A Political History of Religion*. Princeton, NJ: Princeton University Press, 1997.

Geertz, Hildred. "An Anthropology of Religion and Magic, I." *Journal of Interdisciplinary History* 6 (1975): 71–89.

Genette, Gérard. *Mimologics*. Trans. Thaïs Morgan. Lincoln: University of Nebraska Press, 1995.

Gethin, Rupert. "The *Mātikās*: Memorization, Mindfulness, and the List." In Janet Gyatso, ed., *In the Mirror of Memory: Reflections on Mindfulness and Remembrance in Indian and Tibetan Buddhism*, 149–72. Albany: SUNY Press, 1992.

Goodman, Hananya, ed. *Between Jerusalem and Benares: Comparative Studies in Judaism and Hinduism.* Albany: SUNY Press, 1994.

Goudriaan, Teun. *Māyā: Divine and Human.* Delhi: Motilal Banarsidass, 1978.

Gould, Stephen Jay. *The Mismeasure of Man.* Revised ed. London: Penguin, 1997.

Grazia, Margreta de. "The Secularization of Language in the Seventeenth Century." *Journal of the History of Ideas* 41 (1980): 319–29.

———. "Shakespeare's View of Language: An Historical Perspective." *Shakespeare Quarterly* 29 (1978): 374–88.

Greaves, Richard L. "Puritanism and Science: The Anatomy of a Controversy." *Journal of the History of Ideas* 30 (1969): 345–68.

Gustafson, Thomas. *Representative Words: Politics, Literature, and the American Language, 1776–1865.* New York: Cambridge University Press, 1992.

Halbertal, Moshe, and Avishai Margalit. *Idolatry.* Trans. Naomi Goldblum. Cambridge, MA: Harvard University Press, 1992.

Halbfass, Wilhelm. *India and Europe: An Essay in Understanding.* Albany: SUNY Press, 1988.

Hallisey, Charles. "Roads Taken and Not Taken in the Study of Theravada Buddhism." In Donald S. Lopez, Jr., ed., *Curators of the Buddha: The Study of Buddhism under Colonialism,* 31–61. Chicago: University of Chicago Press, 1995.

Hanegraaff, Wouter. "How Magic Survived the Disenchantment of the World." *Religion* 33 (2003): 357–80.

Harrison, John R. *The Library of Isaac Newton.* Cambridge: Cambridge University Press, 1978.

Harrison, Peter. *The Bible, Protestantism, and the Rise of Natural Science.* Cambridge: Cambridge University Press, 1998.

———. *Religion and the Religions in the English Enlightenment.* Cambridge: Cambridge University Press, 1990.

Heckel, David. "Francis Bacon's New Science: Print and the Transformation of Rhetoric." In Bruce Gronbeck, Thomas Farrell, and Paula Soukup, eds., *Media, Consciousness, and Culture: Explorations of Walter Ong's Thought,* 64–76. Newbury Park, CA: Sage, 1991.

Heiler, Friedrich. *Prayer: A Study in the History and Psychology of Religion.* Trans. Samuel McComb. Oxford: Oxford University Press, 1932.

Hill, Christopher. *The English Bible and the Seventeenth-Century Revolution.* New York: Penguin, 1993.

———. *Intellectual Origins of the English Revolution.* Oxford: Clarendon Press, 1965.

Hooper, J. S. M. *Bible Translation in India, Pakistan and Ceylon.* 2nd ed. Oxford: Oxford University Press, 1963.

Horton, Robin, and Ruth Finnegan, eds. *Modes of Thought: Essays in Thinking in Western and Non-Western Societies.* London: Faber & Faber, 1973.

Iliffe, Robert Charles. "The Idols of the Temple: Isaac Newton and the Private Life of Anti-Idolatry." Unpublished Cambridge University Ph.D. Thesis, 1989.

Inden, Ronald. *Imagining India*. Cambridge, MA: Blackwell, 1990.

Indramitra. *Karunasagar Vidyasagar*. Kolkata: Ananda Publishers, 2006.

Iversen, Erik. *The Myth of Egypt and its Hieroglyphs in European Tradition*. Princeton, NJ: Princeton University Press, 1993.

Jacquier, E. "Matthew, Saint, Gospel of." In *The Catholic Encyclopedia*, 10: 57–65. Ed. Charles G. Herbermann et al. New York: Robert Appleton Co., 1911.

Johnson, Paul J. "Hobbes's Anglican Doctrine of Salvation." In Ralph Ross, Herbert W. Schneider, and Theodore Waldman, eds., *Thomas Hobbes in His Time*, 102–25. Minneapolis: University of Minnesota Press, 1974.

Jones, Kenneth W. *Arya Dharm: Hindu Consciousness in 19th-Century Punjab*. Berkeley: University of California Press, 1976.

Jones, Richard Foster. *The Seventeenth Century: Studies in the History of English Thought and Literature from Bacon to Pope*. Stanford: Stanford University Press, 1951.

Jordens, J. T. F. *Dayananda Sarasvati: His Life and Ideas*. Oxford: Oxford University Press, 1978.

Kane, P.V. *History of Dharmaśāstra*. 2nd ed. Poona: Bhandarkar Oriental Research Institute, 1977.

Kaviraj, Sudipta. "The Sudden Death of Sanskrit Knowledge." *Journal of Indian Philosophy* 33 (2005): 119–42.

Keane, Webb. *Christian Moderns: Freedom and Fetish in the Mission Encounter*. Berkeley: University of California Press, 2007.

———. "From Fetishism to Sincerity: Agency, the Speaking Subject, and their Historicity in the Context of Religious Conversion." *Comparative Studies in Society and History* 39 (1997): 674–93.

———. "Religious Language." *Annual Review of Anthropology* 26 (1997): 47–71.

———. "Sincerity, Modernity, and the Protestants." *Cultural Anthropology* 17 (2002): 65–92.

Khan, Mofakhkhar Hussain. *The Bengali Book: History of Printing and Bookmaking 1667–1866*. 2 vols. Dhaka: Bangla Academy, 2001.

Killingley, Dermot. *Rammohun Roy in Hindu and Christian Tradition: The Teape Lectures 1990*. Newcastle upon Tyne: Grevatt & Grevatt, 1993.

King, Richard. *Orientalism and Religion: Postcolonial Theory, India and "The Mystic East."* London: Routledge, 1999.

King, Preston, ed. *Thomas Hobbes: Critical Assessments*. 4 vols. London: Routledge, 1993.

Kitagawa, Joseph M., and John S. Strong. "Friedrich Max Müller and the Comparative Study of Religion." In Ninian Smart, John Clayton, Steven Katz, and Patrick Sherry, eds., *Nineteenth Century Religious Thought in the West*, 3: 179–213. 3 vols. Cambridge: Cambridge University Press, 1985.

Knowlson, James. *Universal Language Schemes in England and France 1600–1800.* Toronto: University of Toronto Press, 1975.

Kopf, David. *British Orientalism and the Bengal Renaissance: The Dynamics of Indian Modernization, 1773–1835.* Berkeley: University of California Press, 1969.

Korshin, Paul. *Typologies in England 1650–1820.* Princeton, NJ: Princeton University Press, 1982.

Kroskrity, Paul V. *Regimes of Language: Ideologies, Polities, and Identities.* Sante Fe, NM: School of American Research Press, 2000.

Lachs, Samuel Tobias. Review of Louis H. Feldman, *Jew and Gentile in the Ancient World. Bryn Mawr Classical Review* 94.05.06.

Laird, M. A. "The Contribution of the Serampore Missionaries to Education in Bengal, 1793–1837." *Bulletin of the School of Oriental and African Studies* 31 (1968): 92–112.

Landy, Joshua, and Michael Saler, eds. *The Re-enchantment of the World: Secular Magic in a Rational Age.* Stanford: Stanford University Press, 2009.

Lanham, Richard A. *A Handlist of Rhetorical Terms.* 2nd ed. Berkeley: University of California Press, 1991.

Laping, Johannes. "Pragmatism and Transcendence: Aspects of Pragmatic Soteriology ('Heilspragmatik') in Indian Tradition." In Detlef Kantowsky, ed., *Recent Research on Max Weber's Studies of Hinduism,* 199–207. München: Weltforum Verlag, 1986.

Lariviere, Richard. "Justices and *Paṇḍitas*: Some Ironies in Contemporary Readings of the Hindu Legal Past." *Journal of Asian Studies* 48 (1989): 757–69.

Latour, Bruno. *We Have Never Been Modern.* Trans. Catherine Porter. Cambridge, MA: Harvard University Press, 1993.

Lawrence, Raymond J. "Faith-Based Medicine." *New York Times,* April 11, 2006.

Leopold, Joan, ed. *The Prix Volney.* 3 vols. Dordrecht: Kluwer, 1999.

Lewis, Rhodri. *Language, Mind and Nature: Artificial Languages in England from Bacon to Locke.* Cambridge: Cambridge University Press, 2007.

Lilla, Mark. *The Stillborn God.* New York: Knopf, 2007.

Lincoln, Bruce. *Theorizing Myth: Narrative, Ideology, and Scholarship.* Chicago: University of Chicago Press, 1999.

Llewellyn, Jack E. *Defining Hinduism: A Reader.* New York: Routledge, 2005.

———. "From Interpretation to Reform: Dayanand's Reading of the Vedas." In Laurie Patton, ed., *Authority, Anxiety, and Canon,* 235–51. Albany: SUNY Press, 1994.

"Long-Awaited Medical Study Questions the Power of Prayer." *New York Times,* March 31, 2006.

Löwith, Karl. *Meaning in History: The Theological Implications of the Philosophy of History.* Chicago: University of Chicago Press, 1957.

Madan, T. N. "Secularism in Its Place." In Rajeev Bhargava, *Secularism and Its Critics,* 297–320. Delhi: Oxford University Press, 1998.

Malinowksi, Bronislaw. *Magic, Science and Religion and Other Essays.* Boston: Beacon Press, 1948.

Malamoud, Charles. *Le Svādhyāya: récitation personnelle du Veda.* Paris: Editions de Boccard, 1977.

Mandair, Arvind-Pal S. *Religion and the Specter of the West: Sikhism, Postcoloniality, and the Politics of Translation.* New York: Columbia University Press, 2009.

Mani, Lata. *Contentious Traditions: The Debate on Sati in Colonial India.* Berkeley: University of California Press, 1998.

Manuel, Frank. *The Changing of the Gods.* Hanover, NH: University Press of New England, 1983.

———. *The Eighteenth Century Confronts the Gods.* Cambridge, MA: Harvard University Press, 1959.

———. *Isaac Newton, Historian.* Cambridge, MA: Harvard University Press, 1963.

———. *The Religion of Isaac Newton.* Oxford: Clarendon Press, 1974.

Marshall, Peter. *The British Discovery of Hinduism in the Eighteenth Century.* Cambridge: Cambridge University Press, 1970.

Masuzawa, Tomoko. *In Search of Dreamtime: The Quest for the Origin of Religion.* Chicago: University of Chicago Press, 1993.

———. *The Invention of World Religions, or, How European Universalism Was Preserved in the Language of Pluralism.* Chicago: University of Chicago Press, 2005.

———. "Our Master's Voice: F. Max Müller after a Hundred Years of Solitude." *Method & Theory in the Study of Religion* 15 (2003): 305–28.

Maw, Martin. *Visions of India: Fulfilment Theology, the Aryan Race Theory, and the Work of British Protestant Missionaries in Victorian India.* New York: Peter Lang, 1990.

McGuire, J. E., and P. M. Rattansi. "Newton and the Pipes of Pan." *Notes and Records of the Royal Society* 21 (1966): 108–43.

McMurtrie, Douglas C. *Early Mission Printing Presses in India.* Rajkot, 1933.

Menski, Werner. "Hindu Law as a 'Religious' System." In Andrew Huxley, ed., *Religion, Law and Tradition: Comparative Studies in Religious Law,* 108–26. London: RoutledgeCurzon, 2002.

Merivale, Patricia. *Pan the Goat-God: His Myth in Modern Times.* Cambridge, MA: Harvard University Press, 1969.

Merton, Robert K. *Science, Technology & Society in Seventeenth Century England.* New York: Harper Torchbooks, 1970.

Meyer, Birgit, and Peter Pels, eds. *Magic and Modernity: Interfaces of Revelation and Concealment.* Stanford: Stanford University Press, 2003.

Mitchell, W. Fraser. *English Pulpit Oratory from Andrewes to Tillotson.* London: Society for Promoting Christian Knowledge, 1932.

Morris, Charles. *Signs, Language, and Behavior.* New York: Prentice-Hall, 1950.

Mulligan, Lotte. "Civil War Politics, Religion and the Royal Society." *Past & Present* 59 (1973): 92–116.

Oddie, Geoffrey. *Imagined Hinduism: British Protestant Missionary Constructions of Hinduism, 1793–1900.* London: Sage, 2006.

———. *Religious Traditions in South Asia: Interaction and Change.* Richmond, UK: Curzon, 1998.

Ohly, Friedrich. *Sensus Spiritualis: Studies in Medieval Significs and the Philology of Culture.* Chicago: University of Chicago Press, 2005.

Olender, Maurice. *The Languages of Paradise: Race, Religion, and Philology in the Nineteenth Century.* Trans. Arthur Goldhammer. Cambridge, MA: Harvard University Press, 1992.

Padley, G. A. *Grammatical Theory in Western Europe 1500–1700: The Latin Tradition.* Cambridge: Cambridge University Press, 1976.

Patrides, C. A. "The Cessation of the Oracles: The History of a Legend." *The Modern Language Review* 60 (1965): 500–07.

Pennington, Brian. *Was Hinduism Invented?: Britons, Indians, and the Colonial Construction of Religion.* New York: Oxford University Press, 2005.

Pierucci Antônio Flávio. "Secularization in Max Weber: On Current Usefulness of Re-Accessing That Old Meaning." *Brazilian Review of Social Sciences,* special issue no. 1 (2000): 129–58.

Pollock, Sheldon. "The Death of Sanskrit." *Comparative Studies in Society and History* 43 (2001): 392–426.

———. "Deep Orientalism? Notes on Sanskrit and Power beyond the Raj." In Carol Breckenridge and Peter van der Veer, eds., *Orientalism and the Postcolonial Predicament,* 76–133. Philadelphia: University of Pennsylvania Press, 1993.

———. "Introduction: Forms of Knowledge in Early Modern South Asia." *Comparative Studies of South Asia, Africa and the Middle East* 24 (2004): 19–21.

———. *The Language of the Gods in the World of Men: Sanskrit, Culture, and Power in Premodern India.* Berkeley: University of California Press, 2006.

Popkin, Richard H. "The Crisis of Polytheism and the Answers of Vossius, Cudworth, and Newton." In James E. Force and Richard H. Popkin, eds., *Essays on the Context, Nature, and Influence of Isaac Newton's Theology,* 9–26. Dordrecht: Kluwer, 1990.

Potts, Daniel. *British Baptist Missionaries in India, 1793–1837.* Cambridge: Cambridge University Press, 1967.

Prakash, Gyan. *Another Reason: Science and the Imagination of Modern India.* Princeton, NJ: Princeton University Press, 1999.

Priestman, Martin. *Romantic Atheism: Poetry and Freethought 1780–1830.* Cambridge: Cambridge University Press, 1999.

Quack, Johannes. *Disenchanting India: Organized Rationalism and Criticism of Religion in India.* New York: Oxford University Press, 2011.

Rabb, Theodore K. "Puritanism and the Rise of Experimental Science in England." *Journal of World History* 7 (1962): 46–67.

———. "Religion and the Rise of Modern Science." *Past & Present* 31 (1965): 111–26.

Radice, William, ed. *Swami Vivekananda and the Modernization of Hinduism.* Delhi: Oxford University Press, 1998.

Robbins, Joel. *Becoming Sinners: Christianity and Moral Torment in a Papua New Guinea Society.* Berkeley: University of California Press, 2004.

———. "God Is Nothing But Talk: Modernity, Language, and Prayer in a Papua New Guinea Society." *American Anthropologist* 103 (2001): 901–12.

———. "Ritual Communication and Linguistic Ideology." *Current Anthropology* 42 (2001): 591–614.

Rocher, Ludo. *Ezourvedam: A French Veda of the Eighteenth Century.* Amsterdam: John Benjamins, 1984.

Rossi, Paolo. *Francis Bacon: From Magic to Science.* Chicago: University of Chicago Press, 1968.

———. *Logic and the Art of Memory: The Quest for a Universal Language.* Trans. Stephen Clucas. Chicago: University of Chicago Press, 2000.

Said, Edward. *Orientalism.* New York: Vintage, 1979.

Saler, Michael. "Modernity and Enchantment: A Historiographic Review." *American Historical Review* 111 (2006): 692–716.

Salmon, Vivian. *The Study of Language in Seventeenth-Century England.* 2nd ed. Amsterdam: John Benjamins, 1988.

———. *The Works of Francis Lodwick.* London: Longman, 1972.

Salmond, Noel. *Hindu Iconoclasts: Rammohun Roy, Dayananda Sarasvati, and Nineteenth-Century Polemics against Idolatry.* Waterloo, ON: Wilfred Laurier University Press, 2004.

Schieffelin, Bambi B., Kathryn Ann Woolard, and Paul V. Kroskrity. *Language Ideologies: Practice and Theory.* New York: Oxford University Press, 1998.

Schopen, Gregory. "Archaeology and Protestant Presuppositions in the Study of Indian Buddhism." In *Bones, Stones, and Buddhist Monks,* 1–22. Honolulu: University of Hawaii Press, 1997.

Schwab, Raymond. *Oriental Renaissance: Europe's Rediscovery of India and the East, 1680–1880.* Trans. Gene Patterson-Black and Victor Reinking. New York: Columbia University Press, 1987.

Searle, John. *Speech Acts: An Essay in the Philosophy of Language.* London: Cambridge University Press, 1969.

Shapiro, Barbara J. *John Wilkins, 1614–1672: An Intellectual Biography.* Berkeley: University of California Press, 1969.

Sharpe, Eric J. *Comparative Religion: A History.* La Salle, IL: Open Court, 1986.

Sheahan, Joseph F. *Vain Repetitions, or The Protestant Meaning of Batta.* New York: Cathedral Library Association, 1901.

Sheehan, Jonathan, ed. "Thinking about Idols in Early Modern Europe." Special issue of the *Journal of the History of Ideas* 67, no. 4 (2006): 561–712.

Singer, Thomas C. "Hieroglyphs, Real Characters, and the Idea of Natural Language in English Seventeenth-Century Thought." *Journal of the History of Ideas* 50 (1989): 49–70.

Slaughter, Mary M. *Universal Languages and Scientific Taxonomy in the Seventeenth Century*. Cambridge: Cambridge University Press, 1982.

Smith, James K. A. *After Modernity?: Secularity, Globalization, and the Re-enchantment of the World*. Waco, TX: Baylor University Press, 2008.

Smith, Jonathan Z. *Imagining Religion: From Babylon to Jonestown*. Chicago: University of Chicago Press, 1982.

———. *To Take Place*. Chicago: University of Chicago Press, 1992.

Snobelen, Stephen D. "'God of Gods, and Lord of Lords': The Theology of Isaac Newton's General Scholium to the *Principia*." *Osiris*, 2nd series, 16 (2001): 169–208.

Sommerville, C. John. "The Secularization of Language." In *The Secularization of Early Modern England*, 44–54. New York: Oxford University Press, 1992.

Springborg, Patricia. "Hobbes, Heresy, and the *Historia Ecclesiastica*." *Journal of the History of Ideas* 55 (1994): 553–71.

———. "Thomas Hobbes and Cardinal Bellarmine: Leviathan and The Ghost of the Roman Empire." *History of Political Thought* 16 (1995): 503–31.

Stark, Rodney. *The Victory of Reason: How Christianity Led to Freedom, Capitalism, and Western Success*. New York: Random House, 2005.

Stephens, James. *Francis Bacon and the Style of Science*. Chicago: University of Chicago Press, 1975.

Stephens, W. P. *The Theology of Huldrych Zwingli*. Oxford: Clarendon Press, 1986.

Stillman, Robert E. *The New Philosophy and Universal Language Schemes in Seventeenth-Century England: Bacon, Hobbes, and Wilkins*. Lewisburg, PA: Bucknell University Press, 1995.

Stimson, Dorothy. "Puritanism and the New Philosophy in 17th century England." *Bulletin of the Institute of the History of Medicine* 3 (1935): 321–34.

Stokes, Eric. *The English Utilitarians and India*. Oxford: Clarendon Press, 1959.

Strenski, Ivan. "Misreading Max Müller." *Method & Theory in the Study of Religion* 8 (1996): 291–96.

———. "The Proper Object of the Study of Religion." In Slavica Jakelic and Lori Pearson, eds., *The Future of the Study of Religion*, 145–72. Leiden: Brill, 2004.

Stroumsa, Guy. "John Spencer and the Roots of Idolatry." *History of Religions* (2001): 1–23.

Studdert-Kennedy, Gerald. *British Christians, Indian Nationalists, and the Raj*. New York: Oxford University Press, 1991.

Sugirtharajah, Rasiah S. *The Bible and Empire: Postcolonial Explorations*. Cambridge: Cambridge University Press, 2005.

————. *The Bible and the Third World: Precolonial, Colonial, and Postcolonial Encoun-ters*. Cambridge: Cambridge University Press, 2001.

————. *Postcolonial Criticism and Biblical Interpretation*. New York: Oxford University Press, 2002.

Sugirtharajah, Sharada. "Colonialism." In Gene Thursby and Sushil Mittal, eds., *Studying Hinduism: Key Concepts and Methods*, 73–85. New York: Routledge, 2007.

————. *Imagining Hinduism: A Postcolonial Perspective*. New York: Routledge, 2003.

Tambiah, Stanley. *Culture, Thought, and Social Action: An Anthropological Perspective*. Cambridge, MA: Harvard University Press, 1985.

————. *Magic, Science, Religion, and the Scope of Rationality*. Cambridge: Cambridge University Press, 1990.

Targoff, Ramie. *Common Prayer: The Language of Public Devotion in Early Modern England*. Chicago: University of Chicago Press, 2001.

Taussig, Michael. *The Magic of the State*. New York: Routledge, 1997.

Taylor, Charles. *A Secular Age*. Cambridge, MA: Harvard University Press, 2007.

Taylor, Mark C. *After God*. Chicago: University of Chicago Press, 2007.

Thapar, Romila. "The Oral and the Written in Early India." in *Cultural Pasts: Essays in Early Indian History*, 195–212. New Delhi: Oxford University Press, 2000.

Thomas, Keith. "An Anthropology of Religion and Magic, II." *Journal of Interdisci-plinary History* 6 (1975): 91–109.

————. *Religion and the Decline of Magic*. New York: Charles Scribner's Sons, 1971.

Tiliander, Bror. *Christian and Hindu Terminology*. Uppsala: Almqvist & Wiksell, 1974.

Trautmann, Thomas. *Aryans and British India*. Berkeley: University of California Press, 1997.

Tucci, Giuseppe. "Nomina Numina." In Joseph Kitagawa and Charles Long, eds., *Myths and Symbols: Studies in Honor of Mircea Eliade*, 3–7. Chicago: University of Chicago Press, 1969.

Tuck, Richard. "The Christian Atheism of Thomas Hobbes." In Michael Hunter and David Wootton, eds., *Atheism from the Reformation to the Enlightenment*, 111–30. Oxford: Clarendon Press, 1992.

————. *Natural Rights Theories: Their Origin and Development*. Cambridge: Cam-bridge University Press, 1979.

Urban, Hugh. *Tantra: Sex Secrecy, Politics and Power in the Study of Religion*. Berkeley: University of California Press, 2003.

Veer, Peter van der, ed. *Conversion to Modernities: The Globalization of Christianity*. London: Routledge, 1995.

————. *Imperial Encounters: Religion and Modernity in India and Britain*. Princeton, NJ: Princeton University Press, 2001.

Vickers, Brian. "Analogy Versus Identity: The Rejection of Occult Symbolism, 1580–1680." In *Occult and Scientific Mentalities in the Renaissance*, 95–163. Cam-bridge: Cambridge University Press, 1984.

————. *Rhetoric and the Pursuit of Truth: Language Change in the Seventeenth and Eighteenth Centuries*. Los Angeles: William Andrews Clark Memorial Library, 1985.

Villamil, Richard de. *Newton: The Man*. London: Gordon D. Knox, 1931.

Viswanathan, Gauri. "Colonialism and the Construction of Hinduism." In Gavin Flood, ed., *The Blackwell Companion to Hinduism*, 23–44. Malden, MA: Blackwell, 2005.

————. *Masks of Conquest: Literary Study and British Rule in India*. New York: Columbia University Press, 1989.

————. *Outside the Fold: Conversion, Modernity, and Belief*. Princeton, NJ: Princeton University Press, 1998.

Voigt, Johannes H. *F. Max Müller: The Man and His Ideas*. Calcutta: K. L. Mukhopadhyay, 1967.

Walker, D. P. *Ancient Theology: Studies in Christian Platonism from the Fifteenth to the Eighteenth Century*. Ithaca: Cornell University Press, 1972.

Ward, John O. "Magic and Rhetoric from Antiquity to the Renaissance: Some Ruminations." *Rhetorica* 6 (1988): 57–118.

Weber, Max. *The Protestant Ethic and the Spirit of Capitalism*. Trans. Talcott Parsons. New York: Charles Scribner's Sons, 1958.

————. *The Religion of India: The Sociology of Hinduism and Buddhism*. Trans. H. H. Gerth and Don Martindale. New York: Free Press, 1958.

————. "Science As A Vocation." In H. H. Gerth and C. Wright Mills, eds., *From Max Weber: Essays in Sociology*, 129–56. London: Routledge, 1991.

————. *The Sociology of Religion*. Trans. Ephraim Fischoff. Boston: Beacon Press, 1964.

Westfall, Richard S. "Isaac Newton's *Theologiae gentilis origines philosophicae*." In Warren Wagar, ed., *The Secular Mind: Tranformations of Faith in Modern Europe*, 15–34. New York: Holmes and Meier, 1982.

————. *The Life of Isaac Newton*. Cambridge: Cambridge University Press, 1993.

————. *Never at Rest: A Biography of Isaac Newton*. Cambridge: Cambridge University Press, 1980.

————. "Newton's Theological Manuscripts." In Zev Bechler, ed., *Contemporary Newtonian Research*, 129–43. Dordrecht: D. Reidel, 1982.

————. *Science and Religion in Seventeenth-Century England*. Hamden, CT: Archon Books, 1970.

Whitney, Charles. *Francis Bacon and Modernity*. New Haven: Yale University Press, 1986.

Wiebe, Donald. *The Politics of Religious Studies: The Continuing Conflict with Theology in the Academy*. New York: St. Martin's, 1998.

Williams, Robert A. *The American Indian in Western Legal Thought*. New York: Oxford University Press, 1990.

Wollock, Jeffrey. "John Bulwer (1606–1656) and the Significance of Gesture in 17th-century Theories of Language and Cognition." *Gesture* 2 (2002): 227–58.

Yates, Frances W. *Giordano Bruno and the Hermetic Tradition.* Chicago: University of Chicago Press, 1964.

Yelle, Robert A. "Bentham's Fictions: Canon and Idolatry in the Genealogy of Law." *Yale Journal of Law & the Humanities* 17 (2005): 151–79.

———. *Explaining Mantras: Ritual, Rhetoric, and the Dream of a Natural Language in Hindu Tantra.* New York: Routledge, 2003.

———. "Hindu Law as Performance: Ritual and Poetic Elements in *Dharmaśāstra.*" In Timothy Lubin, Donald R. Davis, Jr., and Jayanth K. Krishnan, eds., *Hinduism and Law: An Introduction,* 183–92. Cambridge: Cambridge University Press, 2010.

———. "Moses' Veil: Secularization as Christian Myth." In Winnifred Fallers Sullivan, Robert A. Yelle, and Mateo Taussig-Rubbo, eds., *After Secular Law,* 23–42. Stanford: Stanford University Press, 2011.

———. "To Perform or Not to Perform?: A Theory of Ritual Performance versus Cognitive Theories of Religious Transmission." *Method & Theory in the Study of Religion* 18 (2006): 372–91.

———. "The Rhetoric of Gesture in Cross-Cultural Perspective." *Gesture* 6 (2006): 223–40.

———. *Semiotics of Religion: Signs of the Sacred in History.* London: Bloomsbury, 2012.

———. "The Trouble with Transcendence: Carl Schmitt's 'Exception' as a Challenge for Religious Studies." *Method & Theory in the Study of Religion* 22 (2010): 189–206.

Young, Richard Fox. *Resistant Hinduism: Sanskrit Sources on Anti-Christian Apologetics in Early Nineteenth-Century India.* Leiden: Brill, 1981.

Zaleski, Philip, and Carol Zaleski. *Prayer: A History.* Boston: Houghton Mifflin, 2005.

Ziolkowski, Eric J. *A Museum of Faiths: Histories and Legacies of the 1893 World's Parliament of Religions.* Atlanta: Scholars Press, 1993.

Index

Lepsius, Richard, 84, 215nn76–77
Lightfoot, John, 113
Lilla, Mark, 30
linguistic ideology
    definition of, 176n84
    of Hindus contrasted with that of
        British, 36–38, 40, 42
    modernity as, 22
literalism, Protestant. *See also*
    iconoclasm, Protestant; idolatry:
    Christian linguistic explanation of;
    plain style, Protestant; typology,
    Christian; univocal language, idea
    of; vain repetitions, Protestant
    critique of
    and critique of vain repetitions, 108, 132
    as elevation of semantic over pragmatic
        function, 25, 26–29, 107, 133–34
    and iconoclasm, parallels between, 25
    influence on Baconianism, 49,
        74–75, 100, 133
    influence on colonial codification, 73,
        75–78, 79–80
    influence on colonialism, 5, 9–10,
        25–26, 27, 41–42
    influence on Friedrich Max Müller,
        69, 73, 75–77, 78
    influence on modernity, 22–23, 26–29
    and monotheism, 9
    and plain speech, 18, 19–20, 22–24,
        27–29, 41, 49, 51, 69, 70, 138, 161,
        190n84
    in Reformation, 9
    and *sola scriptura* (scripture alone),
        9, 24, 108
Locke, John, 34, 35, 40, 47, 52, 53–54,
    89, 90, 96, 186n66, 218n108
Lord, Henry, 104, 148–49
Löwith, Karl, xiii, 30
Lowth, Robert, 113
Luther, Martin, 9, 24, 95, 151, 158

Macaulay, Thomas B., 33, 73, 84, 95,
    103, 120

Macnaghten, Francis Workman, 144
Maine, Henry Sumner, 145, 146, 147,
    246n53
magic. *See also* disenchantment;
    mantras; natural (iconic) language,
    belief in; vain repetitions,
    Protestant critique of
    in colonial Indonesia, 27
    in contemporary South Asia,
        xi–xii
    disenchantment as decline of, ix, 7,
        13, 14, 15, 17–18, 20–21, 29, 30–31,
        171n56
    and *ex opere operato* (Catholic
        doctrine of ritual efficacy), 115, 133
    and idea of a real character, 88–89
    Protestant critique of vain repetitions
        as, xii, xiv, 9, 16, 25, 104–05, 107,
        115, 116, 117, 119, 120–22, 133, 135
    rejection of, by modernity, 26, 40, 89
    universal languages as, 89
Maimonides, 55
Malinowski, Bronislaw, xii
Mandair, Arvind-Pal S., 10, 128
Manton, Thomas, 113–14
mantras. See also Tantras; vain
    repetitions, Protestant critique
    of: applied to Hinduism; *Vedas*:
    repetition of
    belief in, as magical language, xi,
        16–17, 38–40, 104–05
    Bengali folk (*laukik*), xii
    bīja (seed) mantras, 39, 125
    as diagrams of creation, 16–17, 39
    japamālā (rosary), 39, 121, 122
    mantradoṣa (flaws of mantras), 125
    mantra (word) translated as "magic"
        by British, 117
    oral dimensions of, 125, 127 (*see also*
        Hinduism: orality in)
    poetry in, xi, 16, 39, 125
    prāṇapratiṣṭhā (establishing the
        life-breath), 118, 123
    praṇava (*oṃ*), 38, 125, 236n125